# The Preservation Management Handbook

...........................

# The Preservation Management Handbook

A 21st-Century Guide
for Libraries, Archives,
and Museums

**ROSS HARVEY** and
**MARTHA R. MAHARD**

ROWMAN & LITTLEFIELD
*Lanham • Boulder • New York • Toronto • Plymouth, UK*

Published by Rowman & Littlefield
4501 Forbes Boulevard, Suite 200, Lanham, Maryland 20706
www.rowman.com

10 Thornbury Road, Plymouth PL6 7PP, United Kingdom

British Library Cataloguing in Publication Information Available

**Library of Congress Cataloging-in-Publication Data**
The preservation management handbook : a 21st-century guide for libraries, archives, and museums / [edited by] Ross Harvey and Martha R. Mahard.
     pages cm
 Includes bibliographical references and index.
 ISBN 978-0-7591-2315-1 (cloth : alk. paper)—ISBN 978-0-7591-2316-8 (electronic)
 1. Library materials—Conservation and restoration. 2. Archival materials—Conservation and restoration. 3. Museum conservation methods. 4. Digital preservation. 5. Preservation of materials. I. Harvey, D. R. (Douglas Ross), 1951– editor of compilation. II. Mahard, Martha R., 1948– editor of compilation.
 Z701.P7445 2014
 025.8'4—dc23                                                                                          2013045882

Printed in the United States of America

Dedicated to Wendy Smith, 1943–2006,
for her contributions to improving preservation
practice in Asia, Australia, and the Pacific,
and for her friendship

# Contents

· · · · · · · · · · · · · · · · · · · · · · · · · · · · · · · · · · · · · · · · · · · · · · · · · · · · · · · · · · · · · ·

· · · · · · · · · · · · · · · · · · · · · · · · · · · · · · · · · · · · · · · · · · · · · · · · · · · · · · · · · · · · · ·

# List of Figures

·········································································

·········································································

# Foreword

...............................................................................................

*T*he Preservation Management Handbook: A 21st-Century Guide for Libraries, Archives, and Museums is about planning and managing programs
for the preservation of information resources in libraries, museums,
and archives. *Preservation* is the term that we use to refer to these activities, yet it is
sometimes an elusive subject, touching on many fields, and perhaps, as a result, only a
few people have attempted to write textbooks about it, for a number of reasons. Why?
First, there is its breadth: What is preservation, and what does it cover? Does it refer to
man-made or naturally occurring objects? To the built environment, or only that which
is contained in it? Should a book that focuses on preservation address conservation—the
care and treatment of objects—or focus on the overall management and protection of
collections? How does restoration fit into the larger picture of preservation?

In addition to definition and scope, there is the issue of timeliness. Digital media are
becoming an ever-increasing part of the information landscape. Technologies change
rapidly, but so do the ways in which we interact with them.[1] How do we account for
technology and user behaviors in designing and implementing preservation programs?
And how do we write about technology in a way that will not immediately become
dated?

Third, preservation is a relatively new field, if we define it as the aggregate care of
collections. Prior to the 1970s, cultural heritage institutions focused primarily on the
physical care of their collections. True, institutions reformatted collections and attempted
to "control" the environment, but a comprehensive managerial approach to collections
care was not yet practiced. To wit, rather than textbooks, you have their precursors:
articles and bibliographies. The first edition of George Cunha's *Conservation of Library
Materials: A Manual and Bibliography on the Care, Repair and Restoration of Library Materials* (later, compiled with Dorothy Cunha) was published in 1967; it attempted to be
more comprehensive than an article could.[2] However, the book proved to be more useful
as a bibliography than as a manual, since the manual covered little new territory. The
bibliography is useful even now in taking the measure of conservation and preservation thinking at that time. A second edition of the manual/bibliography was published

...............................................................................................

in 1971.[3] Later, Susan G. Swartzburg and Robert E. Schnare Jr., with George Cunha, published a *preservation* bibliography of works published from 1983 to 1996.[4] This work gives us the measure of the field's growth: 5,358 citations for this thirteen-year period, versus the many fewer, and unnumbered, entries in the first two editions of Cunha.

Fourth, it is difficult to write comprehensively on preservation because to do the topic justice, one needs to look widely at areas of personnel; old, new, and changing technologies; the relationship between the creation of catalogs and finding aids, and access in various forms; funding; physical plant issues; collection development and maintenance issues; environmental standards; disaster preparedness; administrative issues; and so forth.

From the 1960s on, attention to the care of individual objects was augmented by a new focus on institutions and even national and international collections.

But what of textbooks, manuals, and handbooks, then? These books are intended for students and practitioners. In the United States, there were few preservation practitioners or students before 1980. Preservation was not offered as a graduate course in library and information science programs in the United States until the early 1970s, and then, only sporadically. Paul Banks, who offered it at the University of Illinois in 1971, taught the first course "devoted exclusively to the preservation of library materials";[5] George Cunha began teaching a course at the University of Rhode Island in 1974. Most library and information science programs didn't begin offering courses until the 1980s, and that is when preservation textbooks appeared. In *Preserving Library Materials: A Manual* (1980),[6] Susan G. Swartzburg picked up George and Dorothy Cunha's mantle by writing another manual/bibliography. Two things make Swartzburg's book distinctive: the manual section is greatly expanded from Cunha's, and Swartzburg uses *preserving* in the title, jettisoning *conservation* and *restoration* as terms of art. In the preface to her book, Thomas H. Mott Jr. defines preservation this way:

> Preservation concerns not only the conservation of a book, or other object, in its original format but also, quite literally, the preservation of the intellectual content of library materials and the maintenance of the physical plant where library materials are housed. Whether or not librarians have items in their collections that require special conservation, they are responsible for the general preservation of all materials under their care.[7]

Beginning in 1990, three more books were published that were useful for students and practitioners, by Ross Harvey, by John N. DePew, and a collaboratively authored work by John Feather, Graham Matthews, and Paul Eden.[8] The focus in these works was squarely on library preservation, though DePew touched on archives.

Ross Harvey and Martha Mahard take preservation out of an institution-specific setting. In part, this reflects changes that have occurred in the information professions since the 1990s. In library and information science programs, archival science has become an important component, and over the past decade or so, cultural heritage informatics has also joined the curriculum. Changes have also taken place in practice. Consider the collaborations across libraries, archives, and museums that have been made possible because of new digital technologies. Traditional boundaries across cultural heritage institutions are blurring, though certainly not yet disappearing. This book, then, is an outgrowth of the cultural heritage fields today.

It does not strive for comprehensiveness; that would be impossible to achieve. Rather, it aims to address a breadth of areas by focusing on principles and precepts for all materials, digital and analog. Of particular value are the authors' thoughtful discussions about longevity, choice, quality, integrity, and access. The book includes the components one would expect to find in a preservation program: assessment and planning; artifacts and information; risk assessment; the environment; media-specific concerns; and so on.

There is much that still needs to be done to bring together the perspectives of different types of cultural heritage institutions, not just in preservation, but in the areas of collection development and the organization of information as well. Yet librarianship, archives, and museum studies are still separated by different professional associations, practices, and journals. Harvey and Mahard have made an important contribution to preservation by writing a book that will expand the forums in which its basic principles are considered.

On a bibliographic note, it is fitting that Rowman & Littlefield, which now owns Scarecrow Press, is the publisher. Scarecrow's many preservation publications over nearly fifty years have advanced the preservation field. The present volume is a worthy addition to the literature.

Michèle V. Cloonan
Dean Emerita and Professor
Graduate School of Library and Information Science
Simmons College, Boston

## NOTES

1. The bibliographies on digital curation by Charles W. Bailey Jr. demonstrate the flood of publications in this area.

2. George Daniel Martin Cunha, *Conservation of Library Materials: A Manual and Bibliography on the Care, Repair and Restoration of Library Materials* (Metuchen, NJ: Scarecrow Press, 1967).

3. George Martin and Dorothy Cunha, *Conservation of Library Materials: A Manual and Bibliography on the Care, Repair and Restoration of Library Materials*, 2nd ed. (Metuchen, NJ: Scarecrow Press, 1971).

4. Robert E. Schnare Jr., and Susan G. Swartzburg, with George M. Cunha, *Bibliography of Preservation Literature, 1983–1996* (Lanham, MD, and London: Scarecrow Press, 2001).

5. Michèle Valerie Cloonan, "Preservation Education in American Library Schools: Recounting the Ways," *Journal of Education for Library and Information Science* 31, no. 3 (1991): 188.

6. Susan G. Swartzburg, *Preserving Library Materials: A Manual* (Metuchen, NY, and London: Scarecrow Press, 1980).

7. Swartzburg, *Preserving Library Materials*, viii.

8. Ross Harvey, *Preservation in Australian and New Zealand Libraries: Principles, Strategies and Practices for Librarians* (Wagga Wagga, NSW: Centre for Information Studies, 1990), a second edition was published in 1993; John N. DePew, *A Library, Media, and Archival Preservation Handbook* (Santa Barbara, CA: ABC-Clio, 1991); and John Feather, Graham Matthews, and Paul Eden, *Preservation Management: Policies and Practices in British Libraries* (Aldershot, Hants, 1996).

# Preface

.........................................................................................

*T*he *Preservation Management Handbook: A 21st-Century Guide for Libraries, Archives, and Museums* was conceived when the authors were teaching preservation at Simmons College, Boston. For many years the teaching of preservation at Simmons College's Graduate School of Library and Information Science has been a collaborative effort. Located in an area richly populated with libraries, archives, and museums of all sizes, managed by practitioners with a wealth of expertise in many fields, we have had the good fortune to draw on them in our teaching. We have adopted the same approach in preparing this volume. Collaboration is, in fact, an essential characteristic of any successful preservation management program. Cultural heritage professionals—museum curators, museum professionals, archivists, and librarians—use their specialized knowledge to prioritize the needs of their collections. Preservation managers draw on experts in climate control, fire safety, pest management, and other relevant fields in developing an overview of a collection and its needs. Others are experts in all of the many different materials in the collections. In compiling this volume we have sought contributions from colleagues with special expertise in different areas. Our goal has been to organize the contributions into a cohesive volume that is an essential one-stop point of reference for cultural heritage professionals, particularly for those in small- to medium-sized organizations in which resources are limited and professional help is not always at hand, and that is an enduring text for students.

The goal is, indeed, an ambitious one. Preservation, like almost every other area of the cultural heritage domain, has been through enormous change over the past few decades. Technology has allowed us to make significant progress, while at the same time introducing new sets of challenges. Perhaps more than at any other time, today's cultural heritage professionals must have knowledge of a daunting array of materials and media. Archivists open boxes to find reels of nitrate film; librarians have cabinets full of sound recordings, from wax cylinders to vinyl to magnetic tape and CD; and museum curators have always had to deal with books and manuscripts as well as works of art. It is hard to imagine a type of repository that does not have photographs among their collections, and even harder to imagine one without digital assets in multiple formats. In this volume we

.........................................................................................

pull together the analog and digital worlds and present the reality of what is to be found in most collections regardless of their size or type.

The editors of this book and many of its contributors have for many years taught courses in preservation management to graduate students in library, archives, and information science. We have not found a satisfactory text that does what we propose to do here: to introduce the reader to the essential tools and principles of a preservation management program in the 21st century—one that addresses the realities of diverse collections and materials and embraces the challenges of working with both analog and digital collections.

Our focus is on material culture rather than naturally occurring objects, for which we defer to others. Similarly, we will not attempt to provide in-depth advice on furniture, sculpture, and other fine art objects. Those topics are well covered elsewhere and are outside the scope of this volume. The sections on planning and managing a preservation program contain the basic starting point for any kind of collection, regardless of size and content. Written with the small collection in mind, the principles are nevertheless scalable and more widely applicable.

Part I: Fundamentals begins with two chapters that set out the current preservation landscape and consider the ways in which fundamental changes in the cultural heritage world have driven changes in the preservation community. The impact of information technology has been profound in this field, as elsewhere. Technology has introduced many challenges, but it has also placed a new emphasis on the commonalities of practice across libraries, archives, and museums. The lines separating these traditionally siloed institutions are becoming blurred, and preservation practice is one area in which much can be gained from working across old boundaries. Digitization, born-digital objects, and the exponential increase in the number of digital assets in all types of repositories have added significantly to the range of technical expertise that a preservation manager needs. Although conventional wisdom maintains that digital preservation *is* different, it is the contention of this book that digital preservation is *not* different.

It is essential to determine the different issues involved when we look at the preservation of a physical artifact in contrast to the preservation of information. This distinction predates the arrival of digital surrogates. Past outcries about books and newspapers that were discarded after having been microfilmed are evidence that the distinction is important; managers chose the information over the object, but not everyone was convinced this was the right choice. Once digital reformatting became an acceptable option in the preservation toolbox, this distinction became an increasingly critical part of the preservation decision-making process.

The focus in Chapter 3 is on the policy, assessment, and planning aspects of preservation management in libraries, archives, and museums. A precondition for developing a preservation plan is to determine the extent to which preservation is an institutional mandate. The plan needs to be based on clear understandings: it should be grounded in a mission statement and based on clearly articulated policies, and the chapter indicates how this can be done. A preservation assessment provides in-depth knowledge of the collection, building, and operations of the institution, also necessary in an effective preservation plan. Sections on policies, planning, and assessment take the reader step-by-step through a review of the external and internal environment, including risk factors, and through the processes of gaining a thorough overview of collection condition and of assessing the options that will maximize available resources. The chapter concludes with a section about another kind of plan considered essential to preservation—the disaster plan—and notes what should be present in one. The preservation community has developed sophisticated tools for writing disaster preparedness plans, and this chapter reviews the essential steps in ensuring the success of such plans. Of course, no plan, however carefully developed, can cover every eventuality that might occur, which means preparing not only to meet disasters but also to cope with the unexpected, to put the plan into action in difficult circumstances, and to resume operations under less than ideal conditions.

Part II: Collections begins with a chapter on the preservation of artifacts and information in general: the intrinsic characteristics that make them vulnerable to decay and extrinsic factors that will assist with their preservation. Indicators for in-house repair and the choice of conservation treatment options are discussed. The rationale for preserving information by reformatting physical and digital objects is examined, and a range of options for both physical and digital objects is presented.

The next chapter in Part II focuses on the environment, beginning with a look at common practices, basic principles, and risk management. Over the last decade our notion of what constitutes an "ideal" environment has shifted noticeably. This is due in part to a renewed sense of urgency about the sustainability of the world we live in, but it is also based on continuing research and evolving standards. Sections are included on the importance of a holistic approach to the building envelope and structure for the care of physical objects, and of trusted digital repositories for digital assets. Regardless of the type of institution or collection that is responsible for their care, physical and digital objects are vulnerable to many common threats, ranging from pests and mold to the harmful properties of water, humidity, light, and fire. Essential information for recognizing potential and imminent threats is provided, together with information about best practices for avoiding them and coping with the effects of those that are not avoided.

Part III: Materials and Objects consists of a chapter noting the importance of creating objects that are preservation friendly, and it provides examples of such objects. The concept of preservation-friendly objects is particularly important for digital assets, but it is not new; improvements in the quality of paper in printed books are an example of predigital advances in creating preservation-friendly objects. One of the important tools for creating these objects is metadata. The existence of good descriptive, administrative, and technical metadata from the creation of an object onward can improve identification, help verify its authenticity, and facilitate future preservation. We recognize that this is not possible or desirable in every context or for every type of object. Professionals in all areas of libraries, archives, and museums can be (and are) proactive in advocacy and in raising awareness of preservation goals among creators. Collecting essential metadata from the start of a project may be a low priority for creators, but library, archives, and museum professionals can help by demystifying the descriptive process for creators and by becoming partners in assembling the relevant data.

Part IV: Media and Material is the final part of the book. It contains contributions by experts about the preservation concerns of protecting the collections of cultural heritage institutions, and about the preservation of objects commonly found in those institutions. In their contributions about objects, the expert scholars and practitioners have used a template and built on the general guidance given in preceding chapters. Materials that are most commonly encountered are covered here, with the aim of providing basic information that will help nonexperts to recognize what they find and to make appropriate preservation decisions based on an understanding of the characteristics that affect an object's survival. This section is intended for use as a quick reference tool for information about collection objects, covering identification, preferred environment, handling practice, typical characteristics of their decay, and treatments. Recognizing that it is not realistic to present a comprehensive itemization of every type of object likely to be found in collections in libraries, archives, and museums, we have restricted coverage to the types of text-based objects, image-based objects, audio-visual objects, digital files, and artifacts most likely to be found in collections today. We hope *The Preservation Management Handbook: A 21st-Century Guide for Libraries, Archives, and Museums* will become a useful text for students and faculty, as well as for practitioners in the field.

Ross Harvey
Martha R. Mahard

# Acknowledgments

························································································

We are indebted to many people who have assisted us in various ways, both during the preparation of this book and in helping us shape our ideas about preservation. First and foremost, we acknowledge the experts who contributed their specialist knowledge in their contributions in Part IV: Shelby Sanett, Michael F. Knight, Richard Dine, Kevin A. McCoy (Holdings Protection); Donia Conn, Dawn Walus (Paper Objects and Books); Brenda Bernier (Photographic Materials); Elizabeth Walters, Bob Pymm, Matthew Davies (Sound Materials); Liz Coffey, Elizabeth Walters (Moving Image Materials); Leslie Johnston (Digital Storage Media); Frances Lennard (Textiles); and Heather Hole (Paintings).

We also gratefully acknowledge the students, past and present, in preservation courses offered by the Graduate School of Library and Information Science at Simmons College. We also acknowledge with gratitude the adjuncts who have taught, and continue to teach, preservation courses at Simmons College; some of them have written contributions to this book, for which we are doubly grateful. Our Simmons faculty colleagues, past and present, have also provided inspiration and support.

Ross Harvey wishes to acknowledge, with thanks: students in the course LIS 531W Digital Stewardship, especially those in the 2012 Fall semester for their astute comments on definitions; Michael Printy for his comments on preservation-friendly objects; Andra Langoussis, graduate student assistant in Fall 2012 for her assistance; Leah Nickell, whose assistance with another book identified material that has been used in this book. He has learned much from his academic colleagues over the years, and he wishes in this respect to especially express his gratitude for the support and collegiality of Michèle Cloonan. He has been fortunate to benefit from the expertise and support of preservation professionals in many countries, and he acknowledges in particular Jane Hedberg, Seamus Ross, and staff of the National Library of Australia and the National Film and Sound Archive. Most notable in this respect is Wendy Smith, who as a critical friend was influential in forming his thinking about preservation. Some of the material used in this book has its origin in material developed by Wendy and Ross for a workbook on preservation that was not completed.

························································································

Ross Harvey must again acknowledge the unfailing support of Rachel Salmond. He owes Rachel more than he can adequately express here for her continuing support and love over three decades, her editorial assistance, and her patience as the preparation of this book took over normal schedules.

Martha Mahard wishes to acknowledge, in addition to those already mentioned, her deep gratitude for the friendship and support of Michèle Cloonan. She, too, thanks Jane Hedberg for her wisdom, generosity, friendship, and good humor. During her years in the libraries at Harvard University, Martha worked with, and learned from, an array of astonishingly talented and dedicated professionals to whom she remains grateful. Her contribution to this book was forged in those shared experiences. And finally, Martha wishes to acknowledge the daily support and encouragement of Manley Tuttle.

Earlier versions of chapters 1 and 2 were published as Ross Harvey and Martha Mahard, "Mapping the Preservation Landscape for the Twenty-First Century," *Preservation, Digital Technology & Culture* 42 (2013): 5–16. The authors are grateful to the editor and publisher of this journal for permission to use them here.

We also thank the following people and organizations for their assistance and for giving permission to publish: the National Film and Sound Archive (Australia); Melissa Tedone, Conservator, Iowa State University Parks Library Preservation Department; David Broda, Syracuse University Photo and Imaging Center; Eve Neiger; the Philips Company Archive; and the Boston Athenaeum.

# PART I

# FUNDAMENTALS

·····································

# CHAPTER 1

# Mapping the Preservation Landscape for the 21st Century

The reality for preservation management programs at the beginning of the 21st century is one of diverse collections and materials, of convergence of traditionally diverse preservation practices, and of a necessity to embrace the challenges of working with both analog and digital collections. The cultural heritage world is undergoing fundamental change, which is driving corresponding change in the preservation community. The impact of information technology has been as profound in preservation as in other environments. Information technology has raised, and continues to raise, challenges, but it has also demanded that we recognize the commonalities of professional practice among libraries, archives, and museums, including those of preservation practice. The lines that previously separated traditionally siloed institutions are blurring, so that preservation practice once contained in one kind of institution is becoming relevant to other kinds of institutions. Much can be gained from looking across the now-blurring boundaries and adopting or adapting practices previously limited to one specific context. Collaboration is a hallmark of the new, converging preservation environment and an essential characteristic of any successful preservation management program. Cultural heritage professionals—defined in this book as museum professionals, archivists, and librarians—apply their specialized knowledge to prioritizing the needs of their collections, and they collaborate with preservation managers who, in turn, draw on experts in climate control, fire safety, pest management, digital preservation, and more in developing the broader overview of a collection and its preservation needs.

This chapter[1] is the first of three chapters introducing the fundamentals of preservation management in this converging environment. It introduces the preservation landscape we are embracing in the early decades of the 21st century. It contains descriptions and explanations of recent changes in the cultural heritage environment and of the impact of information technology, and it discusses the significant commonalities that are now present in preservation practice in cultural heritage institutions. It presents definitions of preservation terms and concepts that are being reconceptualized in response to the changing environment, comments on the crucial distinction we need to make between the preservation of artifact or the preservation of information content, and observations about in whose professional hands preservation responsibilities lie in the changing environment.

This book is based on the philosophy that there are preservation principles that apply to all kinds of materials, whether digital or analog. The idea that "digital is different" is widespread, and it is generally considered that digital preservation should be handled differently in cultural heritage institutions because of the different nature and characteristics of digital objects. As our understanding of digital preservation matures, we are starting to question some of the assumptions and mantras associated with it and to identify preservation principles and practices that apply to all materials. "Is There Such a Thing as Digital Preservation?" asks Leslie Johnston, a contributor to this book, in a 2013 posting to *The Signal* blog (http://blogs.loc.gov/digitalpreservation/2013/08/is-there-such-a-thing-as-digital-preservation/). Chapter 2 proposes a new set of principles that apply to all materials. Within the context and aims of preservation as we currently understand it, these principles provide a framework for the management of cultural heritage collections.

Chapter 3 considers general aspects of management that are relevant to preservation. Despite their diversity, collections share a number of common objectives such as acquisition, providing access, retention, and keeping objects in fit condition to be used. The purpose of a collection is a determining factor in its preservation needs. Chapter 3 examines these aspects by investigating organizational contexts, assessment, planning, and policies.


## FUNDAMENTAL CHANGE

Almost every aspect of the cultural heritage domain has undergone substantial change in recent decades. Preservation is no exception. Information technology is the main driver of this change, providing opportunities to make significant progress while also introducing new challenges. Digital objects, regardless of whether they are digital surrogates of analog originals or they are born digital, have added to the already wide array of materials and media that today's cultural heritage professionals need to be familiar with. It is now almost impossible to conceive of a collection that does not contain digital objects, most likely in multiple formats.

The main reason for these substantial changes is, as already indicated, information technology—more precisely, information and communication technology. We now inhabit, play, and work in a network society that is still evolving. Characteristics of this new network society, to summarize Hans Hofman, include:

- increasing interconnectivity
- blurring of boundaries between organizations, as well as between public and private domains
- the shift of focus from organizational structures to functions and processes, resulting in changes to traditional organizational structures
- the emergence of the "open" movement (as in open access, open source, open data)
- greater emphasis on transparency, accountability, and freedom of information
- new and innovative ways of working, forced in part by the ongoing financial crisis and reduced budgets[2]

One consequence of the evolving network society is convergence of practices across libraries, archives, and museums, stimulated and enabled by information and communication technology. Professionals in these traditionally discrete institutions are identifying significant areas of commonality in their practices. The increasing permeability of previously rigid boundaries is resulting in cross-fertilization of ideas and practices, and there is much to be gained from working across old boundaries.

Fundamental changes in the cultural heritage domain encourage, or sometimes force, changes in the preservation community. Paul Conway characterizes some of the changes in the preservation community as enhancing preservation outcomes by applying digital technologies and transforming preservation practice.[3] He identifies three ways that preservation outcomes are enhanced by the application of digital technologies. They can be applied to *protecting the originals* (the analog objects) by creating digital surrogates for use, and thereby protecting the originals by limiting access to them. Digital technology has been used to make surrogate copies in the past, although microfilming and photocopying were more widely applied for this purpose. There has, more recently, been a major increase in the use of digitizing to make surrogates. Digital technologies can also be applied to *representing the originals*: here, a digital system represents the information content of the original objects and is used in place of the original objects for searching its information content. They can be applied to *transcending the originals*, providing digital surrogates that enhance what is normally visible. Examples include multispectral imaging to reveal characteristics of an artifact not seen by the human eye, as applied by the British Library to the Codex Sinaiticus.[4]

Conway also identifies how preservation practice is being transformed by applying digital technologies. He notes this in terms of the changes in the fundamental preservation concepts of longevity, choice, quality, integrity, and access. No longer is the *longevity* of the physical object the primary (or sometimes the only) consideration. Traditional preservation practice is based on stabilizing physical objects, housing them in high-quality storage environments, and ensuring they are handled in ways that don't damage them. Standards and guidelines—for environmental control, care and handling, the quality of paper and of archival microfilm—where they still apply, are only a small part of preserving digital storage media with their shorter life spans and, more crucially, the short life expectancy of the systems required to access them and the files stored on them. The concept of longevity is no longer a sufficient basis for preservation. *Choice* as a preservation concept is also being redefined. Collections are developed in libraries, archives, and museums through a process of selection (appraisal in the archives context). Selection and appraisal decisions traditionally came after sufficient time had elapsed for the significance of an object to be determined. We do not, however, have the luxury of time to understand the significance of vulnerable digital objects that will not survive unless they receive attention from an early point in their existence. Selection shifts from a process carried out after time has passed to an ongoing activity, starting as close as possible in time to the digital object's creation. *Quality* of preservation is being redefined, too. All preservation activity is concerned with quality, expressed through standards for library binding, microfilming, and paper quality, among others. But what is quality in the digital world? Quality is not an absolute for digital objects that are copies of an analog object, but it is determined by the technology used to capture the image (or other representation) and to display the result. Conway expresses this succinctly: "Digital conversion places less emphasis on obtaining a faithful reproduction in favor of finding the best representation of the original in digital form."[5] Thus, the emphasis shifts from the quality of the product to the quality of the system that represents it; we might, for example, have a digital image created to a high standard but a computer system that can only display that image at a lower quality.

*Integrity* is probably the concept that has been forced to change the most in a digital world. Traditionally, conservators preserved the physical integrity of an object by trying not to change it at all, and they maintained its intellectual integrity by keeping documentation of its chain of custody and of conservation treatments applied to it. These procedures are not sufficient for digital objects. The principal reason is that preservation procedures for digital objects, such as migration, result in changes to the objects. We cannot, therefore, maintain the physical integrity of a digital object; the best we can do is to scrupulously maintain documentation about the changes and the chain of custody. Conway again: "Ultimately, the digital world transforms traditional preservation principles from guaranteeing the physical integrity of the object to specifying the creation of the object whose intellectual integrity is its primary characteristic."[6]

How we think about and provide *access* has also changed radically. Historically, preservation simply meant collecting and providing safe storage. It was use, principally, that exposed objects to the risks of theft, damage, or misuse, so minimizing use by limiting access, perhaps by making a copy of an original for use, was a key preservation practice. The choice was between preservation and access. Changes in thinking in the 1980s led to an acceptance that preservation and access are not mutually exclusive, famously expressed in Patricia Battin's phrase "preservation is access, and access is preservation."[7] Preservation actions are applied to objects so that they may be used. The focus has moved again with digital objects, where preservation is essential, not optional, for access and use. But new complexities arise: for digital objects, what is it, exactly, that we are providing access to?

The fundamental change in preservation requires us to shift our points of reference dramatically. We need new definitions because digital information is used increasingly in ways that are very different from the ways that physical objects are used. Because of the ease with which small pieces of data can be isolated and reused, understanding the contexts of its creation, management, and use is critical to understanding digital information in the future. The definitions of preservation that we use need to reflect this.

## DEFINITIONS

Changes in preservation principles and practice are reflected in the language adopted to describe them. The preservation function has traditionally been considered central to library practice, as reflected in statements such as "The preservation function—the stewardship of the accumulated knowledge base—represents the central obligation of librarianship."[8] Libraries, archives, and museums endorse the American Institute for Conservation of Historic and Artistic Works' statement that "every institution has a responsibility to safeguard the collections that are entrusted to it. That responsibility includes incorporating preservation and conservation awareness into all facets of the institution's activities so as to ensure the long-term preservation of its collections."[9] Now, in place of the word *preservation* we are likely to see and use *curation* and *stewardship*, which are relatively free from the association with physical objects (especially printed books) that *preservation* has. Using these words encourages a wider view of preservation as not just a set of technical processes isolated from services, policies, and stakeholders, but one that also takes into account of a wide range of stakeholders across disciplinary boundaries— libraries, archives, and museums, as well as funding agencies, government bodies, national data centers, institutional repositories, and learned societies.

Definitions matter, so commonly accepted definitions are needed, as was acknowledged in the OAIS Reference Model (now an ISO standard, ISO 14721),[10] a key standard for building a digital archive. The committee that drafted the OAIS Reference Model in the mid to late 1990s was concerned to provide definitions that applied to a wide range of disciplines, not just to the space data community that developed it, and sought to select terms that were not already heavily entrenched in any specific discipline. The introduction to the OAIS Reference Model provides definitions.[11]

Despite the importance of clear definitions, there is currently a lack of consensus on definitions, as a listserv discussion in October 2012 demonstrates. The question "How does your organization use the term *data curation* vs. *data management*?" was posed,[12] and the discussion led quickly to considering the terms *data stewardship* and *long-term preservation and access*. One participant suggested, "Data curation becomes difficult to unpack for faculty, though generally library folks seem to understand it now." We need to establish a common understanding of the terms and their definitions, because, without it, it is harder to work collaboratively in a context of convergence engendered by a network society.

Before preservation needed to encompass digital objects, there was common agreement about the terms *preservation*, *conservation*, and *restoration*. *Preservation* was allocated the more general, all-encompassing meaning; it "includes all the managerial and financial considerations, including storage and accommodation provisions, staffing levels, policies, techniques and methods involved in preserving library and archive materials and the information contained in them" as defined by the *IFLA Principles for the Preservation and Conservation of Library Materials*.[13] *Conservation* is more specific—the "practices taken to slow deterioration and prolong the life of an object by directly intervening in its physical or chemical make-up"; examples given are repairing damaged bindings and deacidifying paper.[14] *Restoration* refers to the rebuilding, sometimes extensive, of an object, typically using modern materials.[15]

These definitions need to be modified so that they embrace digital technologies. *Preservation* (as in *digital preservation*) is "the series of actions and interventions required to ensure continued and reliable access to authentic digital objects for as long as they are deemed to be of value."[16] (This series of actions and interventions is but a small subset of the activities involved in stewardship or curation.)

*Curation* is a term now in common use, although its meaning is not yet widely agreed on. Many life-cycle models that describe how digital objects are managed over time use this term to encompass not only digital preservation but also activities associated with creating digital objects, selection and appraisal, and enhancing digital objects to enable their use and reuse. Digital curation, then, begins before digital objects are created by setting standards for planning data collection that results in objects that can be maintained and used in the future. The term emphasizes adding value to data, for example through annotations to enhance their reuse, and it involves a wide range of stakeholders from across disciplinary boundaries. The Digital Curation Centre's Curation Lifecycle Model,[17] for example, recognizes the centrality of metadata, planning, and collaboration in managing digital objects over time in all of its key "sequential actions." This inclusive view is also apparent in other definitions of *curation*. The term *curation* is increasingly associated with science and social science data, and a new term, *research data management*, is gaining ground.

The term *stewardship* is also becoming more common. Stewardship is a broader concept than curation, being "an overarching process occurring now but attending to the past and taking into account and influencing the future."[18] Like *curation*, *stewardship* takes a wider view than preservation, which for digital objects is considered as a technical process isolated from services, policies, and stakeholders. It has a strong element of the holding of resources in trust by institutions for use by future generations. Priscilla Caplan notes: "Institutions exercise stewardship, individuals curate or manage data. . . . If you have stewardship of something, you don't dump it in the bit-bucket when your funded research project ends."[19] A strong sense of duty is associated with the practice of stewardship, in that it is the *necessary duty* of everyone involved in managing digital objects—the responsibility of everyone in the community—from the creator of the digital object to the curator, the user, and everyone in between.[20]

In this book we use the terms in this way:

*Digital stewardship*: the cultural, public policy, and ethical questions about how and what we remember and forget (relating to information in digital form). Digital stewardship encompasses the full range of preservation practices and issues applied by information professionals, who have the obligation of keeping collections, and the objects in them, in trust for future generations.

Digital stewardship subsumes *digital curation*: maintaining and adding value to a trusted body of information for current and future use.

Digital curation subsumes *digital preservation*: the technical processes involved in maintaining digital information over time.

## HYBRID COLLECTIONS

All collections in cultural heritage institutions, regardless of size or type, almost always contain both analog and digital media. If they do not currently, it is certain they will in the near future. Engaging with digital materials is no longer optional for cultural heritage professionals; as just one example indicates, 92 percent of respondents to a 2012 survey of Association of Research Libraries (ARL) members already collect born-digital content.[21] Commenting on digitizing, Anderson suggests that archives "have too much to offer, and the public too much to lose, if archives fail to fully engage in this process," and that they need to "ensure that they can provide high-quality digital surrogates that maximize the value of their collections not just in immediate access but also for long-term use and re-purposing."[22] The significant uptake of digitizing is changing the responsibilities of cultural heritage professionals who now help users navigate both physical and digital collections. It also demands knowledge of how to preserve digital objects as well as analog objects.

We are currently in a transitional phase, such as those periods of transition that Rankin views as "historically . . . dangerous times for the preservation of the record." He notes that when managing records there is "the need to handle hybrid information and record systems—paper, unmanaged digital (on hard drives and networked drives) and managed digital." Urgently needed are "the protocols, policies, legislation and behaviours" for handling different kinds of materials.[23] Do the policies and procedures developed for analog materials also apply in the hybrid environment? If they need to change, how do they need to change? How does maintaining physical collections as well as digital resources and their associated infrastructure affect costs? These are just some of the challenges that preservation managers now need to understand and address.

## NEW SKILLS

One consequence of the evolving network society and changing preservation activities is the new demand for cultural heritage professionals to understand a daunting array of materials and media. Preservation managers, who already need to manage a wide range of analog materials, have to add to their knowledge base digital materials—born digital as well as digitized versions of analog materials. The addition of digital objects in all types of repositories has expanded considerably the technical expertise required. Archivists handle digital storage media increasingly as they process collections. Librarians deal more and more with e-journals and e-books, whose publishers may not understand libraries' need to ensure their availability for long periods of time. Museum curators, in addition to the works of art, books, and manuscripts they have always managed, now have to take on board digital objects. It is difficult to imagine a repository with only a single format in its collection; identifying one with no digital assets is even more difficult.

As well as needing to know about more kinds of material and media, cultural heritage professionals also have an increasing obligation to understand how other silos across the cultural heritage landscape function. We are observing increasing commonalities in preservation practice in libraries, archives, and museums, resulting in significant part from practices converging in response to networked computing environments and user demand for digitized objects. This should not be perceived as threatening: the aims of each kind of institution are similar, as they include preservation and basic principles and practices, such as the requirement to provide stable storage environments. In fact, many institutions combine library, archives, and museum functions, which suggests there is a need to identify and implement practices common to all.

From this need an important question arises: What kind of person will develop the new policies and implement the new procedures required to effectively manage, in a range of institutions, both digital materials and analog materials over time? Almost certainly they will need a solid understanding of the principles underlying preservation, regardless of format. Although Australian experts interviewed in 2005[24] were not unanimous, they strongly suggested that an understanding of preservation in general was essential for understanding digital preservation. One expert believed that "a preservation specialist in any medium needs first to understand the purpose of the whole activity," another that "there is a common body of knowledge which can form the basis of a set of competencies." A third, from the audiovisual archiving arena, suggested that "you also need to have the mental framework that understands the nature of the analogue image and sound, the importance of the artefact and so on . . . it's actually an extension of knowledge. It's adding digital knowledge to analogue knowledge, so you can make your judgments on that basis." To illustrate this point, applicants for the position of Director of Preservation Services for the Northeast Document Conservation Center were, according to the Center's website in 2012, required to have "a broad knowledge of and experience in traditional collections preservation and digital curation."

The Australian experts also suggested the need for a strong emphasis on generic skills not specific to discipline or medium. Among desirable characteristics they identified were "the open mind, the inquiring mind, incredibly good project management skills, you've got to have an ability to work across complex organizations without treading on anybody's toes. You've got to be able to write a sentence which more than two people agree with." Thinking holistically was necessary: "the holistic picture, across the whole . . . rather than I'm a librarian, I'm an archivist, I'm the manager of a satellite imagery repository." Preservation personnel needed "IT skills and . . . a pretty good awareness of archival concepts, but . . . also . . . good analytical and writing skills." Added to these were a knowledge of "change management and an ability to liaise with owners and creators . . . to provide ongoing guidance and write comprehensible guidelines for depositors, and to ensure rigorous documentation and ongoing maintenance procedures are undertaken. Working as a team will also be pretty important."

There is no doubt, though, that new specific skills relevant to digital preservation are also required. From the 1990s on, commentators have noted the lack of people with expertise, including people who combine information technology skills with an understanding of long-term preservation. There has been considerable research into identifying the skills needed for digital preservation, most notably that of the DigCCurr (Digital Curation Curriculum) project (www.ils.unc.edu/digccurr) and the DigCurV (Digital Curator Vocational Education Europe) Project (www.digcur-education.org), which has given us a better understanding of the requirements.

What are the new skills? Professional understandings are required, such as an in-depth appreciation of preservation's importance and contribution in the context of a specific profession. Generic skills such as project management and communication and presentation skills are also necessary, as are technical skills at a higher level than have previously been considered relevant. Digital preservation specialists with high-level IT skills are also needed.

There will be change over time in the IT skills required, driven not only by the rapidly changing computer industry with its heavy emphasis on the next new technology but also by our increased understanding of what we need to know. Job descriptions offer guidance about skills that employers think necessary now. IT skill requirements reflected in job descriptions typically stipulate knowledge of specific systems, software, and metadata schema, such as UNIX, DSpace, and PREMIS. Educational and training programs are being developed and offered to meet these needs, and we can expect more to develop and evolve in response to industry needs. These programs will need to impart underlying principles as well as specific skills to ensure graduates have a solid foundation consisting of "a substantial degree of technical familiarity and also self-assurance in resolving problems."[25]

## CONCLUSION

The preservation landscape of the early decades of the 21st century is significantly different from what preceded it. This chapter has introduced the fundamentals of preservation management in the new landscape, which is characterized by an evolving networked environment, the breaking down of distinctions among previous separate sets of practice and between digital and analog materials, and collaboration. The next chapter builds on these fundamentals. It proposes a new set of preservation principles that apply to all materials, whether analog or digital, regardless of whether they are located in museums, archives, or libraries.

## NOTES

1. Earlier versions of this and the following chapter were published as Ross Harvey and Martha Mahard, "Mapping the Preservation Landscape for the Twenty-First Century," *Preservation, Digital Technology & Culture* 42 (2013): 5–16. The authors are grateful to the editor and publisher of this journal for permission to use them here.

2. Hans Hofman, "Rethinking the Archival Function in the Digital Era," paper presented at the International Council on Archives Congress, Brisbane, August 20–24, 2012, accessed January 29, 2014, http://ica2012.ica.org/files/pdf/Full%20papers%20upload/ica12final00187.pdf.

3. Paul Conway, "The Relevance of Preservation in a Digital World" (Andover, MA: Northeast Document Conservation Center, 2007), accessed September 16, 2013, http://www.nedcc.org/free-resources/preservation-leaflets/6.-reformatting/6.4-the-relevance-of-preservation-in-a-digital-world.

4. Barry Knight, "Multi-Spectral Imaging for the Codex Sinaiticus," accessed September 16, 2013, http://codexsinaiticus.org/en/project/conservation_msi.aspx.

5. Conway, "The Relevance of Preservation in a Digital World."

6. Conway, "The Relevance of Preservation in a Digital World."

7. Patricia Battin, "From Preservation to Access: Paradigm for the Nineties," *IFLA Journal* 19 (1993): 367.

8. Commission on Preservation and Access, *Annual Report, July 1, 1989–June 30, 1990* (Washington, DC: CPA, 1990), 1.

9. American Institute for Conservation of Historic and Artistic Works, "Position Paper on Conservation and Preservation in Collecting Institutions," accessed September 16, 2013, http://www.conservation-us.org/index.cfm?fuseaction=Page.viewPage&pageId=619.

10. The version noted here is Consultative Committee for Space Data Systems, *Reference Model for an Open Archival Information System (OAIS): Recommended Practice, CCSDS 650.0-M-2* (Washington, DC: CCSDS, 2012), accessed September 16, 2013, http://public.ccsds.org/publications/archive/650x0m2.pdf.

11. Consultative Committee for Space Data Systems, *Reference Model for an Open Archival Information System (OAIS)*, Section 1.7.2.

12. Megan Toups, October 11, 2012 (9:47 a.m.), posting to acr-igdc-l@ala.org (Subject: Data Curation vs. Data Management).

13. Edward P. Adcock, ed., *IFLA Principles for the Care and Handling of Library Material* (International Federation of Library Associations and Institutions Core Programme on Preservation and Conservation, 1998), 5, accessed September 16, 2013, http://archive.ifla.org/VI/4/news/pchlm.pdf.

14. Adcock, *IFLA Principles for the Care and Handling of Library Material*, 4.

15. Ross Harvey, *Preservation in Libraries: Principles, Strategies, and Practices for Librarians* (London: Bowker-Saur, 1993), 5–6.

16. JISC, "Digital Preservation Briefing Paper," November 20, 2006, accessed September 16, 2013, http://www.jisc.ac.uk/publications/briefingpapers/2006/pub_digipreservationbp.aspx.

17. Digital Curation Centre, "DCC Curation Lifecycle Model," accessed September 16, 2013, http://www.dcc.ac.uk/resources/curation-lifecycle-model.

18. H. Karasti, K. S. Baker, and E. Halkola, "Enriching the Notion of Data Curation in E-Science: Data Managing and Information Infrastructuring in the Long Term Ecological Research (LTER) Network," *Computer Supported Cooperative Work* 15 (2006): 352.

19. Priscilla Caplan, "At the Nexus of Analog and Digital: A Symposium for Preservation Educators, School of Information, University of Michigan, June 5–7, 2011, Panel 1: Definitions," *Preservation, Digital Technology and Culture*, forthcoming.

20. We are indebted to Sari Mauro, a student in a 2012 Digital Stewardship class at Simmons College, for many of these ideas.

21. Naomi L. Shaw et al., *Managing Born-Digital Special Collections and Archival Materials* (SPEC Kit 329) (Washington, DC: Association of Research Libraries, 2012), 11.

22. Ian Anderson, "Archival Digitisation: Breaking Out of the Strong Box," in *Record Keeping in a Hybrid Environment: Managing the Creation, Use, Preservation and Disposal of Unpublished Information Objects in Context*, eds. Alistair Tough and Michael Moss (Oxford, UK: Chandos, 2006), 223.

23. Frank Rankin, "Implementing EDRMS and Shaping the Record" in *Record Keeping in a Hybrid Environment*, 42–43.

24. A summary of these interviews can be found in Ross Harvey, *Preserving Digital Materials* (München: K. G. Saur, 2005).

25. Peter Botticelli et al., "Educating Digital Curators: Challenges and Opportunities," *International Journal of Digital Curation* 6 (2011): 154.

# CHAPTER 2

# Preservation Principles

························································································

Chapter 1 noted that the preservation landscape of the early decades of the 21st century is significantly different from what preceded it. One difference, in particular, concerns us in this chapter—the erosion of distinctions among previously separate sets of practice and between the preservation of digital and analog materials. This chapter proposes and develops a new set of preservation principles that apply to all materials, whether analog or digital, regardless of whether the materials are located in museums, archives, or libraries. These principles are infused throughout the rest of this book.

## THE PRINCIPLES

This book is based on the philosophy that there are preservation principles that apply to all kinds of materials, whether digital or not. Preservation theory and practice normally considers that "digital is different," so writings about digital preservation, curation, and stewardship tend to emphasize the differences, rather than the many similarities. If this is indeed the case, digital stewardship in cultural heritage management institutions should be a separate professional field because of the differences in the nature and characteristics of digital objects. It is commonly contended that digital objects are difficult to preserve because they exist in a large variety of types and representations that quickly become obsolete, they are closely linked to specific software applications or hardware that also quickly become obsolete, they are prone to corruption, they are generally poorly identified with insufficient metadata, and they require more frequent preservation attention than analog objects. There is a lack of infrastructure in place to support digital stewardship activities, any infrastructure that is in place is unlikely to be funded sustainably, and a range of intellectual property rights associated with digital objects restrict our ability to preserve them. Furthermore, we still do not know enough about how to preserve digital objects.

························································································

As our understanding of digital stewardship matures, we can begin to question some of these assumptions and mantras and to develop principles that straddle the analog-digital preservation divide, along with practices that apply to all materials. The reality in the workplace is increasingly of the erosion of distinctions between digital and analog materials and how they are managed. As Tyler Walters and Katherine Skinner contend, "Very few research libraries should have more than half of their infrastructure devoted to physical collections at this point in time. The library needs to think of digital curation as a core function of the library and to invest financial and other resources into it accordingly."[1] Some institutions, such as the Deutsche Nationalbibliothek, are already restructuring to reflect the convergence of digital and analog preservation.[2]

These ideas are not new. In 1993 Michèle Cloonan challenged us to consider how the principles of preservation, "oriented towards the treatment of individual items," translate to the digital world.[3] Gerard Clifton suggested in 2005: "In principle, the actions to preserve digital materials are largely the same as those for traditional materials, although the form that such action may take can be different in the digital environment."[4] The most unequivocal statement is by Paul Conway: "The fundamental principles of preservation in the digital world are the same as those of the analog world and, in essence, define the priorities for extending the useful life of information resources. These fundamental concepts are longevity, choice, quality, integrity, and access."[5] Priscilla Caplan has pointed out some of the similarities: both are "components of institutional stewardship. Both compete for resources against more direct user services. Both must maintain the integrity and authenticity of the information they preserve. Both are concerned with the environmental conditions of storage units . . . and must protect resources against malicious and accidental damage. Both have to cope with media degradation."[6]

A preliminary investigation in 2011 identified many significant common elements in analog and digital preservation practice, concluding, "It is very likely that we can improve the preservation aspects of our digital stewardship practice by adopting and adapting practices from our extensive analog preservation experience."[7] One readily identified principle is the idea that it is worth putting effort into creating long-lived storage media; for example, by encouraging the development and use of permanent paper and creating digital objects in open, well-supported standard formats for which access tools may remain available. Another principle identified was that of redundancy, typically described in terms of keeping multiple copies, providing adequate data backup, keeping original bitstreams as well as migrated copies, or keeping analog versions after they have been digitized. The investigation offered a statement of basic preservation principles and practices applicable to both analog and digital materials, acknowledging it as only a beginning:

- Appraisal is both necessary (because of limited resources) and desirable (to ensure high-quality preservation).
- Materials contain the seeds of their own destruction (inherent vice), so the key to understanding what preservation actions to take is in understanding their structure.

- A clear distinction must be made between artifacts and the information they carry, or between the containers and the content.
- Prefer preservation actions that address large quantities of material over actions that focus on individual objects.
- Preservation actions must take into account the needs of the user.
- Preservation, as a key component in the sustainability of cultural property, is an imperative that transcends national borders and is essential for the maintenance and perpetuation of global cultural heritage.[8]

Other principles identified in the preliminary investigation are not, on the surface, applicable to both analog and digital preservation practice. Of these the best example is *benign neglect*—the idea that most artifacts do not deteriorate rapidly if ignored, thus buying time before preservation attention is needed. Benign neglect has always been a preservation management tool used by libraries, archives, and museums, but we have assumed that it is not a reliable tool for dealing with digital objects. The reasoning behind the assumption is that, because digital objects are in file formats that rapidly become obsolete, are stored on media that deteriorate very rapidly, and rely for access on hardware and software that rapidly goes out of date, benign neglect is out of the question; preservation attention is required at an early stage in the life of any digital object. However, there is some evidence that benign neglect may not be as disastrous for digital objects as previously thought. David Pearson's work at the National Archives of Australia on the recovery of files from several collections of digital storage media from 1970 onward[9] suggests that we may have more time than we have assumed, *if* the media have been housed in high-quality storage. Similar examples suggest the need for more research into data deterioration rates. Benign neglect might just turn out to be more acceptable as a principle on which to base digital preservation strategies than we currently think.

The preliminary statement of basic preservation principles made in 2011 and reproduced above was the starting point for the more comprehensive list of preservation principles and practices applicable to both analog and digital materials used in this book, presented in figure 2.1.

## CONTEXT AND AIMS

The four preservation principles in the first group are about the context and aims of preservation.

*Preservation, as a key component in the sustainability of cultural property, is an imperative that transcends national borders and is essential for the maintenance and perpetuation of global cultural heritage.* The Society of American Archivists' Core Values Statement and Code of Ethics articulates this imperative for archives: "Since ancient times, archives have afforded a fundamental power to those who control them. In a democratic society

## THE CONTEXT AND AIMS OF PRESERVATION

- Preservation, as a key component in the sustainability of cultural property, is an imperative that transcends national borders and is essential for the maintenance and perpetuation of global cultural heritage.

- Preservation actions must take into account the needs of the user.

- Authenticity of the objects needs to be ensured in any preservation action.

- Preservation is the responsibility of all, from the creators of objects to the users of objects.

## GENERAL PRINCIPLES

- Effort put into creating long-lived objects and material reduces the need for preservation attention in the future.
- Collaboration is necessary to ensure preservation.
- Advocacy is necessary to ensure preservation.
- Taking preservation action now is better than doing nothing.
- Preservation requires active, managed care.
- Understanding the structure of materials is the key to understanding what preservation actions to take, as materials contain the seeds of their own destruction (inherent vice).
- Distinguish clearly between objects (containers) and the information they carry (content).
- Prefer preservation actions that address large quantities of material over actions that focus on individual objects.

## SPECIFIC PRINCIPLES

- Appraisal is both necessary and desirable.

- Keep the original.

- Keep multiple copies of objects.

- Do the minimum necessary to stabilize and preserve the object.

- Preservation actions should not exceed the abilities of the personnel who apply them.

- Preservation actions should aim at the highest quality possible.

- Preservation actions should not harm the object.

- Preservation actions should be documented.

- Preservation actions should adhere to ethical considerations.

**FIGURE 2.1.** Preservation Principles and Practices Applicable to All Materials

such power should benefit all members of the community." The statement continues: "Archivists preserve a wide variety of primary sources for the benefit of future generations. Preserving materials is a means to this end not an end in itself. . . . Archivists thus preserve materials for the benefit of the future more than for the concerns of the past."[10]

*Preservation actions must take into account the needs of the user.* A key principle in this book is that the ultimate goal of all preservation is to ensure continued access to information. Everything described in this book is aimed at keeping information accessible for as long as it is needed. Preservation of information that results in reducing or restricting access to that information is usually a waste of resources. The mission statements of many organizations acknowledge this principle: the British Library's Collections Care Department, for example, notes on its website that it is "responsible for protecting and preserving the Library's vast collections and their assets, and enabling them to be used, experienced and interpreted." Professional associations also acknowledge it. The Society of American Archivists' Core Values Statement and Code of Ethics indicates that "recognizing that use is the fundamental reason for keeping archives, archivists actively promote open and equitable access to the records in their care within the context of their institutions' missions and their intended user groups. They minimize restrictions and maximize ease of access. They facilitate the continuing accessibility and intelligibility of archival materials in all formats."[11] *Conservators*, "in collaboration with other professional colleagues involved with cultural heritage, shall take into account the requirements of its social use while preserving the cultural heritage."[12] Preservation of digital objects is no different. It is driven by the imperative to "enhance rather than compromise access."[13]

*Authenticity of the objects needs to be ensured in any preservation action.* Definitions of the term *authenticity* abound, the most succinct being "the verifiable claim that an object is what it purports to be."[14] Ensuring authenticity is arguably the overriding requirement for any action aimed at preserving an object, whether analog or digital. For physical objects, we strive to maintain the authenticity of the artifact—although we acknowledge this isn't always possible—so that its users are assured that they are viewing or handling an original object. Conservators' codes of ethics place a high priority on maintaining long-term access to an item without compromising its integrity or authenticity. The point to note here is that maintaining the integrity of the artifact in its original state also maintains its authenticity. This concept is not transferable to digital objects because the physical media in which their information content is stored will change from time to time. Precisely what constitutes authenticity for a preserved digital object is a problematic concept, but authenticity does, nevertheless, need to be demonstrated for digital objects.

*Preservation is the responsibility of all, from the creators of objects to the users of objects.* This principle highlights one of the differences traditionally identified between preserving analog and digital objects. Preservation of analog objects was carried out usually after they had been determined to be worth adding to a collection and had been taken into the collection. It was typically the province of conservators or preservation administrators. Incorporating digital objects into the collections of museums, archives, and libraries requires both the timing of and responsibility for preservation to shift. Information professionals must now acknowledge that preservation is a responsibility they all share, whatever their role in an organization—whether they are creators, curators, producers, collection managers, registrars, catalogers, or conservators. A specific action based on this principle is encouraging creators of digital objects to use open, well-supported standard formats for which access tools may remain available longer, rather than proprietary formats where there is less assurance that access will continue to be possible. Other specific actions are noted elsewhere in this and later chapters.

## GENERAL PRINCIPLES

In the second group of preservation principles, eight general principles are given, whose relevance has been enhanced or reinterpreted in the digital domain.

*Effort put into creating long-lived objects and material reduces the need for preservation attention in the future.* This principle, the focus of chapter 6, is long established in preservation practice. As the American Library Association's Preservation Policy acknowledges, "Manufacturers, publishers, distributors and purchasers of information products must work in tandem to improve the usability, durability, and longevity of the media (e.g., paper, film, magnetic tape, optical disk) that ensure the persistence of these products."[15] A well-established example of this principle is the use of permanent paper in creating documents and printing books. This paper is manufactured to standards that specify characteristics such as its alkalinity and strength, resulting in a product that is considerably more likely to remain usable in the future (although it is hardly permanent). The principle that lies behind the use of permanent paper is relevant to digital objects. For example, when creating digital objects in a digitization process, selecting well-supported, stable, open file formats, digitizing at an image quality recommended by relevant guidelines, and avoiding lossy compression algorithms are intended to increase the usability and extend the longevity of the master files created.[16]

*Collaboration is necessary to ensure preservation.* Cultural heritage professionals increasingly realize the need for collaborative efforts to ensure adequate preservation of their collections. Collaboration is, in fact, well established in most preservation management programs. For example, preservation managers collaborate with experts in climate control, fire safety, pest management, and other areas in gaining an understanding of a collection and its preservation requirements. Although the sheer quantity of digital objects already in collections now underscores the need for collaboration, its importance has long been well understood, and collaborative activities have been implemented, well in advance of the full recognition of the challenges of digital stewardship. The Brittle Books Program in the United States is an example. Funded in 1988 for twenty years by the National Endowment for the Humanities (NEH), the program sought to address paper deterioration in books in library collections in the United States by reformatting the content of these books to microfilm, and libraries and library consortia in most states participated.[17] Conservators recognize this imperative, too; the Professional Guidelines of the European Confederation of Conservator-Restorers' Organisations state, "Where necessary or appropriate, the Conservator-Restorer shall collaborate with other professionals and shall participate with them in a full exchange of information."[18]

There is an abundance of digital stewardship collaboratives. One of them, LOCKSS (Lots of Copies Keep Stuff Safe), states the imperative to collaborate clearly: "No single library can achieve robust long-term preservation alone."[19] The Digital Preservation Network (d-p-n.org), launched in 2012, works collaboratively to preserve the scholarly record. In its "Community Watch and Collaboration" action, the DCC Curation Lifecycle Model emphasizes the importance of collaboration, particularly participation in "the development of shared standards, tools and suitable software."[20] A 2012 Online Computer Library Center (OCLC) report also argues for collaboration aimed at providing and maintaining software and workstations for obsolete technology.[21]

*Advocacy is necessary to ensure preservation.* It was stated in the first group of four principles that preservation is the responsibility of all, from the creators of objects to the users of objects. An aspect of the responsibility is that all parties must advocate for preservation. Awareness of the urgency in addressing preservation issues, especially digital stewardship issues, needs to be raised at all levels of society, from the general public, who create objects, to governments, who fund national preservation programs. Many professional organizations acknowledge the need for advocacy in policy statements. The *IFLA Principles for the Care and Handling of Library Material* state the importance of raising awareness "among the general public and those who are in a position to fund preservation programs. Governments must play an active role in ensuring the welfare of a nation's heritage. National preservation offices, financially supported either by government or private funding, are essential if a country's written heritage, in whatever format, is to survive."[22] The American Library Association's Preservation Policy is more specific: "Libraries have an obligation (a) to inform donors, users, administrators, and local officials about the ephemeral nature of primary source materials, (b) to promote strategies for the proper care, handling, and storage of these materials, and (c) to recommend the use of durable media and methods of documentation."[23]

*Taking preservation action now is better than doing nothing.* We don't know everything we need to know about the long-term effects of some preservation processes and actions. In some cases, common understandings have led to decisions about preservation that have not stood the test of time; an example is the previously widespread copying of highly flammable cellulose nitrate film to acetate film. We now know that acetate film is also unstable, and that it deteriorates, resulting in a greater loss of film than would have occurred if the nitrate film had been kept under appropriate, secure storage.[24] We certainly don't know all that we need to about digital stewardship. Colin Webb's 2004 summary of a significant body of experience asserts that action is possible now, even if we do not have all of the answers.[25]

*Preservation requires active, managed care.* The challenges of digital stewardship highlight the need for active care of digital objects, ideally from the point of their creation, and this care must be managed. "Move it or lose it" was one of three aphorisms developed from the experiences of participants in Canadian Conservation Institute workshops. (The others were "something is better than nothing" and "don't throw out the original.")[26] The requirement for active, managed care is already well understood in the context of preserving analog objects. It has given rise to an emphasis on preservation procedures intended to stabilize physical objects, improve storage environments, and maintain high-quality climate control. What is different about digital objects is their inherent instability; they are unlikely to remain readable and understandable unless they are actively managed from an early stage of their existence.

*Understanding the structure of materials is the key to understanding what preservation actions to take, as materials contain the seeds of their own destruction (inherent vice).* Knowledge of the structure of materials that constitute the collections of cultural heritage institutions is essential for all information professionals concerned with preservation. Such knowledge allows an information professional to understand why some preservation actions are effective. Objects in collections need to be viewed as significant not just for the information they contain and how that information can be used, but also as physical objects governed by the same laws that affect all organic materials. Deterioration is defined in this book as a loss of quality in any material that decreases its ability to carry out its intended function. It results in part from inherent instability of the materials, such as the acidic nature of some kinds of paper, the light-sensitive nature of the silver halide image-bearing layer of a photograph, or the deterioration in the protective polymer layer on a compact disk. Paper deterioration has been commented on for centuries and more recently investigated scientifically, most notably by William Barrow. As understanding of the chemical and physical realities of paper deterioration deepened, fruitful efforts were made to improve the manufacture of paper, especially by reducing its acid content. For digital objects, understanding how file formats are constructed and controlled by their owners is a key to creating or selecting formats that stand the best chance of being preserved in the future.

*Distinguish clearly between objects (containers) and the information they carry (content).* The realization in the 20th century that reformatting—copying information content to a more durable medium—was an acceptable preservation action was revolutionary. Copying has a long tradition; the copying of palm leaf manuscripts in Southeast Asia is but one example of copying as a response to damage and deterioration of information resources. Printing facsimiles (often applying photographic printing techniques such as photolithography) was used to make copies of fragile physical objects for use or exhibition purposes. What changed is that reformatting techniques were developed that enabled much larger numbers of objects to be reformatted. First came microfilming, and then digitizing, both of which create surrogates for use and thereby protect the originals by limiting access to them. It is important to realize that "digitization is not preservation—it is simply a means of copying original materials. In creating a digital copy, the institution creates a new resource that will itself require preservation."[27]

*Prefer preservation actions that address large quantities of material over actions that focus on individual objects.* This principle is based on economic necessity. Given limited financial resources and skilled personnel, preservation actions that deal with large numbers of objects result in a more favorable cost-to-benefit ratio. For analog materials, this is demonstrated by giving priority to preventative conservation measures that aim to limit further deterioration, such as putting photographic materials in cold storage. An example of the principle's application to digital objects is making sure they are created in open, well-supported standard formats for which access tools are more likely to remain available.

## SPECIFIC PRINCIPLES

The nine preservation principles in the third group describe specific principles for preservation that apply equally to the preservation of analog and digital objects.

*Appraisal is both necessary and desirable.* It is essential to set priorities for resource allocation for effective and responsible stewardship, as there is simply too much to keep. There is a strong economic rationale for this principle, as there is for the last principle in the previous group, although it is by no means the only reason for its prominence. Archivists and museum curators have long realized that appraisal—the process of identifying materials that have sufficient value to be accessioned into a collection[28]—is an essential component of their professional practice. Archivists determine the value of objects in relation to criteria such as provenance, content, authenticity, and intrinsic value, and they make their decisions in conjunction with other stakeholders.[29] Museum curators select exemplars that best illustrate outstanding quality, or have historic, artistic, scientific, or social significance, among other factors. Librarians select information resources based on the relevance of the information content to their collections and users. Appraisal is receiving renewed attention as more digital objects are incorporated into collections. In a survey reported in 2012, historians and information professionals "expressed a clear desire for the selection of digital data to mirror the analogue world: *there is no sudden change, just because the format of the material has evolved.*"[30] The appraisal of digital objects is not substantially different from the appraisal of analog materials, although there is a difference in emphasis of some of the criteria over others.[31]

*Keep the original.* The primary focus of the stewardship of materials of any kind, whether analog or digital, is keeping materials for the long term. (It is not stewardship's only focus, as noted elsewhere in this chapter; providing access over time is another key aim.) The practice of preserving originals wherever possible provides an example. For example, if a newspaper is microfilmed or digitized, it is now common practice to keep the original after it has been reformatted, perhaps in low-cost storage, allowing us to go back to the original if necessary to make another copy. For digital materials, whose preservation is inextricably tied to copying, the practice is to keep the original bitstream. This principle faces significant challenges in the stewardship of very large data sets, where the cost of keeping a copy on a "just in case" basis is very high. The principle was also frequently challenged in its application to analog materials when an original object was heavily deteriorated and the process of reformatting it hastened its deterioration to the extent it became unusable. For example, preparing very brittle newspapers for copying and handling them while making copies can reduce an original to a pile of small paper fragments.

*Keep multiple copies of objects.* This principle is typically referred to as redundancy, or sometimes diversification. The more copies of an object are available, the less likely it is the object will become unavailable and inaccessible in the future. For analog objects, copies are made, usually by digitizing the object, and housed in different locations so that damage to a copy at one location is not duplicated at another. For digital objects, the principle is interpreted as providing adequate data backups and ensuring that backups are stored at geographically dispersed locations. This principle is the basis of preservation programs, such as LOCKSS (www.lockss.org), which apply decentralized and distributed preservation by copying material at multiple sites so that damaged versions at one site can be restored from a copy at another site.

The remaining six preservation principles in this group form a subset of specific principles that apply equally to analog and digital objects. This subset is based closely on the codes of ethics of professional conservators, which are broadly similar regardless of country of origin.[32]

*Do the minimum necessary to stabilize and preserve the object.* Conservators apply the principle of minimal intervention, which is doing as little as possible in order to stabilize, conserve, or preserve an object. It is sometimes stated as limiting the treatment to "only that which is necessary."[33]

*Preservation actions should not exceed the abilities of the personnel who apply them.* The "Code of Ethics and Guidelines for Practice" of the American Institute for Conservation of Historic and Artistic Works (AIC) requires the conservation professional to "practice within the limits of personal competence and education as well as within the limits of the available facilities."[34] A much-publicized example in which limits of competence were exceeded is the amateur conservation work applied to a fresco in a Spanish church.[35]

*Preservation actions should aim at the highest quality possible.* This principle applies to all professional activities engaged in by cultural heritage professionals. Conservators' ethical codes acknowledge that, even though there may be circumstances that constrain preservation actions, such as limited resources, the work carried out must always be of the highest possible quality within any constraints. The AIC's "Code of Ethics and Guidelines for Practice" puts it this way: "While circumstances may limit the resources allocated to a particular situation, the quality of work that the conservation professional performs shall not be compromised."[36]

*Preservation actions should not harm the object.* The interests of the object being preserved are paramount. The AIC's "Code of Ethics and Guidelines for Practice" indicate that conservators "must strive to select methods and materials that, to the best of current knowledge, do not adversely affect cultural property or its future examination, scientific investigation, treatment, or function."[37]

*Preservation actions should be documented.* Conservators record their actions as a matter of course. Photographs of an analog object are taken before, during, and after preservation treatment, and reports carefully document the condition of the object and of procedures and materials used in treatment. The same principle applies to the preservation of digital objects, but with added force. Records of the preservation actions applied to digital objects are essential for the determination of important characteristics of those objects, including authenticity. Chapter 6 considers documentation of digital objects in more detail.

*Preservation actions should adhere to ethical considerations.* The final principle we note is in the nature of a metaprinciple reinforcing all of the previous principles—be ethical in the choice and application of all preservation actions.

## ARTIFACT OR INFORMATION?

We understood better how to incorporate digital objects into our preservation worldview once we distinguished between preserving the physical object and preserving the information represented in, or by, the physical object. Although distinguishing between artifact and information content is not a new concept, it is one whose significance we have had to relearn and reassess. We are used to considering a book as both a physical object (a material container) and a text (information content). With an e-book there is no physical object, so an e-book is best considered as a text that may exist in a number of digital formats.

Historically, preservation referred only to collecting and providing safe storage for physical objects, as noted in chapter 1. Analog preservation's emphasis on physical objects relies on the fact that most analog materials stay reasonably stable over time. We see this expressed in the concept of benign neglect, outlined earlier in this chapter. It is also apparent in procedures that stabilize physical objects—for instance, deacidifying paper. The integrity of a physical object is maintained as far as possible by practices such as storage in an optimum controlled environment. The assumption is that by doing this its information content will remain readable. This way of thinking and working cannot be applied to digital objects without major modification. One of the key characteristics of digital objects is their heavy reliance on sophisticated equipment that rapidly evolves, with high rates of obsolescence. Unlike most analog objects, simply storing digital objects does not provide a high likelihood of their information content remaining accessible in the future. A different approach needs to be taken.

Although the predominant emphasis of preservation was on preserving the physical object, it coexisted with techniques for preserving the information content. Copying of manuscripts has a very long history, although its accuracy was frequently suspect. Cicero, writing in the first century BCE, complained, "I no longer know where to turn for Latin books, the copies on the market are so inaccurate" and called these copies "books full of lies."[38] The fascinating story of the preservation of texts written by the mathematician Archimedes because a medieval prayer book was copied over them is told in *The Archimedes Codex*.[39] With the development of printing techniques, especially photolithographic techniques in the latter half of the 19th century, it became commonplace to print photographic facsimiles of a rare text. The 1976 edition of *Facsimiles of the Declaration of Independence and the Treaty of Waitangi*, seminal documents for New Zealand, is a facsimile of the first edition produced by photolithography in 1877.[40] Although the reason for making copies was predominantly the dissemination of information content, copying also served a preservation purpose by making multiple copies available and minimizing further damage to the originals. Microfilming was used for preservation purposes in libraries and archives from the 1930s, as photocopying was later.[41] Microfilming has been almost completely superseded by digitizing, and digitizing of objects in the collections of libraries and archives is increasing at a dramatic rate. (Reformatting is noted in more detail in chapter 4.)

The focus of digital stewardship cannot be on preserving the physical object—that is, the medium on which the digital object is stored. Initially, digital stewardship thinking was based on analog preservation understandings, so early practice concentrated on developing long-lived digital storage media and storing digital storage media in high-quality environmental conditions. Digital objects were often preserved by printing them out to paper or microfilm because it was considered that paper and microfilm were more stable than digital storage media. Research was undertaken into developing long-lived storage media, such as the HD-Rosetta (www.norsam.com/rosetta.html) and Arnano processes (www.arnano.fr), both based on microscopic processes that engrave data onto long-lasting bases. Although these processes have not been widely adopted, the thinking underlying them persists in recommendations to use gold CDs for long-term storage of data. Tests of gold CDs show they are more durable than other kinds of CDs and DVDs, although there is considerable variation in durability among the products of different manufacturers.[42] Recommending gold CDs for long-term preservation ignores the issue of obsolescence of software, hardware, and file formats, which will render digital objects stored on any CD, gold or otherwise, unreadable long before the storage media deteriorate. Similarly, storing digital media in high-quality environmental conditions may slow down the rate at which the media deteriorate, but it is no guarantee that the content will remain accessible.

Digital materials are difficult to preserve for many reasons. They exist in a large variety of types and representations, which quickly become obsolete; they are closely linked to specific software applications or hardware, which quickly become obsolete; they are prone to corruption; they are generally poorly identified, with insufficient metadata; there is a lack of developed infrastructure to support digital stewardship activities; any infrastructure that is present for digital stewardship is not funded so it is sustainable; and there are often intellectual property rights that restrict our ability to preserve them.[43] For these and other reasons, the stewardship of digital materials needs to focus on the content of digital objects. Gerard Clifton suggests two requirements: "Preserve the data streams that encode the digital information, and maintain a way of interpreting the preserved data so that the encoded information can be presented in the future."[44] The National Archives of Australia has articulated the requirements as the "performance" model: "The preservation of digital records should focus on maintaining the *performance* of a record over time, rather than attempting to preserve the specific combination of source data and technology that supports a record at its creation. This fundamental idea, now adopted by a number of archival institutions around the world, remains central to everything we have done since then."[45]

## STARTING POINTS

The view of the preservation landscape ahead of us is encouraging. We have developed better understandings of what a digital archive might look like (as in the Trusted Digital Repository concept) and have developed and applied concepts of *digital stewardship* (as distinct from the more limiting concepts of *digital preservation*). We have a much better understanding of how to handle data that are different from "library-based" (and "museum- and archives-based") objects. While our practice to date has been founded on how to preserve documents (usually static, text-based material such as pages from books, or image files) on a relatively small scale, we are slowly appreciating what it means to handle large data sets generated in e-science environments, and learning how to deal with very large, curated databases (such as genome databases) that are the product of many hands and change constantly.

The notion that cultural heritage professionals must become actively involved at the very earliest stages of record creation was underlined by Hywel Gwynn Williams and Anna Henry, who note that "[a] holistic approach is important which acknowledges the need to influence the practices of creating agencies and agents, re-evaluate the processes and tools for receiving records and data into archival control, and ensure the efficient and effective description and on-going management of data and digital records within their context and provenance."[46] The principles outlined in this chapter provide a template for future practice that embraces the diversity of cultural property at the same time as it emphasizes the commonalities across materials, domains, and cultures.

The next chapter considers general aspects of management relevant to the preservation of collections in every kind of cultural heritage institution. Collections share a number of common objectives: acquisition, providing access, retention, and keeping objects in fit condition to be used. The purpose of a collection is a determining factor in its preservation needs. Chapter 3 examines these aspects by investigating organizational contexts, assessment, planning, and policies.

## NOTES

1. Tyler Walters and Katherine Skinner, *New Roles for New Times: Digital Curation for Preservation* (Washington, DC: Association of Research Libraries, 2011), 57.

2. Reinhard Altenhöner, "Preservation and Conservation as an Integrated Process in the German National Library: Status Quo and Outlook," paper presented at IFLA WLIC 2013, Singapore, accessed September 28, 2013, http://library.ifla.org/247/1/146-altenhoener-en.pdf.

3. Michèle Valerie Cloonan, "The Preservation of Knowledge," *Library Trends* 41 (1993): 594.

4. Gerard Clifton, "Risk and the Preservation Management of Digital Collections," *International Preservation News* 36 (2005): 21.

5. Paul Conway, "The Relevance of Preservation in a Digital World" (Andover, MA: Northeast Document Conservation Center, 2007), accessed September 16, 2013, http://www.nedcc.org/free-resources/preservation-leaflets/6.-reformatting/6.4-the-relevance-of-preservation-in-a-digital-world.

6. Priscilla Caplan, "At the Nexus of Analog and Digital: A Symposium for Preservation Educators, School of Information, University of Michigan, June 5–7, 2011," Panel 1: Definitions," *Preservation, Digital Technology and Culture*, forthcoming.

7. Jeannette Bastian, Michèle Cloonan, and Ross Harvey, "From Teacher to Learner to User: Developing a Digital Stewardship Pedagogy," *Library Trends* 59, no. 4 (2011): 611.

8. Bastian, Cloonan, and Harvey, "From Teacher to Learner to User," 612.

9. David Pearson, "Preserve or Preserve Not, There Is No Try: Some Dilemmas Relating to Personal Digital Archiving," presentation at DigCCurr 2009: Digital Curation Practice, Promise and Prospects, April 1–3, 2009, Chapel Hill, NC, accessed September 17, 2013, http://www.ils.unc.edu/digccurr2009/6a-pearson.pdf.

10. Society of American Archivists, "SAA Core Values Statement and Code of Ethics," approved May 2011, accessed September 17, 2013, http://www2.archivists.org/statements/saa-core-values-statement-and-code-of-ethics.

11. Society of American Archivists, "SAA Core Values Statement."

12. European Confederation of Conservator-Restorers' Organisations, "E.C.C.O. Professional Guidelines," adopted March 1, 2002, accessed September 17, 2013, http://www.ecco-eu.org/about-e.c.c.o./professional-guidelines.html, Article 6.

13. Douglas Elford et al., "Getting the Whole Picture: Finding a Common Language Between Digital Preservation and Conservation," National Library of Australia Staff Papers 2012, accessed September 17, 2013, http://www.nla.gov.au/openpublish/index.php/nlasp/article/viewArticle/2458, 6.

14. Abby Smith, "Authenticity and Affect: When Is a Watch Not a Watch?" *Library Trends* 52 (2003): 172.

15. American Library Association, "Preservation Policy, Revised 2001," accessed September 17, 2013, http://www.ala.org/alcts/resources/preserv/01alaprespolicy.

16. Clifton, "Risk and the Preservation Management of Digital Collections."

17. Abby Smith, *The Future of the Past: Preservation in American Research Libraries* (Washington, DC: Council on Library and Information Resources, 1999), accessed September 17, 2013, http://www.clir.org/pubs/reports/pub82/pub82text.html.

18. European Confederation of Conservator-Restorers' Organisations, "E.C.C.O. Professional Guidelines," Article 13.

19. LOCKSS, "Preservation Principles," accessed September 17, 2013, http://www.lockss.org/about/principles/.

20. Digital Curation Centre, "DCC Curation Lifecycle Model," http://www.dcc.ac.uk/resources/curation-lifecycle-model.

21. Ricky Erway, *Swatting the Long Tail of Digital Media: A Call for Collaboration* (Dublin, OH: OCLC Research, 2012), accessed September 17, 2013, http://www.oclc.org/content/dam/research/publications/library/2012/2012-08.pdf.

22. Edward P. Adcock, ed., *IFLA Principles for the Care and Handling of Library Material* (International Federation of Library Associations and Institutions Core Programme on Preservation and Conservation, 1998), 12.

23. American Library Association, "Preservation Policy."

24. Heather Heckman, "Burn After Viewing, or, Fire in the Vaults: Nitrate Decomposition and Combustibility," *American Archivist* 73 (2010): 483–506.

25. C. Webb, "The Malleability of Fire: Preserving Digital Information," in *Managing Preservation for Libraries and Archives: Current Practice and Future Developments*, ed. J. Feather (Aldershot, Hants: Ashgate, 2004), 27–52.

26. T. Strang, "Choices and Decisions," in *Symposium 2003: Preservation of Electronic Records: New Knowledge and Decision-Making*, Ottawa, September 15–18, 2003: preprints.

27. Janet Gertz, "Preservation and Selection for Digitization" (Andover, MA: Northeast Document Conservation Center, 2007), accessed September 17, 2013, http://www.nedcc.org/free-resources/preservation-leaflets/6.-reformatting/6.6-preservation-and-selection-for-digitization.

28. Modified from the definitions in Richard Pearce-Moses, *A Glossary of Archival and Records Terminology* (Chicago: Society of American Archivists), accessed September 17, 2013, http://www2.archivists.org/glossary.

29. Society of American Archivists, "SAA Core Values Statement."

30. Lena Roland and David Bawden, "The Future of History: Investigating the Preservation of Information in the Digital Age," *Library & Information History* 28 (2012): 226 (emphasis added by the authors).

31. Ross Harvey, "Instalment on 'Appraisal and Selection,' January 2007," in *DCC Curation Reference Manual*, accessed September 17, 2013, http://www.dcc.ac.uk/webfm_send/121.

32. The examples examined included the Codes of Ethics of the AIC (www.conservation-us.org/index.cfm?fuseaction=page.viewPage&PageID=858&E), ECCO (www.ecco-eu.org/about-e.c.c.o./professional-guidelines.html), CAC and CAPC (www.cac-accr.ca/files/pdf/ecode.pdf), and AICCM (http://www.aiccm.org.au/who-we-are/code-ethics-and-code-practice).

33. European Confederation of Conservator-Restorers' Organisations, "E.C.C.O. Professional Guidelines," Article 8.

34. American Institute for Conservation of Historic and Artistic Works, "Code of Ethics and Guidelines for Practice," accessed September 17, 2013, http://www.conservation-us.org/index.cfm?fuseaction=page.viewPage&PageID=858&E.

35. "Amateur Restoration Botches Jesus Fresco in Spain," *PRI's The World*, August 23, 2012, accessed September 17, 2013, http://www.theworld.org/2012/08/amateur-restoration-botches-jesus-fresco-in-spain/.

36. American Institute for Conservation of Historic and Artistic Works, "Code of Ethics."

37. American Institute for Conservation of Historic and Artistic Works, "Code of Ethics."

38. *Ad Quintum*, iii, 5, quoted in David Diringer, *The Book before Printing* (New York: Dover, 1982), 237–38.

39. Reviel Netz and William Noel, *The Archimedes Codex: How a Medieval Prayer Book Is Revealing the True Genius of Antiquity's Greatest Scientist* (Boston: Da Capo Press, 2007).

40. *Facsimiles of the Declaration of Independence and the Treaty of Waitangi* (Wellington, New Zealand: Government Printer, 1976).

41. Policy statements and guidelines for preservation photocopying abound, for example, from the Library of Congress (www.loc.gov/preservation/care/photocpy.html) and National Archives (www.archives.gov/preservation/holdings-maintenance/photocopying.html).

42. Library of Congress, "Frequently Asked Questions: Audio Recording and Moving Image Media," accessed September 17, 2013, http://www.loc.gov/preservation/about/faqs/audio.html.

43. Gerard Clifton explains these issues in more detail: Clifton, "Risk and the Preservation Management of Digital Collections."

44. Clifton, "Risk and the Preservation Management of Digital Collections," 21.

45. Michael Carden, "Digital Archiving at the National Archives of Australia: Putting Principles into Practice," paper presented at the International Council on Archives Congress, Brisbane, August 20–24, 2012, accessed September 17, 2013, http://www.naa.gov.au/about-us/partnerships/conferences/michael-carden-digital-archiving.aspx.

46. Hywel Gwynn Williams and Anna Henry, "Building a Digital Archive: Integrating Theory and Implementation," paper presented at the International Council on Archives Congress, Brisbane, Australia, August 20–24, 2012, 2, accessed September 17, 2013, http://ica2012.ica.org/files/pdf/Full%20papers%20upload/ica12Final00280.pdf.

# CHAPTER 3

# Managing Preservation

......................................................................................

## Policy, Assessment, Planning

The preservation needs of any collection are determined in part by the purposes for which it has been acquired or assembled. Although the contents and purposes of collections may be very diverse, they share a number of common objectives, including acquisition of materials, retaining them, providing access to them, and keeping them fit for use. Stewardship of cultural heritage collections of any type implies a broad managerial commitment. Stewardship is the necessary duty of everyone involved in the community supporting or engaged with those collections, from the creators of objects that might end up in the collections to curators, catalogers, exhibition planners, users, and many others. This broad view of stewardship encompasses areas that may be new to preservation managers trained to focus on one format or category of material. New skills and new ways of thinking about collections are required, particularly as preservation managers assume responsibility for digital materials.

Chapter 3 examines the profound impact this broad, holistic view has on the management of cultural heritage collections, focusing on policy, assessment, and planning. Although those responsible for collection management may not be formally designated as preservation managers, their responsibilities will certainly extend to many of the issues discussed here. The chapter expounds further on the preservation principles articulated in chapter 2, especially

- Preservation is the responsibility of all, from the creators of objects to the users of objects.
- Preservation requires active, managed care.

For many decades cultural heritage professionals have understood that preservation is a management responsibility that applies to all stages in the life of an object or document. A clearly expressed preservation plan that is funded as part of the ongoing budget cycle is essential. It is well understood, as the first of the two principles notes, that all stakeholders must be engaged and must support the plan, whether they are patrons, volunteers, or staff at every level and in every process in the organization. To put the second principle noted above into practice, it is necessary to gain a thorough understanding of the collection and its environment. A thorough assessment of the collection is a vital first step in gaining control, as it provides the data needed for appropriate policymaking and planning.

In 1993 Harvey asserted that all collections need a preservation plan and that it must be adequately funded as part of the ongoing budget.[1] In the intervening two decades much more has been learned about the nature of materials in cultural heritage collections and about the science underlying their maintenance. We now have many proven models of what a well-funded, well-run preservation management program can accomplish.

## PRESERVATION AS INSTITUTIONAL MANDATE

Cultural heritage professionals consider that the act of acquiring an object constitutes an ethical obligation to care for that object for a clearly specified period of time, if not in perpetuity. (This concept is embedded in the preservation principle "Preservation actions should adhere to ethical considerations.") By accepting responsibility for objects, no matter what state we receive them in, we are agreeing to protect and preserve them and, in most cases, to make them available to those for whom the objects have significance and interest. In a sense we are making an implicit promise or contract with the objects, as we take on an ethical, or in many instances fiduciary, responsibility for the collections in our care.

This implicit contract with the objects immediately presents us with a managerial dilemma. For all but the most robust objects, regular handling accelerates deterioration. Some objects suffer if they are merely displayed for long periods of time; some deteriorate in the dark; and some age prematurely through being too hot or too dry. Consequently, cultural heritage professionals face the challenge of providing the best access to the objects in their care, while at the same time protecting them for future generations.

For cultural heritage professionals it is axiomatic that preservation without access is pointless. Nevertheless, many institutions have withdrawn materials from public display or use because of deterioration caused by exposure to airborne pollutants, light, environmental changes, and inappropriate handling. In some cases the physical object is so precious and so endangered by frequent use that researchers now have access only to the information content by means of a surrogate or facsimile. For example, the Musée Condé caused a stir in 1987 when its director announced that the manuscripts *Les Tres Riches Heures du Duc de Berry* and the *Ingeburge Psalter* would no longer be available for public or scholarly access. The British Library's Janet Backhouse stated at the time, "If no one has access to a manuscript there is no reason for it to exist."[2] Today there is an abundance of exquisitely produced facsimiles of rare manuscripts available to collectors and cultural heritage institutions, and in many cases the originals are still available for consultation, even though there may be more restrictions on their use. The existence of facsimiles and increasing numbers of digital surrogates has radically changed the study of early manuscripts, at the same time introducing new concerns. Some libraries now require that visitors exhaust all available resources before being permitted direct access to original manuscripts. The New York Public Library's guidelines exemplify this requirement:

- Researchers will be required to consult and exhaust all available resources—such as departmental files, catalogues, facsimiles, transparencies, digital images, microfilms, and the 10,000 detailed slides that the Library has for use—prior to inspecting a manuscript at first hand.
- Direct access to the original manuscripts for individual study will be restricted to qualified scholars, with a demonstrated need to consult the manuscripts at first hand, and experience in handling such materials.
- Certain highly fragile and extensively studied manuscripts, such as the Tickhill Psalter (NYPL Spencer 26; *Splendor* cat. No. 41), are not available for direct consultation.[3]

The availability of digital surrogates and high-resolution viewing equipment has made the art and the information in these manuscripts available to users worldwide, regardless of their level of scholarship or sophistication, but the fact remains that the original object must be maintained and preserved. Preservation managers now have the double duty of maintaining both the physical object and the digital surrogate.

Institutions dedicated to preserving cultural heritage may be a small unit in a large organization, a single house museum, a small local history collection, an academic library, a government-run museum, or any number of other configurations. Preservation activities and responsibilities are directly linked to the mission and goals articulated by an organization's governing body. The addition of materials to a collection is underpinned by an implicit understanding that the materials will be properly cared for in the public interest. Although most cultural heritage institutions acknowledge this understanding, some may not always demonstrate this understanding in properly planning for the preservation of their collections. Any cultural heritage institution whose mission includes collecting, preserving, and providing access to cultural materials should have a preservation plan that guides the management of its collection.

The managers of most institutions share the realities of limited financial resources, staffing, and space. No matter what budget constraints it faces, any library, archive, museum, and historical society can still develop a preservation plan to meet at least some of the preservation needs of its collections.

The process of developing a preservation program, plan, or policy can be a very positive one for an institution. It raises awareness about the collections among staff and patrons and provides a framework upon which sound practice can be built. Through their involvement in the process, staff at all levels gain a sense of ownership of the preservation responsibility, greatly improving the chances of the planning process's success. Even more critical is the impact of good planning on managing financial resources. Difficult choices must be made about the allocation of resources, and a carefully considered policy will help prioritize the needs of different parts of a collection.

Mirjam Foot stresses the supremacy of institutional purpose in determining a comprehensive preservation policy: "Different formats and different media may need different strategies and demand different technical solutions, but the aims and the purpose of the library or archive and its functions determine its preservation policy, which must cover all formats and all media."[4] An understanding of an institution's aims, purposes, and functions is at the heart of any institution's mission statement. It is that mission statement that sets the course for any policy and planning document throughout that institution, including any preservation policies and plans.

## MISSION STATEMENTS

The words *preserve*, *preserving*, or *preservation* are to be found in the mission statements of most libraries, archives, and museums. Usually prepared in the first stage of any strategic planning process, a mission statement declares an organization's primary reasons for its existence. A good mission statement can be a public relations tool, educating users about the collection's purpose and about its importance and value. It should answer in broad terms questions such as *whom* do we serve, and *what* do we do? The specifics of *how* a mission is accomplished are expressed as goals and objectives, and they do not belong in a mission statement. A mission statement that is adopted and supported by an organization's governing body and administration will lead to policies and activities that are focused within institutionally acceptable limits. For example, a mission statement purporting to provide access to the entire world of knowledge would be inappropriate for a small public library, and a local history museum with no stable funding whose mission statement asserts that it will preserve and provide access to a collection of local artifacts cannot fulfill its mission until such time as funding becomes available for proper housing and storage for that collection.

Whether or not preservation is actually an intrinsic aspect of an institution's mandate needs to be considered when preparing a mission statement. Although it may seem obvious that preservation is an essential function for archival collections, it should be stated. Different types of libraries are likely to have very different functions, and will, therefore, have different preservation models and needs. The American Alliance of Museums advises its members to study themselves thoroughly before drafting a mission statement. Thorough assessment of purpose and activities is useful in strategic planning in any organization and can be particularly beneficial when a mission statement needs to be created or revised.

The mission statement stands as a promise to the collections and to the public and places the trustees, administrators, and staff under an ethical obligation to see that it is honored. As David Carr puts it,

> The museum's statement of mission is a public expression of promise; therefore, it is an obligation under the care of administrators, trustees, employees, and volunteers. An articulate mission makes clear that all of the museum's work is done in the presence of an obligation to adhere to its aims; therefore, the first criterion of ethical practice is the prominent embodiment of mission in even the smallest of the museum's plans and activities.[5]

Management decisions, collection policies, and access to materials must be made in the context of this obligation, in all types of cultural heritage organizations. Melissa Mannon extends Carr's contention:

> When properly written, the mission statement defines a clear path for policies and procedure. The mission should be understandable, concise, and all-encompassing. It should distinguish the institution it represents from other similar organizations. When necessary, the revision of a mission should aim to clarify it rather than changing the core concepts that are important to the institution. These core values should only be changed if major revisions to the institution itself take place, such as a merger.[6]

## Sample Mission Statements

Mission statements are typically written in broad terms, whereas the specifics needed to meet the obligations expressed in them are left to goals, objectives, and policy statements. Input from across the institution is essential when drafting a mission statement for the first time. Investigating the mission statements of other institutions is helpful; a range of examples available on institutions' websites follows.

The Morgan Museum and Library (www.themorgan.org/about/mission.asp) declares that its mission "is to preserve, build, study, present, and interpret a collection of extraordinary quality, in order to stimulate enjoyment, excite the imagination, advance learning, and nurture creativity." In an elegant and simple statement, the Morgan accomplishes a great deal in one sentence. In answer to the question "what do we do?" the Morgan's statement uses five action verbs (*preserve*, *build*, *study*, *present*, *interpret*) to describe the institutional commitment or promise to its "collection of extraordinary quality." The second promise refers to an unspecified public, who may be stimulated, excited, educated, and nurtured by that collection. How this will be achieved is left for other documents or policies to articulate.

The mission of Massachusetts Institute of Technology (MIT) Libraries (libraries.mit
.edu/about) "is to create and sustain an intuitive, trusted information environment that
enables learning and the advancement of knowledge at MIT. We are committed to developing innovative services, strategies, and systems that promote discovery, preserve knowledge, and improve worldwide scholarly communication. We empower MIT through
knowledge." This more complex mission statement emphasizes learning and knowledge
(mentioned three times) without reference to collections. Stewardship is implied by the
verbs *create* and *sustain* in the first sentence of the statement. The deliberate use of the
phrase *preserve knowledge* frees the libraries from the issues of formats and containers of
knowledge, without committing to specific media or formats for delivery in the future.

The Minnesota Historical Society states its mission on its website (www.mnhs.org/
about/mission) as: "Using the Power of History to Transform Lives. Preserving—
Sharing—Connecting." To understand this epigrammatic statement one must also read
the values and vision statements presented with the mission statement. The Massachusetts
Historical Society also gives a lengthy vision statement on its website (www.masshist.org/
mission), preceded by a mission statement that can stand on its own: "The Massachusetts
Historical Society is an independent research library that collects, preserves, makes accessible, and communicates manuscripts and other materials in order to promote the study
of the history of Massachusetts and the nation—a mission it has pursued since 1791."

The brief mission statement of Dallas Municipal Archives (www.ci.dallas.tx.us/cso/
archives.html) provides links to the charter and city codes of the City of Dallas, as well as
information on ethics, conflict of interest, and records management. The statement itself
is concise: "The mission of the Dallas Municipal Archives is to document and preserve
the permanently valuable and historical records of the government of the City of Dallas,
and to effectively provide access to information to citizens and city employees." In other
contexts involving government documents and records, city and state archives' mission
statements may include the statutory mandate under which they are formed. For example, the City of Boston's Archives and Records Management Division (www.cityofbos-
ton.gov/archivesandrecords) cites the statute under which they are charged with the care
of municipal government records, and it makes explicit the nature of the public trust
they represent as the third component of its lengthy mission statement:

> The City Archives is a public trust, which plays a key role in fostering effective
> and responsible government through management of the lifecycle of records and
> through sustained access to historically valuable municipal records. These records
> enable people to inspect what Boston municipal government has done, allow officials
> and agencies to review their actions, and help citizens hold government account-
> able. These records are rich and varied sources of information used to answer ques-
> tions about the past of the City, the nation and society.

These examples indicate the wide variety of mission statements of cultural heritage
institutions. The word *preserve* appears in all of them, whether in reference to physical

collections or to the knowledge they contain. The mission statements of public libraries, however, which emphasize meeting the needs of a specific community, often do not
include any reference to preservation. Typical of a large city public library, the Worcester
(Massachusetts) Public Library (www.worcpublib.org/about/about.htm) states that it

> serves as a gathering place that actively promotes the free exchange of ideas in our
> democratic society. The Library makes information and services available to all
> people while fostering intellectual freedom, protecting privacy, encouraging per-
> sonal growth and enrichment, and celebrating our diverse community heritage.

The need to support a growing and diverse population and to deliver information
services through new media is prompting many public libraries to produce mission statements that promise to meet their community's current and changing information needs,
without reference to books or documents. Among the mission statements of academic
libraries, historical societies, and museums, however, are many examples that retain
phrases like the Morgan's—*preserve*, *build*, *study*, *present*, and *interpret*,—with action
verbs that can be associated with collections of materials.

### Developing a Mission Statement

There are many helpful guides to developing a mission statement, or revising an
existing one, although few address specifically the requirements of cultural heritage
institutions. Professional organizations offer helpful resources for certain types of
institutions, but often the advice they give can be applied more broadly. Investigating
the available literature, both in print and online, before beginning is recommended.
Engaging a professional facilitator with experience in this type of work may also be
helpful.

The process of writing a mission statement inevitably encourages an organization to
think deeply about its purpose, its goals, and its vision for the future. It can be a useful
public relations exercise and can also reveal tension and dysfunction in the organization
that may be difficult to address. The process will lead to the consideration or reconsid-
eration of every one of the collection's policies and practices.

Once in place, the mission statement serves as a guide for the development of all the
organization's policies, and it can be used as a measure of how well the organization is
meeting its goals and responsibilities.

## POLICIES

Helen Forde noted the role of preservation policies as "a tool to be used by institutions
dedicated to ensure the survival of material entrusted to their care. Museums, galleries, libraries and archives are all seeking to express their policies in [preservation] and

to demonstrate their capabilities."[7] Once a general preservation policy has been developed that is in tune with the institution's mission statement, implementation strategies, best practice, goals, and objectives can be formulated. A clearly articulated preservation policy will help all stakeholders understand their role and the importance of their contribution to the overall goal. Mission statements and preservation policies can also be useful documents for the public. A preservation policy will articulate for the governing board, trustees, staff, volunteers, donors, and other administrative bodies the aims and objectives of an institutional preservation program. A well-written policy can help demonstrate the responsible use of resources, set appropriate priorities, and point out areas where additional funding is needed.

A preservation policy lays out clearly and succinctly what needs to be preserved, the purposes for which it is preserved, and for how long. Having a preservation policy in place establishes a framework for practice, and it demonstrates that collection managers understand the need for accountability. It also establishes parameters that can be monitored and assessed. An established preservation policy is the first step in more comprehensive preservation planning and program development.

A number of national organizations offer suggested standards and guidelines for developing a preservation policy.[8] Some organizations begin their own policies by indicating that they adhere to nationally and professionally accepted standards and techniques. For example, the preservation policy of the National Archives in the United Kingdom asserts that it accords with "existing preservation policies from the archival and preservation sectors."[9] To its policy it has appended a list of specific standards and policies referred to in its development.[10]

Because not all readers of the policy will be experts in preservation, it may be necessary for a policy to provide definitions of terminology. A policy should also identify the roles and responsibilities of staff in relation to its implementation. Some policies include procedures for implementation; others refer to a more detailed set of best practices and guidelines. Ideally, a preservation policy should be general, rather than specific, and be accompanied by separate documents giving best practices and guidelines. A strategic plan will set out specific goals and time lines for assessment.

## Sample Preservation Policies

The Wellcome Library's "Preservation Policy for Materials Held in Collections"[11] includes a section of general policy statements covering retention, access, benefits of the preservation policy, exhibitions and loans, disaster preparedness, financial policy, standards, and monitoring and review of the policy. Separate sections for physical resources and digital resources follow the general policy, each of which covers principles, handling and transportation, storage, collections preservation, preservation treatments, and preservation research. Appendices cover terminology, long-term storage of digital materials, sources, specific standards cited, related internal documents, and a list of relevant external conservation and preservation organizations. The complete document is less than fourteen pages long, yet it gives a very clear overview of the Library's "commitment to the life cycle management of the materials in its collections."

The preservation policy of the National Library of Australia is intended

> to define the Library's preservation responsibilities, and to provide guidance to Library staff engaged in making decisions and undertaking other activities that may have an impact on collections. It is also a fundamental accountability document concerning one of the Library's core business functions, and is intended to serve as the basis for communication with a range of external stakeholders.[12]

The Archives Centre of Churchill College, Cambridge, states these principles in its preservation policy:

> Preservation is a fundamental responsibility through which the Archives Centre ensures the continued availability and authenticity of the archival records that it holds in trust for present and future generations. The Archives Centre recognises that preservation is a pervasive function and works to ensure that it remains an integral part of all archive activities from acquisition through to access. Without preservation there can be no access.[13]

Essential in a preservation policy is a clear statement of institutional mission or strategic goals, often followed by definitions of terms and a statement of general principles. The National Library of Australia's policy makes it clear their preservation policy is central to the Library's business functions. The excerpt from Churchill College's Archives Centre emphasizes the integral part that preservation plays in all activities "from accession to access." In these examples, the preservation policy is closely linked to the acquisition process, as well as to policy on retention.

## Practical Considerations

If an institution asserts its intention to provide sustainable access to its collections, it is implying a limit to what it acquires that is determined by financial resources in the future. Consider the offer of a large collection of piano rolls from the estate of a local collector, but no funds are available to support the acquisition of the necessary playback equipment, and the rolls are not in good condition. Even if a vintage player piano could be acquired, it could not responsibly be used to play the old rolls, as that might further damage them in ways that are beyond the institution's ability to repair. A preservation policy is intended to provide a framework for decision making in situations such as this. If a library, archive, or museum routinely accepts photographic materials, a policy covering the preservation of such materials should be in place. The preservation of photographic negatives, for example, generally requires special housing, and older negatives, such as those made of cellulose nitrate and of cellulose acetate, have severe preservation problems and should not be accepted into a collection unless it has the ability to care for them properly. Similarly, a policy on digital materials should be in place that notes preferred formats and what types of media requiring special playback equipment are to be accepted. A policy covering digital materials needs to be regularly reviewed in order to keep abreast of rapid change in technology.

Acquisition and retention decisions in a public library or an undergraduate library will differ considerably from those made in a research library, a historical society, or an archive. A research library may regularly acquire out-of-print books, in which case a policy about what physical condition is acceptable should be in place. Many libraries use a formula to determine what percentage of their acquisition funds should be dedicated to preservation or conservation activities. The Association of Research Libraries, for example, "has determined that an appropriate amount is 3–5 percent of the library's acquisitions budget."[14] Unfortunately, what started as a rule of thumb is arbitrarily applied as a ceiling that is too low for the level of resources that are actually needed.

Because terminology can vary across different types of institutions, it is often necessary to establish what is meant in a particular instance. As cultural heritage institutions are increasingly working together, we should beware of jargon that is used in one type of institution. Libraries have *collection development* policies, which frequently address the issues of formats, condition, duplication, and retention. Archives are more likely to have *acquisition* policies, which may specify the importance of physical condition as a priority in materials proposed for acquisition. Larger collections will have separate policy statements for different types of materials; an example is the National Archives and Records Administration's gift collection acquisition policy for motion pictures and sound and video recordings.[15] *Retention* policies, though not unheard of in libraries, are more often associated with records management, while libraries often refer to *weeding* or *deselection* of a collection. Library weeding projects may identify books that need to be replaced because they are in poor condition, but they also help maintain an appropriately focused collection and an uncrowded storage facility. Archives look at different levels of retention, most commonly in three categories: transient materials; materials in which the information is more important than the container; and items whose content must be retained, as well as the original format. In terms of acquisition and retention, preservation policy is closely linked to collection development policy and must be developed with reference to it.

A survey of European and British research library collections conducted in the 1990s found that, where preservation policies existed, they did not conform to a standard model, and that the majority of respondents did not follow the UNESCO *Guidelines on Preservation and Conservation Policies in the Archives and Libraries Heritage*.[16] Many libraries had separate policies on security, disposal, reprography, and exhibitions; survey results supported the idea that the best preservation policies are "firmly linked to collection development and retention policies."[17] Since that survey was conducted, many more institutions have developed preservation policies, as administrators and professional accrediting organizations became aware of the need for them. By the end of the

20th century, a more comprehensive approach to national and international preservation policies and programs had become evident, influenced in part by rising awareness of the complexity of providing long-term access to digital materials,[18] and in part by the significant number of useful guides to their preparation available through the Internet since the early 1990s.

Following to the letter guidelines such as the UNESCO *Guidelines* and the British Library Preservation Advisory Centre's *Building a Preservation Policy*[19] may seem too daunting a task for smaller collections. There is no need, however, to tackle all the elements such guidelines propose at once. Being aware of what is considered best practice for a policy and working on a framework that suits a specific institutional situation reduces the sense of challenge. The process will be significantly aided if there is already a clear idea of how preservation fits into the overall goals of the institution. Beginning by tackling the preservation concerns involved in acquisition and retention decisions will enable significant early progress. If staff resources permit, divide up responsibility for different aspects of the policy, such as security, handling, and photocopying, among personnel who are most closely involved with each of these aspects. Encourage them to locate examples of similar policies from other similar institutions and then develop a statement that is aligned with the institution's mission and philosophy.

The preservation principles articulated in chapter 2 provide some useful points of reference for the preparation of a preservation policy. Three principles in particular are relevant: "Preservation actions must take into account the needs of the user"; "Authenticity of the objects needs to be ensured in any preservation action"; and "Preservation is the responsibility of all, from the creators of objects to the users of objects." To implement a preservation policy, a thorough assessment of the collection and of its building and storage environments is essential for developing priorities and an action plan.

## Related Policies

As already noted, large institutions may have separate policies for a number of different areas that are considered within the purview of a preservation program, such as security, storage and environmental control, exhibitions, and loans. The preservation policies of smaller institutions often include sections on security, the environment, guidelines for proper handling, the conditions under which photocopying is permissible, the use and creation of surrogates, access to original materials, and sections on exhibition and loans.

All policies should be reviewed and, if necessary, revised or updated to make clear their connection to the preservation policy. Collection development (or acquisition) policies are extremely useful complements to preservation policies. Most collection development policies specify areas of collecting strength and identify areas that are considered out of scope; many also clarify what types of media are collected. When such things are clearly documented in collection development policies, they can provide information for use in conjunction with the preservation policy to ensure that whatever is acquired can be properly cared for. Sustainability has always been a significant consideration for any effective collection management policy, and it is even more so for digital collections. Well-planned acquisition strategies usually take into consideration the resources available for maintaining the collection, but they may require further specification in the context of a preservation program, which presents an excellent opportunity for collaboration among staff and managers.

Like other policy documents, collection development policies require regular review and updating. A collection development policy written in the 1990s and not revisited since is unlikely to adequately consider digital objects. All policy documents must be kept up-to-date as practice may have evolved and overtaken the policy.

Some related policies may have evolved in an ad hoc manner, and some of them—for example, a reading room's policy on photographic reproduction—may be candidates for incorporation in the preservation policy. Others may not be true policies at all but are really statements of best practice or practical guidelines, such as handling guidelines for shelvers.

## ASSESSMENT: BUILDING, CONTEXT, ENVIRONMENT

Preservation assessments are an early step in developing a preservation plan and are essential for establishing a point of reference, or a baseline, from which to evaluate current conditions and monitor the effect of changes. A preservation assessment provides an opportunity to examine needs and resources, and it provides information for determining preservation priorities, planning ongoing programs, and in seeking funding.

In libraries, the brittle book crisis of the 1970s highlighted the need for a more holistic approach to the care of collections. In archives, emphasis on the permanence of records resulted in attempts to stabilize deteriorating documents and to improve the containers housing the documents. In both contexts, acute awareness of collection-wide deterioration led to significant advances in understanding the impact of storage environments on collections and the need for an administrative infrastructure to support long-term preservation goals. Museums have traditionally had a greater understanding of overall collection needs, while at the same time they have spent considerable resources on improving the condition of individual items requiring conservation and restoration work.

### Conducting the Assessment

A preservation assessment typically begins with a survey of the building in which collections are housed, starting with its geographical location and surroundings. A description of the general characteristics and condition of the building, both inside and outside, is the next component of the assessment. There are weak points in most structures, as any homeowner knows, many of which are easily identified and rectified with a minimum outlay of resources. For example, shrubs and bushes too close to a building make it vulnerable to undesirable insects of all sorts; overhanging trees may be an open invitation for squirrels to take up residence in an attic; a drain that is not directing water far enough away from a building can result in water in the basement. Adequate roof maintenance, proper insulation, window placement, and secure entrances and exits are all of concern. Knowing what the fabric of a building is will lead to an understanding of strengths and weaknesses inside the building as well.

A typical checklist for the assessment of a building's exterior includes: date of construction; information on additions and renovations; plans for future renovations; predominant building materials; and overall condition and maintenance. Records of past problems such as roof leaks, flooding, electrical problems, or mold growth all contribute to an informed overview. Professional inspection of the roof and drains is recommended as part of the assessment. If this is not possible, observable conditions and signs of damage can be noted, along with any history of leaks or water accumulation. Ascertain the age of the roof, bearing in mind that most modern roofing materials have an anticipated life span of no more than twenty years. Note special features such as skylights, as these are often vulnerable to leaks. Examine the exterior surfaces of the building, looking for missing boards and shingles, crumbling brick and masonry, peeling paint, or mold or spots that might indicate water and other problems. The building's foundations may also need professional assessment; some signs of deterioration may be obvious, but others are not. The location and direction of output from drains is important to determine, as they must reliably direct water away from the building.

Inside the building, note overall conditions, especially major service systems, such as plumbing and electrical systems. Inspect attic and basement areas, which are not generally recommended for storage of collections but must be kept clean and dry if they are used for this purpose. Look for any signs of mold, insects or rodents, water leaks, and condensation inside the building. Establish whether insulation and vapor barriers have been installed, and include in the assessment file a photographic record of what is observed. The results of the assessment of the building allow for a list of maintenance and repair needs to be developed and prioritized.

A major concern for the well-being of collections is the maintenance of a stable and appropriate climate within their storage areas. Measuring the temperature and relative humidity inside the building daily is a critical early task. Data for each separate area in which collections are stored or used, including work areas and reading rooms, need to be collected.

A variety of devices are available for recording daily temperature and relative humidity conditions. They may be stand-alone units or networked systems and can provide a wealth of detail. Until recently, temperature and relative humidity in collection spaces was monitored by the use of the hygrothermograph (thermohygrograph in some parts of the world), which combines the functions of the thermograph, recording temperature, and the hygrograph, recording relative humidity. The convenience of collecting these data on one chart overrode the need for regular calibration, inking, and reloading paper.

Digital data loggers, battery-powered devices that monitor and record temperature and relative humidity, are now widely used. Data can be downloaded from data loggers to a computer and analyzed. They may also be linked to alarms and to environment management systems for the adjustment of humidity levels when needed.

By assembling accurate data on daily and seasonal fluctuations in temperature and relative humidity, an understanding of a collection's environment can be reached. Inappropriate levels of heat and humidity, and especially their fluctuations, are the most common risks that collections are exposed to. Maintaining a stable environment is the cornerstone of preventive preservation efforts. Chapter 5 provides more information.

The data collected on temperature and relative humidity help monitor the condition and performance of heating, ventilation, and air-conditioning (HVAC) systems. Other data to be gathered in the process of getting a good overview of potential weak points or areas of concern relate to: housekeeping details, such as how often storage areas and public access areas are cleaned; any special training the cleaning staff are given; the use of cleaning chemicals that might be harmful to objects in the collection; the acceptability or otherwise of food and drink in any part of the building; security systems installed; and alarm systems for fire and water detection.

## External Risk Factors

Many libraries, museums, historic houses, and archives have suffered traumatic damage as the result of earthquakes, floods, and other natural disasters. In the first decade of the 21st century alone, devastating earthquakes and floods have affected a large number of cultural heritage institutions. A very short list includes institutions in Haiti (earthquake, January 12, 2010), Chile (earthquake and tsunami, February 27, 2010), Iowa (extensive flooding, August 10, 2010), Washington, D.C. (earthquake, August 2011), and the eastern Atlantic seaboard of the United States (Hurricane Sandy, October 25, 2012). Nevertheless, we continue to build on major geological fault lines, in flood plains, in hurricane zones, and near the ocean. In some earthquake-prone areas building codes have resulted in the construction of buildings in which structural damage caused by earthquakes is minimized. For example, steps have been taken in Turkey, after decades of increasingly devastating earthquakes, to mitigate damage to that nation's museums.

The geographical and geological conditions of an area, particularly any potential for the occurrence of floods and earthquakes, need to be understood in a preservation assessment. In the United States, the Federal Emergency Management Agency website (www.fema.gov) provides information about threat and hazard identification and risk. Other potential sources of information are local and state hazard mitigation offices; local fire, police, and health departments; the U.S. Geological Survey; and the U.S. Environmental Protection Agency.

Threats and hazards may have technological or human causes and may be intentional actions or accidents, such as a plane crash or a power failure. The humidity of tropical climates, air pollution, fire, drought, armed conflict, civil disorder, terrorism, and construction in the immediate vicinity of a building all threaten the ongoing security and maintenance of cultural heritage institutions and collections.

## ASSESSMENT: COLLECTION CONDITION

Gathering data about what is in a collection, what its storage conditions are, and about existing and potential problems with both is the next step in a preservation assessment. Many approaches to gathering these data can be taken, from using a sampling method to comprehensive examination of a whole collection. An example of a comprehensive examination was reported by one curator, who dedicated every Friday afternoon to working through the collection, a few boxes at a time, thus building familiarity with the collection as well as developing a list of priorities for collection rehousing and repair.

### Determining What Is in the Collection

Of primary concern is gathering quantitative data about the types of objects, materials, and formats in a collection. For example, in a collection of photographs, it is useful to know such things as: how many daguerreotypes, albumen prints, Polaroids, and negatives are held; how many of the negatives are safety film and how many are nitrate based; whether they are 35mm strips or 4 x 5-inch sheet film. The collection can be measured in linear feet, as is common in archival practice, or by whatever type of count is most useful to an institution, which may even be simply the number of shelves and drawers, boxes, or oversized file drawers. For some collections it may be appropriate to use different measures for different formats and media; for example, to use linear feet for text-based archival materials and number of boxes for photographs. In estimating the total number of objects in a collection, an average can be calculated by counting the contents of three or four boxes and multiplying that by the number of boxes in the collection. Determining the number of digital assets in a collection is also necessary, although the process has some additional challenges. The number of floppy discs, Zip discs, CD-ROMs, DVDs, and other digital storage media containing data currently in the collection needs to be known before any planning for their preservation and access can be done, and the required storage capacity (in megabytes, terabytes, or even petabytes) estimated. Information about the age range of digital storage media also needs to be gathered. Some experts suggest starting an examination of media by dividing them according to the machine needed for access or playback.[20] While gathering quantitative information about the items and media in a collection, information about their storage conditions, whether new boxes or folders are needed, and indicators of potential problems can also be gathered.

Developing good observation skills is invaluable, as observing indicators of threat to collections can result in the early application of cost-effective measures to prevent the progression from threat to damage and disaster. Unusual smells can be indicators of problems. The vinegary smell of vinegar syndrome, for example, may indicate a problem with cellulose-acetate photographic negatives. Other smells may indicate the presence of mold or pests. Condensation on windows indicates a problem with the relative humidity balance. Accumulation of dirt particles around air vents suggests that a particulate filtration system is not performing as it should. Training staff to observe and understand signs of potential problems has an important role in disaster prevention.

In addition to assessing the overall condition of the collection, regular review of the contents of boxes and other storage areas may help staff maintain an awareness of materials for which there is insufficient metadata in the institution's catalogs, inventories, or registration systems. The inadequacy of finding aids is a preservation issue because incomplete descriptions of collection contents can result in excessive handling of materials as a researcher attempts to determine which items in a collection are relevant to their information need.

## SURVEY TOOLS

Several different approaches to collection assessment and preservation planning have been developed, some of which are particularly useful for large collections with primarily paper-based holdings, such as books and manuscripts, while others have been designed for specific types of objects, such as digital or audio media. Many methods use random sampling and require a basic knowledge of statistics. An item-by-item survey may be possible in small collections or for small groups of particular types of material within a larger collection.

An understanding of what each of the survey tools available seeks to quantify is necessary when selecting the tool best suited to the types of materials in a collection to be surveyed. Typically a survey attempts to establish an overview of the condition of materials in a collection, identify the quantity of materials in need of care, determine primary risk factors or potential threats to a collection, and recommend and prioritize the actions needed. Some surveys also examine intellectual and physical access to collection materials, and some may assess their potential research use. The data collected will inform management decisions related to environmental control, disaster preparedness, security, reformatting, and conservation treatment.

CALIPR (www.lib.berkeley.edu/preservation/CALIPR), a software package developed by the library at the University of California, Berkeley, is an example of a survey tool. CALIPR uses a random sampling methodology that is beneficial for gathering information about large collections, but it may be less useful for small institutions. Sherelyn Ogden's 1997 workbook *Preservation Planning: Guidelines for Writing a Long-Range Plan* remains a useful guide.[21] Checklists in the Northeast Document Conservation Center's online tutorial Preservation 101 (unfacilitated.preservation101 .org) are applicable in surveys of smaller collections or subsets of larger collections. Columbia

University Libraries (library.columbia.edu/services/preservation/survey_tools.html) and New York University (library.nyu.edu/preservation/archivespreservation.html) have both made available a Special Collections Materials Survey tool, based on a model developed by the Historical Society of Pennsylvania. Although the software can only be used in a Microsoft computing environment, the guidance given in its manual is more widely applicable. Columbia subsequently developed a survey instrument for audio and moving image collections (library.columbia.edu/services/preservation/audiosurvey .html).

## REVIEWING STORAGE CONDITIONS

The importance of monitoring the internal environment of collection storage areas has already been noted. In addition to stable temperature and relative humidity, proper housing, enclosures, and shelving must be considered in a preservation strategy for physical objects.

Libraries often take a major step in the preservation of newly acquired books by rebinding, inserting security monitoring devices, bookmarks, ownership stamps, and shelf numbers. As digital objects and digital storage media are taken into collections, however, it is not tenable to delay intervention in these media and their storage in the same way. The preservation of digital materials calls for emphasis on the active, managed care stated in the principle "Preservation requires active, managed care," from the earliest possible point in their acquisition process.

A collection assessment must consider how all items, whether digital or analog, are stored. Many national and international standards for housing particular kinds of materials exist, and professional organizations and regional preservation centers can provide advice about appropriate furniture, enclosures, and boxes. Some examples are noted here. NARA provides detailed information about standards and their application in its storage facilities (www.archives.gov/records-mgmt/storage-standards-toolkit). The Council of State Archives provides a state-by-state listing of links on storage conditions and standards (www.statearchivists.org/arc/states/res_stor.htm). Among the many relevant standards issued by the International Organization for Standardization (ISO) are ISO 11799:2003 *Information and Documentation—Document Storage Requirements for Archive and Library Materials*, ISO 18918:2000 *Imaging Materials—Processed Photographic Plates—Storage Practices*, and ISO 18911:2010 *Imaging Materials—Processed Safety Photographic Films—Storage Practices*. Standards are described further in chapter 4.

Among other storage problems that a collection assessment will bring to light are overcrowding of shelves or boxes, books that are not properly supported, oversized materials stacked on top of each other, books and boxes stored on the floor, and highly acidic storage envelopes and boxes. Actions to address such problems, and thus reduce the potential for any damage they may cause, need to be prioritized in a preservation plan.

## Determining Value

A survey of the collection will identify and quantify components of the collection at risk and enable preservation priorities to be established. Determining the value of a collection of historical materials is, however, a much more elusive and subjective undertaking. Although monetary value cannot always be ignored, other values of collection materials are more commonly focused on, such as their evidentiary, informational, artifactual, associational, functional, or institutional values. An academic library or special collection may also take into account the value of materials in the pedagogical context of an educational institution.

Any record of the past use of a collection for research and any predictions of its future use will also influence the assessment of its value. Many archivists and special collections librarians have deep subject expertise that enhances their ability to evaluate potential research interest in the items and records in their collections. Keeping a record of circulation requests and research questions enables collection use and trends to be tracked. Professional organizations and their journals are also important resources in maintaining awareness of research developments in different fields. Enduring value is harder to predict and is inevitably based on what we know of current use and value.

A daguerreotype serves as an interesting example of the different ways that value may be determined. First, it is a unique object by virtue of the technology involved in its creation: it is a direct positive—that is, there is no negative involved. The piece of metal with the image on it was in the camera at the time the image was exposed. As a unique object, the daguerreotype may have artifactual value as well as informational value. Just as the binding of a 16th-century book imparts particular information to the researcher, so does the protective case that holds the daguerreotype. Much is now known about these cases and how they were made, and this information can help establish a probable date for the daguerreotype. Associational value may be added when a lock of the subject's hair is found to have been preserved in the case, or when we are able to determine a photographer's name or location. Not every object in a collection falls into more than one of these categories of value, but we must remember that potential research use often lies in unexpected areas.

The assessment process produces a quantity of useful information. When it is accumulated it firmly places a building or collection storage area in context and enables a clear understanding of risk factors inherent in the climate and environment of that context. While some risk factors may be beyond our ability to influence, knowledge of a building or storage area helps in preparing for the unexpected. If it is understood that a nearby construction project can pose a threat to a collection, steps can be taken to increase the protection of the collection for the duration of that project. On an altogether more dramatic scale are examples of protective steps such as those taken to protect the Bactrian hoard of thousands of Bronze Age gold pieces; they survived years of violent civil war in Afghanistan because the last communist president of the country had ordered their transfer from the national museum to an exceptionally secure underground vault beneath the Central Bank of Afghanistan.

The assessment may also reveal areas in which security systems need to be improved or reconsidered. For example, for many years the staff of a major rare books and manuscripts library were issued keys that let them into the building outside normal hours. They went in and out of the building through an unattended service door and routinely took the keys home with them. Following the appointment of a new director, a more secure system was instituted, requiring staff to turn in their keys at night. (Chapter 7, "Holdings Protection" provides more information on this topic.) Many practical housekeeping matters may also surface as a result of the assessment and lead to the revision of housekeeping routines and training.

## DEVELOPING A PLAN

Thorough assessment of a building's exterior and interior and of the collection it houses generates a significant amount of data that can be used in conjunction with the institution's mission statement and preservation policies to establish priorities for preservation action. Some priorities will inevitably require immediate action, while others will simply not be affordable. For example, collections of photographic materials may contain nitrate negatives that will need immediate action. An example of unaffordable action might be the improvement of environmental control in buildings without the essential infrastructure to provide the necessary control. Factors such as funding availability, staff time and levels of expertise, and current and potential user demand for the collections also need to be accounted for in the preservation planning process.

A case study describes the results of a preservation assessment survey conducted at the National Library of Ireland in 2007 to 2008. Although there were few surprises for the Library's staff, the survey provided external validation of their concerns and "heightened and strengthened the need to take action."[22] They faced problems not uncommon for large, historic collections in equally historic buildings, such as having no storage area that met the recommended preservation and archival standards for environmental control and monitoring. The survey heightened managerial awareness of the scope of the problem, and it also placed preservation issues higher on the Library's agenda. Preservation planning was given the highest priority, resulting in the writing of a disaster plan and a preservation policy, both of which are now in place. Initiating action on environmental control and monitoring proved more difficult, but plans to address storage conditions for the newspaper collections and to build high-density, archival standard offsite storage were developed. A fire risk assessment, improved security measures, extensive staff training, and the establishment of an onsite box-making laboratory were other outcomes of the assessment.

The Northeast Document Conservation Center's online tutorial "Preservation 101" provides a list of criteria for establishing priorities (unfacilitated.preservation101.org/ session8/prac_prep-setting.asp), which are divided into "collection-specific criteria" (use, storage, condition, value, and format) and "overall criteria" (impact, feasibility, and urgency).[23] Inevitably, actions with high impact and high feasibility will rise to the top of the list of priorities, and it is likely that heavily used materials in poor condition may warrant preservation action ahead of materials of high monetary value. By methodically prioritizing preservation need, it is possible to identify tasks that can be completed in-house, those that can serve as projects for properly trained and supervised volunteers and interns, and objects that are in need of specialist professional intervention.

Once a preservation assessment has been completed, a preservation policy developed, and preservation priorities determined, a strategy for implementing the prioritized actions should be drawn up. A preservation policy sets out general principles to be followed in a preservation program; a strategic plan must set achievable goals, objectives, and action-based outcomes. A comprehensive strategy encompasses overall collection condition; current and potential preventive and stabilization procedures, repair, conservation, and reformatting procedures; and environmental monitoring. It should also cover facility improvements and other large collection management issues that may require considerable resources to address.[24] Consequently, the strategic plan must address how appropriate levels of funding will be found and sustained; it must also be consistent with the overall mission of the organization and the preservation policy.

Although it is the plan of a very large organization, NARA's strategic plan for 2006 to 2016 is an informative example of the product of a thorough and structured strategic planning process. It provides details of NARA's goals, "the strategies we will use to achieve these goals, and the measures by which we will evaluate our progress."[25] It states six goals that are clear and focused, addressing leadership and the management of federal government records, as well as NARA's responsibility to the public. Specific strategies for the accomplishment of each of those goals are clearly stated, and very specific long-range performance targets are committed to. The final section of the report reviews accomplishments for each goal in 2006 to 2009, the first three-year period of the plan's implementation.

Preservation management encompasses a wide range of concerns, including environmental control, security, disaster planning, and proper storage and handling, that affect, to varying degrees, all types of collections. Different types of institutions or collections have different responsibilities, users, and priorities, which means that a one-size-fits-all template for strategic planning is unlikely to be useful. In historical collections and archives, a long-term preservation obligation may be assumed, in which case strategic planning is likely to emphasize broad issues such as environmental control and emergency preparedness. A small undergraduate library or a public library is likely to be committed to maintaining a circulating collection for current use, which will highlight in their strategic planning the need for basic book repair and the need to replace out-of-date and brittle items with new copies and digital surrogates.

Points of difference in the strategic plans of myriad types of institutions will, of course, be consistent with the differences in their mission statements. If an institution's mission statement emphasizes making information readily available to a community, the goals expressed in a strategic plan for preservation will reflect the need to facilitate access to a collection while maintaining its security. If that institution's preservation assessment has identified collections of interest to a community that are unprocessed, a goal in its strategic plan might be to secure the funding necessary to make those collections available within a specified time frame.

## Building a Realistic and Supportable Plan

Each goal in NARA's strategic plan had long- and short-term outcomes, as well as indicators for measuring achievement. By keeping goals focused over a set time period of between five and ten years, they are unlikely to be overambitious and are, therefore, likely to win the support of those at the highest level of an institution's governance and administration. A recent report on the preservation of media in the Indiana University Bloomington's collections clearly connects preservation needs and goals to their specific institutional context by aligning them with four documents:

- The Indiana University president's core *Principles of Excellence*
- University Information Technologies Services' *Empowering People: Indiana University's Strategic Plan for Information Technology 2009*
- The Office of the Vice Provost for Research *Five-Year Strategic Plan 2008–2013*
- The IU Libraries *Mission Statement*[26]

Because the report calls for major commitment of staff and financial resources, this level of alignment is critical to the success of the strategy. Throughout the report collaboration within the university and with other peer institutions is emphasized; at the same time, even though the task force had a university-wide mandate, the important decision-making role of curatorial or custodial staff at the collection level is underlined.

## Staff

Some organizations have established broadly based preservation programs, frequently with a dedicated manager and staff, offering a wide range of services including staff training, emergency preparedness, 24/7 availability for emergency response and salvage expertise, collection surveys, environmental monitoring, and digital reformatting. Some institutions may have on-site conservation treatment laboratories and the capacity to carry out stabilization of materials in their general collections. (An example is the Weissman Preservation Center at Harvard University.) Collections with fewer resources may not have a designated preservation officer, relying instead on staff to shoulder a range of responsibilities. No matter what the resourcing circumstances of an institution, a good preservation plan is key to progress and achievement. A senior staff member should hold responsibility as preservation officer, or an equivalent title, and this role should be included in their job description. Having a preservation plan allows for the definition of specific preservation-related staff roles and for the commitment to provide training when it is needed. Establishing relationships with professional organizations, local vendors, emergency responders, and recovery services is also a part of preservation planning.

A preservation program needs to engage every member of staff. All staff, from student workers reshelving library books to the exhibition curators deciding what type of lighting to use in a display case, share responsibility for maintaining sustainable and accessible collections and for ensuring that they are used without risk.

Recognizing this fact means that the daily routines of all staff and the workflow of all processes must be considered in preservation planning. For example, in circulating collections staff is often trained in making decisions about routing books for repair. An archivist appraising a collection of papers for potential acquisition will consider the condition and potential preservation problems of that collection, and as the collection enters the institution, additional staff may be involved in preservation-related activities as the papers are processed. Managers need to be aware of the many ways in which all collection objects are handled as they are processed and used in an institution so that they can identify potential problems and bottlenecks and adjust training as necessary.

## STAFF TRAINING

Education for librarians, archivists, and museum professionals typically exposes them to the basic principles of good collection care and handling. It is reasonable to expect professional staff to know what best practices are and to implement them when they are working directly with collections. Few new professionals, however, will have the in-depth knowledge to administer a comprehensive preservation program without some additional level of directed study.

Staff and users need to be given appropriate training in the preservation aspects of their work. Another of the preservation principles this book is based on is relevant here: "Preservation actions should not exceed the abilities of the personnel who apply them." Actions can be as simple as taking care to turn out unnecessary lighting in closed stack areas, or requiring users to wash their hands before handling certain materials. For a preservation program to be effective, everyone must understand how his or her particular role contributes to the preservation whole.

Given the likelihood of regular turnover in staff positions at all levels, it can be a management challenge to ensure that all staff receive appropriate training and updating. Self-guided staff wiki sites, staff manuals, video and slide presentations, demonstrations and exhibitions, and other training materials can be made available for staff in most institutions. Local preservation centers, continuing education programs—both online and face-to-face—at schools of library and information science, workshops and conferences, and webinars offered by professional organizations are some of the many options for advancing and refreshing staff knowledge and skills.

Ensuring appropriate training for all staff does not have to be a big item in the preservation manager's budget. Many large academic libraries, state archives, and historical societies make their training materials available on the Web, and many workshops, conferences, and refresher courses offer good value. Improperly trained staff, however well intentioned, can have a serious, negative impact on the collections and consequently on available funding. The example of a well-intentioned, but undertrained and undersupervised, volunteer in a special collection is salutary; the volunteer used duct tape to repair the spines of several shelves of 19th-century books, an action that was discovered when the volunteer sought to have the cost of the duct tape reimbursed. The repairs to the damaged books cost considerably more than what a half-day training session in appropriate treatments would have cost.

## DISASTER PLANNING AND RECOVERY

Disaster planning and recovery has a prominent role in preservation planning. The efficient restoration of services is the aim of recovering from a disaster. To achieve this a plan that covers physical and virtual collections, services, administration, cash flow, and people is essential. A disaster plan is now an accepted component of every cultural heritage institution's preservation program (although it is often neither present in the program nor kept up-to-date). It is a set of rehearsed actions that minimizes the effect of a disaster, whatever its magnitude, on the institution, and it drives the process of restoring the institution and its collections and services in as short a time as possible. This section introduces the need for a disaster plan and explains its major components, but it is no substitute for careful study of the many guides to preservation planning available in print and on the Internet.

The term *disaster* may be misleading. A disaster in this context is "an unexpected event with destructive consequences to . . . holdings," ranging from "a small-scale incident [to] a full-blown emergency," but whatever its scale, it demands "prompt action to limit damage."[27] Disasters in cultural heritage institutions are common; their frequency is indicated by a partial list of libraries and archives destroyed in the 20th century.[28] Small leaks, spills, and floods are likely to occur in any building; major catastrophes will occur less frequently or, ideally, not at all. In most disasters, whatever their size, water and fire are most likely to be the cause of damage, but the physical destruction of buildings by earthquakes, war, hurricanes, and the like is, unfortunately, not uncommon.

### Minimizing Risks

A disaster plan consists of two sets of actions: preventive—minimizing the likelihood of a disaster by planning, reducing vulnerabilities, and establishing procedures; and reactive—putting into practice already established and rehearsed procedures to recover from a disaster and resume normal service. The best protection against disasters is to reduce the risk of their occurrence. Actions that minimize this risk include what should be normal good practice in managing a cultural heritage institution: regular housekeeping; appropriate construction, fitting out, and maintenance of buildings; and well-trained staff.

Inspecting the building from the viewpoint of disaster prevention will help identify risks so they can be addressed. (This has been covered in more detail in the section "Assessment: Building, Context, Environment" earlier in this chapter.) Fittings and materials, such as combustible furnishings or nitrate film, in the collection may pose risks. Regular housekeeping and building maintenance ensures that the potential for risk is monitored by identifying areas where problems might occur. Staff training is another important preventive activity; for example, regular instruction in fire prevention procedures and in the use of fire extinguishers.

## Response

What needs to happen when a disaster occurs? A disaster plan should be available; planning is noted below in the section "Developing a Disaster Plan." With the plan in place, the first steps are to raise the alarm and assemble staff, according to well-rehearsed procedures. When the site of the disaster is declared safe to enter, a preliminary assessment of the extent of damage and equipment and supplies required is made. Damaged material should then be packed, details recorded, and removed. A treatment area close to the disaster site should be set up where treatments that can be carried out immediately, such as air-drying wet, paper-based materials, take place.

## Recovery

Once damaged materials have been removed from the site and treated or stabilized for treatment in the future, the disaster site needs to be made ready for reoccupation.

First, decisions can be made and action plans developed, taking into account the causes of the disaster. From the assessment of causes, future actions, such as relocating shelves away from water pipes and raising materials off the floor, might be determined. Decisions about which materials are restored to usable condition first, and how (preferably with the advice of a conservator or a specialist in specific object types) need to be made. The disaster site is made habitable by clearing debris or drying carpets, among other steps. Environmental conditions should be checked particularly carefully to ensure that they have settled down to acceptable levels. Restoring an acceptable relative humidity level is vital because of the possibility of rapid mold growth if it is too high. Materials should not be put back in place until environmental conditions have settled. A debriefing, with input from all staff involved with the disaster, will help to improve the disaster plan.

The contributions in Part IV provide expert advice on disaster response actions that should be applied to specific object types. Further relevant information about controlling mold and stabilizing temperatures can be found in chapter 5.

## Developing a Disaster Plan

A formal and publicly available disaster plan is indispensable in preparing for and responding to the occurrence of disasters. It acknowledges the possibility of disasters happening, that the organization is committed to action if they do happen, that decision making is relevant, and that damage to collections can be reduced and costs contained. On a practical level, a disaster plan provides staff with step-by-step instructions.

A disaster plan assumes that general emergency procedures covering situations that threaten the safety of people are in place and addresses what needs to happen after people are safe. The principal activities in preparing a disaster plan are: forming a disaster response team; compiling documentation (for example, building floor plans, a list of personnel and their contact details, a list of equipment, and lists of suppliers of items needed during an emergency); arranging for access to freezer capacity and other services; making financial provisions to pay for emergency needs; taking preventive measures to ensure that damage is minimized if a disaster happens (for example, raising collection materials off the floor); and testing and regularly updating the plan.

Lists of key personnel, services, and sources of equipment must be compiled and available at designated locations both inside and outside the building. Other lists to compile include: the location of building features, such as electrical switchboards, gas mains, taps, and water stopcocks; services and sources of equipment, such as freezing and cold-store facilities, local equipment-hire businesses, plumbers, electricians, and locksmiths; and people in the area with training or experience in disaster response, together with their contact information. The need to keep all lists up-to-date cannot be emphasized enough.

Training of staff, and especially of those in the disaster response team, is critical to the success of a response to a disaster. Training in how to enter a disaster site, identifying materials at risk, removing materials, and making decisions about recovery techniques is needed, and it must be refreshed and updated regularly.

It is helpful to have on hand equipment needed in the recovery phase. Smaller incidents can often be handled using the contents of a disaster box, consisting of items to clear up liquid spills (bucket and mop, paper towels, sponges), material to cover parts of the collections to prevent further damage (polythene sheeting, scissors, polythene bags), and items to help organize activities during a disaster (pencils and writing paper, protective gloves). Large and more costly cleanup and recovery items, such as plastic crates, wet-dry vacuum cleaners, pumps, dehumidifiers, and fans, can be housed in a central store.

It is crucial that the disaster plan and its lists are kept current. A timetable for regular checking of the plan must be established, and a staff member (probably a member of the disaster response team) should be designated to update it.

Each institution will determine the components to include in its disaster plan documentation. Typically found are:

- clear summary of emergency procedures (for both human life and the collections) to be followed for each likely type of disaster—fire, water damage, bomb threats, etc.
- list of personnel to be contacted if an emergency occurs
- list of regional and national consultants and services
- lists of equipment and supplies on hand, and of sources for equipment not on-site
- procedures for getting emergency funds from the parent organization
- floor plans of the institution with locations of priority materials and equipment for salvage clearly marked
- summary of insurance coverage and insurers
- list of arrangements made for regular building inspections, covering building maintenance, plumbing, electrical facilities, roofs, drainage, water pipes, etc.
- list of arrangements made for regular inspection of security equipment such as alarm systems and fire detection and fire extinguishing equipment[29]

Anyone who is developing a preservation plan is well served by examining a range of plans from other institutions and adopting and adapting the features and presentation best suited to their requirements. Useful templates to assist with disaster planning may be found online, such as *dPlan: The Online Disaster-Planning Tool for Cultural and Civic Institutions* (www.dplan.org), computer software designed for this purpose, and local and regional collaboratives, such as COSTEP: Coordinated Statewide Emergency Preparedness (www.nedcc.org/free-resources/costep) in Massachusetts. Collaboration with other staff of their institution in developing the plan will also have the positive benefits of increasing general preservation awareness and of disaster response in particular.

## CONCLUSION

A preservation plan based on clear understandings is essential for effective preservation. It should be grounded in a mission statement and clearly articulated policies. Turning the mission statement and preservation policies into an actionable plan requires in-depth knowledge of the collections, the building, and the operation of the institution, for which a thorough preservation assessment will establish a baseline. Current conditions can be evaluated and the effect of changes monitored through the preservation assessment, which also serves as the cornerstone for long-range preservation planning.

The next chapter examines how we choose between preserving the physical objects in collections, or their information content, and how in some cases we choose both. It considers what influences the survival of objects in collections of cultural heritage institutions, especially the storage environment, quality of the material from which objects are made, the enclosures they are housed in, and how they are handled. The rationale for preserving objects or information content is examined, and an overview of the range of options for preserving artifacts and information is given.

# NOTES

1. Ross Harvey, *Preservation in Libraries: Principles, Strategies, and Practices for Librarians* (London: Bowker-Saur, 1993), 211.

2. Paul Lewis, "Preservation Takes Rare Manuscripts from the Public," *New York Times*, January 25, 1987, accessed October 1, 2013, http://www.nytimes.com/1987/01/25/books/preservation -takes-rare-manuscripts-from-the-public.html.

3. New York Public Library, "The Medieval and Renaissance Western Manuscripts of the New York Public Library," accessed October 2, 2013, http://www.nypl.org/locations/tid/36/node/29598.

4. Mirjam M. Foot, *Building a Preservation Policy* (London: British Library Preservation Advisory Centre, 2013), 4.

5. David Carr, *The Promise of Cultural Institutions* (Walnut Creek, MD: AltaMira Press, 2003), 119.

6. Melissa Mannon, *Cultural Heritage Collaborators: A Manual for Community Documentation* (Bedford, NH: ArchivesInfo Press, 2010).

7. Helen Forde, "Preservation Policies—Who Needs Them?" *Journal of the Society of Archivists* 18 (1997), 165.

8. For example, Foot's *Building a Preservation Policy*, published by the British Library.

9. The National Archives, *Preservation Policy* (London, 2009), 3, accessed October 1, 2013, http://www.nationalarchives.gov.uk/documents/tna-corporate-preservation-policy-2009-website -version.pdf.

10. The National Archives, *Preservation Policy*, 10–12.

11. Caroline Checkley-Scott, and Dave Thompson, *Wellcome Library Preservation Policy for Materials Held in Collections* (London: Wellcome Library, 2007), accessed October 1, 2013, http:// wellcomelibrary.org/content/documents/policy-documents/preservation-policy.

12. National Library of Australia, "Preservation Policy," reviewed 2009, accessed October 2, 2013, http://www.nla.gov.au/policy-and-planning/preservation-policy.

13. Churchill College, Cambridge, "Preservation Policy," updated 2011, accessed October 2, 2013, http://www.chu.cam.ac.uk/archives/about/preservation.php.

14. Patricia K. Turpening, "Essential Elements for Starting a Library Preservation Program," *Abbey Newsletter* 26, no. 6 (2003), accessed October 1, 2013, http://cool.conservation-us.org/byorg/ abbey/an/an26/an26-6/an26-608.html.

15. National Archives and Records Administration, *National Archives Gift Collection Acquisition Policy: Motion Pictures and Sound and Video Recordings* (General Information Leaflet 34) (Washington, DC: 1990), accessed October 1, 2013, http://www.archives.gov/publications/general -info-leaflets/34-media.html.

16. UNESCO, *Guidelines on Preservation and Conservation Policies in the Archives and Libraries Heritage* (Paris, 1990) accessed October 1, 2013, http://unesdoc.unesco.org/images/0008/ 000863/086345eo.pdf.

17. Mirjam M. Foot, "Towards a Preservation Policy for European Research Libraries," *Liber Quarterly* 9, no. 3 (1999), 324.

18. Maja Krtalic and Damir Hasenay, "Exploring a Framework for Comprehensive and Successful Preservation Management in Libraries," *Journal of Documentation* 68, no. 3 (2012): 354.

19. UNESCO, *Guidelines on Preservation*; Foot, *Building a Preservation Policy*.

20. PrestoSpace, "Deliverable D14.1 Preservation Guide: General Guide to Audiovisual Preservation (Web Report)" (2006), 16, accessed October 1, 2013, http://prestospace.org/project/deliverables/D14-1.pdf.

21. Sherelyn Ogden, *Preservation Planning: Guidelines for Writing a Long-Range Plan* (Washington, DC: American Association of Museums and the Northeast Document Conservation Center, 1997).

22. British Library Preservation Advisory Centre, *National Library of Ireland: Preservation Assessment Survey Case Study*, 1, accessed October 1, 2013, http://www.bl.uk/blpac/pdf/nli.pdf.

23. The priorities list is based on Ogden, *Preservation Planning*.

24. *To Preserve and Protect: The Strategic Stewardship of Cultural Resources: Essays from the Symposium Held at the Library of Congress October 30–31, 2000* (Washington, DC: Library of Congress, 2002).

25. National Archives and Records Administration, *Preserving the Past to Protect the Future: The Strategic Plan of the National Archives and Records Administration, 2006–2016,* revised 2009 (Washington, DC, 2009), iii, accessed October 1, 2013, http://www.archives.gov/about/plans-reports/strategic-plan/2009/nara-strategic-plan-2006-2016-final.pdf.

26. Indiana University Bloomington Media Preservation Initiative Task Force, *Meeting the Challenge of Media Preservation: Strategies and Solutions* (Bloomington, 2011), 15, accessed October 1, 2013, http://www.indiana.edu/~medpres/documents/iu_mpi_report_public.pdf.

27. Hazel Anderson and John E. McIntyre, *Planning Manual for Disaster Control in Scottish Libraries and Record Offices* (Edinburgh: National Library of Scotland, 1985), 9.

28. Hans van der Hoeven and Joan van Albada, *Lost Memory: Libraries and Archives Destroyed in the Twentieth Century* (Paris: UNESCO, 1996), accessed October 6, 2013, http://unesdoc.unesco.org/images/0010/001055/105557e.pdf.

29. Based on a list in Research Libraries Group, *RLG Preservation Manual*, 2nd ed. (Stanford, CA, 1986), 132–33.

# PART II
# COLLECTIONS

# Artifacts and Information

··························································································································

Chapter 4 first considers the factors that have the greatest impact on the survival of objects in the collections of cultural heritage institutions: their storage environment, the quality of the material from which they are made, the enclosures they are housed in, and how they are handled. The rationale for preserving the information content of physical objects, rather than the objects themselves, by reformatting them is then examined. An overview of the range of options for preserving artifacts and information concludes the chapter.

This chapter is underpinned by the preservation principles articulated in chapter 2, emphasizing three in particular:

- Preservation requires active, managed care.
- Understanding the structure of materials is the key to understanding what preservation actions to take, as materials contain the seeds of their own destruction (inherent vice).
- Distinguish clearly between objects (containers) and the information they carry (content).

Other preservation principles relevant to this chapter are:

- Taking preservation action now is better than doing nothing.
- Prefer preservation actions that address large quantities of material over actions that focus on individual objects.

## CONCEPTS

To make informed decisions about how best to preserve objects in the collections of cultural heritage institutions, we must first understand what contributes to their survival:

··························································································································

the storage environment, the quality of the material from which they are made, the enclosures they are housed in, and how they are handled. When thinking about these factors it is helpful to distinguish between *preventive preservation* and *active treatment*. Wherever possible, we should attempt to prevent damage to the objects, or delay or minimize damage, rather than repair them later—this is *preventive preservation*. If objects become damaged or are at risk of total disintegration, we may decide to apply repairs or conservation processes or to reformat them—this is *active treatment*. Active treatment is expensive, typically costing significantly more than preventive preservation. Figure 4.1 provides examples of preventive preservation actions and active treatments.

Preventive preservation, applied prospectively, is the goal of most preservation programs, rather than active treatment, applied retrospectively. It is always better to prevent damage from occurring than to deal with damage after it has happened. It is also cost-effective; as already noted, active treatment typically costs significantly more than preventive preservation. Two preservation principles come into play: "Preservation requires active, managed care"; and "Prefer preservation actions that address large quantities of material over actions that focus on individual objects."

Three characteristics common to physical (analog) and digital objects mean they will not last as long as we want without preservation attention. First, they are usually inherently fragile and unstable, or obsolescent (that is, in the process of becoming obsolete). The material they are made of, and how well they are made, directly affects how they deteriorate; for some materials, the availability of equipment and software

| Preventive preservation | Actions that aim to prevent, delay, or minimize damage occurring include: |
|---|---|
| | • Identifying what collections are made of and how the information in them has been recorded. |
| | • Improving the way collections are stored or housed. |
| | • Controlling the environment around collections—heat, humidity, light, dirt, animals, and insects. |
| | • Educating staff and users about the best ways to handle, display, and use collections. |
| | • Being prepared to act if any disaster threatens collections. |
| Active treatment | Active treatments, usually carried out after damage has occurred, include: |
| | • Repairing damaged items, preferably when the damage is first found. |
| | • For very special materials, having them treated to full conservation standards. |
| | • Making new copies of materials that cannot be used or displayed in their original form. |

FIGURE 4.1. Preventive Preservation and Active Treatment

needed to use them affects whether we can use them. Second, they are affected by the natural and built environments that surround them, so how they are stored directly speeds up or retards their deterioration. Third, the ways in which they are used directly affects their longevity. The care with which they are handled and used is a key factor in deterioration.

The statement that objects "are usually inherently fragile and unstable, or obsolescent" calls for further scrutiny. Most objects in the collections of cultural heritage institutions consist of organic materials that deteriorate, decay, and ultimately disintegrate. For these objects to be available indefinitely, their preservation needs to be actively considered immediately. If the original objects cannot be preserved in their current format, the information they contain must be migrated to another format. For some materials, such as newspapers, this is already common practice. For some objects there is the added complication of the need for a playback device to access and make readable the information they contain. Videotapes and audiotapes, for example, require specialized equipment for capturing the information placed on them, and for accessing, reading, and rendering that information. The specialized equipment is often obsolescent or may have already become obsolete (that is, not in common use or not commonly available). Digital objects also need specialized equipment for capturing, accessing, and rendering the information they contain; they have the further complication of needing software to access and interpret the information stored in them. If any one of several components is missing, the information cannot be accessed. These factors illustrate one of the preservation principles on which this book is based: "Preservation requires active, managed care."

Another preservation principle helps in analyzing the statement that "the material objects are made of, and how well they are made, directly affects how they deteriorate." This principle is "Understanding the structure of materials is the key to understanding what preservation actions to take, as materials contain the seeds of their own destruction (inherent vice)." This principle is noted with reference to specific materials and object types in Part IV. Because most objects in the collections of cultural heritage institutions are made from organic materials, they are affected by the conditions in which they are stored. Most materials survive longer if the temperature at which they are stored is kept low and stable, the relative humidity is kept moderately low, the air around them meets clean air standards, and the building in which they are housed is fireproof, weatherproof, and safe from natural disasters. Many examples are provided in Part IV of this book.

The statement that "the ways in which objects are used directly affects their longevity" is just common sense. Heavy use puts greater stress on objects, adding to the likelihood that they will be damaged, to the extent that the information they contain is lost. Two examples illustrate this point. Some information storage media have moving parts that are subject to wear and will eventually damage the information-bearing layers of the media. For example, jolting or dropping a hard-disk drive may result in the misalignment of its rotating disks, which will badly affect their performance. Inappropriate handling of an optical disk (such as a DVD or CD-ROM) can leave an oily residue, which corrupts the digital information stored on it.

Given all of these factors and the myriad complications they raise, how do we determine what preservation actions to take? Do we preserve the information content of the object, or the object itself, or perhaps both? How does the access we require to objects affect their preservation?

## INFORMATION OR ARTIFACT?

A crucial distinction to make is between preservation of the artifact (the physical object) and preservation of the information content residing in the artifact, expressed in the principle "Distinguish clearly between objects (containers) and the information they carry (content)." Recognizing this distinction and its implications was one of the most important preservation understandings in recent decades, and it has proved crucial to developing effective digital preservation approaches. Preservation was historically considered as collecting and providing safe storage of physical objects. Physical objects were kept intact, and it was assumed that the protection of intact objects would guarantee they remained usable. Preservation procedures, such as storing objects in an optimally controlled environment, aimed to stabilize physical objects. Underlying these procedures was the further assumption that the objects would stay reasonably stable over time. This second assumption was extended to an acceptance that most objects do not deteriorate rapidly if ignored—the basis of the concept of benign neglect introduced in chapter 2.

Digital objects challenge these assumptions and their relevance for preservation. Digital objects rely on sophisticated equipment with high rates of obsolescence, and on equally obsolete or obsolescent applications and file formats. Simply storing them and hoping that they will remain usable in the future is a risky approach to take for their preservation. Even if the discs or other media on which digital files are stored are kept in high-quality environmental conditions, the obsolescence of software, hardware, and file formats is very likely to cause the digital objects stored on these media to be unreadable long before the media deteriorate. For these reasons, in preserving digital materials the focus must be on information content.

Techniques for preserving the information content rather than the artifact were (and still are) applied to analog objects. Copying of manuscripts has a very long history, as noted in chapter 1. Microfilming was used in libraries and archives from the 1930s, and photocopying at a later date. Reformatting—copying the information content of an object to another format—is now a standard preservation technique, and digitizing objects in the collections of libraries and archives is now the copying method of choice.

### Access Requirements and Preservation

How, then, do we decide whether to allocate preservation resources to physical objects or to their information content? When is it possible to allocate resources to both? One answer is to separate and treat materials according to access requirements, all the while applying an understanding of the role and purpose of the cultural heritage institution that has responsibility for them, and of the needs and expectations of that institution's users.

For library and archives collections, determining the uniqueness of the types of information in collections may guide decision making. Figure 4.2 indicates some factors to consider.

However, only considering the type of information when we determine appropriate preservation attention is not sufficient. We also need to take account of the institution: what kind it is, the needs of its users, the types of materials in its collections, and the resources (space, finance, staff) available. This section is, of necessity, written in general terms and does not reflect the combined and converging responsibilities and foci of some institutions.

*Libraries* have traditionally been considered as places with collections of books that are made available for users to consult and read, either in-house or on short-term loan. Until relatively recently, library collections consisted mainly of books and other printed materials. Some libraries also held collections of special materials, such as manuscripts, pictures, and maps. Today, audio, video, photographic materials, and digital materials are being collected in libraries in ever-increasing amounts. Online resources no longer need to be consulted at a particular location, as they can be made available at almost any location.

| Type of Information | Examples | Preservation Focus |
|---|---|---|
| Primary | Eyewitness accounts, oral histories, manuscripts, letters, photographic negatives, original sound recordings, archival records | Original or unique, so requires the highest level of preservation attention. It is common practice to make a surrogate copy ("use" copy). |
| Secondary | Most published books, serials, encyclopedias, distribution copies of sound recordings, photographic prints | Almost always exist in multiple copies. It is important to know that one copy exists somewhere and that a commitment to preserve it forever has been made. |
| Tertiary | Bibliographies, indexes, and abstracts, used to find information | Almost always exist in multiple copies. It is important to know that one copy exists somewhere and that a commitment to preserve it forever has been made. |

**FIGURE 4.2.** Types of Information in Libraries and Archives

Many different types of library exist, and the type of library and the way it is used will define the preservation needs of its collections. Public libraries, for example, typically contain recreational reading (fiction, general interest materials) and a small, current reference collection. These are secondary materials for which the preservation focus is on maintenance and repair to keep the materials in use for as long as the library and its users need them. A local history study collection will have some primary materials, with higher levels of preservation need. Research libraries, such as national libraries, some state libraries, and some academic libraries have the primary purpose of facilitating research. They are likely to contain a broad range of materials, both current and retrospective. Much will be primary materials with high levels of preservation need. Some libraries (usually national or state libraries) have legal deposit collections, amassed to ensure that all the published output of a country or state is retained permanently. Legal deposit collections require the highest levels of preservation attention.

*Archives* preserve corporate and individual memory, usually in the form of administrative records and cultural, historical, and personal records, which are nearly always unique. These records have been selected as important in some way, and their preservation is one of the major responsibilities the archive has toward them. Records come in all shapes and formats. Although traditionally paper based, they can also include objects, such as personal effects like clothes, jewelry, and badges of rank, and increasingly they include digital objects.

Librarians select what to acquire from the world's output of published materials in building the collections of libraries; archivists, especially those in official archives, determine what to discard in the process of identifying what records need to be kept to preserve memory. In some organizations, particularly government archives, archivists have much greater involvement in the creation of records than librarians ever have in the creation of library materials. Most government archives services play a significant role in influencing the creation of records for long-term retention; for example, by advising on the papers and inks used, and on the file formats used for digital records. Archivists in some types of archives may have a legal responsibility to preserve the records they hold in perpetuity, which has major implications for the preservation actions they must apply in those archives. Only those libraries with a legal deposit role have a comparable obligation to maintain their deposit collections in perpetuity.

*Museums* collect materials, typically tangible objects, but increasingly also audio, visual, and digital objects, selected according to their aesthetic value or educational value. They acquire objects that provide material evidence of people and their environment, for the purposes of study, education, and enjoyment. Heavy emphasis is placed on keeping the collection in excellent shape and ensuring the authenticity of objects in that collection. The handling of objects is usually restricted to museum staff or bona fide researchers who have proven credentials. Members of the public can see objects when they are exhibited, but they cannot handle them. The objects in a museum's collection may have been selected and acquired because they are exemplars, and they are often unique. Because most objects are original or unique, they receive the highest level of preservation attention.

In summary, the choice of preservation actions depends on several factors: the materials from which an object is made; how (and how frequently) it is used; the kind of cultural heritage collection it resides in; and the reasons for its selection and addition to that collection. Once these factors are understood, the choice of how to preserve objects can be made.

## PRESERVING ARTIFACTS

The rationale for preserving artifacts is based on the concept that the information content on an artifact coexists exactly with the artifact, and is understandable. (The fact that this is not always the case is usually conveniently ignored, as demonstrated by two examples. The three scripts on the Rosetta Stone, an ancient Egyptian stone stele inscribed with a decree issued in 196 BCE, aroused widespread public interest from its reappearance in 1799 CE. Although the artifact was preserved, its information content was not fully deciphered for many years. The Phaistos Disc, a clay disc from the Minoan palace of Phaistos on Crete, possibly dates from the second millennium BC. Although the artifact has been preserved, its purpose and the meaning of the inscribed symbols on it remain unclear.) Following this reasoning, keeping an artifact becomes the equivalent of preserving the information content of that artifact and is the principal concern, often the only concern, of the preservation actions applied. Heavy emphasis is therefore placed on keeping artifacts in the best possible condition by providing ideal storage conditions, keeping them in nonharmful enclosures, and handling them in ways that do not damage them.

Hand in hand with this rationale is the concept of benign neglect, introduced in chapter 2 and commonly used as a preservation management tool in libraries, archives, and museums. Many artifacts stay reasonably stable over time and do not deteriorate rapidly, thus requiring no immediate preservation attention. Benign neglect buys time. The validity of benign neglect as a preservation tool is enhanced if materials are manufactured from stable materials, as noted in detail elsewhere in this chapter. However, although benign neglect has been applied in analog object preservation, it is not usually considered valid for digital objects, which demand preservation attention early in their life because of the rapid obsolescence of file formats, storage media, and hardware and software. This claim is being challenged as our understanding of digital preservation improves.

The next two sections consider some general aspects of preserving artifacts. The first section describes *intrinsic* factors, characteristics of objects that stem from their manufacture. It describes the materials that objects are made of and specifies the effect of quality of materials and of the manufacturing processes. The second section describes *extrinsic* factors, in particular the effects of storage environment; shelving and enclosures such as boxes, containers, and encapsulation; and handling. These sections are concerned only with general principles: specific practices, recommendations, and standards for specific object types are noted in Part IV.

## Intrinsic Characteristics

All materials have built-in decay characteristics, determined by the kinds of materials used to make them and how they are manufactured. Because materials and manufacturing processes have a direct effect on how long objects last, understanding materials and processes allows us to develop effective preservation practices. The notion that materials contain the seeds of their own destruction is sometimes referred to as inherent vice. The preservation principle relevant here is "Understanding the structure of materials is the key to understanding what preservation actions to take, as materials contain the seeds of their own destruction (inherent vice)." Paper-based materials are used here as an extended example, as they still predominate in the collections of library and archives, requiring that we understand them. To understand how to preserve paper-based materials—and ultimately the information they are being used to record—we need to know what they are made out of, how they deteriorate, and how they can be manufactured better. Described here are the papers and cardboards used, the materials used to record the information (such as inks) and the physical construction of objects. Paper-based materials are noted in more detail in the sections "Paper: Library and Archives Materials" and "Paper: Works of Art on Paper" in chapter 8.

## Paper Manufacture and Quality

Two key components of paper affect its survival potential: the fibers it is made from, and the additives or processing chemicals used during its manufacture. The fiber source has major implications for paper quality. Early Western papers, made almost entirely out of old rags, have lasted for centuries. Most book papers from the mid-19th century, made from wood pulp, last only for decades. The quality of wood-pulp paper depends heavily on the processes used to extract cellulose fibers from wood and remove impurities, especially lignin. The characteristic yellowing of newsprint when it is exposed to sunlight results from degradation of lignin in the paper.

Materials are added during the papermaking process to make paper better to write and print on, to prolong its life, and to improve its aesthetic appearance. Some of these additives are acidic. The presence of acid or acid-forming substances causes partial decomposition of the cellulose fibers over time, weakening the paper. Acid can also be introduced into the paper sheet from gases in the environment, such as sulfur dioxide, nitrogen oxides, and ozone. Excluding acidic, or potentially acidic, substances during manufacture can increase the life expectancy of paper. International standards for permanent paper specify that the paper is buffered with an alkaline additive to counteract the effects of external acidity from the environment, has less than 1 percent lignin, and meets strength requirements.[1] "Permanent" papers are expected to last for several hundred years without significant deterioration under normal use and storage conditions. Many papers currently manufactured now meet these standards.

## Putting the Image onto Paper

Information is recorded on paper by printing, writing, or drawing, using a variety of colored materials held on the paper surface by some form of binder. Two characteristics are important for the long-term preservation of information recorded on a paper base:

- the stability of the colored materials themselves—Will they change color or fade with time (particularly when exposed to light), or will they cause any damage to the substrate?
- the binding of the colored materials onto the paper substrate—How well are they bound onto the substrate? Will the agent binding them onto the substrate fail? Can they be brushed off, erased, or washed off?

Two examples illustrate how these characteristics affect longevity. Iron gall writing inks, in use from at least the first century BCE to the early part of the 20th century, were produced by the reaction of acid and iron salts in the presence of oak galls. A dark, brownish-black color develops as the ink ages. Writing using iron gall ink was far more permanent than other early writing inks, but there can be problems: where applied heavily, iron gall ink creates areas of text burned out of the paper; and where weakly applied, it fades to such a pale yellow that it becomes almost illegible. Thermal faxes (Thermo-Fax was one common trade name) were in use from 1954 to around 1969. They consist of a thin, color-forming layer made up of a colorless dye and a color-forming agent, coated onto a paper base. If the paper is exposed to a heat source, residual dye can develop, because the agent that develops the dye is heat activated, causing the image to deteriorate. Thermal faxes are also vulnerable to water, which may cause the coated layer to lift off, or copies to stick together.[2]

## Book Structure

Books provide another example of how understanding the material informs how we manage their preservation. The binding process fixes the text block (the pages secured together) in one place and helps secure the text's integrity. The binding usually helps preserve the printed material in the text block, but some binding styles have the opposite effect, leading to damage. For example, a book that is bound too tightly is often damaged when it is heavily used or photocopied. If the gutter (the gap between the text and the spine of the book) is too narrow, readers damage the book when they force it open to read the inner edges of the text near the spine.

How the pages of a book are prepared for binding, and how the covers are attached to the text block, directly affect how long books last. The pages may be section-sewn, glued, or side-sewn (stab-sewn), and the resulting text block may be attached to the covers using tight-back binding, case binding, glued ("perfect") bindings, wire, plastic, and other materials and methods. Each of these has different characteristics that influence longevity. For example, perfect binding, used in modern paperbacks, uses adhesive to join single sheets together at the spine edge. Older adhesives were rubber based and became brittle as they aged, causing pages to become detached from the spine. Modern synthetic adhesives, such as hot melts and emulsions, are more stable. Tight-back bindings, used since medieval times, have the covering material attached solidly to the spine of the book and are considered to be the most durable of hand bindings. However, books bound this way do not always open easily, and as the leather covers of older books deteriorate they tend to become detached from the spine. Books are noted in more detail in the section "Books" in chapter 8.

## Other Materials in Paper-Based Collections

Collections that contain mostly paper-based materials, typically in libraries and archives, include other materials whose manufacture and decay characteristics need to be understood so we can preserve them effectively. Figure 4.3 illustrates how preservation decisions and processes are assisted by knowledge of the materials. Further information on different kinds of materials is noted in Part IV.

## Extrinsic Factors

Cultural heritage professionals typically do not have much control over how objects in the collections of cultural institutions are made and what they are made from, although they constantly seek to influence the creators of objects to ensure their objects will last longer. Another set of factors—extrinsic factors—also influence how long objects in collections last. Cultural heritage professionals have more control over these factors. Two extrinsic factors are especially influential: how objects are stored, and how they are handled.

Many intrinsic factors cause paper to deteriorate, to continue the extended example. Paper's lignin content causes it to yellow, lose strength, and become brittle; and acidic papers do not last as long as alkaline papers. Extrinsic factors exacerbate intrinsic factors: high storage temperatures speed up chemical reactions that lead to embrittlement and loss of strength; high humidity allows mold growth and also leads to loss of strength; inappropriate storage and handling result in tears, crumpling, and holes in paper; insect pests create holes in paper (or even totally destroy it); and disasters can result in severe damage and loss. Some inks and paints, especially if colored, fade when exposed to light, and they may dissolve in high humidity. Storage and handling are principal causes of damage to books: thin paper covers will not stand up to heavy use; some paperback bindings (perfect bindings) become brittle and fail, so that pages fall out; large, flat-sheet materials, such as maps, are difficult to handle and store safely. The impact of extrinsic factors can be minimized by attending to storage environments appropriately and by careful handling.

This section introduces the role of storage environment in preservation (chapter 5 examines it in more detail). Related to storage environment are enclosures, such as boxes,

| Material | Where Found | Stability | Deterioration |
|---|---|---|---|
| Leather | In bindings of most books published before the 20th century | Vegetable-tanned goatskin is one of the most stable leathers for bookbinding. Other leather is less stable, especially if acids are used in their manufacture, or if they have been stored in an acidic environment. | Leather on the spine and hinges of covers usually fails first. Damage is typically seen as "red rot"; the top surface hardens and cracks, releasing a powdery, red dust. This damage is untreatable. |
| Parchment, Vellum | Used until recently for official documents (for example, land titles, deeds) | Made from specially prepared animal skins, traditionally calfskin. Very durable, but subject to damage by both high and low humidity. | If humidity levels are too high or low, parchment expands or shrinks. |
| Bookcloth | In the covers of books, in place of leather covers from about 1820 | Traditionally made of cotton or linen with additional fillers (typically pyroxylin or starch) to provide smoothness and strength. Bookcloth comes in a wide range of weights, finishes, and colors. | Some bookcloths are especially prone to mold in high humidity, others to grazing attack by insects. They are subject to damage by light, fading, and degrading, especially on their spines, resulting in covers becoming detached. |
| Adhesives | In bindings | Animal glue was traditionally used to adhere the spine to the text block. Modern adhesives are usually based on polyvinyl acetate (PVAc) and are applied as a hot or cold emulsion. | Animal glue becomes very brittle with age, causing the text block to become detached from covers. Modern emulsion adhesives perform better over time than animal glues, but hot melt adhesives can fail, particularly if they have been kept at an elevated temperature for too long during binding processes. |

**FIGURE 4.3.** Other Materials in Paper-Based Collections

containers, and encapsulation. Shelving plays an important role in preservation, as does the handling of materials.

## Storage Environment

Controlling the environment in which collections are stored so that optimal conditions are provided is essential for preservation. Temperature and relative humidity, light, and pollutants are three environmental factors that need to be controlled. Providing optimal storage environments illustrates two of the preservation principles on which this book is based: "Preservation requires active, managed care," and "Prefer preservation actions that address large quantities of material over actions that focus on individual objects."

Temperature and relative humidity must be discussed together, because it is difficult to separate their effects on how materials deteriorate. Temperature and moisture content in storage areas influence how objects deteriorate. If both the temperature and the relative humidity are too high, mold is more likely to grow. Very high humidity levels cause water-soluble inks to run, pages coated with china clay or chalk to stick together, and polymer binders in magnetic tapes to soften or become brittle, so that the binder sticks to the equipment's tape heads ("sticky tape" phenomenon) and information is lost from dropouts. Rapid changes in temperature are particularly damaging because they cause expansion and contraction, placing mechanical stress on materials. It is therefore essential to control the rate at which temperatures change in order to reduce deterioration. As a general guideline, the lower the storage temperature, the better. The optimal temperature and relative humidity levels in which to store collections vary according to the kinds of material collection objects are made of. For storage areas that include multiple kinds of material, compromise is called for, as noted in chapter 5. Recommendations for each kind of material are noted in Part IV.

Light is a form of energy and, as such, can trigger the chemical reactions that cause deterioration. The shorter the wavelength of the light, the greater is the energy level. Visible light has the longest wavelength of the usual sources of light; the most harmful is the shortest. Exposure of paper to light speeds up oxidization and chemical breakdown. Paper may get bleached and, if it contains any lignin, will darken. Inks may fade, reducing the legibility of text and image. Photographs are especially susceptible to damage from exposure to light. Light levels should be kept as low as possible to prevent the harmful effects of light on materials in collections. More on this topic is noted in chapter 5, and recommendations for each kind of material are noted in Part IV.

Pollutants in the air cause considerable damage and are a particular problem for collections located in densely populated areas. Pollutants can be gaseous or solid, are often acidic, can cause oxidization, or can be abrasive. The most common gaseous pollutants are sulfur dioxide, nitrogen dioxide, and hydrogen sulfide, by-products of the combustion of coal and petrol. Ozone is another. Solid pollutants such as dirt, dust, sand, and oily soot particles cause damage by their abrasive action, by providing nutrients that encourage growth of mold and fungi, or by forming acid. Abrasion may cause scratches on photographic materials and magnetic tapes and damage to paper. Oily soot can disfigure paper. Airborne pollutants may also affect staff and patrons adversely. Deterioration caused by pollutants is controlled by filtering air intakes into storage areas and by regular cleaning of collection areas. Chapter 5 provides more information on this topic.

Controlling temperature and relative humidity, light, and pollutant levels also minimizes deterioration caused by biological agents—mold and fungi, insects, rodents, and other animals. Biological agents thrive where there are high temperature and relative humidity levels, inadequate ventilation, and dust. They feed on the plentiful organic matter in collections: paper, leather, and wood are food sources for bacteria, molds, fungi, and insects. Mold and fungi spores, always present in the air, grow wherever conditions are favorable. They require warmth (about 75°F or 24°C and higher), moisture (about 70 percent RH or higher), darkness, and limited air circulation. Molds stain and weaken the material on which they grow and can destroy images on photographic materials and paper. To minimize their effect, repositories need to maintain temperature and relative humidity at levels that discourage growth and remove dirt, dust, and other solid particles. Insects, too, thrive in conditions similar to those that encourage mold growth. The presence of insects means that storage and environmental conditions are inappropriate. Insect damage is usually irreversible: text or images destroyed when holes are eaten through paper cannot be restored. Keeping storage areas clean helps control insects, as do low temperatures. Rodents, typically rats and mice, and many other locally specific pests damage collections by tearing up paper and by the corrosive effects of their droppings.

## Enclosures

Objects are often stored in boxes or containers, and, if they are single sheets of paper, they are sometimes encapsulated (enclosed in sheets of inert transparent polyester film such as Melinex). Enclosures protect objects from the normal wear and tear of being handled and stored. Additionally, the microenvironment within an enclosure acts as a buffer to slow down the rate of change in temperature and relative humidity. Enclosures also provide protection from water, smoke, and heat, which is an important consideration in preventing damage if disaster strikes. Enclosures in common use include encapsulation for single paper sheets, folders for unbound documents, boxes for larger items and for bound items whose bindings are in poor condition, slipcases for bound items, and shrink-wrapping for low-use materials and to provide protection when objects are moved.

Bindings are protective enclosures, too. Libraries may bind items (for example, paperbacks) to strengthen them and to group together smaller items or items issued serially, and they may rebind books with worn bindings that no longer protect their text block. Each of these binding decisions has its own requirements. Binding a book to maximize the number of times it is issued in a circulating collection has different requirements from binding an item in a special collection, where features of the item and its previous binding are kept for evidential and, perhaps, aesthetic reasons. Binding of materials that are likely to be photocopied (such as textbooks and periodicals) needs to allow the book to open flat on the platens of photocopiers. Essential further readings about library binding are the ANSI/NISO/LBI library binding standard[3] and Merrill-Oldham and Parisi's guide to that standard.[4]

## Shelving

Attention to shelving processes and to how shelving is constructed minimizes the risk of damage. Careful, harmless shelving practices need to be learned and consistently practiced. Best practice varies from one type of material to another, but it must ensure that the object, whatever the material it is made of, is not damaged. For example, flat sheets should be shelved flat and supported by rigid, inert material, and books should be kept upright to minimize strain on spines, sewing, and edges. Shelving must not be constructed with sharp edges or corners, must be fully supported so it will not become unbalanced and collapse, and should not be located in areas in which there are potential dangers to the materials it will house. Shelving recommendations for specific object types are noted in Part IV.

## Handling

A major source of damage to materials is the handling they receive from both staff and users. We preserve materials so they can be used, but, paradoxically, use results in damage. Careful, appropriate handling is one way to reduce the deterioration of objects, but it does not come naturally and must be taught. This section notes basic principles; handling practices for specific object types are noted in Part IV.

Care with handling starts as soon as an object enters a collection. Apparently insignificant practices, such as carefully removing a book from its shelf, not opening a tightly bound volume too far, or not touching the surface of an optical disk contribute considerably to reducing deterioration rates. Modifying the behavior of cultural heritage professionals and users of their collections is key to reducing deterioration caused by improper handling, and here education plays a significant role. Professionals are not able to directly intervene in the mishandling of material on loan; the best they can hope for is to influence through education. In library and archives buildings there are more possibilities, such as monitoring reading rooms and stack areas. Examples of inappropriate handling of library materials include stacking books insecurely, folding corners of pages, leaving books open face down, forcing bound volumes onto the platens of photocopiers, spilling liquids and leaving food fragments on material—the list is long. The surfaces of CDs and DVDs should not be touched, but they should be handled only at their center hole and outer edge, and they should be returned to storage cases immediately after use. Special handling may be required for rare and valuable material—for example, weak older bindings, where high-density foam or wooden supports should be available when they are opened for use.

## Standards

Standards have been developed for many of the extrinsic factors and for some of the intrinsic factors. Standards specify how some materials should be manufactured: two standards for permanent paper (ANSI NISO Standard Z39.48-1992 and ISO 9706:1994) have already been noted in this chapter. The manufacture of microfilm has generated many standards, among them ANSI/AIIM MS23-2004 *Standard Recommended Practice—Production, Inspection, and Quality Assurance of First-Generation, Silver Microforms of Documents* and ISO 6200:1999 *Micrographics—First Generation Silver-Gelatin Microforms of Source Documents—Density Specifications and Method of Measurement*.

Standards that indicate best practices for many of the extrinsic factors are available, playing an influential role in determining appropriate conditions for storage environments and offering useful advice for handling. The most important examples are standards that recommend environmental conditions, such as ANSI/NISO Z39.79-2001 *Environmental Conditions for Exhibiting Library and Archival Materials*. Standards that specify requirements for storage equipment include ANSI/NISO Z39.73-1994 *Single-Tier Steel Bracket Library Shelving*. Binding standards are also relevant: examples are ANSI/NISO Z39.66-1992 *Durable Hardcover Binding for Books* and ANSI/NISO/LBI Z39.78-2000 *Library Binding*.

Standards relevant to specific materials are noted in Part IV, and all of the standards noted in this book are also listed at the end of the book.

## Routine Collection Maintenance

A regular cleaning program is an important part of collection maintenance. In larger collections the primary responsibility of a staff member could be to clean, tidy, and carry out minor repairs; in smaller collections goals could be set, perhaps that a particular part of the collection is examined and maintenance carried out on specified dates. Ideally, every item in a collection should be examined once every two years at a minimum.

Minor repairs such as repairing damaged items, preferably when the damage is first noticed, should be routine in libraries and archives. The costs of and staff training in minor repairs are minimal, especially in comparison with full conservation treatments that may be needed if damage is left untreated. Treating objects to full conservation standards may also be part of the range of strategies used, but it is expensive and requires expert skills. Objects may also be reformatted, usually by digitizing them (but microfilming and photocopying are sometimes used). Careful coordination between in-house repair, collection maintenance operations, and other parts of the preservation program is essential to produce the most cost-effective results. Repair of specific materials is noted in Part IV.

The decision about whether an object requires simple in-house repair or conservation attention is based on its physical condition, value, and use, and on the preservation and collection development policies of the institution responsible for it. For books in a library's circulating collection, repairs are intended to keep books in usable condition, not to retain their original features. Typical in-house repairs address common problems, such as loose hinges on bindings, paper tears, and damaged spines. For books with special value to a collection, full-scale treatment (disbinding, deacidification, paper repair, rebinding, or constructing a protective enclosure) may be warranted. For archives material on paper, simple in-house repairs include surface cleaning, mending paper tears, foldering, and boxing. Simple in-house repairs are cost-effective: five minutes spent tightening the hinges of a binding costs significantly less than rebinding the book at a later stage, which has the added problem that the book is not available for days or weeks. It is essential to use only high-quality materials for repairs and nothing that could be harmful to objects. For example, paper used in repairs should be alkaline-buffered so that acid is not introduced to the object being repaired. The advice of a conservator should be sought when setting up a repair program. Keep in mind the preservation principle "Preservation actions should not exceed the abilities of the personnel who apply them."

Decisions about which treatment to apply need to be supported by an understanding of what is feasible in technological, financial, and practical terms, as well as of the value of the object to a collection. Policies and guidelines can be developed to enable speedy and effective decision making. For example, a policy could be to put all thin pamphlets in acid-free envelopes, and another to repair all paper tears in manuscripts with Japanese tissue paper. The advice of an experienced conservator is helpful when establishing policies and guidelines.

Refurbishing a library, archives, or museum collection in poor physical condition overall may be warranted. This could entail cleaning all items in the collection and its physical surroundings; applying protective measures to damaged items, such as enclosures for damaged or fragile items; identifying items in need of more advanced conservation work; and reshelving the refurbished items.

Trained and experienced conservators are not commonly located in any but the largest or well-endowed cultural heritage institutions. The reality is that preservation is usually the responsibility of cultural heritage professionals without specific preservation training. They must become informed and stay informed about preservation principles and current practice. One way to keep current is to seek advice from a conservator, perhaps on a regular consultancy basis. A conservator should also be hired at the initial stages of setting up a repair and maintenance program.

## PRESERVING INFORMATION

Distinguishing between preserving the artifact and preserving information content is one of the preservation principles this book is based on: "Distinguish clearly between objects (containers) and the information they carry (content)." Its history is noted briefly in chapter 2. The rationale for preserving the artifact is that the artifact's information content coexists exactly with the artifact, so keeping the artifact becomes the equivalent of preserving its information content. The fact that many, perhaps most, artifacts stay reasonably stable over time and do not require immediate preservation attention supports this rationale. It is difficult or impossible to halt the deterioration (and therefore information loss) of some artifacts for more than a short period. Among such artifacts are digital objects, which deteriorate rapidly because of obsolescence of file formats, storage media, and hardware and software, and artifacts on low-quality, typically acidic, paper, which deteriorates rapidly, especially if heavily used. For these vulnerable artifacts a different approach is needed; we concentrate on preserving their information content, rather than the artifact in or on which the information resides. Transferring the information to a longer-lasting storage medium or more stable file format is the mechanism used.

We recognize that a book—an artifact consisting of sheets of paper fastened together—contains a literary work or text. The literary work or text may be available as a physical book, serialized in a printed newspaper or an electronic version of a newspaper, as an e-book, as an audio recording on CD, and as a digital file. Alexander McCall Smith's novels serialized in *The Scotsman* newspaper, where they were available as both text and audio, and later published in book form, are an example. In preservation the distinction between object and information content has been long appreciated. Reformatting—copying information content to a more durable medium—has been a common preservation action for millennia.

When the focus is on preserving information content, rather than the artifact, different approaches to preservation are needed. There is, however, no "one-size-fits-all" approach. The information content may be copied to a longer-lasting information storage media, such as when printed material on paper is microfilmed and attention is then given to keeping the new, more durable media in the best environmental conditions so it lasts. In other cases, most notably when digitizing is used to copy information content, the commitment is to keep the digital product in such a way that ensures it is available, usable, and understandable in the future. To achieve this, digital objects must be actively managed, so they are copied on a regular basis to new storage media. (This brings into play another preservation principle: "Preservation requires active, managed care.") Attention has shifted well away from keeping the artifact as the sole focus of preservation activities.

As our experience with preserving digital objects increases, there is some evidence (albeit limited) that the life of digital storage media may not be as short as we have assumed. For example, the data on 91 percent of three hundred data carriers (magnetic tape, floppy disks, and diskettes) dating back to 1970 and stored in secure, controlled environment conditions, were 100 percent readable, with only 2 percent failing completely;[5] and, according to a posting to the Digital Curation blog in April 2009, a thirteen-year-old floppy disk, kept under poor storage conditions, was found to be readable using inexpensive hardware on a modern Windows PC. Benign neglect has always been an important preservation tool for analog materials and may yet be found to be applicable to digital objects. However, we must not ignore the other factors that make digital objects more prone to becoming unusable—obsolete file formats, hardware, and software that rapidly goes out of date, and lack of metadata and other contextual information. Until we have collected more evidence about the life span of digital storage media, we cannot base our preservation practices for digital objects on benign neglect. We must heed the preservation principle "Taking preservation action now is better than doing nothing."

## Reformatting Physical Objects

Reformatting is the process of copying at-risk objects to more durable objects. The most common reformatting processes are digitizing, microfilming, photocopying, and photography. Reformatting is typically applied when there is a need to save an artifact from further wear, perhaps because it is too fragile to allow further handling. (Extending and improving access to information, usually by digitizing, is also a reason for reformatting, but since it is not principally concerned with preservation it is not considered here.) Some artifacts merit both reformatting and conservation treatment because they have special value as physical objects, arising from such things as their aesthetic qualities, rarity, historical and bibliographical significance, and high monetary value.

It is usual to distinguish between master surrogate copies and copies for dissemination and use. For digitizing, the master digital file, uncompressed, could be kept in a preservation-focused digital repository, and use copies made at lower resolutions, say PDF. For microfilming, the silver halide master microfilm is kept in a low-temperature-controlled environment, whereas diazo or vesicular use copies are kept in the normal repository environment. Correct storage of master copies is a vital part of any reformatting program, as their continued protection allows copies for use to be made into the future.

Other reformatting considerations are intellectual property rights, the existence of other copies, and making others aware of what has been reformatted. For some materials there may be legal constraints on reformatting, so an awareness of legal provisions governing ownership of copyright and reproduction rights is essential. For some objects, typically published material held in library collections, a reformatted version—such as a reprint of a book, a microfilm version, or another copy of the book—may be available for purchase and is often a less expensive option than reformatting. Locating existing reformatted versions requires a mechanism for determining their existence and location, which, in turn, means that an institution engaged in a reformatting program should contribute details of the objects it reformats to an accessible, shared, federated database of some kind.

Reformatting is one component of an integrated preservation program, with equal status given to other components: environmental control, careful handling and storage, education and training, disaster preparedness planning, and a maintenance and repair program.

## Target Formats

The most common target formats (the formats that are the outcome of reformatting) are digital objects, microfilm, and photocopies, with photographs and facsimile reprints of books less common. The rapid development of 3-D copiers may mean that surrogate copies of museum objects can be reproduced.[6] Currently the most popular target format is digital objects (the output of digitizing), followed at a distance by microfilms and preservation photocopies. Much less commonly, preservation photography is used for original black-and-white photographic prints and facsimile publishing for works on paper. Questions to consider when selecting a target format include: How and where will the reformatted version be used, and by whom? Does the new format allow ready access? How heavily will the item be used? Technical questions to ask are: What is the format's life expectancy? What are optimum conditions for storage and access? Will further format conversion be needed, and how frequently? Cost factors—the costs of conversion and costs associated with storage, maintenance, and cataloging of the new format—also need to be considered. In practice, though, the selection of format is made on the basis of current popularity and of the significant advantages digital copies provide over other formats. The National Library of Australia's *Preservation Copying of Collection Materials Policy*[7] is an excellent overview of the factors to be considered when selecting target formats.

## Digital Objects

Digitizing physical artifacts is currently by far the most popular reformatting method. Examples abound: a 2012 survey of about two thousand European cultural heritage institutions noted that 83 percent of institutions have a digital collection or were currently involved in digitization activities, with photographs the most digitized objects;[8] and in the United States, the Stanford Media Preservation Laboratory in 2011, according to a posting to the Media Preservation blog in December 2012, "hit its digitization stride," digitizing 3,115 items, an 88 percent increase over the previous year. Reasons lie in large part in the improved access digital objects provide over other reformatting target formats, especially the ease of transmitting them through communication networks and searching their contents. But digitizing to improve access is not the same as digitizing for preservation, which must adhere to very high standards of production, storage, and management.

Physical objects that are digitized are usually paper based—books, manuscripts, and images on paper. Digitization is rarely applied to physical objects such as museum artifacts, although images of the objects are increasingly provided in the collections databases of museums (which does not constitute reformatting).

The equipment for digitization is readily available. High-quality scanners or cameras should be used, not low-end consumer equipment. Output files should adhere to the highest standards possible. Adequate metadata must be assigned to the files at the time they are created. (These requirements are noted in more detail in chapter 6.) Current guidelines for digitizing need to be located and their recommendations followed. There are many helpful case studies in the considerable literature about digitizing. Digitizing can be outsourced to vendors who specialize in preservation digitizing. If their services are used, it is incumbent on the commissioning institution to know the standards that need to be met and to ensure that the vendor meets those standards.

Digital files produced from digitizing must be scrupulously stored and managed. While short-term storage of digital files is well understood—geographically distributed multiple backups and checksums are a part of what is required—the challenges lie in long-term retention of digital files over time. (This is covered in more detail in the section "Reformatting Digital Objects" in this chapter, and in the section "Digital Files" in chapter 12.) Questions to be addressed include: Where will the high-quality digital files that result from digitizing be kept? How will they be kept? Many institutions now consider that digital copies can be preservation masters. One is the National Library of Australia, whose *Preservation Copying of Collection Materials Policy* notes its "informed commitment to producing digital copies that can be preserved, and [that it has] invested in preserving both their data integrity and means of accessing them. For this reason the Library accepts its digital copies as preservation copies."[9] Considering the medium in or on which the digital files are stored (such as CD, flash drive, or hard disk) as the object that needs long-term preservation is not adequate for long-term preservation, because of the inherent fragility of these media and other factors, in particular hardware obsolescence. The focus must be on the files themselves, regardless of the media on which they are currently stored. More detailed discussion of these issues, and guidelines for best practice, are noted in the section "Digital Files" in chapter 12.

## Microfilm

Microfilming, once the dominant reformatting procedure, has been almost completely superseded by digitizing. Many legacy collections of microform are being digitized. In many countries it is now difficult to locate companies that carry out microfilming. The "Microform" section in chapter 9 gives further information about microforms.

Microfilm and microfiche are the output formats of microfilming most commonly encountered in collections. Three types of film were used—silver-gelatin, diazo, and vesicular—but only silver-gelatin film, carefully processed to appropriate standards, should be used for the production of preservation-quality master negatives. To achieve maximum longevity, silver-gelatin master negatives must be carefully stored and handled to minimize damage from fungi, water, and mechanical abrasion. Use copies can be diazo or vesicular film, which are less expensive but have a shorter life. The filming process is straightforward, but processing is crucial to the longevity of the negative master. If residual chemicals are present, the film continues to develop after processing is completed, resulting in staining and fading of the image. Testing and inspection of the developed film is an essential part of producing preservation microfilms. There are many standards covering microform production and storage, and they should be followed to ensure the longest possible life for microform. If processed, stored, and handled to relevant standards, microform has an estimated lifetime of five hundred years.[10] Although the equipment needed to access them is relatively simple, microforms are considered difficult to use and are not popular with users and staff.

## Preservation Photocopies

Preservation photocopying is essentially the same process as normal photocopying, except that it uses alkaline paper of appropriate archival quality. The copies may be bound if required. No special skills are required for this copying process, but the photocopy machines must be well maintained. Preservation photocopying is especially useful for smaller and medium-sized libraries and archives that already own or have access to a photocopier. It is most appropriate for reformatting heavily used smaller items, but it is less suitable for works with high-quality black-and-white illustrations or colored illustrations (unless the photocopier handles color). The handling of the original during photocopying may damage fragile items.

## Other Formats

Preservation photography is typically used to reformat original black-and-white photographic prints by producing a master negative plus another negative (the interim master negative) for making prints from when needed. The master negatives must be kept in the best possible storage conditions (at a low temperature with appropriate relative humidity and light levels).

Facsimile reprints of books, manuscripts, or other works on paper are expensive to produce. This process is typically applied to reformatting manuscripts and works with extensive manuscript additions. Because of its expense, it is usually selected only when it is likely that the cost can be recouped from sales of the facsimile publication.

## Reformatting Digital Objects

Reformatting of digital objects, whether born digital or digitized versions of analog originals, is in essence the same as reformatting physical objects—the process of copying at-risk objects to more durable objects. Copying (also called migration) is currently the most common standard practice used for preserving digital objects.

Copying digital objects is a necessary preservation measure for many reasons. The key issue is that they are especially vulnerable to loss and destruction because storage media are fragile. The media deteriorate rapidly and may suddenly fail for a variety of reasons: poor manufacturing quality, how heavily they are used, how carefully they are handled, the temperature and humidity levels at which they are stored, and the quality of the equipment used to access them.[11] There are no exceptions—all digital information storage media are vulnerable. (Despite advertising that attempts to convince consumers to the contrary, "archival" gold CDs are vulnerable, too.) It is salutary to note the example of magnetic disks (for example, hard disks), which have an expected usable life of around five years.[12] However, the actual life span of the media is not the most important determinant for how long digital objects are accessible and usable. Life spans of the media are often longer than the length of time the media can be read because of hardware and software obsolescence.

In order for reformatted digital objects to be long lasting and preservation friendly, certain requirements need to be met. (Chapter 6 addresses these requirements in greater detail.) The target file formats should be carefully decided on, the chief requirement being that they stand a high chance of being understandable in the future. To achieve this they will normally be in widespread use, open rather than proprietary, be able to work on a wide range of operating systems, and be able to be processed with well-documented, preferably open source, software. Another important requirement is that sufficient metadata is generated and kept about the digital objects. The metadata needs to provide a detailed description of the files, details of their creation, representation information (information that allows users to understand their meaning), and an indication of their structure and content. Also recorded in metadata are actions applied to files, such as when reformatting was carried out, what software and hardware was used, and other relevant technical details. Metadata is essential for the effective preservation of digital objects. The ability of an institution to preserve them will be seriously compromised if sufficient metadata is not available.

Three sets of actions are typically applied when reformatting digital objects: refreshing, normalizing, and migration.[13] Refreshing refers to copying digital files from one medium onto another of the same type: for example, from a flash drive onto a new flash drive. There is no change to the bitstream, and checksums are applied to verify that the data have been copied accurately. Refreshing does not address obsolescence. Normalizing addresses the proliferation of file formats and the proprietary nature of many of them. Preferred file formats are identified, and digital objects that use other file formats are converted to these preferred formats. Normalizing is based on the assumption that preservation difficulties will be minimized if preservation-friendly file formats with characteristics such as openness, portability, functionality, longevity, and preservability are used. Widely implemented with normalizing is the practice of restricting the range of file formats accepted and managed by the digital archive. Digital objects are converted into these preferred formats.

Migration, in the context of digital preservation, has various definitions. Central to these definitions are that migration addresses technological obsolescence, doing so through procedures that are carefully designed, tested, and implemented and carried out regularly. During migration, digital files are converted from one hardware/software configuration to another, or from one generation of computer technology to a subsequent generation, with the aim of preserving the migrated digital objects' intellectual content as well as their ability to be retrieved, displayed, and used by those who need them. Migration is not the same as refreshing, which is more limited, addressing only obsolescence of the physical medium. Migration also addresses obsolescence of data formats, with the aim of keeping them usable and understandable. A common example of migration is version migration, converting files from one version of software to a later version, needed because software manufacturers do not always provide backward compatibility for all versions of their product.

Migration is a common preservation procedure for digital archives. It has a long history of use, so experience and expertise in its application is available. Software tools are available to assist with migration, such as the open source ImageMagick for image format migration. Successful migration requires written policies and guidelines, rigorous documentation of procedures, strictly applied quality-control procedures, keeping the original bitstream, and testing the migration process before it is fully implemented.[14]

Migration does, though, pose significant challenges. Because it requires careful documentation of processes and careful checking of their output for quality, it is labor intensive. The need for future migrations implies ongoing costs, and rights management may not allow the migration of some materials. The strongest argument against migration is that the process changes data because the digital encoding of the objects being migrated is usually changed to make them more suitable for preservation or processing; further, every time objects are migrated more changes are made to them. Despite these challenges, migration is the most commonly applied preservation procedure for digital archives.

## CONCLUSION

How we distinguish between preserving artifacts and preserving the information content in them is a fundamental question that we need to address before coherent, sensible preservation plans can be developed. Once the distinction is made and the preservation option (or options, if it is decided to preserve the artifact and information) selected, there are other considerations. For preserving artifacts, an understanding of materials used in the manufacture of artifacts is vital for determining what preservation actions to apply. Knowing how environmental conditions and handling affect objects allows us to develop storage and handling procedures that minimize deterioration. For preserving information content, there is a range of processes, each of which has its own set of considerations.

The next chapter builds on the introduction to environmental conditions in this chapter and examines in more detail the ideal storage environments for artifacts and why compromise is often required. It also notes what is required for secure, preservation-focused storage of digital objects.

# NOTES

1. ANSI NISO Standard Z39.48-1992, *Permanence of Paper for Publications and Documents in Libraries* (Bethesda, MD: NISO Press, 1993); ISO 9706:1994, *Information and Documentation—Paper for Documents—Requirements for Permanence* (Geneva: ISO, 1994).

2. Ian Batterham, *The Office Copying Revolution* (Canberra, ACT: National Archives of Australia, 2008), 117.

3. ANSI/NISO/LBI Z39.78-2000, *Library Binding* (Bethesda, MD: NISO Press, 2000).

4. Jan Merrill-Oldham and Paul Parisi, *Guide to the ANSI/NISO/LBI Library Binding Standard, ANSI/NISO/LBI Z39.78-2000* (Chicago: Preservation and Reformatting Section, Association for Library Collections and Technical Services, 2008).

5. David Pearson, "Preserve or Preserve Not, There Is No Try: Some Dilemmas Relating to Personal Digital Archiving," presentation at DigCCurr 2009: Digital Curation Practice, Promise and Prospects, April 1–3, 2009, Chapel Hill, NC, accessed September 17, 2013, http://www.ils.unc.edu/digccurr2009/6a-pearson.pdf.

6. Jimmy Stamp, "3D Printing During the Renaissance," March 20, 2013, accessed September 18, 2013, http://lifewithoutbuildings.net/2013/03/3d-printing-from-the-renaissance-to-today.html.

7. National Library of Australia, *Preservation Copying of Collection Materials Policy*, June 2007, accessed September 18, 2013, http://www.nla.gov.au/policy-and-planning/preservation-copying.

8. Natasha Stroeker and René Vogels, *Survey Report on Digitisation in European Cultural Heritage Institutions 2012* (London: ENUMERATE Thematic Network, 2012), 4, accessed September 18, 2013, http://www.enumerate.eu/fileadmin/ENUMERATE/documents/ENUMERATE-Digitisation-Survey-2012.pdf.

9. National Library of Australia, *Preservation Copying*.

10. ISO 18901:2010, *Imaging Materials—Processed Silver-Gelatin-Type Black-and-White Films—Specifications for Stability* (London; Geneva: BSI; ISO, 2010), Section 8.2 Accelerated Ageing Test.

11. Ross Harvey, *Preserving Digital Materials*, 2nd ed. (Berlin: De Gruyter Saur, 2012); chapter 3 expands on these reasons.

12. National Library of Australia, *Guidelines for the Preservation of Digital Heritage* (Paris: UNESCO Information Society Division, 2003), 113.

13. Harvey, *Preserving Digital Materials*, 2nd ed., chapter 8 provides more information about these actions.

14. Based on Digital Preservation Coalition, *Preservation Management of Digital Materials: The Handbook* (York: DPC, 2008), 112–13, and National Library of Australia, *Guidelines*, 135.

CHAPTER 5

# The Environment

·································································································

The importance of the role the environment plays in preservation cannot be overstated. As James Reilly indicates, "Preservation takes many forms, but none is as far-reaching or fundamental as the storage environment."[1] All except one of the expert contributions in Part IV of this book[2] emphasize that the single most important action in preservation is maintaining an appropriate environment in which to store the objects in a collection. We have known for decades that temperature and humidity are primary factors in the deterioration of cultural heritage collections of all types of media. Monitoring other environmental factors, in particular light, airborne, or gaseous pollutants, and particulate pollutants (such as dust) is also important. All of these factors are interrelated; too much light will generate additional heat, high humidity will cause changes to pollutants, and so on. Uncontrolled extremes of temperature and humidity can lead to obvious problems such as mold and insect infestations, but they are also at the heart of less obvious, but equally damaging, chemical changes that occur within all materials in collections.

Research undertaken in the past two decades has changed our understanding of the long-term impact of different environmental conditions on cultural heritage collections and has led to the development of sophisticated tools for predicting the impact of environmental conditions on natural aging processes. Reilly notes that our expectations for the longevity of library materials have been based on the survival of books and manuscripts over several centuries. The fact that these survivors are made of inherently durable materials, such as parchment, and were stored for much of their lives in cooler environments than they are now is often overlooked. Reilly found that:

> the low annual average temperature in unheated stone buildings of northern Europe, for example, together with effective means—albeit low-technology methods—to shield them from periods of high humidity, produced a much slower rate of chemical decay than any modern storeroom operated at pleasant and unwavering room temperature. The rare book room kept to tight tolerances at sixty-eight degrees

Fahrenheit, 50 percent RH causes the books to deteriorate three to four times faster than their former home in the unheated church or manor house. As a consequence, as much deterioration has occurred in the last fifty years of "good" storage as happened in the previous two centuries.[3]

Adding to this gloomy picture is the reality that maintaining climate-controlled storage facilities is a high-energy undertaking. In response to concerns about protecting the natural environment by minimizing the use of fossil fuels for energy generation, greener storage facilities for cultural heritage materials continue to be developed. We must find ways to combine our need to preserve our cultural heritage documents and objects with responsible use of the earth's resources.

This chapter identifies and explains the basic principles and common practices of achieving appropriate environmental control. It is underpinned by the preservation principles articulated in chapter 2. Four are especially applicable:

- Taking preservation action now is better than doing nothing.
- Preservation requires active, managed care.
- Understanding the structure of materials is the key to understanding what preservation actions to take, as materials contain the seeds of their own destruction (inherent vice).
- Prefer preservation actions that address large quantities of material over actions that focus on individual objects.

## COMMON PRACTICES

One of the significant commonalities in practice among all types of cultural heritage institutions is a focus on maintaining a stable environment for collections. (The principles "Preservation requires active, managed care" and "Prefer preservation actions that address large quantities of material over actions that focus on individual objects" come into play.) Twentieth-century researchers established guidelines for optimum temperature and relative humidity levels that gradually acquired prescriptive authority. These "ideal" levels of temperature and relative humidity are difficult to maintain in some climates and are often in conflict with the demands of human comfort. Rigid controls set to a standardized ideal are seldom achievable, extremely costly to maintain, and often at odds with the capacity of buildings housing collections. More advanced methods of monitoring environments (at both the micro and the macro levels) and the search for greener solutions have caused a significant shift in thinking. It is no longer deemed necessary or practical for a library, archive, or museum to maintain the same climate throughout galleries, public reading areas, stacks, offices, and storage facilities. The ability to monitor and control separate zones of a building makes it possible to use resources more efficiently and in ways appropriate in differing situations.

Practices in environmental monitoring and control across libraries, archives, museums, and galleries are based on the same research and standards. For example, there is general agreement (supported by existing standards) that temperatures of 65°F (18°C) or lower are best for most documents, and low relative humidity is better for overall chemical stability. A. D. Baynes-Cope expresses these commonalities in a commonsense statement about the fundamentals of safe storage, applicable to all artifacts in collections and not just to the books he refers to:

1. The buildings must be sound in all respects.
2. The rooms used as a store must be sound in all respects.
3. The room must be easy to keep clean and inspect thoroughly.
4. The free circulation of air is probably the most important single factor in the climatic condition of the safe storage of books.
5. Every effort should be made to ensure an even climate, changing as slowly as can be managed, throughout the room.
6. The room is better cold than warm.[4]

## Risk Management

Museums often divide the types of objects in their collections very broadly by their component characteristics into organic, inorganic, and composite. Libraries and archives are likely to have a preponderance of organic materials. In assessing the risks and determining compromises involved in environmental control of a collection, the focus is on the objects in that collection and their basic composition (as encapsulated in the preservation principle "Understanding the structure of materials is the key to understanding what preservation actions to take, as materials contain the seeds of their own destruction [inherent vice]"). Materials may be vulnerable to pollutants that come in from outside or that are generated inside the building. Storage furniture and enclosures have frequently been found to be culprits. Even the long-trusted Solander boxes, used in museums for decades, have been the source of damaging gaseous pollutants in specific instances.[5] In assessing the potential problems caused by pollutants, we must look at the collection; its storage furnishings and enclosures; the rooms in which the collection is stored, displayed, or processed; the building itself; and finally the external conditions in which the building is located. Chapter 3 provides more information about assessing buildings and collections.

Compared with objects made from organic materials, objects made from inorganic materials are relatively unreactive to the environmental conditions in which they are stored. Light, temperature, humidity levels, and animal and insect pests do not generally introduce risks to their preservation. Nevertheless, there are some risk factors that need to be assessed and accommodated when determining appropriate environmental conditions for the storage and display of objects made from inorganic materials. For example, metal objects suffer from deteriorative effects of air pollution, handling, and inappropriate cleaning; because of their fragility glass and ceramic objects can break if handled or stored inappropriately; and objects made of precious metals and stones may have high monetary value and thus are at high risk of theft.

## Agents of Deterioration

Collections are vulnerable to a wide range of potentially harmful agents and conditions. Polluted air may introduce gaseous, liquid, or solid contaminants. Radiation in the form of ultraviolet or excessive visible light causes harm, on its own and in combination with other threats. Inappropriate temperature and humidity levels are well-known enemies, and achieving appropriate levels is often challenging. Independently and in combination, the effects of these environmental factors will cause or accelerate the chemical and mechanical changes and the biological processes that threaten collections.

Some notoriously short-lived collection objects are self-destructive by the very nature of their chemical makeup, and they are extreme examples of "materials [that] contain the seeds of their own destruction (inherent vice)," as noted in one of the preservation principles underlying this chapter. These objects are made of such things as cellulose nitrate and cellulose ester film, wood-pulp paper, many 20th-century plastics, and magnetic media. If stored at room temperature they might survive in an undamaged state for a few years, but certainly not for as long as cultural heritage collections typically require. Many of these materials can be stabilized and their deterioration slowed with proper storage conditions, usually involving lower than usual temperature and relative humidity levels.

As objects and documents in our care are processed, handled, circulated, used in a controlled reading room, moved from stack area to work area, placed on display, and loaned to other institutions—in short, throughout their life cycle—they are subject to deterioration. The impact of poor handling can be minimized with protective enclosures. Placing a fragile scrapbook or photograph album in a box that is made with acid-free or alkaline-buffered, lignin-free barrier board, rather than leaving it standing on the shelf, will protect it from dust, light, and other potential problems. The box can be retrieved and transported without adding to the wear and tear on the album.

Minimizing the impact of the many and varied agents of deterioration is the principle goal of preventive preservation.

## Monitoring

If appropriate control of a collection's environment is to be achieved, accurate data about the conditions of that environment need to be collected. A wide range of data-monitoring equipment is available that makes gathering information about very specific areas straightforward, either continuously or in spot checks. As conditions are adjusted and compliance with accepted standards achieved, continuing data collection will provide evidence of good collection stewardship and inform planning for preservation management. For example, if monitoring shows one storage area to be drier and cooler than others, that area might be determined as particularly suitable to store certain types of objects that will benefit from these conditions.

Monitoring environmental conditions need not be expensive. Temperature can be measured using a wide range of devices, from simple thermometers to sophisticated data loggers that store the data collected. Air pollution can be monitored using the white glove test (putting on a white glove and running a finger along a spot to see how much dirt is present). The presence of water can be assessed by observation, or by devices such as water alert monitors. Observation will determine where sunlight falls on collections and where mold is growing or where insect pests or rodents have been. Some environmental factors, such as relative humidity, ultraviolet light, and air quality, are harder to measure, and expert advice or equipment may be required.

## The Ideal Environment

The long-term effects of exposure of objects in collections to heat, light, humidity, water, air pollution, and animals and insects can be severe. They are usually insidious and gradual and, by the time they are obvious, it is often too late to save the collections. The prescriptive levels for optimum temperature and relative humidity levels noted earlier in this chapter are difficult to achieve and, if they are achieved, expensive to maintain. Debate about the best conditions for collections storage continues, with expert opinions often differing considerably.

Consequently, the ideal environment is no longer expressed in terms of absolute temperature, relative humidity, light, and air quality levels. Instead, we aim at providing an environment that is achievable in relation to a building's structure, the local climate in which the building is located, and available resources. Awareness of ideal levels is helpful, but compromise is necessary when attempting to implement them, as a perfect environment is not achievable. Reaching compromise is where risk management comes into play, as it is essentially a process of balancing what is achievable and affordable against acceptable risks to the objects in a collection. In order to make decisions about risks, knowledge of what is in the collection and what they are made of is essential. With this knowledge (which can be gained for different types of objects from Part IV of this book), decisions can be made about which environmental factors are the most important to attempt to control for a specific collection.

As already noted, stable internal environmental conditions are acknowledged as necessary for keeping collections over time. Stable temperature and relative humidity levels are typically managed by the use of heating, ventilation, and air-conditioning (HVAC) systems, especially in affluent countries with temperate climates, such as the United States and Britain and Europe. Increasingly, though, there is concern about whether the "perfect" conditions that HVAC systems provide are in fact the best conditions. There is also concern about the environmental impact of running energy-hungry HVAC systems continuously. In response to this concern, buildings are being designed "to create conditions that require the least change from external environmental conditions and also a reasonable environment for collections. The results tend to be stable buildings, with minimal plant and equipment, which are less prone to disastrous changes if power supplies are lost for any reason."[6]

The aim of environmental control is, simply stated, to maintain storage areas that are kept cool and dry and work areas that are comfortable for humans. We know that nearly all cultural heritage materials will survive longer if the temperature they are stored in is kept low and stable, the relative humidity is kept fairly low, the air around them meets clean air standards, and the building in which they are housed is fireproof, weatherproof, and safe from natural disasters. James Reilly proposes the following rules of thumb for minimizing the impact of the various types of deterioration to which most collection materials are subject: chemical change, biological processes, and mechanical or physical change.

- For minimizing chemical decay:
  - make it as cool as you can without causing mechanical, or biological damage
  - keep summertime dew points as low as possible
- For minimizing biological decay:
  - minimize risk by avoiding high RH at moderate temperatures
  - keep excursions above 65% RH to a few days or less
  - keep summertime dew points low
- For minimizing mechanical damage:
  - keep excursions below 20% RH or above 70% RH as short and infrequent as possible
  - keep wintertime dew points from being too low and summertime dew points from being too high.[7]

Setting achievable targets is essential. Fixed formulas that accommodate little variance are, in reality, very difficult and expensive to achieve with any consistency. As Reilly's rules of thumb indicate, we need to be less dogmatic and more practical in our approach.

## BUILDING ENVELOPE AND STRUCTURE

Attaining achievable targets for environmental conditions can be significantly assisted by the design of the building in which collections are stored. Ensuring that the building is in good shape is the first step toward providing an appropriate environment for storage of collections, as indicated in more detail in chapter 3. Attainable targets for storage conditions must be set with the characteristics of the building and its location in mind—its local climate, human comfort, technology available for controlling the environment, limitations imposed by the existing building, construction materials, and cost.

## Impact of Local Climate

Most of the recommendations about environmental control are based on conditions in temperate climates, even though many collections are not located in such climates. For example, for temperature levels in reading rooms, recommendations from North America, Britain, and Europe are for temperatures in the range 65°F (18°C) to 70°F (21°C), but in tropical regions, where outside temperatures are usually higher, readers will consider 70°F (21°C) to be too cold.

Temperatures and relative humidities in tropical climates will almost certainly be higher than in temperate climates, with relative humidities in particular being very high indeed, especially during monsoons or wet seasons. Recommendations developed for temperature and relative humidity levels in temperate climates are difficult to achieve in tropical climates. The costs of purchasing, installing, and running HVAC systems is high, especially if electricity supply is intermittent. The *IFLA Principles for the Care and Handling of Library Materials* provides examples. In humid climates relative humidity seldom goes below 65 percent and is usually much higher than that. Achieving a level below 65 percent is unrealistic unless air-conditioning runs continuously. In arid climates relative humidity is usually below 45 percent and maintaining a level consistently between 40 to 45 percent is a realistic expectation, without the assistance of expensive systems. In both cases it is important to avoid fluctuations in relative humidity.[8]

In some regions light levels may be high, with high ultraviolet light levels that are very damaging. Limiting the exposure of objects to light is important, and building design is one way of achieving it; for example, by reducing the number and size of windows.

## Human Comfort

Appropriate temperature and relative humidity levels for storing objects may not be appropriate for human comfort. Buildings may need to maintain different levels in different zones. For a large institution the zones could be general storage areas, specialist storage areas for object types that need lower humidity and/or temperatures or cold storage, and work areas. For smaller institutions, only one zone may be feasible, requiring a practical compromise between the comfort of humans working in and visiting the institution and the storage requirements of collections.

## Design and Construction of Buildings

The characteristics of existing buildings are a significant determinant in how achievable appropriate storage is. Their orientation is one of these characteristics. Orientation of buildings so that there are few or no windows on the side of a building most frequently exposed to sun reduces the amount of light and heat that enters that building.

The materials that buildings are constructed from affect the targets that need to be set for optimal storage conditions. In many circumstances, careful selection of building materials can produce satisfactory internal environmental conditions and do away with the need for HVAC systems. Traditional building materials sourced locally may often provide for better storage conditions than those introduced from elsewhere. Local building designs developed to provide comfortable dwellings for local conditions are well worth considering when constructing storage facilities for cultural heritage materials.

Building traditions from subtropical, tropical, and arid regions provide examples. The thick limestone walls of Maltese buildings provide excellent storage for library materials,[9] and materials with high thermal mass such as these limestone walls are used in many parts of the world to slow down the rate of temperature fluctuation. Traditional Thai building styles concentrate on shade and airflow; the concept of spaces within spaces is used to protect palm-leaf manuscripts. In arid regions, building underground provides the same thermal buffering as building using materials with a high thermal mass does. Controlling airflow with a system of fans and louvers, as in the University of the South Pacific Library, Suva, Fiji, is often used in tropical areas.

## Cost

Already noted, but worth reiterating, is that HVAC systems are costly to purchase, install, commission, and run. In an era of diminishing fossil fuel supplies and growing awareness of climate change, in which we can no longer rely on the availability of cheap energy to run HVAC systems, efficient use of resources and the constructions of "green" buildings are increasingly emphasized. Cultural heritage institutions are not immune from the impact of this emphasis. For example, the British National Museum Directors' Conference (NMDC) issued its *Guiding Principles for Reducing Museums' Carbon Footprint* in 2009, in recognition that "seeking to achieve an internationally agreed narrow environmental standard for temperature and relative humidity has resulted in an unnecessarily high energy use."[10] The literature of sustainability in libraries, archives, and museums clearly demonstrates an increasing awareness of the need to reduce the environmental impact of buildings.[11]

## Renovating an Existing Building

The principles of achieving environmental control through building design can be applied when renovating an existing building to provide more suitable storage conditions for cultural heritage materials. Renovation might, for example, include installing ventilation in an attic space to reduce heat conduction through the roof, using window coverings to reduce light levels, or sealing an area within the building to provide for closer temperature and relative humidity control for specialist material.

The first and most important step when renovating is to seal the structure. This action reduces pest access, reduces heat loss or gain, reduces the amount of air and particulate pollution entering the building, and reduces the sources of moisture, thus achieving a significant reduction in relative humidity levels. Specific actions that can be considered are given in the *IFLA Principles for the Care and Handling of Library Materials*:

- Use draft excluders and weatherstripping to make the building weathertight.
- Ensure windows and doors fit securely.
- Ensure good air circulation by appropriate use of fans and windows.
- Use dehumidifiers and humidifiers to reduce or increase relative humidity.
- Use insulation methods to reduce heat gain or loss.
- Use UV-filters on windows and fluorescent lighting.
- Use screens, blinds, shutters (preferably outside the windows, as this reduces solar heat gain), and heavy curtains to keep out direct sunlight.
- Ensure storage facilities are dark.
- Paint the outside of the building with a pale-coloured light-reflecting paint in hot climates.
- Be aware that while trees and vegetation near buildings can reduce heat gain, they can also encourage insect and pest activity.
- Locate plumbing and heating pipes outside storage areas.
- Locate sanitary premises and sinks outside storage areas.[12]

Two further points made by the *IFLA Principles* are significant. The first is "Ensure buildings are properly maintained to keep out dampness during rainy periods." There are other reasons for being vigilant about building maintenance, of course, but the fact remains: regular maintenance of the building is essential. The second is "Use close-fitting enclosures (boxes and envelopes) wherever possible to protect important and valuable library material. These can create a microclimate around the object, which delays the effects of changes in temperature and relative humidity. They also shield the item from light, and can act as a buffer against atmospheric pollutants and prevent particulate deposits."[13] The point made here (and elsewhere in this book) is that the concept of spaces within spaces, whether boxes around objects or a room within a building, can be used to protect materials and provide them with acceptable climate conditions when providing acceptable conditions for the whole room or building is not possible.

## New Buildings

The extensive literature on designing new buildings and experts in their planning and construction must be consulted when a new building is being planned. There is often a tension between what is best for preservation and what an architect proposes, which may call for compromise and diplomacy. Building codes will probably prescribe standards for building materials and construction that address local conditions, such as specifications for minimizing damage in earthquakes. The points that follow cover only a few of the kinds of preservation considerations relevant in designing a new building.

Building design has a significant impact on the security of collections. Reducing the number of entrances and exits, including windows, service ducts, and sewers, in a building can minimize the possibility of theft. (See chapter 7, "Holdings Protection" for further information.) Choosing building materials, fittings, and furnishings that are not combustible can minimize fire risk. In libraries, ensuring that book returns are isolated from the rest of the library also reduces fire risk.

Risk of water damage can be minimized by ensuring that there are no drainage sumps in storage areas. Keeping the number of windows to a minimum can reduce the exposure of collections to the deteriorative effects of light. Pests can be excluded by ensuring that floors, walls, ceilings, and window frames are sealed and have no gaps in them. Air circulation can be improved by not placing shelving along walls, because pockets of stagnant air, in which insects and mold thrive, can form behind it.

A holistic approach to environmental control must be one of the key drivers when planning new buildings for cultural heritage institutions. It must go beyond planning for the installation of an HVAC system, which is increasingly secondary to incorporating control of interior climate by natural methods through the application of passive building design principles. Consideration of an integrated pest management program also has high priority in the design of new buildings.

## Integrated Pest Management

Integrated pest management (IPM) is an excellent example of a holistic approach to building design and management. Whereas in the past insect infestations would have been addressed by applying pesticides that were often also harmful to humans, the IPM approach takes a much wider view by finding out why pests are present and addressing the conditions that encourage them to thrive. IPM is based on the principle that prevention is better than treatment (keeping in play here two of the preservation principles underpinning this book: "Preservation requires active, managed care"; and "Prefer preservation actions that address large quantities of material over actions that focus on individual objects"). An IPM program has four pillars: knowledge of pests that occur in the region where the institution is based and of their life cycle; good housekeeping and cleanliness; controlling the environment within and outside the building; and control methods.[14]

By knowing what pests occur in the region where the institution is based and understanding their life cycle, we can determine the conditions in which they thrive and take steps to change these conditions and to provide traps or other means of killing them. It is, therefore, important to identify any pests that are found, which may require the services of an expert, such as an entomologist, or a specialist pest eradication company.

Good housekeeping and cleanliness are basic to an IPM program, as they are also to other preservation endeavors. Frequent and regular inspections of storage areas for evidence of damage by pests or evidence of infestation, such as body parts and frass (debris or excrement produced by insects), are required. Floors must be kept clear and clean; a vigilant cleaning program that covers grilles, corners, ledges, and furniture must be in place; trash and waste must be removed promptly; food and drink in the building must be either completely disallowed or only consumed in specified areas; and, above all, all these activities should be constantly monitored. The full cooperation of all staff in maintaining good hygiene (such as taking care when discarding food) and in spotting and reporting evidence of pests is vital to successful pest control.

The first step in controlling pests inside and outside a building is to prevent their entry and to minimize the attraction of the interior of the building to any pests that do get inside. Minimize pest intrusion into the building by not having plants near or inside the building as they may attract birds, animals, and insects;[15] ensuring outside trash cans are emptied expeditiously; good building maintenance practices, such as keeping gutters clear of debris; and ensuring that outside lighting is located so that it does not attract too many insects. Inside the building, the key to reducing pest damage is to control temperature and humidity levels to prevent them multiplying, as well as preventing their entry. Air movement also discourages pests. (Appropriate temperature and humidity levels are noted later in this chapter, and in the contributions about specific object types in Part IV.) Perimeter repellents and insecticides can deter pests, and sticky mats that can give early warning of insects can be used at points of ingress.

Control methods, especially chemical control methods, are the last resort in an IPM program; a "least chemical" approach must be taken. Many of the pesticides freely applied in the past are now unacceptable for health and safety reasons, and many are banned in most jurisdictions. Where control methods are needed, physical methods of control should first be applied, the most effective being control of temperature and relative humidity levels, as already noted, and the use of barriers and traps. Other physical control methods are creating a low oxygen environment and insect-desiccating irritant dusts and powders. Biological methods of control, such as the cautious introduction of natural predators, are also possible, but expert advice is needed. Repellents may be applied, such as naphthalene, camphor, or local plant materials known to repel specific insects. Because of their toxicity, chemical control methods are a last resort and should be applied only by licensed pest controllers.

## TRUSTED DIGITAL REPOSITORIES

Planning for storage of analog objects focuses on providing appropriate environmental conditions, as noted above. Appropriate storage of digital objects (digital files) takes on a different meaning. As explained elsewhere in this book (in particular the "Digital Files" section in chapter 12, Part IV), the provision of excellent conditions in which to store physical objects (the information storage media) cannot be the major emphasis of keeping digital files. To store digital files, a storage facility must meet other criteria. These criteria are articulated in the concept of the Trusted Digital Repository (TDR).

## Definition of a TDR

A Trusted Digital Repository is a repository "whose mission is to provide reliable, long-term access to managed digital resources to its designated community, now and in the future."[16] The influential 1996 Task Force on Archiving of Digital Information defined the concept of trusted digital repositories and noted that there should be a number of trusted organizations with the capacity to store, migrate, and provide access to digital materials. Trusted repositories, which should undergo a process of certification to ensure trust, are crucial for effective digital preservation.[17]

## Principles of TDRs

To be trusted, a digital repository needs to meet requirements specified in the *Trustworthy Repositories Audit & Certification: Criteria and Checklist* (TRAC) publication.[18] These include:

- the repository's compliance with the OAIS Reference Model
- a structure that supports the long-term viability of the repository as well as the digital information for which it has assumed responsibility
- demonstration of financial responsibility and sustainability
- systems that meet commonly accepted standards to ensure the ongoing management, access, and security of the digital materials accepted by the repository
- implementation of system evaluation methodologies
- clearly stated policies

The Open Archival Information System (OAIS) Reference Model[19] is a key standard in digital preservation. This model was initially developed by the space data community to provide a common framework for digital archives, but its value to other communities was soon realized and it was widely adopted, eventually becoming an ISO standard (ISO 14721:2012). The OAIS Reference Model is influential in many respects. It establishes a common language for discussion of digital preservation, so that all parties (cultural heritage professionals, computer specialists, funding agencies, for instance) can understand one another. It distinguishes between simple data storage and long-term preservation, important because how to store data is well understood but long-term preservation of digital objects is not. It articulates and describes in detail seven functions that a digital archival system needs to perform: ingest; archival storage; data management; administration; access; preservation planning; and common services. The concept of "information package" is fundamental to the OAIS Reference Model. The digital object being preserved is much more than just the content represented by the bitstream; we also need to preserve, with the bitstream, information that tells us what we did to preserve it, information about its attributes, information about how to render (or represent) the bitstream in the future so it can be understood, and more. Cultural heritage professionals who wish to specialize in digital preservation must understand the OAIS Reference Model.

## Auditing and Certification

The key word in any discussion of digital archives is *trust*. If we are to submit our digital files to a repository, perhaps one that we do not control, how do we know we can trust it to preserve our files? The 1996 Task Force on Archiving of Digital Information noted the importance of a process of certification to ensure trust. Certification requirements were defined in the 2007 TRAC document.[20] Tools to assist with auditing and certification are available, such as the online interactive tool DRAMBORA (Digital Repository Audit Method Based on Risk Assessment, www.repositoryaudit.eu). An important development is ISO 16363:2012, a standard for auditing and certification of trusted digital repositories, which supersedes TRAC. Not only is certification required so that creators, owners, and users of digital materials can trust digital repositories, auditing is also required to monitor their ongoing trustworthiness.

The first TDRs to meet certification requirements were certified in 2010. Meeting the requirements is arduous, and only a few have met them to date. Those that have are either partnerships, such as Portico (libraries and publishers), HathiTrust (academic and research libraries), and Scholars Portal (Ontario Council of University Libraries), or service providers (Chronopolis). It is likely that there will only ever be a small number of certified TDRs and that those institutions using them will participate in them on a contract or collaborative basis. It is also likely that the very largest institutions will manage their own collections of digital files and will not use a TDR.

# PRINCIPLES AND BEST PRACTICES

This section summarizes the effects of environmental factors on the deterioration and longevity of material in collections and notes principles and best practice in managing these factors. These are the general principles that apply to providing appropriate storage conditions for nearly all kinds of objects. (Relevant is the preservation principle "Preservation requires active, managed care.") For the appropriate storage conditions for specific object types, refer to Part IV.

Temperature and water are considered first because they (usually in combination) are the catalysts of deterioration. Light, a source of energy needed for many deteriorative processes, is considered next, followed by air quality. The section concludes with comment on fire damage and prevention.[21]

## Heat

Controlling the temperature in which objects are stored is essential to their longevity. Too much heat causes some materials to become desiccated and brittle, and it increases the rate of deterioration because the energy that heat provides speeds up the chemical reactions that cause damage. When the temperature and the relative humidity are too high, mold can grow. Fluctuations in temperature that are too rapid also have deleterious effects, placing physical stress on some object types. (The effects of temperature on specific object types are described in the contributions in Part IV.) As a general guideline for preserving materials in cultural heritage collections, the lower the storage temperature and the less fluctuation, the better.

There is general agreement about desirable temperature ranges for collection storage but no agreement about precise levels. In fact, attaining precise levels is difficult (noted above in the section "The Ideal Environment").

Active control by installing and running an HVAC system, which must be reliable and run continuously to be effective, is one of several approaches taken to control temperature. A temperature that is constantly above recommended levels in an environment with no HVAC system is preferable to widely fluctuating temperatures caused by an HVAC system that fails frequently or is only run during opening hours. By contrast, passive control applies actions such as building design, site location, creating microclimates around objects in the collection, increasing air circulation, and using insulation and window coverings to reduce heat gain. There may be scope to control temperature only in smaller areas of a building; for example, collections at greatest risk of deterioration can be placed in rooms or areas with the least temperature fluctuation (likely to be inner spaces) or with an HVAC system installed to control that area, and not the whole building.

Suitable means of monitoring and recording temperature levels and fluctuations must be applied so that problems can be identified and the effectiveness of solutions monitored. Equipment to monitor temperature ranges from the relatively simple, such as a thermometer, to the more sophisticated data logger and fully automatic electronic sensing equipment linked directly to the HVAC system.

## Water

Water causes deterioration of material in collections in both its gaseous state (water vapor) and its liquid state. Controlling the humidity (the amount of water vapor in the air) in which objects are stored is, like temperature, also essential to their longevity. Too much humidity causes information loss in some materials; for example, water-soluble inks run, paper coated with china clay or chalk blocks (pages stick together), emulsion lifts from photographs, and magnetic tape delaminates. Mold growth is the most serious threat for most materials when humidity levels are too high. When the relative humidity is too low, some materials become desiccated and brittle. Rapid fluctuations in humidity also have deleterious effects, so constant levels are essential in order to avoid damage such as that caused by physical stress when rapid changes occur. (The effects of relative humidity levels on specific object types are described in the contributions in Part IV.)

Temperature and relative humidity need to be discussed together because relative humidity is defined in terms of temperature and because it is often difficult to separate their deteriorative effects. It is "the amount of water vapor in a volume of air, expressed as a percentage of the maximum amount that the air could hold at the same temperature."[22]

The warmer the air, the more moisture it is able to hold; so, if the temperature rises but no extra moisture is added, the relative humidity decreases. Suddenly lowering the temperature in a room with fixed moisture content causes the relative humidity to rise and water to condense on the surfaces of objects. Water damage in the form of staining may occur, and hygroscopic organic materials (those that expand and contract as moisture levels rise and fall), such as paper and vellum, shrink or swell as relative humidity changes. These changes in internal stresses in the objects cause damage over time. The harmful action of acid hydrolysis on paper and other materials is both water and temperature dependent. (More examples are found in the sections on specific object types in Part IV.)

Optimum levels of relative humidity vary according to the material, and compromise is necessary. Relative humidity below 30 percent is unacceptable because materials dry out and become brittle; above 75 percent means that mold is more likely to grow. Maintaining relative humidity somewhere between 40 percent and 60 percent is practical and economical for most collections. Keeping levels constant is the ideal to minimize damage caused by the physical stress of shrinking and swelling, but it is difficult to maintain.

Running an HVAC system continuously may control relative humidity. Many institutions are limited by financial resources or by an unhelpful local climate, and they use other means to control relative humidity, such as ensuring suitable air circulation by using fans and windows, using dehumidifiers in badly affected areas of the storage facility, and ensuring that buildings are properly maintained.

Monitoring of relative humidity levels, as it is with temperature, is imperative. Monitoring equipment ranges from a simple sling psychrometer to the more sophisticated recording thermohygrograph (digital models have now mostly replaced mechanical models) and fully automatic electronic sensing equipment linked directly to an HVAC system.

As well as controlling humidity (water vapor), collections must be sheltered from water in its liquid form, which will damage almost all types of objects. To minimize the risk of water damage, constant vigilance is essential to spot leaks, storm damage, blocked drains, and similar issues. Storage areas should not be located in areas of a building prone to floods or leaks. Roofing, gutters, and plumbing must be regularly maintained. Objects should never be stored on the floor or directly under a roof, and boxing or wrapping of materials most at risk from water damage can be considered.

## Light

Extended exposure to excessive light has the potential to damage collection materials; very little exposure to light has positive benefits. Some kinds of light are more harmful than others; ultraviolet (UV) light is more damaging than visible light. Light is one form of the radiant energy needed for chemical reactions that cause deterioration, such as the breakdown of complex cellulose molecules to simpler molecules of embrittled paper. Exposure to direct sunlight, fluorescent light, and ultraviolet light causes damage to most materials in collections. The effects include severe loss of strength, change in color by bleaching or fading, change of the color balance by selective changes in one color, and yellowing of some lighter-colored materials.

Controlling light levels is in practice straightforward. The aim is to keep them as low as possible, preferably excluding light altogether. There are many simple ways to do this. Avoid direct sunlight by using curtains, blinds, or shades inside and awnings or shutters on outside windows, covering skylights, or adding UV-excluding film to windows. Time switches or motion sensors can be fitted in storage areas so that there is no light when no one is in that area. The number of lights can be reduced, or lights can be refitted with lower wattage bulbs. Light levels can be monitored with a UV meter, light meter, or Blue Wool Fade Cards (the Blue Wool Scale measures and calibrates the permanence of colors).

Objects being exhibited need special attention to minimize damage from light. The total light exposure over the period of exhibition is the measure and needs careful monitoring. The higher the lux (a measure of light level), the shorter the allowable time on display. The section "Photographic Materials and Negatives" in chapter 9, Part IV explains this in more detail.

## Air

Poor-quality air carrying gaseous and airborne solid pollutants causes materials in collections to deteriorate. By-products of burning fossil fuels (coal, petrol, oil), such as sulfur dioxide, nitrogen dioxide, and hydrogen sulfide, are common gaseous pollutants; another is ozone, produced by photocopiers and electrostatic filters in some air-conditioning units. The most common solid pollutants are dirt, dust, sand, and oily soot. The list of sources of pollutants is even longer: "human and animal metabolism, combustion, cooking, introduced materials and chemicals, and not least outgassing from the building's materials and contents, including items in the collection and their display and storage cases" are potential sources.[23]

Gaseous pollutants, such as the sulfur dioxide and nitrogen oxide from burning fossil fuels, combine with water in the air to form acidic gases that cause materials to degrade. Office copiers give off ozone, which is very aggressive and causes oxidization and embrittlement of paper and leather. Many of the materials frequently used in the construction and fitting out of museums, galleries, archives, and libraries produce gases that are potentially harmful; wood, wood products, and certain adhesives and sealants give off acetic acid; and formic acid is produced from some woods and when oil-based paint dries. Airborne solid pollutants may rub and scratch materials. Dust, commonly a mixture of many particles including fragments of skin, textile fibers, soot, soil, grease, and salts, is usually hygroscopic, attracting moisture that mold may thrive in; it may also be abrasive. Airborne salt causes damage to some materials, especially metals. Smoke from fires, cooking, and cigarettes not only darken and disfigure objects but also can leave oily deposits. If airborne particles containing acidic substances adhere to the surfaces of objects, the pH of the object (especially if it is made of paper) may be altered, resulting in deterioration, especially in moist conditions.

Controlling damage caused by pollutants is aimed at lowering the risk they pose to materials in collections by minimizing the amount of pollutants that enter a building or storage area and also by reducing pollutant-generating sources inside the building. In addition, an effective regular cleaning program is essential for the removal of accumulated pollutants. Other actions, such as sealing materials most at risk in enclosures, can also be used. Where an HVAC system is installed, filters that are typically part of the system control pollutants entering a building or storage area. When there is no HVAC system installed (and even when there is), windows and doors can be adjusted to seal tightly and filters placed over windows to minimize the entry of pollutants. Actions to reduce the generation of pollutants inside the building include restricting cooking and smoking in the building, keeping storage areas clear of the location of electrical plant and equipment, and paying particular attention to gases given off by a building's construction and furnishing materials.

## Mold

Mold growth is encouraged in conditions where temperature and relative humidity levels are high, the air is stagnant, and nutrients are available. Always present in the air, the spores of mold and other fungi grow whenever favorable conditions are reached. To generalize, they require temperatures above about 75°F (about 24°C), relative humidity of about 70 percent or higher, darkness, and poor air circulation; some may require nutrients found in leather, vegetable paste, cellulose, sizing, gelatin emulsions on photographs, or solid airborne pollutants. Mold has many deleterious effects on most types of collection objects, including weakening and staining of paper, obliteration of photographic images, and foxing (small brownish patches) on paper and card.

Avoiding the growth of mold and other fungi in the first place is by far the best approach. Temperature and relative humidity levels in storage areas need to be maintained at levels that discourage growth; dirt, dust, and other solid particles need to be removed; and good airflow is required. Controlling the relative humidity in particular is crucial: most mold and other fungi grow well when relative humidity rises above 80 percent. When mold or other fungi are detected, changing the environmental conditions that allowed the growth and, if necessary and safe, cleaning the affected area thoroughly, are essential first steps. Relative humidity levels can be controlled by using fans to keep air flowing, applying water-sealant paint in damp areas to floors and walls, removing ornamental fountains and other water sources, and removing plants to reduce the quantity of water released into the air. When an outbreak of mold or other fungal growth is detected, it may be necessary to use chemical treatment to kill the growth. Expert advice should be sought.

## Pests

The presence of pests (insects, rodents, and birds) in collection storage areas is usually the result of inappropriate environmental conditions. They flourish in conditions that are dusty, poorly ventilated, and poorly lit, and with high temperature and relative humidity. For many pests, dead organic matter (in paper, wood, and leather, for example) is a food source. It is important to identify each pest observed in order to determine the best approach to minimizing its effects or eradicating it. This can often be done by knowing what kind of materials particular pests prefer and the kinds of damage they do. Bird droppings, for example, cause staining; rats and mice chew up almost anything, with paper a favorite, and they also cause staining and corrosion through their droppings; silverfish graze on the surface of paper and thrive in damp conditions. Some pests, such as termites, rats, and mice, can totally destroy objects. The damage insects cause—holes eaten through books, images eaten off photographs, permanent acidic fly-spots—is irreversible.

While some of the insect pests encountered are specific to a locality, others are widespread. Some are almost omnivorous; others are more selective in their preferences. Commonly found are:

- cigarette beetles, drugstore beetles, spider beetles; preferring a wide variety of plant- and animal-based materials
- carpet beetle larvae; preferring mostly animal-based materials (wool, silk, fur, hair, feathers, insects, animals)
- common clothes moths, case-making clothes moths: preferring mostly animal-based materials (wool, silk, fur, hair, feathers, insects) and cellulosic textiles, particularly if soiled
- borers, timber beetles; preferring wood, books, papers
- termites; preferring wood, books, papers
- cockroaches; preferring almost anything and causing staining through their eating habits
- silverfish; preferring mostly cellulosic materials (paper, textiles, pastes, and sizes)

As with other causes of deterioration, insect pests are controlled by maintaining appropriate environmental conditions and by good housekeeping, especially cleaning. Insects prefer warm, dark, damp, poorly ventilated, and dirty conditions. Some, such as silverfish and booklice, need moist conditions to thrive. The presence of some insects is an indicator that conditions in the storage area are inappropriate: for example, silverfish indicate that relative humidity is too high, at least 75 percent. Fumigation and the use of insecticides, applied only after expert advice has been sought, may be needed to eradicate insect pests. Once eradicated, regular inspections are needed to make sure they do not reappear. Rodents and birds are controlled by eliminating points at which they can enter a building, by setting traps, and by good housekeeping.

## Fire

Preventing damage to collections from fires has an extensive literature and many experts, who should be consulted when installing or updating fire detection and suppression procedures and equipment. Building codes also set requirements that must be met.

Preventing fires from starting in the first place is by far the best approach. For a new building or during a renovation, select building materials and fittings that are not combustible. Install fire doors and ensure that ducting for electrical services does not pass through storage areas. Any equipment that might cause a fire needs to be regularly maintained. Flammable materials, such as nitrate film, should be removed to specialized storage. Chemicals and combustible materials should, if possible, be kept away from collection storage areas. Smoking in all parts of the building must be banned and the ban rigorously enforced.

Fire detection equipment needs to be selected from the wide variety available and matched to the needs of the storage area and the materials in it. Expert advice should be sought in determining appropriate equipment. Detection equipment ranges from basic smoke detectors to early-warning air-sampling systems linked to fire alarms.

Fire suppression devices use either water or gas; again, expert advice needs to be sought when selecting from the wide range available and when installing and testing them. Modern water-based sprinkler systems are more sophisticated and more effective than older systems. Halon and carbon dioxide gas extinguishing systems are now considered environmentally unacceptable, are expensive to install and maintain, and are rarely recommended.

The keys to fire prevention are building maintenance and regular checking of equipment. Potential sources of fire, such as electrical wiring, kitchen facilities, and chemical stores, need to be checked. Fire detection and suppression equipment must be regularly checked and maintained. The location of fire suppression equipment should be well marked, and all staff should be instructed in its use, regularly and frequently.

## CONCLUSION

The most significant points made in this chapter are summarized in the following guidelines for minimizing the damaging effects of harmful environmental factors:

- Avoid wide variations in and extremes of temperature and relative humidity. (The variation in temperature and relative humidity is every bit as significant as their actual values.)
- Keep temperature stable, with as little variation as possible. Ideal temperature goals may need adjusting to achieve ideal relative humidity goals.
- In humid environments aim at a relative humidity level between 50 percent and 60 percent; in dry climates, aim at a level between 30 percent and 40 percent. Stability is more important that the actual value chosen.

- Reduce or eliminate exposure to direct sunlight or prolonged exposure to strong artificial light. Keep lighting levels low and eliminate the UV component.
- Keep objects in a clean environment, free from dust, fumes, and smoke and free from animal and insect pests.
- Aim at a zero body count for insects and animals in the building.
- Ensure good air circulation to prevent mold growth. Check regularly for mold.
- Use building design, as well as building siting and location, to enhance environmental control.

The next chapter moves from the consideration of environmental conditions in which objects are stored to a focus on the objects. It introduces the concept of preservation-friendly objects and provides examples. It also gives an explanation of why the concept of preservation friendliness is essential to the preservation of objects and why it is incumbent on cultural heritage professionals to influence the way that objects are created.

## NOTES

1. James M. Reilly, "Measuring Environmental Quality in Preservation," *Journal of Library Administration* 38 (2003): 135.

2. The exception is "Digital Files," for reasons explained at the start of that contribution.

3. Reilly, "Measuring Environmental Quality," 138.

4. A. D. Baynes-Cope, *Caring for Books and Documents*, 2nd ed. (London: British Library, 1989), 40.

5. Andrea Wise, Caitlin Granowski, and Belinda Gourley, "Out of the Box: Measuring Microclimates in Australian-Made Solander Boxes," in *Art on Paper: Mounting and Housing*, ed. by Joanna Kosek, Judith Rayner, and Birthe Christensen (London: Archetype Publications, 2005), 55–58.

6. Jane Henderson, *Environment* (London: British Library Preservation Advisory Centre, 2013), 8, accessed October 7, 2013, http://www.bl.uk/blpac/pdf/environment.pdf.

7. James M. Reilly, "Specifying Storage Environments in Libraries and Archives," in *From Gray Areas to Green Areas: Developing Sustainable Practices in Preservation Environments, 2007, Symposium Proceedings*, ed. Melissa Tedone, 3–4 (Austin, TX: Kilgarlin Center for Preservation of the Cultural Record, 2008).

8. Edward P. Adcock, *IFLA Principles for the Care and Handling of Library Material* (International Federation of Library Associations and Institutions Core Programme on Preservation and Conservation, 1998), 25–26, accessed September 16, 2013, http://archive.ifla.org/VI/4/news/pchlm.pdf.

9. Helmut Bansa, "The Conservation of Library Collections in Tropical and Sub-Tropical Conditions," *IFLA Journal* 7 (1981): 264–67.

10. National Museum Directors' Council, "NMDC Guiding Principles for Reducing Museums' Carbon Footprint," 2009, 1, accessed October 7, 2013, http://www.nationalmuseums.org.uk/media/documents/what_we_do_documents/guiding_principles_reducing_carbon_footprint.pdf.

11. Rebecca Meyer, Shannon Struble, and Phyllis Catsikis, "Sustainability: A Literature Review," in *Preserving Our Heritage: Perspectives from Antiquity to the Digital Age*, ed. by Michèle Cloonan (Chicago: ALA Neal Schuman, 2014 forthcoming).

12. Adcock, *IFLA Principles*, 33.

13. Adcock, *IFLA Principles*, 33.

14. The extensive literature about IPM should be consulted before implementing an IPM program, especially control methods. A good starting point for archives is chapter 12 of Helen Forde and Jonathan Rhys-Lewis, *Preserving Archives*, 2nd ed. (London: Facet, 2013).

15. This action is one that may call for compromise, as the planting of shade is also considered beneficial in the temperature control of a building.

16. RLG/OCLC Working Group on Digital Archive Attributes, *Trusted Digital Repositories: Attributes and Responsibilities* (Mountain View, CA: Research Libraries Group, 2002). The section on TDRs is based on Ross Harvey, *Preserving Digital Materials*, 2nd ed. (Berlin: De Gruyter Saur, 2012), especially 97–98.

17. Task Force on Archiving of Digital Information, *Preserving Digital Information* (Washington, DC: Commission on Preservation and Access, 1996), 37.

18. RLG-NARA Task Force on Digital Repository Certification, *Trustworthy Repositories Audit & Certification: Criteria and Checklist* (Chicago: Center for Research Libraries, 2007), accessed October 7, 2013, http://www.crl.edu/sites/default/files/attachments/pages/trac_0.pdf.

19. Consultative Committee for Space Data Systems, *Reference Model for an Open Archival Information System (OAIS): Recommended Practice, CCSDS 650.0-M-2* (Washington, DC: CCSDS, 2012), accessed September 16, 2013, http://public.ccsds.org/publications/archive/650x0m2.pdf. This section on OAIS is based on Harvey, *Preserving Digital Materials*, especially 80–82.

20. RLG-NARA Task Force on Digital Repository Certification, *Trustworthy Repositories*.

21. The summary in this book can be supplemented by the many sources available. An excellent starting point among the many books on the topic is Ted Ling, *Solid, Safe, Secure: Building Archive Repositories in Australia* (Canberra, ACT: National Archives of Australia, 1998). Searching the Internet for material about passive building design of museums, libraries, or archives will bring up informative material.

22. Mary Lynn Ritzenthaler, *Preserving Archives & Manuscripts*, 2nd ed. (Chicago: Society of American Archivists, 2010), 97.

23. Nigel Blades, Tadj Oreszczyn, Bill Bordass, and May Cassar, *Guidelines on Pollution Control in Heritage Buildings* (London: Council for Museums, Archives and Libraries, 2000), 6. Accessed October 7, 2013. http://discovery.ucl.ac.uk/2443/1/2443.pdf.

# PART III

# MATERIALS AND OBJECTS

........................................

# CHAPTER 6

# Creating Preservation-Friendly Objects

·······················································································

This chapter introduces the concept of preservation-friendly objects and provides examples. Some definitions are in order:

- An *object* is the unit being preserved; for example, book, print, website.
- A *preservation-friendly object* is an object that has a better chance of being accessible and usable in the future because it has been created with its longevity in mind. The idea of the preservation-friendly object has a long history, as noted in this chapter, and it has assumed greater importance in recent decades because of the fragility of digital objects.
- *Metadata* is "structured information that describes, explains, locates, or otherwise makes it easier to retrieve, use, or manage an information resource,"[1] and it is essential for preservation-friendly objects.

Specifications have been developed for many kinds of preservation-friendly objects and materials, including paper. Cultural heritage professionals, in conjunction with publishers and authors, advocated strongly for the development and use of permanent paper to ensure that books were more preservation-friendly. It takes more than attention to specifications for longevity, however, to create an object that is preservation-friendly. Hand in hand with these specifications goes metadata. An object must have adequate and appropriate descriptive, administrative, and technical metadata associated with it so that it can be identified and have its authenticity established and verified. Curators working with performance art, installation art, and digital art are already energetically seeking new ways to document information about artists' intent and technical requirements, which is crucial for their preservation. Photographers are embedding metadata in their digital images to make them more retrievable and are actively promoting the use of photographic papers of archival quality for their prints, thereby demonstrating a commitment to extending the life of what they create.

While it is not always possible to meet the full specifications, any efforts made to ensure that objects are preservation-friendly are worthwhile. Curators will not always be in a position to influence the creators of objects that eventually enter their collections, but in circumstances in which they can have some influence, much can be accomplished. Although assigning essential metadata when objects are created may be a low priority for creators, cultural heritage professionals can help by demystifying the process and become partners with creators in collecting relevant metadata.

This chapter is based on the preservation principles articulated in chapter 2. It addresses, in particular, one principle: "Effort put into creating long-lived objects and material reduces the need for preservation attention in the future." Other principles relevant to this chapter are:

- Authenticity of the objects needs to be ensured in any preservation action.
- Preservation is the responsibility of all, from the creators of objects to the users of objects.
- Collaboration is necessary to ensure preservation.
- Advocacy is necessary to ensure preservation.
- Preservation actions should be documented.

This chapter notes the rationale underlying two key concepts: promoting the development of preservation-friendly objects, and the crucial role that metadata plays. It examines contexts in which creating preservation-friendly objects is most feasible, as well as the kinds of objects that can be designed to be preservation-friendly. The locus of responsibility for creating preservation-friendly objects is noted, and particular emphasis is given to the advocacy and education roles of cultural heritage professionals. The kinds of metadata that are needed to make objects preservation-friendly are examined in some detail, as is best practice in assigning them. Examples of preservation-friendly objects are given.

## RATIONALE

"Effort put into creating long-lived objects and material reduces the need to apply preservation attention to them in the future," states the preservation principle on which this chapter is based. Longevity, however, is not sufficient for preservation, although for preservation purposes it is a highly advantageous characteristic for an object or material to have. The term *preservation-friendly* expresses more accurately what we are aiming at. Gold CDs and DVDs are long-lived, with estimated life spans that exceed those of their standard counterparts several times over, but they are not preservation-friendly. The data stored on them are very unlikely because of the obsolescence of file formats, software, and hardware to be accessible and usable after the one hundred years that is often claimed.

Applying techniques that improve our ability to access and use in the future objects that end up in permanent collections is worth the effort because it reduces the preservation attention we need to pay to them. It is for this reason that a whole chapter of this book is devoted to preservation-friendly objects and material. A book printed on low-quality paper provides an example. The process by which acidic paper deteriorates is now well understood, thanks to research by William Barrow and others. We know that careful handling, storage in a controlled environment, and deacidification of acidic paper can slow down the rate of the book's deterioration, but that ultimately this is not enough. The paper the book is made of will eventually become brittle, possibly to the extent that it will be impossible to handle the book anymore because the paper is breaking into small pieces. In this case the only preservation options we have for this book are the expensive and time-consuming copying processes of digitizing or microfilming it—processes that would have been avoided if the book had been printed on longer-lasting paper.

Cultural heritage professionals play an essential role in advocating for the development and use of preservation-friendly objects and materials. One way to do this is to ensure that objects that are likely to end up in collections are created using materials that will last. Another way is to ensure that appropriate metadata is associated with the objects we preserve. Metadata allows us to record characteristics of the object: a description; its relationship to other objects; what has happened to it while in our care; and who treated it and when. Recording metadata assumes greater importance for the preservation of digital objects, where it is one of the key tools used to demonstrate authenticity.

Making a commitment to ensuring that objects are preservation-friendly has many positive consequences. Preservation-friendly objects have a longer life and deteriorate more slowly. They are more easily identified—an important point in a collection consisting of tens of thousands of similar objects. Maintaining a history of actions applied to objects helps verify their authenticity, especially for digital objects. Recording information about their manufacture and structure facilitates future preservation.

## CONTEXTS AND MATERIALS

The contexts most suited to emphasizing, planning, and creating preservation-friendly objects are those in which close contact with creators is possible. In some contexts creators may even be required to create objects according to preservation-friendly criteria—for example, by legislation—although persuasion is generally considered more effective than coercion. If as many creators of records as possible, whether they be on paper or in digital forms such as digital photographs and word-processed documents, are encouraged to create records that are preservation-friendly objects, their incorporation into collections of cultural heritage professionals is much more straightforward. An underlying principle demonstrated here is "Collaboration is necessary to ensure preservation"—in this case, collaboration among creators of objects (who may be members of the public), developers of standards, and cultural heritage professionals.

In ensuring that objects are preservation-friendly, the materials from which they are made need to be considered. A book, for example, is constructed from paper, ink, adhesive, and/or thread, and its binding, which may consist of many materials, among them cloth, paper, adhesives. The preservation-friendly characteristics of each component should be specified, in addition to the characteristics of the composite object. Standards have been developed for paper, bindings, adhesives, and other materials used in book manufacture. They are noted elsewhere in the book, especially in the "Paper" and "Books" sections in chapter 8, Part IV.

While creating preservation-friendly objects is a worthy goal for cultural heritage professionals, it is not possible in every context. It may even be undesirable in some contexts, such as those involving creative artistic expression, where insistence on specific requirements could stifle innovation. Not all objects are suitable or amenable to intervention at the creation stage. Examples are experimental or artistic works, which are often made of found objects or other materials not normally associated with recorded information. The objects most amenable to intervention at the creation stage, and with which we have experience when it comes to creating preservation-friendly objects, are paper-based objects, digital objects (both born digital and digitized versions of analog objects), photographs (both digital and prints), and, slowly but increasingly, digital art.

## RESPONSIBILITIES

Three of the principles on which this book is based are especially germane to the question of who should be responsible for preservation: "Preservation is the responsibility of all, from the creators of objects to the users of objects"; "Collaboration is necessary to ensure preservation"; and "Advocacy is necessary to ensure preservation." How do these translate into practice?

The answer to the question of who is responsible is simply stated: everyone associated with the object. Responsibility no longer lies primarily or solely with cultural heritage professionals, who typically assumed responsibility when objects entered a collection. For digital objects in particular, any effort put into creating them as preservation-friendly is well worthwhile, which places responsibility for preservation clearly with the creator. Although an object (digital or analog) may have been used before it enters an institutional collection, careful storage and handling helps keep it in good condition, and a clear record of its use and of changes made to it helps demonstrate its authenticity, should the need arise. Assigning additional metadata to an object when it is added to the collection may also assist to demonstrate authenticity.

With so many potential participants in preservation, collaboration becomes necessary to ensure objects are successfully preserved. Institutions often decide to collaborate in order to maximize the number of objects that can be preserved and to minimize the costs of preservation.[2] This is evident in many digital preservation collaborations, of which LOCKSS (www.lockss.org) and HathiTrust (www.hathitrust.org) are just two examples. Joint storage facilities for physical objects also demonstrate collaboration; an example is the Harvard Depository (hul.harvard.edu/hd), which offers high-quality storage on a contract basis to libraries within the Harvard system. Similar joint storage facilities operate on a citywide or regional basis. The need for collaboration is increasingly recognized and implemented in digital preservation, in large part as a response to the costs involved, and it is articulated in this book as the principle "Collaboration is necessary to ensure preservation."

Energetic advocacy efforts are needed to ensure positive preservation outcomes (encapsulated in the principle "Advocacy is necessary to ensure preservation"). Too few creators of objects understand the link between materials and longevity. Many who do understand it fail to put it into practice, often because it costs more or is time-consuming. This is especially the case with digital objects, which, if they have insufficient metadata, may be impossible to understand and use. Howard Besser and students from New York University's Moving Image Archive Program investigated the issues arising from archiving the records of the Occupy Wall Street Movement, a protest movement in New York's financial district in late 2011. Besser notes characteristics of the material produced, much of which was directly uploaded from iPhones to YouTube, Flickr, and other social networks: large quantities of material were produced; it lacks consistent quality, file formats, and metadata; metadata is stripped out during uploading processes; and many participants in the Occupy movement were suspicious of organizations such as libraries and universities. Guidelines in development for archiving the material include best practice for content creators and the use of Creative Commons licenses. "Tips on Outreach to Communities" include the need to build trust and to focus on content, metadata, and rights.[3]

Advocacy efforts are needed in at least three key areas. The first is to increase all stakeholders' understanding of the vulnerability of materials. The second is to promote widespread knowledge of preservation-friendly formats, material, and objects, once again to all stakeholders. The third is to promote understanding of appropriate storage and handling procedures for material in personal collections. Although there are many preservation advocacy activities already and many more proposed, the audiences they reach need to be expanded significantly.

Hand in hand with advocacy goes education. Forums for educating stakeholders about preservation range from university-based education programs offering formal credentials to informal events that seek to promote preservation knowledge and skills. Preservation education and training is available in a wide range of short courses, increasingly offered online. They sometimes lead to a qualification, but usually do not, and are offered by professional associations (for example, the American Association for State and Local History, www.aaslh.org), educational institutions, such as colleges and universities, and local interest groups. The education of users of cultural heritage institutions presents an opportunity for promoting awareness of preservation, especially the education of users of libraries and archives. For example, Digital Preservation in a Box (dpoutreach.net/) was developed by the National Digital Stewardship Alliance, as stated on its website, "to support outreach activities that introduce the basic concepts of preserving digital information." Museums often provide educational programs for their visitors that explain a specific conservation effort, make their conservation laboratories visible to the public, and offer educational material about conservation. The Smithsonian American Art Museum's Lunder Conservation Center (americanart.si.edu/lunder/index.cfm) is an example of such public outreach. A further source of preservation training is on-site and in-house training for those working in cultural heritage institutions.

Programs to educate and train information professionals typically include some coverage of preservation, although it is not always a requirement for students to graduate. Library and information science programs are likely to offer a range of preservation courses, most commonly covering preservation administration but often with more advanced offerings. They increasingly offer courses in digital preservation or with a significant digital preservation component, acknowledging the urgent need for this expertise. Archives programs typically require students to take a preservation course, reflecting the prominent role of preservation principles in archival practice. Museum studies programs usually have a preservation component, in a course often named Collections Care. Advocacy topics may be addressed in these courses, although not necessarily labeled as such. Topics may include influencing stakeholders, user education, and making a case for more resources. Conservation programs can include similar topics; for example, the program in art conservation at Buffalo State, part of the State University of New York (SUNY) system, notes "assisting the public to better understand conservation principles" in its website summary of a course on professionalism in conservation (artconservation.buffalostate.edu/courses).

Informal forums, in many formats, advocate for preservation. Websites provide helpful information. In the United States, the Library of Congress offers advice for preserving personal digital materials through its "Personal Archiving: Preserving Your Digital Memories" website (www.digitalpreservation.gov/personalarchiving) and runs an annual Personal Digital Archiving Day. The American Library Association (ALA) promotes an annual Preservation Week and provides resources for libraries and other cultural heritage institutions to develop local activities. The ALA began Preservation Week in 2010 in acknowledgment of the extent of the preservation problem in collections, noting on its website (www.ala.org/alcts/confevents/preswk) that "some 630 million items in collecting institutions require immediate attention and care. Eighty percent of these institutions have no paid staff assigned responsibility for collections care; 22 percent have no collections care personnel at all. . . . These resources are in jeopardy should a disaster strike. Personal, family, and community collections are equally at risk."

Advocacy efforts to raise awareness among all stakeholders are essential. For digital preservation needs, one target group comprises those responsible for public policy and deciding what resources should be directed toward preservation. Driving this advocacy focus are the massive costs associated with effective digital preservation. The Blue

Ribbon Task Force on Sustainable Digital Preservation and Access is an example of this advocacy. Its activities began in 2007 and culminated in the 2010 report *Sustainable Economics for a Digital Planet*, which includes an agenda for action aimed at decision makers.[4]

The example of digital art—artistic works in which the creative and/or presentation process requires the use of digital technology—is instructive. Digital art demands fresh ways of thinking about preservation; a major aspect of current approaches is collaboration with creators. Traditional preservation practice envisages preservation as ensuring that the physical object survives, which for museums means stabilizing works of art and providing secure and environmentally appropriate storage. Works of digital art are often not intended by their creators to survive, and the media on which they are stored or by which they presented are expected to become obsolete. The focus is not, therefore, on preserving the original creation. Instead, institutions work closely with artists to create plans of action as early as possible in the life of digital artworks. When the inevitable happens, the institution can replace, repair, or upgrade components of the work while still maintaining the artist's original intent. Richard Rinehart, former director of Digital Media for the Berkeley Art Museum and Pacific Film Archive, is often quoted on this issue: "With digital art, there's no room for things to fall between the cracks. . . . If you don't do something to preserve it within a span of five years, it's not going to survive."[5] As curators of digital art acknowledge, some innovative thinking about preservation, particularly in terms of what it means to preserve, has resulted. The artist's intent comes to the fore, and keeping the physical object, storage media, and presentation technology are deemphasized.

Prioritizing the intent of artists in preservation calls for strong advocacy. The input of artists is crucial, so strong relationships between artist and curator must be cultivated to ensure that the challenge of getting artists to take action based on their artistic intentions is met. Artists need to be proactive, to understand and envisage what is likely to happen to their artworks as a result of digital obsolescence, and then to establish plans to address the issues. The Variable Media Initiative exemplifies this approach:

> For creators working in ephemeral formats who want posterity to experience their work more directly than through second-hand documentation or anecdote, the variable media paradigm encourages creators to define their work independently from medium so that the work can be translated once its current medium is obsolete. This requires creators to envision acceptable forms their work might take in new mediums, and to pass on guidelines for recasting work in a new form once the original has expired.[6]

Documentation is essential in this approach in order to record intent and alternative forms of presentation that accord with a creator's intent. The emphasis has shifted from keeping artifacts to proactive thinking about preservation at the time of the planning and creation of digital objects.

# INTELLECTUAL ACCESS AND CONTROL

Metadata is an essential component of what constitutes a preservation-friendly object, noted several times in this chapter already. This section examines the kinds of metadata that need to be assigned to objects to make them preservation-friendly and briefly notes best practice in assigning them. Three of this book's principles are most relevant to this section: "Preservation actions must take into account the needs of the user"; "Authenticity of the objects needs to be ensured in any preservation action"; and "Preservation actions should be documented."

Metadata needs to be sufficient and appropriate. What kinds of metadata should it be? How much metadata do we need? What does metadata allow us to do? It is crucial for the preservation of an object that adequate and appropriate metadata serving four purposes is associated with that object: to describe the object; to indicate its relationships with other objects; to record the history of the object; and to explain how the object is managed and used. Not all objects require the full range of metadata for their preservation, so it is important to understand what kinds are available, the uses we make of them, and their role in preservation, particularly with respect to digital objects.

This section gives an overview of why metadata are needed. It does not intend to be a guide to applying metadata, of which many are readily available.[7]

## Kinds of Metadata

### DESCRIBING OBJECTS

Metadata that allows us to identify and locate objects is called, not surprisingly, *descriptive metadata*. It allows the persistent identification of an object. The important word here is *persistent*: the description of the object and its location is known at all times. This is especially important when managing digital objects, which will probably be moved from one server to another several times during their lifetime, so we need to know precisely where to find them. Descriptive metadata also allows the unique identification of an object so it cannot be confused with similar objects. Descriptive metadata, then, needs to describe an object clearly and unambiguously.

Typical descriptive metadata elements are:

- unique identifiers: for example, web addresses derived from the PURL (Persistent Uniform Resource Locator) service (purl.oclc.org)
- physical attributes: for example, media, dimensions, condition
- bibliographic attributes: for example, title, author/creator, language, keywords[8]

### INDICATING RELATIONSHIPS AMONG OBJECTS

*Structural metadata* indicates how an object is related to other objects, allowing users of the object to understand the context in which it was created and managed. Structural metadata can be outward-facing—for example, indicating the larger group of objects to which a specific object belongs and describing its relationship with the larger group; or it can be more inward-looking—for example, describing how the parts of a complex object made up of several simple objects are related to each other.

Typical structural metadata elements are:

- information about the internal structure of resources: for example, page, section, chapter numbering, indexes, table of contents
- information about relationships among materials: for example, photograph A was included in manuscript B
- information that fixes relationships of files: for example, File F is the JPEG format of archival image File G

## RECORDING THE HISTORY OF OBJECTS

Because preservation is an activity that takes place over time, it is vital to record accurately the history of preservation and other actions applied to objects. *Administrative metadata* records the history of an object: for example, when and how it was created, preservation actions applied to it, who applied these actions and when, and who has accessed it. Administrative metadata is especially important for establishing and verifying the authenticity of objects. This authenticity role assumes greater importance with digital objects; a detailed record in metadata of actions that have been applied to them is crucial to understanding the inevitable changes that are made as a result of those actions. For example, recording details of the migration of a digital object—the applications used, dates, input and output formats, and so on—is a vital part of establishing whether a digital object is what it claims to be.

Typical administrative metadata elements are:

- technical data about creation and quality control: for example, scanner type and model, resolution, bit depth, color space, file format, compression, light source
- rights management, access control and use requirements: for example, owner, copyright date, copying and distribution limitations, license information
- preservation action information: for example, refreshing cycles, details of migration processes

## MANAGING AND USING OBJECTS

Typologies of metadata typically agree on three principal types: descriptive, structural, and administrative, but the agreement ends there. *Preservation metadata* is sometimes considered as a specific kind of administrative metadata, but its exact classification is not important. What does matter is that there is sufficient metadata providing the information we need to manage the preservation of an object. This metadata might, for example, provide the technical information needed to use a digital object, identify who is responsible for the management and preservation of an object, or describe the legal rights applying to an object, which may determine what can be done to that object.

## REPRESENTATION INFORMATION

We also need to acknowledge a relatively new player in the metadata arena: *representation information*.[9] Representation information is the information needed to understand and render (display, play, or use as originally intended) a bitstream, and thereby make the digital object represented by that bitstream meaningful to users. Without representation information, the bitstream is meaningless. Representation information comes from the OAIS Reference Model, a key standard in digital preservation.[10] What constitutes representation information is only loosely defined: it is any information that helps us ensure the bitstream is accessible and understandable over time. It can be as simple as file format information, or more complex, such as information about operating system and hardware dependencies, character encoding, and algorithms. A statistical database in digital form illustrates why representation information is needed; unless we know the meaning of the variables, the database is unusable.

## Other Metadata Considerations

How much metadata is sufficient? There is no single answer to this question, as many variables come into play, such as the kinds of objects, the preservation actions applied, and the requirements of future users. A book in a lending collection, where preservation actions are limited to running repairs and basic preventative actions so that the book can be issued as many times as possible, requires only descriptive metadata: what the object is, and where it can be found. A manuscript in a library's special collections may, in addition to descriptive metadata, need administrative metadata indicating restrictions on its use.

An analog object that has received conservation treatment needs more metadata than just descriptive metadata. It needs administrative metadata, such as conservation documentation records that describe the object, especially its physical condition, and give information revealed by the object, such as the material it was made from. Conservation documentation typically includes some or all of the following information: the existing condition of an object; condition of an object after treatment; material composition and technology; conservation methods used; materials used during treatment; and administrative details (for example, the date of conservation treatment, name of the conservator, accession number and other identifying numbers, relevant dates such as when an object entered the laboratory, deadlines, and date of completion of conservation work). Other metadata might also be collected, such as information about insurance on an object and visual documentation in the form of photographs and sketches.[11]

Metadata is especially relevant to ensure adequate description and control of digital objects over the long term. The types of metadata required for digital objects are: descriptive metadata, to describe them and refer to their location; technical metadata, to provide technical information needed to use digital objects; preservation metadata, to record and describe what happened to digital objects as they move through their life cycle; and representation information, to understand and to render (display, play, or use as originally intended) digital objects. To put it another way, metadata for digital objects is needed to:

- persistently identify a digital object
- maintain reliable links to that object
- describe clearly what an object is
- identify precisely the technical characteristics of a digital object
- identify who is responsible for the management and preservation of a digital object
- describe what can be done to a digital object
- describe what is needed to represent a digital object to the standard required by its users
- record the history of a digital object
- document a digital object's authenticity
- allow users to understand the context of a digital object and its relationship to other objects

Best practice in applying metadata is governed by a bewildering proliferation of standards. Listings of metadata standards for digital preservation are available on the Web. The DCC's list of digital curation standards includes metadata standards,[12] and the Library of Congress lists standards for which it takes responsibility.[13] Two key standards for applying metadata in the context of digital preservation are METS (Metadata Encoding & Transmission Standard; www.loc.gov/mets)—a structure for encoding descriptive, administrative, and structural metadata—and PREMIS (Preservation Metadata; www.loc.gov/standards/premis)—a data dictionary and supporting XML schemas for core preservation metadata needed to support the long-term preservation of digital materials.

## CREATING PRESERVATION-FRIENDLY OBJECTS: EXAMPLES

The creation of preservation-friendly objects, so that preservation attention needed by objects is minimized in the future, has a long history. Some examples follow.

## Medieval Scribes' Choices of Material

Standard practice for medieval scribes, when creating manuscripts, was to select materials on the basis of their longevity. As paper became more readily available in the West, the choice of paper rather than the traditional parchment was debated. Use of paper was forbidden for documents with legal authority. Clemens and Graham note edicts of Frederick II in the kingdom of Sicily in 1231 and an ordinance of Alfonso X of Castille in 1265.[14] Even when paper became more readily available, parchment continued to be widely used and was preferred for more prestigious manuscripts. The preference for parchment transferred to early printed books, for those who could afford the more expensive material. In the polemic *De Laude Scriptorum* (In Praise of Scribes), written in 1492, Johannes Trithemius commented on the success of printing, which was primarily on paper. He compared paper and parchment: "If writing is put on parchment it may last for a thousand years, but how long is it going to last if it is printed on such a thing as paper."[15]

## Charles Darwin's Notebooks

In 2009, the bicentenary of the birth of naturalist Charles Darwin, there was much published about him, including about his working practices. Darwin made conscious decisions about the materials he used in order to ensure the longevity of his field notes. He used notebooks identified as "Type 5." On their inside covers are the words "So prepared as effectually to secure the writing from erasure;—with a METALLIC PENCIL, the point of which is not liable to break. The point of the pencil should be kept smoothly scraped flat & in writing it should be held in the manner of a common Pen." The authors of an analysis of Darwin's notebooks observe:

> The pages of the notebook were treated or coated to react with the metallic pencils, now lost. The paper remains bright white and has a silky or velvety feel. . . . Although the writing in these books looks at first like graphite pencil it is in fact a reaction between the metal of the pencil point and the chemicals with which the paper was treated. This was meant to render the writing indelible.[16]

Darwin also applied the principles "Preservation requires active, managed care" and "Keep multiple copies of objects," as demonstrated in his working practice on the exploratory voyage of the HMS *Beagle*:

> It may be wondered why Darwin did not use one notebook until it was full, rather than keep switching between notebooks. We believe that the main reason he kept switching was that for document security he would only take one notebook onshore, so once he was back on board after an excursion he would start to use the notebook just used as the basis for his various diaries and specimen lists. . . . Since this process might take weeks, and therefore was often not completed before his next excursion,

he preferred to take a notebook with him ashore which [he] had already finished with, rather than risk losing field notes which had not yet been copied out.[17]

Possibly Darwin was no different from his contemporaries in taking such care to ensure the security and longevity of his field notes. He was significantly concerned with how long they would last, taking great care to ensure that they were created in a preservation-friendly way, making multiple copies to ensure their security and storing them securely.

## Library Editions

From the early 19th century it was recognized that books produced by newly introduced mechanical means were deteriorating much faster than their handcrafted antecedents. Paper quality was the initial focus of concern and, by the early 20th century, it had extended to include bindings. Among suggestions to address the issue was the manufacture of preservation-ready books: "There was some thought that publishers should bring out a few copies of every title 'supposed to have permanent value' on linen or cotton paper to purchase by libraries" or just for "the important public libraries."[18] Although preservation-ready books were not manufactured, specifications for book cloths and publishers' edition bindings were developed. The American Library Association's Committee on Bookbinding (1905) was one demonstration of librarians' keen interest in extending the useful life of books and periodicals. From 1904 the firm of Cedric Chivers introduced machine-produced oversewn bindings, widely adopted by libraries for rebinding books. The Library Binding Institute (www.lbibinders.org), established in 1935, has produced eight editions of its standard for library binding, the most recent of which is ANSI/NISO/LBI Library Binding standard Z39.78-2000 (R2010).

## Microfilm

The production of microfilms is, like permanent paper, another process in which a focus on the development of standards has resulted in material that is exceptionally long lived. Although there are three main types of microfilm (silver-gelatin, diazo, and vesicular), standards for long-lived archival microfilm masters specify only silver-gelatin film carefully processed to the appropriate standards. Standards for postmanufacture storage, handling, and checking of microfilms have also been developed. Producing microfilm to such a high level of preservation readiness requires careful attention and strict adherence to standards at every stage. It can be expensive, and it is difficult to maintain consistency.

In preparing materials for microfilming, close attention to collation is required, as the items to be microfilmed should ideally be complete and metadata needs to be prepared. As filming proceeds, care must be taken to produce a high-quality result. Processing the film is of utmost importance in determining the archival life of microfilm. Tests to determine whether levels of residual chemicals are acceptable must be applied.

Inspection of the developed film is also essential to test for chemical stability, to check for physical damage of the film, to make sure density readings are acceptable, and to make sure that no pages have been missed.[19]

Standards applicable to all aspects of microfilm production and storage cover four areas: vocabulary, quality, compatibility, and specific applications. Vocabulary standards specify standard symbols, terms, and orientation of images on the film. Quality standards cover methods of processing and storage. Compatibility standards ensure that all microforms are manufactured to the same sizes, using reels of the same dimensions. Standards about specific applications describe what should be done when newspapers, press cuttings, technical drawings, and other similar kinds of materials are filmed. The standards have been issued by standards organizations in many countries and by the ISO (International Standards Organization). A list of standards is given in *Preservation Microfilming* (1996).[20] Standards are constantly revised and updated, so the latest version should be identified in planning for preservation microfilming.

## Permanent Paper

Paper quality is not the only measure of how long paper-based objects will last, storage and handling also being influential factors, but it is a major determinant in their longevity.

Calls for improvements in the quality of paper, especially paper used in book manufacture, have been made for well over a century, and they were made on a concerted basis from the 1980s. The American Library Association passed a resolution in 1980 calling for improvements in the quality of book production, noting the need for "volumes free from self-destructive substances for all texts of lasting usefulness" and for "permanent/durable paper." A "Resolution on Use of Permanent Paper in Books and Other Publications" was passed in 1988,[21] and another in 1990.[22] At its 1989 conference, the International Federation of Library Associations and Institutions (IFLA) approved resolutions urging the use of permanent paper by governments and publishers, the rapid completion of an international standard for permanent paper, and that IFLA itself use permanent paper for all its publications and documentation.[23] Authors and publishers joined forces with librarians to promote the use of permanent paper, government printers undertook to use permanent paper, and professional societies adopted it.

The key to switching to manufacturing permanent paper was advocacy: promoting changes in paper manufacturing methods from acidic- to alkaline-based paper manufacturing processes. (It is not, however, a coincidence that economic factors also encouraged these changes.) Understanding why paper deteriorated and what constitutes paper acceptable for long-term preservation was based on work by William Barrow and others. Barrow's 1960 "Tentative Specifications for Durable, Non-Coated, Chemical Wood Book Papers"[24] stated that no groundwood and unbleached fibers should be present, and the pH must be not less than 6.5 at the time of manufacture. Further research resulted in the publication in 1984 of the standard ANSI Z39.48-1984, *Permanence of Paper for*

*Printed Library Materials* (further developed in 1992 and revised in 2009 as *Permanence of Paper for Publications and Documents in Libraries and Archives*). This standard specifies that pH should be a minimum of 7.5, that no groundwood or unbleached pulp should be present, that specified levels of fold endurance and tear resistance should be met or exceeded, and that an alkaline reserve at a minimum prescribed level is present. Standard testing methods are also described. Further development of permanent paper standards continued, and their scope was expanded; for example, by standards for permanence of paper used in documents.

### Film

A revealing example of recognizing the consequences of not using preservation-friendly material, and of advocacy to make changes, comes from the movie industry. Color fading in color film has long been recognized as a problem of that medium, but it was brought to the attention of a wider audience, including the movie studios, by director Martin Scorsese. Scorsese's efforts included "The Moving Image: Cultural Suicide" program at the 1980 New York Film Festival, which showed excerpts from films that proved how color was fading. Eastman Kodak introduced a low-fade film stock, adopted by the industry, which has a longer life span than film stock that had been used before, even though it was still subject to fading.[25]

### Long-Lived Digital Storage Media

Chapter 1 noted that early digital preservation developments focused on long-lived digital storage media. One product was HD-Rosetta, which has been adopted in the Long Now Foundation's Rosetta Disk, a product of the Rosetta Project (rosettaproject.org), "a global collaboration of language specialists and native speakers working to build a publicly accessible digital library of human languages." The material used in the Rosetta Disk is exceptionally long-lived solid nickel onto which text is microscopically engraved. Its thirteen thousand pages document over 1,500 languages and can be read using a scanning electron microscope. The HD-Rosetta product was used for material in a time capsule produced by the *New York Times* in 1999.[26] Its developers note that "the durability of this high-density technique is so great that one observer suggested that 'long-term' should be replaced by 'geologic,' when describing the longevity of this data storage method," and that its life can be measured in thousands of years.[27]

### Digital Objects Created from Digitizing

When producing digital versions of analog objects, we are in a position to create preservation-friendly digital objects by adopting best-practice guidelines. Guidelines abound and can easily be located through a Web search. It is vital to identify and implement guidelines that are up-to-date because specifications change as technology develops and users' requirements are better understood. Guidelines typically specify equipment requirements, calibrations of equipment, workflows, metadata requirements, storage requirements for the digital output, and recommended minimum capture standards for various kinds of material. Two examples of the many sets of guidelines available are the Federal Agencies Digitization Guidelines Initiative (FADGI) guidelines,[28] and the *Minimum Digitization Capture Recommendations* issued by the Association for Library Collections and Technical Services' Preservation and Reformatting Section.[29]

Metadata is an important component of preservation-friendly digital objects and, therefore, of digitizing guidelines, such as the FADGI guidelines, which identify common metadata types and provide examples. For descriptive metadata FADGI recommends Dublin Core Metadata Element Set Version 1, plus local fields, and its advice on administrative metadata notes, among other elements, audit trails, persistent identifiers, documentation of imaging process, and information about source materials. The guidelines emphasize the significance of rights information in digital imaging projects, as there are complex legal issues in making objects available online. Technical metadata needs to describe the attributes of digital images to ensure they will be rendered accurately, the image capture process, and image quality.

## Born-Digital Objects

Born-digital objects present many preservation challenges that can be minimized if attention is paid to creating them in a preservation-friendly way. One characteristic of preservation-friendly digital objects is their file formats. Those selected should be the formats most likely to be understandable in the future. They are typically in widespread use, open (with a publicly available specification), independent of specific operating systems, robust, and able to be processed with well-documented software programs, preferably open source. One of many recommendations about preferred file formats for preservation is The National Archives' *Selecting File Formats for Long-Term Preservation*.[30] JPEG (ISO/IEC 10918-1:1994) and PDF (ISO 32000-1:2008) are examples of preferred file formats for preservation use. The public availability of documentation about open file formats makes them important in preservation. If documentation about file formats is available to curators, tools enabling their migration can be developed in the future. By comparison, proprietary file formats make curation difficult and sometimes impossible because their structure cannot be accessed for preservation purposes. Furthermore, backward compatibility of software packages—that is, their ability to import and handle data created in their earlier versions—is typically not guaranteed for any length of time. Consequently, it is common preservation practice to convert data to standard formats that can be interpreted by more than one software application.

Another characteristic of preservation-friendly digital objects is the ready availability of metadata for and about them. Metadata provides a detailed description of the objects, indicates how they were digitized or created, provides information that allows the user to understand their meaning, notes their structure and content, and records actions applied to the objects. Metadata is best assigned to digital objects when they are created and then as their preservation proceeds. It is essential for the effective preservation of digital objects. An institution's ability to preserve digital objects will be seriously compromised if insufficient descriptive, structural, and administrative metadata.

Ideally creators of digital objects should have the knowledge to create preservation-friendly objects, but this is not always the case. How might it be possible to influence them? The promotion of guidelines for best practice is one way, and in some jurisdictions it may be possible to mandate adherence to these guidelines. Guidelines offering advice about digital object creation include the Paradigm Project's *Guidelines for Creators of Personal Archives*[31] and the InterPARES Project's *Creator Guidelines*.[32]

## CONCLUSION

This chapter covers why it is important, even essential, to concentrate attention on the concept of preservation friendliness, on creating objects that are preservation-friendly, and on influencing the creation of objects. Although technical aspects, such as paper quality and file formats, are emphasized in this chapter, we must also acknowledge the importance of social aspects as part of the concept of preservation friendliness. People and institutions need to collaborate in the development, adoption, and revision of the protocols, standards, and models used in preservation. Collaboration—agreeing to work together now and in the future—is difficult to manage and depends in part on an acknowledgment of mutual benefit. It also depends on ideology, whether the free market will evolve to provide solutions or whether solutions are possible only with significant government assistance. About the social aspects of creating preservation-friendly objects there is much less certainty.[33]

While we are building the collaborations that will provide major benefits to the preservation efforts of cultural heritage institutions, we can still do many things at the local level. Jessica Phillips promotes the need for community instruction: "By educating the community today on how to protect the treasures in their care, we have the potential to minimize the repairs needed for these items in the future."[34] Such instruction imparts an understanding of basic preservation issues and describes ways to counteract and prevent damage of objects while they remain in the care of the community.

## NOTES

1. NISO, *Understanding Metadata* (Bethesda, MD: NISO Press, 2004), accessed September 24, 2013, http://www.niso.org/publications/press/UnderstandingMetadata.pdf.

2. This concept is explored in Tyler Walters and Katherine Skinner, "Economics, Sustainability, and the Cooperative Model in Digital Preservation," *Library High Tech* 28 (2010): 259–72.

3. Howard Besser, "Archiving Media from the Occupy Movement: Trying to Involve Participants in Making Their Creations More Preservable," paper presented at the American Library

Association Conference, Seattle, WA, January 26, 2013, accessed September 24, 2013, http://besser.tsoa.nyu.edu/howard/Talks/12ala-occupy-seattle-outreach.pdf.

4. Blue Ribbon Task Force on Sustainable Digital Preservation and Access, *Sustainable Economics for a Digital Planet: Ensuring Long-Term Access to Digital Information* (San Diego, CA: Task Force, 2010), 82–84, accessed September 24, 2013, http://brtf.sdsc.edu/biblio/BRTF_Final_Report.pdf.

5. Kendra Mayfield, "How to Preserve Digital Art," *Wired*, July 23, 2002, accessed September 23, 2013, http://www.wired.com/culture/lifestyle/news/2002/07/53712.

6. Variable Media Network, "Definition," accessed September 24, 2013, http://www.variablemedia.net/e/.

7. Two of the many available online are: Tony Gill et al., *Introduction to Metadata*, Version 3.0 (Los Angeles, CA: Getty Research Institute, 2008), accessed September 24, 2013, http://www.getty.edu/research/publications/electronic_publications/intrometadata/index.html; JISC Digital Media, *An Introduction to Metadata*, accessed September 24, 2013, http://www.jiscdigitalmedia.ac.uk/guide/an-introduction-to-metadata.

8. The examples in this section are derived from table 5.1 in Anne R. Kenney, Oya Y. Rieger, and Richard Entlich, *Moving Theory into Practice: Digital Imaging Tutorial* (Ithaca, NY: Cornell University Library Research Department, 2000–2003), accessed September 24, 2013, http://www.library.cornell.edu/preservation/tutorial/contents.html.

9. Representation information is noted in more detail in chapter 6 of Ross Harvey, *Digital Curation: A How-To-Do-It Manual* (New York: Neal-Schuman, 2010).

10. Consultative Committee for Space Data Systems, *Reference Model for an Open Archival Information System (OAIS): Recommended Practice, CCSDS 650.0-M-2* (Washington, DC: CCSDS, 2012), accessed September 16, 2013, http://public.ccsds.org/publications/archive/650x0m2.pdf.

11. Michelle Moore, "Conservation Documentation and the Implications of Digitisation," *Journal of Conservation and Museum Studies* 7 (2001): 1–19.

12. Digital Curation Centre, "List of Standards," accessed September 24, 2013, http://www.dcc.ac.uk/resources/metadata-standards/list.

13. Library of Congress, "Standards at the Library of Congress," accessed September 24, 2013, http://www.loc.gov/standards/.

14. Raymond Clemens and Timothy Graham, *Introduction to Manuscript Studies* (Ithaca, NY: Cornell University Press, 2007), 6. (A distinction was made in the 1265 ordinance between charters made on leather parchment ("cartas las unas factas en pergamino de cuero") and those on cloth parchment, that is, paper ("las otras en pergamino de paño").

15. Clemens and Graham, *Introduction to Manuscript Studies*, 7.

16. Gordon Chancellor, John van Wyhe, and Kees Rookmaaker, "Darwin's *Beagle* Field Notebooks (1831–1836)," *Darwin Online*, accessed September 24, 2013, http://darwin-online.org.uk/EditorialIntroductions/Chancellor_fieldNotebooks.html.

17. Chancellor, van Wyhe, and Rookmaaker, "Darwin's *Beagle* Field Notebooks."

18. Barbra Buckner Higginbotham, *Our Past Preserved: A History of American Library Preservation 1876–1910* (Boston: G. K. Hall, 1990), 143.

19. These processes are explained in detail in Lisa L. Fox, ed., *Preservation Microfilming: A Guide for Librarians and Archivists*, 2nd ed. (Chicago: American Library Association, 1996).

20. Fox, *Preservation Microfilming*, Appendix A.

21. "Good Resolutions," *Abbey Newsletter* 12, no. 2 (1988): 29–31.

22. "ALA's Third Resolution on Permanent Paper," *Abbey Newsletter* 14, no. 1 (1990): 2.

23. "IFLA Permanent Paper Resolutions," *Conservation Administration News* 40 (1990): 22.

24. W. J. Barrow, *The Manufacture and Testing of Durable Book Papers* (Richmond: Virginia State Library, 1960), 31.

25. Anthony Slide, *Nitrate Won't Wait: A History of Film Preservation in the United States* (Jefferson, NC: McFarland, 1992), 107–8.

26. "Design Is Selected for *Times* Capsule," *New York Times*, December 2, 1999, accessed September 24, 2013, http://www.nytimes.com/1999/12/02/arts/design-is-selected-for-times-capsule.html.

27. Roger A. Stutz and Bruce C. Lamartine, "Estimating Archiving Costs for Engineering Records," paper presented at the annual meeting of the American Association of Cost Engineering, Dallas, TX, July 1997, accessed September 24, 2013, http://www.osti.gov/scitech/biblio/484529.

28. Federal Agencies Digital Guidelines Initiative, *Guidelines*, accessed September 24, 2013, http://www.digitizationguidelines.gov/guidelines/.

29. Association for Library Collections and Technical Services, *Minimum Digitization Capture Recommendations*, June 2013, accessed September 24, 2013, http://www.ala.org/alcts/resources/preserv/minimum-digitization-capture-recommendations.

30. Adrian Brown, *Selecting File Formats for Long-Term Preservation* (London: The National Archives, 2008), accessed September 24, 2013, http://www.nationalarchives.gov.uk/documents/selecting-file-formats.pdf.

31. Paradigm Project, *Guidelines for Creators of Personal Archives*, accessed September 24, 2013, http://www.paradigm.ac.uk/workbook/appendices/guidelines.html.

32. InterPARES Project, *Creator Guidelines: Making and Maintaining Digital Materials: Guidelines for Individuals*, accessed September 24, 2013, http://www.interpares.org/ip2/display_file.cfm?doc=ip2(pub)creator_guidelines_booklet.pdf.

33. We are indebted to Michael Printy, a student in a 2013 class in Digital Stewardship at Simmons College, for this observation.

34. Jessica Phillips, "Educating the Community: Preserving Tomorrow's Treasures Today," in *Preserving Local Writers, Genealogy, Photographs, Newspapers, and Related Materials*, edited by Carol Smallwood and Elaine Williams (Lanham, MD: Scarecrow Press, 2012), 296.

# PART IV

# MEDIA AND
# MATERIAL

· · · · · · · · · · · · · · · · · · · · · · · · · ·

## INTRODUCTION

The expert contributions that follow are of two kinds. The first contribution notes a general preservation concern that affects all collections in cultural heritage institutions; the rest of the contributions describe the preservation of objects commonly encountered in collections. These contributions are written by experts—for the first, in protecting an institution's holdings; and for the rest, in the preservation of objects commonly found in the collections of cultural heritage institutions.

The expert contributions covering commonly encountered objects are based on a template, and they build on the general guidance covered in preceding chapters. Their aim is to provide basic information that will help nonexperts to recognize what they find and to make appropriate preservation decisions based on an understanding of how the characteristics of an object affect its survival. The intention is that these sections are used as a quick reference tool for information about collection objects, ranging from identifying characteristics to their preferred environment, handling practice, and typical decay characteristics. A comprehensive itemization of every type of object likely to be found in collections in libraries, archives, and museums is unrealistic, so we have kept to the types of text-based objects, image-based objects, audio-visual objects, and man-made and naturally occurring artifacts most likely to be found in collections today. It is worthwhile noting that there is useful information about specific object types in more than one contribution: for example, CDs are noted in the contributions about photographic materials, sound materials, and moving image materials.

Each contribution is based on a template, given in figure IV.1. Not all headings are relevant for every kind of material.

The first expert contribution covers an area of preservation activity that affects all collections in cultural heritage institutions: holdings protection, and the actions that can be taken to develop and implement a robust, sustainable plan that reflects equally the need to protect the objects in collections yet still allows stakeholder access to the objects.

The rest of the expert contributions cover the preservation of objects commonly encountered in cultural heritage collections.

## Paper Objects and Books

- Library and archives materials: manuscripts, letters, newspapers, ephemera, pamphlets, architectural reproductions, scrapbooks, albums
- Works of art on paper: prints, drawings, watercolors, pastels, posters, wallpapers
- Books: unique and mass-produced books comprised mostly of paper and parchment, proto-books, e-books

## Photographic Materials

- Cased photographs: daguerreotypes, ambrotypes, tintypes; Negatives: paper negatives, glass-plate negatives, cellulose nitrate film, cellulose acetate film, polyester film; Photographic prints: albumen prints, cabinet cards, carbon prints, gelatin silver developed-out prints, salted paper prints, platinum prints, cyanotypes, "crayon portraits," chromogenic color prints, Polaroid SX70

---

Material
Purposes
Dates in Use
Identification
Representation in Collections
Environment and Storage
    Preferred Environment
    Recommendations for Storage
Handling
What Staff Needs to Know
What Users Need to Know
Disaster Response
Decay
Treatments
Standards and Further Reading

---

**FIGURE IV.1.** Template

- Microform: roll microfilm (16 and 35mm), microfiche, aperture cards, micro-opaques (also called microcards)

## Sound Materials

- Magnetic media: open-reel tape formats (notably ¼-inch audiotape); compact cassettes (more commonly referred to as audiocassettes); small-cassette formats such as minicassettes, microcassettes, and digital audio tape (DAT); other early cassette and cartridge formats; wire recordings; magnetic dictation belts and disc
- Mechanical formats: wax cylinders, 78rpm shellac discs, 16-inch transcription discs, 12-inch 33rpm vinyl LPs, 7-inch 45rpm single discs
- Compact discs: CD-A, CD-ROM, CD-I, CD-R, CD-RW, CD-V, CD-Extra, SACD

## Moving Image Materials

- Motion picture film: 8mm, Super 8, 16mm, 35mm, 70mm
- Magnetic media: analog open-reel formats such as 2-inch Quaduplex, 1-inch SMPTE Type C, and ½-inch EIAJ Type; analog and digital cassette formats such as U-Matic, VHS, Betacam SP, Digital Betacam, Hi8, and MiniDV

## Digital Storage Media and Files

- Magnetic formats: hard disc drives; SyQuest, Bernoulli, Zip, Jaz discs; floppy discs (8-inch, 5¼-inch, 3½-inch, SyQuest); magnetic tape (DAT, DLT, LTO)
- Optical and magneto-optical formats: CD-ROM, DVD, CD-R, DVD-R, CD-RW, DVD-RW, BD-R, magneto-optical discs
- Flash storage: SSD drives, USB flash drives, memory cards
- Digital Files: any of the myriad file formats found in cultural heritage collections, most commonly files created by office productivity software, image files, audio files, video files, and HTML

## Textiles

- Historic dress, accessories, and shoes, tapestries, flags, and banners, samplers and embroideries, rugs and carpets, household textiles

## Paintings

- Works of art, framed or unframed, created with oil, acrylic, tempera, or other paint, often on a canvas or wooden support

The reader needs to be aware that there is overlap in these expert contributions. For example, magnetic media are covered in several contributions: "Sound Materials:

Magnetic Media," "Moving Image Materials: Magnetic Media," and "Digital Storage Media: Magnetic Formats." These can profitably be read together.

The contributions do not cover every type of object found in the collections of cultural heritage institutions. We have attempted to provide useful information about the most commonly encountered objects. For some objects and materials not included, there is mention in some contributions, and readers should refer to the book's index. For example, the "Books" contribution notes leather, and also newspapers and journals, which do not have their own contributions.

CHAPTER 7

# Holdings Protection

Shelby Sanett, Michael F. Knight, Richard Dine,
Kevin A. McCoy

## INTRODUCTION

Cultural heritage institutions, public and private alike, are vulnerable to losses from their collections from both external threats (researchers, stakeholders) and internal threats (staff and management). Building a holdings protection program is a two-track process that addresses both types of threats, with the double objective of deterring theft and collecting evidence should a theft take place. A robust holdings protection program can reduce the risk of loss and still strike a balance between allowing access to items in collections and safeguarding them.

Loss of materials severely impacts the integrity of collections, the reputations of institutions, and the confidence of stakeholders and staff, that cultural heritage institutions can protect historically important and valuable records in perpetuity. Balance can be achieved by developing a comprehensive, sustainable holdings protection plan through a partnership among management, staff, and stakeholders that reflects equally the need to protect material in collections and the need for stakeholders to have access to them. The basic elements of holdings protection are scalable from small, private cultural heritage institutions with few staff or resources, a narrow collections focus, and a relatively small numbers of records, to government repositories with several thousand staff and millions of cubic feet of records in many different types of media.

On June 12, 2012, Barry Landau was sentenced to seven years in prison for conspiracy and theft of historical documents from cultural heritage institutions around the United States. He was caught in the act by astute staff at the Maryland Historical Society, with timely assistance from the National Archives and Records Administration's (NARA) Office of the Inspector General and Holdings Protection Team (HPT), and the world of cultural heritage institutions learned an important lesson—we are all in this together. Landau stole over ten thousand items from dozens of U.S. institutions, including NARA.[1] At the beginning of October 2012, two men were arrested for stealing irreplaceable Second World War documents concerning the Nazi occupation of Denmark from the Danish state archives over several years. The thefts may have gone on for as long as a decade, and the documents have probably been sold. The state archives director concluded "that our security has not been good enough to prevent this."[2]

Only if all institutions take security seriously and share best practices can we limit the risk of theft and damage at all of our institutions. There is an urgent need for a developing conversation on best practices balancing access to and protection of valuable holdings.

## HOLDINGS PROTECTION PROGRAM ELEMENTS

The elements of a holdings protection program should include:

- a concept or mission statement for the program, ideally connected to the institution's mission and strategic plan
- an analysis of current policies and procedures
- a training component
- a physical collections security component
- policy to support new and revised procedures
- a method to monitor and evaluate progress
- a plan for the future after the program is established

### Policy

There are several types of policies to consider that are appropriate for a holdings protection program, including: access control; research or reading room operations (such as line-of-sight observation of users, no pens, use of lockers); exit screening; registration procedures; and transportation of collection materials, loans, and exhibits.

When the program is being developed, existing policies and procedures should be reviewed for effectiveness. Procedures should not be retained simply because they support the way things have always been done. A fresh look may be needed. Policy supports the program and formalizes procedures. When policy is being developed, there is often tension between the ideal and the achievable, and there are often constraints on such things as budget and staff. Realistic discussion is necessary about what can be achieved with the resources available, such as the scope for staff coverage in a research room and alternative forms of surveillance if cameras cannot be purchased right away. Among other tensions to take into consideration when developing policy are balancing access and protection, displaying trust for staff while establishing rules, and balancing donor/stakeholder wishes with advice from security experts. Policies can be updated when circumstances change. The important point is that policies must be realistic and that they must apply to everyone, with no exceptions.

It is useful to share best practices with other institutions, as such cooperation has the added bonus of offering networking opportunities with other institutions and professionals with similar interests. Additional resources for developing holdings protection policy and procedures include: paid security experts; security associated with the parent institution (if applicable); local police; and federal law enforcement agencies. Professional organizations, such as the Society of American Archivists' Security Roundtable (www2.archivists.org/groups/security-roundtable), ASIS International (www.asisonline.org), and the International Foundation for Cultural Property Protection (www .ifcpp.org/), are also excellent resources.

## Program Development

Program development includes determining which organizational department or element will host the program, and within that, which position(s) will be responsible for the program and manage it. Program objectives and goals should be consistent with those of the institution. Special training may be needed for the person who will implement and manage the program, and specific skills and training may be necessary for staff. Staff needs knowledge of the collection (and how it is processed and made available to the public); knowledge of security procedure, best practices, and technology; and communication skills to engage staff and stakeholders in the effort. No single person, or even a single team, will be likely to have all the skills, so it will be necessary to develop partnerships.

One part of program development is the operations/implementation component, including the allocation of resources. How will the program be funded, and who should be included in that conversation? Staffing: how many? What skills are needed? Holdings protection comes at a cost, in money, time, and service. Even a minimal holdings protection program at a very small institution will require some money for locks, surveillance (burglar and fire alarms), a system for recording items pulled from the stacks, and staff time. A larger institution will want to consider cameras, lines of sight for observation in the research room (affecting design and furniture), and other detection equipment. It will take staff time to understand the risks to their collections and to develop the appropriate policies and training. Researchers may feel inconvenienced by additional procedures and restrictions to protect the collections, but at the same time they, and other members of the public, may feel reassured by the knowledge that the institution is properly safeguarding their cultural heritage.

Getting the resources needed—money, time, access controls—requires the careful building of a business case, so that management and funding sources understand the importance of protecting the holdings and appreciate how to balance protection with access and how to balance the costs of protection with other budget priorities. Increased reporting of thefts from archives has had the beneficial effect of encouraging greater recognition of the risk of thefts from any cultural heritage institution, which should in turn encourage a realistic assessment of budgets and risk. External funding sources, such as grants and commercial sponsorship, might be available to supplement program start-up costs and should be explored if funding is needed.

Program development must also incorporate the consideration of how the program's effectiveness will be monitored and what metrics might be used in measuring effectiveness. This is noted further in the section "Evaluating Progress and Measuring Success."

## Training

Training should be required for all staff and for researchers, patrons, and collection users. Staff training should include the orientation of new employees, annual and refresher training, and, especially, training in enhanced customer service techniques. Not all of the training needs to be formal. Training of researchers, patrons, and collections users is necessary as they need to know the institution's rules and staff expectations, as well as the consequences of not following the rules. Signage is a good way to communicate institutional rules and expectations to collection users.

Once the core parameters of the holdings protection program have been established, staff must be trained on how to implement it. The first step is to apply ADDIE (Analyze, Design, Develop, Implement, Evaluate), a simple but powerful model for developing workplace training that can be used by professional instructional designers and novices alike.[3] Its five stages are summarized as:

> *Analyze*: Understand the training objectives and existing capabilities of the target audience (the employees, volunteers, stakeholders, visitors).
> *Design*: Consider the institution's training budget, class size, and skill of the trainers. Decide if workplace aids (summaries of the rules or procedures staff can keep with them as they go through their day) might be helpful.
> *Develop*: After designing the broad outline of the training, write it out and create graphics and other tools. Ensure that there are opportunities for interaction during the training, as staff members may have good ideas to improve the overall holdings protection effort.
> *Implement*: Schedule formal training sessions. Make sure staff members realize that training is important.
> *Evaluate*: Give staff the opportunity to provide feedback, both immediately after the class and a couple months later. Are they using what they learned? Do they need more training or workplace aids?

The scope and nature of the training will vary in ways that depend on the needs and rules of each institution. In most training programs, three key goals need to be accomplished.

First, the knowledge and skills of staff are to be improved. To achieve this, holdings protection procedures should be straightforward enough for staff to learn and understand, so make sure they understand the rules. Have staff practice some specific techniques, such as how to approach a customer or researcher who is breaking the institution's rules. To reinforce teaching, after explaining and modeling a technique, divide the class into customers and staff and have them practice on each other. Experiencing both sides of a procedure will leave a more lasting impression. It is important that skills are kept up-to-date. The skills involved can degrade over time, especially as it is likely that months may go by without incident and with no need to exercise additional caution or to report vulnerability. Incident-free periods can lull staff into a false sense of security that causes them to miss warnings and fail to act when suspicious activity or an incident occurs. Requiring training at least annually is one way to reinforce the skills; another strategy is occasional testing or monitoring of staff. Developing a response action plan and training to that plan, perhaps using a checklist approach to ensure that all tasks are identified and carried out, is a recommended strategy.

Second, make sure that your staff buys into the training program. Most cultural heritage professionals learn little about holdings security during their education, and many have taken an informal approach to it or have emphasized access to collections over their security. When a holdings protection program is implemented, some staff may question whether the institution trusts them. Discussing actual cases of theft and damage can help, especially since the cases show that theft by all sorts of people can happen at any institution.

Third, focus on audience requirements. Staff (professional, volunteer, full time, and part time) are not the only audience; it is important to instill good practice in researchers using the facilities as well. Make sure the materials that deliver the holdings protection rules and any other policies are professionally presented, and have researchers sign a form acknowledging they have read the materials or understood whatever personal briefing they might have been given. If possible, include other stakeholders in the training. Governance and structure will vary from one institution to another, but, where appropriate, consider inviting board members or senior managers to a training session, perhaps to introduce it. This will further your efforts to engage them fully with the holdings protection rules and remind them that they must follow these rules as well.

## Physical Security

The physical security component of the program includes tools such as cameras and intrusion detection systems, access control (internal and external) incorporating exit screening and tracking the movement of materials, and a list of banned researchers, with their photographs. An institution's particular vulnerabilities and resources will determine which specific components will be most effective and cost-effective for it. Partnerships with in-house physical security personnel, local and federal law enforcement agencies, and other cultural heritage institutions and repositories are helpful both in providing security and in determining which components are most appropriate.

## Personnel Security

The institution should conduct background investigations on all staff members. Human resources departments usually take the lead on conducting such investigations. Personnel with responsibility for collections protection should meet with human resources staff and determine both the level of background investigation that should be conducted and suitable criteria for having access to collections. For example, an employee with a credit history problem may be suitable for general access work but not necessarily suitable for work that requires access to restricted areas or holdings until their financial distress has been appropriately mitigated.

## Evaluating Progress and Measuring Success

Evaluating the program's progress is important, but there are a number of challenges in measuring progress, among them the lack of item-level control in some institutions and the cost of monitoring tools. Some evaluation methods to consider are the use of checklists, visual inspections and observations, and the use of outside observers and testers of procedures, such as the staff's enhanced customer service techniques. Evaluation must be built into the program so that it can be properly monitored and adjusted as necessary.

Because most cultural heritage institutions with holdings of archives, records, and other objects, unlike retail stores, do not have item-level control of their materials, they may not become aware that something has been stolen for some years. Since theft cannot be measured directly by simple means such as stock takes, a tempting approach is to test the system with the equivalent of secret shoppers—that is, people brought in to pretend to steal to see if they get caught. This is not, however, an ideal approach, since it can be demoralizing for staff to be tested in this way, and the secret shoppers may not apply strategies that a real thief might use. Similarly, outside auditors or security specialists can try to assess the system, but they may or may not use a realistic set of criteria. A third approach is for designated staff or outside security experts to periodically monitor the facility by walking through the research or reading room, looking into stack and processing areas and watching CCTV output, to see if rules are being followed and if the right balance is being struck between facilitating access to collections and ensuring their protection. This approach is most effective in identifying significant weaknesses and in determining whether staff has generally become lax. A fourth approach is to survey stakeholders—staff, researchers or customers, leadership—to see if they feel that security has been improved and that thieves are more likely to be deterred or caught. Self-monitoring such as this may not be perfect, but it will give some sense of whether various stakeholders think the program is working and provide an opportunity to gather any useful recommendations they may have for improvements to the program.

In the end, in the absence of one perfect solution to the evaluation challenge, a mix of all these techniques will help evaluate the effectiveness of the training. Proper procedures and formal training will do much to improve the institution's awareness and control over the many potential risks to its collections.

### Planning for the Future

This element of the program needs to focus on three areas: program sustainability; future challenges; and outreach. Program sustainability involves determining what will be needed to keep the program going—funding, staff, policies, training, partnerships, and so on. The challenges that institutions face in the future will vary widely, but preparations that can be made to address some of them might include developing a database of banned researchers (with photographs), developing a cross-institutional missing documents list, and building a recovery program. The third area, outreach, includes developing relationships with other institutions, professional organizations, and law enforcement agencies.

Complacency is the greatest threat to sustainability. Sustained vigilance is a perishable commodity, and procedures need to be tested as part of an ongoing protocol to monitor and evaluate the holdings protection program. Months or years might pass without any detection of theft. Other priorities and initiatives will absorb the attention of staff and stakeholders. Achieving sustainability lies in part in following the program's procedures outlined above. It may also be maintained by keeping abreast of news of thefts in other institutions, reminding staff and stakeholders that they cannot assume their institution to be immune from similar incidents, and of the damage that even one thief might cause to their institution's collections and its reputation.

## PHYSICAL SECURITY ELEMENTS OF A HOLDINGS PROTECTION PROGRAM

Deterrence and collection of evidence of system breaches are among the objectives of a holdings program. Program elements aimed at meeting these objectives are presented below; they are intended for implementation in cultural heritage institutions of all sizes.

### Signage

The process of alerting visitors to an institution's established holdings protection rules begins before they enter the building. Research and facility regulations should be posted on the institution's website; early notification of rules can facilitate clearer understanding of behavioral expectations. In exhibit areas and research rooms, signage that reinforces rules should be displayed prominently. For example, signs at entrances that let researchers know they are under constant surveillance when they are using collection materials are a significant deterrent. Because of the threat posed to collection materials when researchers photocopy or scan them, often leaving original documents on the machines they use, signage that reinforces rules related to photocopying and scanning is essential.

It is critical for researchers to receive comprehensive information describing rules for using the collections, which may include rules about the number of items they can have on their table at any one time and about handling fragile materials. The materials that researchers bring into a research room introduce a threat to collection materials, which may engender prohibitions on bringing bags, some types of clothing, files and folders, and electronic equipment into the room. Rules can be presented in several ways, on paper or in digital form. Researchers should be required to sign an acknowledgment that they have read and understood any research room rules.

## Cameras, Monitors, and Digital Video Recorders

Cameras, monitors, and digital video recorders (DVRs) are critical tools in the deterrence of theft from collections. Cameras in research rooms, exhibit areas, and at collection area access points can also be used to provide evidence when theft is suspected. For this reason the use of fake or inactive cameras is strongly discouraged. Cameras must be maintained regularly and tested, as a camera that is not actively recording cannot provide staff and law enforcement agencies with the evidence needed to recover and prosecute and, in some jurisdictions, it could prevent an institution from taking legal action.

Cameras in areas where access is restricted to staff should be positioned to monitor points of entry and exit in order to determine which staff gained access to an area at a particular time. Installing cameras in conservation and preservation processing areas and stack areas is not recommended because the large number of cameras needed to cover blind spots and obstructed angles of viewing means that they are not usually cost-effective. They also tend to foster distrust between managers and staff, who may suspect management of using them to monitor workflow. Cameras that pan, tilt, and zoom provide a broader range of views down corridors, in exhibit areas, and of multiple research desks. Fixed-view cameras may be a more affordable alternative. Lighting, particularly in exhibit spaces, should be considered when choosing cameras. In research rooms, a minimum of two cameras is optimal for monitoring. It is essential to also have a monitor on a research room's staff desk so staff can monitor activities. DVRs set to overwrite collected data in a minimum of sixty days allow staff and law enforcement agents to view suspected incidents throughout the facility and to create copies for evidence purposes.

It is imperative that research room staff and management be trained to use cameras, monitors, and DVRs for better monitoring of their areas of responsibility. In a strategy taken directly from the retail profession, the installation of monitors near the research rooms and exhibit entrances, which display camera feeds publicly and are visible to visitors, can add another level of deterrence by reminding visitors they are under surveillance at all times in these areas.

## Research Room Furniture

Research room furniture should also be carefully considered with collections protection in mind. Research room staff need to monitor the room from an elevated desk and chair so that they can see researcher activities better. The staff desk should be equipped with a duress button to alert local law enforcement agents or the in-house crime prevention unit that an incident is occurring. It enables the staff to request help without escalating the situation with the researcher. If a research room staff member also needs to contact a manager or supervisor, they should get a co-worker to cover for them and then initiate the contact according to their institution's procedures. The duress button should not be used to contact a manager or supervisor. Researcher desks should be arranged so that staff have unobstructed views of the desktops.

## Access Control

Controlling access to a cultural heritage institution's collections is critical in discouraging and obstructing theft. Limiting staff and public access to the collections is an inexpensive way to protect materials. Maintaining a log and/or using keypads and card readers are useful tools to monitor who had access to restricted areas, and when. Only staff with a valid need to have direct access to collections should be granted access, and their names should be recorded on a roster that is regularly updated. This allows for greater awareness of movements and unusual behavior in restricted areas. If holdings are identified as missing, having a list of names of staff with access to restricted areas can help reduce the number of potential interviewees at the outset of an investigation.

## Security Locks

All stack and collections processing areas must be protected by a security locking system. In cultural heritage institutions with more modest budgets, this may come in the form of simple key or cipher locks (locks opened with a programmable keypad). An institution's security personnel or supervisor must maintain strict control of assigned keys. Key distribution lists are as critical as lists of staff with access to restricted areas and must be maintained in a similar fashion. Conducting periodic inventories of all keys, whether issued or not, is important to ensure the integrity of key controls. For institutions with greater resources, keypads or card readers provide an added level of security by recording who accesses a restricted area at any given time (particularly after hours). Cultural heritage institutions may also consider a combination of security lock features. For example, key or cipher locks could secure office areas, and card readers could secure stack areas.

## Screening

When they leave research or reading rooms, researchers must be screened to make sure they have none of the collection's holdings in their possession. Screening serves as a strong deterrent to potential thieves by providing another level of staff review before they exit. Research or reading room exit screenings are more effective if researchers are required to make copies of original documents on colored paper, which makes it easier for staff to distinguish original documents from copies and notes made by researchers. To manage internal risk, it may be appropriate to institute exit inspections of staff by trained security officers who inspect all bags, folders, and outer clothing that the staff might have with them as they leave. Exit inspection stations should be maintained wherever staff is allowed to enter and exit in normal, nonemergency circumstances.

## Tracking

Because many institutions lack intellectual control of their collections down to the item level, it is imperative that all institutions maintain a means of tracking the movement and use of their collections. Loans of collections for exhibits must be thoroughly documented and the documentation shared with those staff who have responsibility for holdings protection. Any items that are loaned must be copied or digitized. If institutions lend items from their collections to other institutions, it is vital that there is a process for alerting staff when those items are overdue for return.

Researchers must be required to identify themselves with government- or academic-issued identification. The researcher's identity and contact information must be recorded and filed so that they are available in the event of any investigation necessary in the future. Staff must also preserve all tracking information related to the records accessed by researchers for as long as possible, because thefts often go undetected for years.

## Collaboration with Security and Law Enforcement Personnel

Cultural heritage institutions can benefit from establishing partnerships with local security and law enforcement agencies. Pursuing such relationships incurs relatively little cost beyond staff time and is vital for institutions that do not have their own security force. Establishing relationships with law enforcement agencies can foster an understanding of an institution's mission and collections and will enhance reaction times in the event of a theft or emergency, because first responders will be familiar with the layout of a facility, will know who to contact, and will be better placed to facilitate any investigation. Institutions housed in their own independent buildings or campus will derive great value from inviting local first responders to conduct their training at a facility during hours when it is not open to the public. In the event of an emergency, first responders will be familiar with the building and will have met staff members.

It should, however, be noted that physical security protocols are ultimately no substitute for staff who are aware of their surroundings. There must be an expectation that staff will circulate regularly through exhibit spaces and research areas to monitor visitor activities and to ensure the safety of collections.

## STAKEHOLDERS

One person or team or department cannot build a holdings protection program alone; almost everyone who supports the institution is involved. Staff must learn to be vigilant, management and funding sources must provide resources and program support, and facility managers must help ensure the building has the proper physical safeguards. The public needs to understand the reason for policies and can often be used as a source of information in identifying potential threats. Figure 7.1 shows many of the parties involved, and the arrows emphasize that the many relationships that need to be fostered are two-way streets, with the person or group charged with developing the program giving information to all of the key players and at the same time learning from each of them.

## SCALABILITY

Much of what has been written here is based on the authors' experience at NARA, gained over more than three years as an eight-member team devoted solely to developing a holdings protection program for NARA's 3,500 staff and twelve billion items spread throughout forty-four locations in the United States. Much of this experience, including outreach efforts to share best practices with other institutions, is scalable to institutions large and small. The core elements of the program are necessary whatever the size of an institution: policy; physical security; personnel security; staff training; stakeholder buy-in; and vigilance. The precise form each of these elements takes will depend on the institution's size, the nature of its holdings, and its tolerance for risk.

The key to a scalable program is having the right expertise when it is being designed. The three core skill sets needed to build the program are in security management; management of archives, libraries, or museums; and materials' process management. It is unlikely any one member of an institution has all three skill sets, and smaller institutions are most likely to lack security expertise. If security expertise is lacking, many sources of this expertise are available, although the ability to use these sources will depend on the size, nature, and resources of an institution and its resources. If an institution is part of a larger institution (for example, a university or a government entity), it may be possible to tap the expertise of its security service. For very small institutions, working with local police and fire departments should go a long way toward getting the information and advice they need. Organizations such as the American Society for Industrial Security (ASIS), an organization that manages the certification of protection professionals, may have useful resources or consultants; the Society of American Archivists' Security Roundtable can also provide advice and possible contacts. The institution can obtain a free crime-prevention assessment by contacting their local ASIS chapter, which will authorize a security professional to conduct the assessment in exchange for a letter from

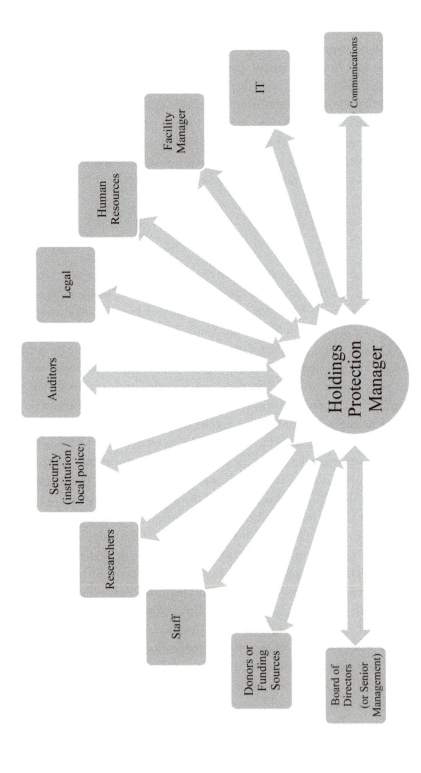

**FIGURE 7.1.** Stakeholders in a Holdings Protection Program

the institution stating that the crime-prevention assessment has been done, which the security professional uses to maintain professional certification.

## GETTING STARTED

Once policies have been established, the initial training developed, management support and funding sources obtained, and plans communicated, it is time to implement the holdings protection policies and procedures. Do not expect everything to go exactly according to plan, and be willing to revise policies, procedures, and training. Learn from feedback.

One of the most important tenets to cling to during implementation is not to allow staff and other stakeholders to develop workarounds for the new procedures. When people make exceptions to rules they introduce one of the greatest risks to holdings protection. Make it clear to all that if a policy seems unworkable they should consult with the holdings protection experts, who can either decide to modify the rules or explain why that policy should remain in place without change. For example, at NARA head coverings were banned from its research rooms, but people who wore them for religious reasons requested exemptions from this ban. NARA's holdings protection team worked closely with NARA legal and security experts to revise the policy so that religious needs were respected while the needed security continued to be provided.

If high levels of potential resistance to new holdings protection requirements are anticipated, consider using a change management model. It must be acknowledged that change is often difficult, and, depending on how ingrained past practices and expectations are, there may be a need to overcompensate in communicating the holdings protection message and to meet frequently with stakeholders to address their concerns and to reinforce the importance of integrating holdings protection into everyone's daily tasks.

## CONCLUSION

Those who steal from cultural heritage institutions often target more than one. One of the most recent examples of that is the convicted felon Barry Landau, mentioned at the beginning of this chapter, who was caught stealing from the Maryland Historical Society and was then found to have stolen from dozens of institutions around the United States, including NARA. We are, indeed, all in this together. It is important that institutions share information and best practices, which is the imperative that is our prime motivation in contributing this chapter and sharing some of the lessons we have learned with the wider cultural heritage community. In the process of developing and refining a holdings protection program, try to organize meetings with other local or regional institutions to share best practices and discuss common issues. There is no need for you to go it alone.

# FURTHER READING

Baker, Paul R., and Daniel J. Benny. *The Complete Guide to Physical Security*. Boca Raton, FL: Auerbach Publications, 2012.

Benny, Daniel J. *Cultural Property Security: Protecting Museums, Historic Sites, Archives, and Libraries*. Boca Raton, FL: CRC Press, 2012.

Griffith, Anna. "Learning from the Holdings Protection Team at the National Archives and Records Administration (NARA), USA." *Australian Library Journal* 62 (2013): 148–57.

National Archives and Records Administration. "Recover Lost and Stolen Documents." Accessed September 30, 2013. http://www.archives.gov/research/recover/.

National Archives and Records Administration, Office of the Federal Register. *Code of Federal Regulations Title 36: Parks, Forests, and Public Property, Part 1254. Using Records and Donated Historical Materials*. Washington, DC, 2012. Accessed September 30, 2013. http://www.gpo.gov/fdsys/pkg/CFR-2012-title36-vol3/xml/CFR-2012-title36-vol3-part1254.xml.

National Park Service. "Care and Security of Rare Books." *Conserve O Gram*, 19/2 (1993). Accessed September 30, 2013. http://www.nps.gov/history/museum/publications/conserveogram/cons_toc.html.

Ritzenthaler, Mary Lynn. *Preserving Archives and Manuscripts*. 2nd ed. Chicago: Society for American Archivists, 2010.

"Security in Museums and Galleries: Access to Collections: A Practical Guide." London: Arts Council England; Collections Trust, 2013. Accessed September 30, 2013. http://www.collectionslink.org.uk/media/com_form2content/documents/c1/a842/f6/PracticalGuide_Access_to_Collections_01.pdf.

"Security in Museums and Galleries: CCTV Systems: A Practical Guide." London: Arts Council England; Collections Trust, 2013. Accessed September 30, 2013. http://www.collectionslink.org.uk/media/com_form2content/documents/c1/a844/f6/PracticalGuide_CCTVsystems_02.pdf.

Strassberg, Richard. "Library and Archives Security." In *Preservation: Issues and Planning*, edited by Paul N. Banks and Roberta Pilette, 166–77. Chicago: American Library Association, 2000.

*To Preserve and Protect: The Strategic Stewardship of Cultural Resources: Essays from the Symposium Held at the Library of Congress October 30–31, 2000*. Washington, DC: Library of Congress, 2002.

Trinkaus-Randall, Gregor. *Protecting Your Collections: A Manual of Archival Security*. Chicago: Society of American Archivists, 1995.

# NOTES

1. "NARA Returns Landau Docs," *History News Network*, May 14, 2013, accessed September 30, 2013, http://hnn.us/articles/nara-returns-landau-docs.

2. "'Irreplaceable' Nazi-era Documents Stolen from Danish Archives," *Telegraph*, October 25, 2012, accessed September 30, 2013, http://www.telegraph.co.uk/history/world-war-two/9634459/Irreplaceable-Nazi-era-documents-stolen-from-Danish-archives.html.

3. For more information about ADDIE, see chapter 3 of Chuck Hodell, *ISD from the Ground Up: A No-Nonsense Approach to Instructional Design*, 3rd ed. (Alexandria, VA: ASTD Press, 2011).

# CHAPTER 8

# Paper Objects and Books

······················································································

Donia Conn, Dawn Walus

## PAPER: LIBRARY AND ARCHIVES MATERIALS (DONIA CONN)

*Dates in use*: approximately 100 BCE to the present.
*Formats*: Manuscripts, letters, newspapers, ephemera, pamphlets, architectural reproductions, scrapbooks, albums.

### Material

#### PAPER

Paper is formed from a pulp of cellulosic fibers derived directly from plant materials or pulped from rags. The cellulosic pulp is formed on a mold, pressed to encourage hydrogen bonding between fibers, and dried. Sheets formed from nonplant sources or from sources other than pulp are not true paper. Older handmade paper and modern hand- and machine-made rag paper is predominantly made from long, strong strands of cellulose derived primarily from cotton, flax, and hemp.

Wood-pulp papers, such as newsprint and much of the commercial paper made since the 1860s, contain lignin. The presence of lignin in paper shortens its overall life span, as it reacts with relative humidity and light to form acidic products, which then attack and shorten the cellulose fibers. In the manufacture of permanent paper pulp, lignin is removed through chemical processes using alkaline or sulfur compounds. In addition to cellulose, paper contains sizing, either internal or externally applied, to prevent inks from feathering (having a fuzzy or indistinct edge), and a multitude of other fillers to give it required characteristics for use.

Blank sheets of paper are not common in collections, so it is also important to understand some of the other materials associated with paper objects, as they too have an

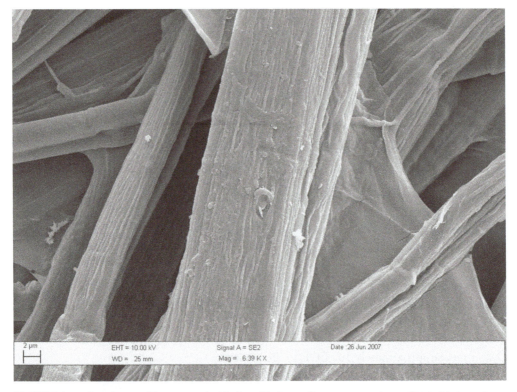

**FIGURE 8.1.** Rag Paper. Photograph, Melissa Tedone, Conservator, Iowa State University Parks Library Preservation Department

impact on paper's longevity. Documents, manuscripts, letters, scrapbooks, and other collection items contain ink, and often adhesives, at a minimum.

## INKS

Ink is a colorant (pigment or dye) suspended in a vehicle. Pigments are dry colorants ground into a fine powder and are insoluble, resulting in a suspension that is not deeply absorbed into the paper. In contrast, dyes form a solution with their chosen vehicle and are absorbed into the paper, resulting in deeply saturated colors. Most pigment-based inks are permanent, but some, along with most dyes, are fugitive and will fade, shift color, or darken over time.

The earliest inks were carbon-based inks. Carbon was collected by burning bones, ivory, and various tars. The soot, sometimes called lamp black or carbon black, was collected and mixed with the vehicle, usually a gelatin for Asian ink sticks and gum arabic for fluid inks. Carbon ink was widely used through the 19th century, when it was replaced by dye-based inks. Carbon ink is permanent and lightfast. Carbon inks are also known as Chinese or India ink.

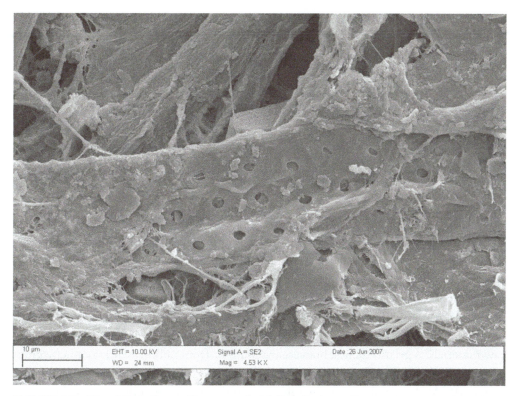

**FIGURE 8.2.** Wood-Pulp Paper. Photograph, Melissa Tedone, Conservator, Iowa State University Parks Library Preservation Department

Another very common ink encountered in historic collections is iron gall ink. The ink was generally prepared by adding some iron (II) sulfate to a solution of tannic acid created by the crushing and boiling of oak galls. Iron gall ink was widely used for over a thousand years. Unlike carbon inks, iron gall ink has a high acidity that gives it a "bite," meaning it could adhere better to parchment and could only by erased by scraping a thin layer off the writing surface. Iron gall ink use started to decline in the 20th century when other non-water-soluble, permanent inks were developed. Iron gall ink is very unstable, changing chemically in the presence of oxygen and high relative humidity into hydrated iron oxide (rust). As the iron gall ink breaks down, it also produces sulfuric acid, which degrades the substrate underneath, leading to bleed-through and eventually causing letters to drop out of text.

With the introduction of aniline dyes in the 1860s, pigments were used less in ink manufacture, and synthetic dyes in aqueous or solvent solutions, with additives to give the ink the characteristics that writing implements needed, were used instead. These dye-based modern inks can be found in felt-tip pens, ballpoint pens, and highlighter pens. Sometimes, inks that appear to be carbon black are, in fact, blue-black dye inks. To identify them, look at the edge of the ink under magnification. Carbon ink will be uniformly black, while the dye-based ink will show blue and black at the edge where it feathers into the paper.

Printing ink, like early manuscript ink, was made from carbon black. Unlike manuscript ink, its vehicle is linseed oil, which hardens by oxidation and, when manufactured correctly, produces a permanent, stable, and lightfast image. Do not assume all historic printing inks used stable linseed oil. Often, whatever oil was on hand was used, and additives were put in to get the desired characteristics. Modern printing inks, especially the less expensive ones, contain both lamp black and dyes and are thus less permanent than earlier inks.

## ADHESIVES

Adhesives are made from starches (paste), animal products (glue), or are purely synthetic. They work by forming a bond, either chemical or mechanical, between two surfaces. In cultural heritage collections many different adhesives will be found in bindings, scrapbooks, and photograph albums, and in the myriad of repairs that have been done over the years. Pastes are made from pure starch or flour and can have all sorts of unknown additives, as most were homemade. Animal glues were made from the same raw materials as gelatin (bones, hooves, and skin) or from milk (casein). Synthetic glues come in the form of methylcellulose, pressure-sensitive tapes, rubber cement, polyvinyl acetate (PVA), Magic photo album adhesives, and many, many other forms. The most stable and reversible adhesives in use today are starch paste and methylcellulose. Some gelatin-based glue is stable if prepared properly, and modern PVAs are stable but not reversible. Many adhesives are the cause of considerable damage to collections, such as acid migration and staining, damaging residues, poor repairs, and damage caused by the loss of adhesion over time.

## REPROGRAPHIC PROCESSES

Among paper-based materials in collections will be examples of a wide range of reprographic processes. The earliest copy method was copying documents by hand onto a new substrate. This method was replaced in 1780 when the wet transfer method of copying letters was developed. This process involved using a special ink to write the document. A page from a letter copying book was dampened, the document placed inside, and the book placed in a copying press. The damp page absorbed some of the ink, and the pressure from the press prevented too much bleeding or feathering so as not to damage the original document. The pages of the letter copying book were very thin and translucent, so that the mirror image could be read through the page once an opaque sheet was put behind it. After the advent of aniline dyes, the ink was replaced with a copying pencil containing the dye. A copying pencil looks like a regular pencil in form, and the marks it leaves on the page look like pencil marking, too. These pencils were sometimes mistakenly used as regular pencils, so use caution if dry-cleaning collections with graphite markings. When documents written with copying pencils are dry-cleaned, their markings will smear blue and will be very difficult to remove.

The products of mimeographs (in use 1890–2000s) and ditto machines (in use 1923–2000s) are both common types of reproductions found in historic collections. Mimeographs forced ink through a stencil on a rotary drum to make a copy. Wax with aniline dye combined with solvents to make a copy on the rotary drum of a ditto (or spirit duplicator) machine. The inks used in both methods fade in ultraviolet (UV) radiation, and the paper used is generally of poor quality, turning yellow and becoming brittle.

Electrostats (in use 1950s–present), more commonly known as Xerox copies or photocopies, work by exposing an original to light that reflects onto a positively charged drum. The reflected light from the blank areas changes the drum's charge to negative, leaving only the images to print from the negatively charged toner. The image is transferred to paper and passed through the fuser (heated rollers). The toner is carbon black pigment and holds to the paper with the binder that is fused at the last step. The pigment is stable, but problems can arise if the fuser is not hot enough to set the ink to the paper.

## Purposes

Paper is the foundation for a high proportion of collection materials in libraries and archives. Manuscripts, newspapers, documents, letters, business records, architectural reproductions, tickets, posters, broadsides, and much more are written or printed on paper.

## Dates in Use

Paper made from pulp was first developed in China. Archaeological remnants of paper made from hemp dating to the Han dynasty (estimated 100 BCE) have been excavated in Shannxi Province. Papermaking technology was a closely guarded secret for many years in Asia, but eventually it made its way west over the Silk Road, arriving in the Middle East in the eighth century CE and in Europe in 1151, when the first paper mill was established in Spain. Again, the technology was closely guarded, and it took 340 years to spread across Europe to England and a further two hundred years to reach the North American colony of Pennsylvania.

Asian papers are traditionally made with native hemp, *kozo*, *gampi*, or *mitsumata* fibers. These fibers are derived from the bast (the inner bark layer) fibers of the plant. Early Western pulp was made from linen or hemp. Rather than harvest the fibers directly from the plant, Europeans processed the fibers into clothing, sails, sacks, and other textiles first and used them until they wore out, at which point they made their way to the papermaker's vat.

Paper quality varied in the handmade rag era, as it does today. Many book and writing papers came from the highest quality rags and remain strong and durable to this day. Some printed materials, such as chapbooks, schoolbooks, and broadsides, were not intended to be of high quality and needed to be less expensive, so paper from lower-quality rags was used.

Changes in the longevity of paper over time can be seen as new innovations were introduced. Beginning around 1789, to speed production, rags were bleached with sodium hypochlorite (the active ingredient in a common household bleach, Clorox) when it became commercially available. Unfortunately, if not rinsed thoroughly enough, chlorine remaining in the paper would slowly break down the paper fibers, leaving a brittle mess behind. Alum rosin sizing was introduced into the papermaking process in 1807. Its use for sizing improved efficiency, as it sized the paper in the vat rather than necessitating hand dipping the sheets in warm gelatin after formation and drying. An excess of alum results in a more acidic paper, especially over time.

As literacy levels increased dramatically around the world in the early 19th century, the demand for paper grew rapidly. To reduce dependency on rags for paper, a new source of pulp was sought. After much trial and error, the paper industry turned to wood fibers. Wood pulp started being processed in the United States in 1867, but it was not for another twenty years that the pulp became widely available.[1] The high yield of wood pulp made it particularly appealing for many types of paper, as it brought the overall cost down. Wood pulp was not suitable, however, for fine book and writing papers because of its high lignin content, which persisted as a problem in the paper for many years.

In 1984, in response to the brittle paper problem, the United States adopted a national standard for permanent papers. The standard, ANSI/NISO Z39.48-1992 (R2009), limited the lignin content of the pulp to 1 percent, required a minimum alkaline reserve of 2 percent, and required the pH of the final paper to be between 7.5 and 10, resulting in papers that are acid-free, lignin-free, and alkaline-buffered.

## Identification

Some materials in collections may be mistakenly referred to as paper when they are not. Papyrus, tapa, amatl, and pith paper are not papers because they do not fit the definition of paper (the dispersion of cellulosic fibers that have been reduced to a pulp and formed into a sheet). They have not been formed into a sheet from pulp, but they are strips of cellulosic fibers beaten into sheets and overlapped perpendicularly with other strips of cellulosic fibers to form larger sheets. Parchment, the processed skin of animals (predominantly calf, sheep, or goat) is not paper.

## Representation in Collections

As noted, paper is the foundation for a high proportion of collection materials in libraries and archives. Other commonly encountered paper-based objects are architectural drawings and scrapbooks.

## ARCHITECTURAL DRAWINGS

Blueprints, diazotypes, and drafting cloth are the most common architectural drawings found in historic collections, with drafting film becoming more common from the 1950s.

Drafting cloth (in use 1860s–1980s) is a linen or cotton fabric that has been starched or sized and calendered for printing or drawing. Drawings on drafting cloth are susceptible to mold, insects, and water/moisture damage, and the ink on their surface may smear or wash off when it gets wet.

Drafting film (in use 1950s–present) is an acetate or polyester film, coated on one or both sides to accept ink. Cellulose acetate film can become brittle and discolored and may shrink, which is detectible by a vinegar odor. Polyester films can yellow slightly from long-term exposure to UV light, and the matt surface on polyester films from the 1960s and 1970s can flake off.

Blueprints (in use 1870s–present) are drawings on a translucent support, placed in contact with paper sensitized with ferric ammonium citrate and potassium ferricyanide and exposed to sunlight or a lamp. The unexposed ferric salts are washed out in a water bath, leaving white lines on a blue background. Blueprints are very susceptible to light and will fade if on display for an extended period. The poor-quality paper used after the 1920s also becomes brittle.

Diazotypes (in use 1900s–present) are similar to blueprints. A drawing on a translucent support is placed in contact with paper sensitized with diazonium salt, which decomposes in contact with light. The exposed copy is washed in a chemical solution, reacting with the diazo salt to form a dye and thus an image. Later, a dry process was developed that uses ammonia gas. Because of the chemical processing this reprographic process is one of the least stable. The poor-quality paper becomes brittle, and the residual chemicals in the paper give off gases that can lead to the deterioration of other paper items stored with diazotypes.

## SCRAPBOOKS

Many historical collections include scrapbooks, which pose challenging preservation problems because they often contain a variety of structures, components, and adhesives. Full scrapbooks can stress the binding on structures with tight, rigid spines and on books that were never intended for use as scrapbooks. Support pages were often made from low-quality paper to keep the cost down, and they become brittle over time. Scraps may be paper, textiles, metal, photographic, dried plant material, and just about any other material imaginable. They may be three-dimensional, have multiple or moving parts, and may be damaging to the other scraps due to their composition or shape. Methods of attachment involve an endless variety of adhesives, but the most commonly used are flour paste, hide glue, mucilage, rubber cement, tape, and photo corners.

# Environment and Storage

## PREFERRED ENVIRONMENT

Managing the environment is one of the best ways to protect and preserve collections. For collections with a wide variety of materials, a single setting for temperature and relative humidity (RH) will not be safe or sufficient; different materials require different environments. Each institution must determine the varied needs of its collections. For paper-based collections, the ideal conditions for storage are:[2]

Combined use and storage areas: 70°F (21°C) maximum, 30 percent to 60 percent RH

Dedicated storage, no work spaces: 35°F (2°C) to 65°F (18°C), 30 percent to 60 percent RH

Allowable monthly drift: ± 4°F (± 1°C), ± 8 percent RH

Current research into environmentally sustainable conditions for storage environments is resulting in less rigid approaches to ideal temperature and RH levels, as noted in chapter 5. If temperatures are too high, chemically unstable materials, such as acidic paper, deteriorate more rapidly. As a rule of thumb, for every increase of 18°F (10°C) the rate of deterioration doubles; if temperatures are lowered, the rate decreases proportionately. To avoid problems, use thermometers, data loggers, temperature monitors, and alarms to monitor temperatures before temperature changes cause problems. Relative humidity (RH) levels that are too high can cause paper to cockle, while levels that are too low cause loss of flexibility. High RH can also attract pests detrimental to collections. A prolonged period of RH readings of over 65 percent is considered dangerous because it allows mold growth.

In addition to temperature and RH, light needs to be managed. The intensity and amount of light to which objects are exposed should be controlled. Paper should be put in folders and boxed, and lights kept off in unoccupied storage areas when they are not needed. When paper items are exhibited, a maximum of 50 lux is recommended for very sensitive materials like watercolors and 150 lux for less sensitive materials. UV radiation from windows, skylights, and lighting fixtures should be filtered, and objects should be protected from sunlight by closing curtains, blinds, or shutters. Light levels can be monitored with a UV meter, light meter, or Blue Wool Standard cards.

Air quality also needs to be managed. Dust, volatile organic compounds (VOCs), and pollution will affect the air quality and the rate of deterioration of collections, and it can be a direct cause of many types of damage. Airborne pollutants such as sulfur dioxide and nitrous oxides, by-products of burning fossil fuels, and ozone ($O_3$), a byproduct of electrical equipment, are strong catalysts of chemical deterioration. These airborne pollutants, in conjunction with RH, react with chemicals in paper, producing sulfuric acid and nitric acid, and they lead to embrittlement and discoloration.

VOCs are produced by the gases given off by storage units and display cases made from oak, medium density fiberboard (MDF), or plywood, and by paints, adhesives, carpet, vinyl flooring, PVC and other plastics, and other materials. Careful selection of materials can reduce the production of VOCs, but when less-than-ideal materials must be used, allow enough time between their installation and their use for them to give off their gases.

Dust can damage paper by abrasion, and it can also encourage the increase of moisture on the surface, leading to problems with mold growth. Where possible, filter incoming air to reduce dust. If resources are available, excluding airborne pollutants with HEPA (high-efficiency particulate air) filtration is desirable. When it is not possible to filter incoming air, store collections in acid-free, lignin-free, and alkaline-buffered folders and boxes.

Cleaning products, such as Pledge and Lysol, and lotions and hand sanitizers, can leave a chemical residue that can be transferred to paper. Liaison with housekeeping and cleaning staff is recommended to ensure that cleaning products are not used unnecessarily, and never where collections are stored.

## RECOMMENDATIONS FOR STORAGE

*Documents.* Manuscripts and other unbound documents are often vulnerable to damage from inappropriate storage and handling practices because of the brittle and fragile nature of the paper. To protect loose sheets during storage and handling, some basic practices need to be followed. They include foldering and boxing in chemically stable materials, removing corroded fasteners, storing materials by size and type, and encouraging staff and users to handle them safely.

Unbound documents should be housed in lignin-free, alkaline-buffered file folders. If their paper is stable, several sheets can be stored in one folder, whose bottom is creased to accommodate the thickness of the group of sheets of paper. If their paper is fragile, it may be necessary to place fewer sheets in a folder or to place each in an individual sleeve. Folded documents and manuscripts should be unfolded for storage, if this can be done without splitting or fracturing them. If a fragile paper sheet resists unfolding, or if unfolding may result in damage, it may require humidification and flattening. Letters that have been unfolded should be stored with their envelopes.

Ideally, every fastener on historic documents would be removed when they are processed. If the institution has chosen to follow the advice of Mark Greene and Dennis Meissner,[3] staff and administration need to discuss the implications of their advice and the importance of removing already corroded staples, paper clips, and pins to prevent further damage. Any fastener that is not of stainless steel on documents that are to be stored in an uncontrolled or unstable environment should also be removed to prevent inevitable corrosion in the future. If papers need to remain clipped together, either place an acid-free, lignin-free, buffered paper, or polyester (Melinex) barrier between the papers and the clip, or use stainless steel paper clips or staples. Never use plastic clips, as they cause considerable deformity.

Folders should be kept in chemically stable document storage boxes. All folders inside a single box should be the same size, and they should fit the size of the box rather than the size of the sheet. Flat and upright boxes that are suitable for document storage are available.

No more than three flat boxes should be stacked on top of each other in order to facilitate access and prevent crushing of boxes. In upright storage boxes, documents and folders should be well supported to prevent slumping and deformity of the contents. Spacers made from chemically stable materials can be used to fill empty space in boxes and to support the folders. Care should also be taken not to overfill boxes or file drawers, as damage may be caused when items are removed or replaced from tightly packed boxes or drawers.

Many historical collections include ephemera (for example, trade cards, Valentines, patterns, paper dolls). Unbound ephemera should be grouped by size and type (photographs, printed material, manuscripts, and so on), individually enclosed to protect items from acid migration and mechanical damage, and stored in a way that will support them structurally. Some vendors of archival supplies offer standard-sized storage boxes and sleeves for common ephemera such as postcards and stereo views. Some vendors can produce custom-sized enclosures in quantity to meet special needs.

*Unbound, Oversized Materials.* Maps, newspapers, architectural drawings, and other oversized objects create storage problems for any institution. They are unwieldy and, therefore, vulnerable to damage, especially if they are not mounted or backed. Oversized objects are best stored unrolled and flat in map-case drawers or in large, flat archival boxes.

Inside drawers or boxes, individual sheets need the additional protection of enclosures such as folders, polyester sleeves, or window mats. Folders are the most commonly used enclosure for archival collections, as they are lightweight and do not take up much space. Like storage boxes, folders should be chemically stable and made of lignin-free, alkaline-buffered stock. Certain objects such as blueprints are alkaline sensitive. For these, interleave with unbuffered tissue.

Folders should be cut to fit the size of the drawer or box, rather than the size of the item. This prevents damage to items when they slip out of folders in a drawer or box. Works of art with delicate surfaces, fragile sheets, and very large or thick objects should have individual folders. Other materials of similar size may share a folder. Significantly smaller objects should be housed separately so that they are not overlooked in a stack. Interleaving with chemically stable paper is recommended, especially if the objects are subject to abrasion. Acidic and otherwise chemically unstable materials should be interleaved to avoid contact staining and deterioration. The number of objects per folder should not exceed ten, and the number of folders per drawer or box should be such that all folders fit below the top of the drawer at their thickest point. As a general principle, do not overcrowd folders, drawers, or boxes. Each object must be stored so that it can be retrieved without damage.

Folders should be clearly labeled toward the front, with all contents listed, to eliminate disruptive and possibly damaging rummaging. They should be labeled in pencil or waterproof ink. Avoid self-adhesive labels, because their adhesives may stain and migrate into the folder and will weaken, causing the label to fall off.

Polyester sleeves may be used for fragile and heavily used oversized objects, but it is best to keep sleeved materials inside folders as well, because stacks of sleeves can be slippery to handle and often get very scratched. Items that have been conserved can be encapsulated, but untreated, acidic materials should not be encapsulated, or even put in sleeves, as it increases the speed of their degradation.

For objects larger than any drawers that are available, rolling is a common storage solution. Though not ideal, in some institutions it may be the only practical means of storing oversized materials. Rolling saves space and is satisfactory for materials that are flexible enough to withstand unrolling and rerolling. It is especially suitable for items that are seldom consulted. Related items, such as groups of architectural drawings, can be rolled together on a tube. Rolling very large objects is often a two-person job. Roll oversized materials around the outside of a lignin-free tube three to four inches in diameter at the very least. If a lignin-free tube is not available, use a regular tube and, before rolling any items on it, cover it with polyester film secured with double-sided tape completely underneath the polyester. The polyester should be larger than the paper object rolled onto the tube, and, to prevent crushing, the tube should extend beyond the sheets by at least two inches at each end.

Normally, objects are rolled front side in, with a single sheet of archival-quality interleaving paper covering the entire back (outer) side. Avoid using several smaller sheets because they can be dislocated, crumpled, and bunched during rolling. When rolled, the interleaving paper serves both as a barrier and as a cushion. Finally, the assembly should be wrapped in archival-quality paper, cotton muslin (washed and dried without fabric softener), or polyester film to protect against abrasion, dust, and pollutants. The outer wrapper may be secured with ties of undyed fabric tape or white polyester ribbon. Ties should be at least half an inch wide. For additional protection, store tubes wrapped with archival-quality materials inside larger-diameter tubes. Tubes should be stored horizontally, never vertically, as the rolled materials may slip down. Shelves should be deep enough so that the tubes do not extend into the aisles, where they may be bumped. Tubes can also be stored by inserting a pole through each and resting the ends of the pole on wall brackets.

Folding oversized items is not recommended. Some objects, such as newspapers, are designed to be folded once. Such sheets may remain that way but should not be folded a second time. If they have already been folded more than once, unfold them cautiously, as they may have become brittle and resist unfolding, and they may break in the process. If that is the case, they need the professional treatment of a conservator. Do not unfold oversized objects until you have figured out how to store them afterward.

*Scrapbooks.* Scrapbooks can be individually stored in custom-fitted boxes, especially those that are of special historic value in their original form. Many vendors sell boxes of this type at reasonable prices. When measuring scrapbooks for custom boxes, the most important thing to remember is to measure the maximum width and height and the thickest point in the binding. Scrapbooks that are very damaged and do not have value to the institution as an object in its original form can have their pages numbered, put into individual folders, and boxed to protect the contents and provide easier access.

*Encapsulation.* Encapsulation in Melinex, a clear, flexible, inert polyester film, is an attractive solution for materials, especially if they are fragile or frequently handled. The object is sandwiched between two sheets of film slightly larger than the object. The edges of the plastic are sealed either with ultrasonic welding equipment or with a heat welder. Polyester film provides excellent protection for objects when they are handled.

Encapsulation is not suitable for acidic objects, however, or for those with powdery or loosely bound media. Because polyester contains a static charge, friable media such as pastel, charcoal, soft pencil, and flaking paint can be easily dislodged by static electricity. Because most old, untreated papers are acidic to some extent, objects should be sent to a conservator for treatment to remove accumulated acid in the paper before encapsulation. Once encapsulated, an object can never be rolled, as the encapsulation will deform and the welds will break.

When deacidification is not possible, a sheet of buffered or MicroChamber paper placed behind the object in a polyester sleeve can be a good alternative. Polyester sleeves come in many sizes and are available from preservation suppliers.

## Handling

Careless or inattentive handling of documents and manuscripts can cause damage, resulting in the loss of information or in the need for expensive treatments before items can be used again. When working with documents in folders, work on a flat table and keep items in the folder to maintain order. If papers are brittle or difficult to separate, turn them using a page-turner, which can be a microspatula, a thin Teflon folder, or simply made of stiff paper—basically anything inert, nonabrasive, and thin to slip in between pages. When using documents and manuscripts, handle only blank areas of the page. After use, pages should be stacked neatly in their folders and the folders returned to their proper places in their box. When handling oversized materials, be sure to have adequate room for unrolling, handling, and viewing.

Unbound documents and manuscripts can be damaged during copying or scanning. Care should be taken when handling any brittle materials to prevent tears or loss. Page-turners should be available to help lift fragile paper, and the paper should not be allowed to slide under the frame of the platen. Multiple-page documents should never be sent through the form feed of a copier or scanner.

## WHAT STAFF NEED TO KNOW

Staff training for safe handling practices is important for ensuring that materials will be preserved during processing, and also when being used by the public.

## WHAT USERS NEED TO KNOW

Users should be instructed in the careful handling of unbound documents on paper in an initial orientation, and when they are using formats that require different handling practices.

*A Note on Wearing White Cotton Gloves.* In many institutions, users are required to wear white cotton gloves when handling paper-based materials. This practice has fallen out of favor because white gloves provide limited protection for collections and reduce tactile sensitivity, making it difficult to handle collections carefully, and ultimately they increase the chances of physical damage. Cotton gloves have many small hairs that can easily catch on brittle edges or worsen existing tears. Cotton is also very absorbent and thus easily soiled, picking up dirt, dust, and other materials that can be transferred to an item when it is handled. When gloves must be worn for the protection of the user or the collections (photographs, film, and metals), lint-free cotton or nitrile (in case of latex allergies) gloves should be worn.

Instead of wearing gloves, it is recommended that users be required to wash and dry their hands carefully before using collections and to rewash them whenever their hands begin to feel dirty. Hand washing is preferable to using alcohol-based hand-sanitizing gels, which may be effective in killing germs but do not remove dirt and leave behind lotions and oils that can damage collection materials.

## Disaster Response

Unless the collection is reduced to a pile of ash, there are few paper-based materials that cannot be salvaged. The ability to salvage depends on how important that collection is to your institution, and how much time and money you can invest in the salvage process. There are four options for the salvage of cultural heritage collections: dehumidification, air-drying, freezing, and vacuum freeze-drying. Select the technique that will minimize physical damage (cockling of paper, warping of covers, and distortion of the binding) and bleeding of soluble inks and colorants. Vacuum thermal drying is not recommended for collection materials that are to be retained for the long term. It is important to understand that no drying method restores collections to their predamaged condition. However, if stabilization and recovery are achieved quickly, paper-based materials can often be dried and returned to the shelves with little discernible damage.

*Air-drying* is the most common in-house method of dealing with small batches (fewer than one hundred items) of water-damaged materials. Depending upon how successfully wet materials are stabilized and dried, the average amount of additional shelf space required after drying is 20 percent. *Freezing* is a good option for stabilization of wet materials with bleeding inks and can be used for drying, but it takes a long time. *Vacuum freeze-drying* is the preferred method for large numbers of wet records and for materials with water-sensitive inks and coated paper. If materials have been frozen quickly after becoming wet, very little extra shelf or storage space (8 percent or less) will be required when they are dry.

## Decay

Paper is always deteriorating. We cannot completely stop its deterioration, but we can slow it down by following the recommendations in the "Environment and Storage" section above.

Paper is especially vulnerable to attack by pests and mold. Rodents, such as mice, rats, and squirrels, will damage paper and packaging materials, primarily by shredding it for bedding and nesting. Mold, like pests, will eat away at paper, and they become problematic when the temperature and RH remain high for an extended period of time.

Paper that is mostly cellulose will remain strong and flexible over time if stored and treated properly. Wood-pulp papers of the late 19th and 20th century are susceptible to yellowing and brittleness because of their lignin content. Paper is also susceptible to foxing when stored in high RH environments. Foxing usually occurs in machine-made paper of the late 18th and 19th centuries, and it is not completely understood. It is likely that its cause is fungal in nature. It will always be reddish-brown in color, will look like it is integral to the fibers of the paper, and will often appear in patchy locations on one page but not in the same patches on adjacent pages.

Many inks are susceptible to fading from light exposure and bleeding when they get wet. Adhesives cause acid migration and staining in paper, and they leave damaging residues.

## Treatments

Staff can be trained to perform in-house some basic procedures, including tear repair, humidification and flattening, surface cleaning, and removal of damaging fasteners. Any treatment required on anything very significant or valuable, or involving the removal of tape and other stains, should be left for a conservator to carry out. Sources for guidance about basic procedures that can be carried out in-house includes Balloffet and Hille's *Preservation and Conservation for Libraries and Archives*[4] and the websites of Indiana University Libraries (www.indiana.edu/~libpres/manual/mantoc.html) and Dartmouth College Library (www.dartmouth.edu/~library/preservation/repair).

# PAPER: WORKS OF ART ON PAPER (DONIA CONN)

*Dates in use*: approximately 100 BCE to the present.
*Formats*: prints, drawings, watercolors, pastels, posters, wallpapers.

## Material

### PAPER

Paper is formed from a pulp of cellulosic fibers derived directly from plant materials or pulped from rags. The cellulosic pulp is formed on a mold, pressed to encourage hydrogen bonding between fibers, and dried. Older handmade paper and modern hand- and machine-made rag paper is predominantly made from long, strong strands of cellulose derived primarily from cotton, flax, and hemp. Wood-pulp papers, such as those used for printing posters, contain lignin. The presence of lignin in paper shortens its overall life span, as it reacts with relative humidity and light to form acidic products, which then attack and shorten the cellulose fibers. In addition to cellulose, paper contains sizing, either internally or externally applied, to prevent inks from feathering (having a fuzzy or indistinct edge), and a multitude of other fillers to give it required characteristics for use. For further information about the characteristics of paper, refer to the more detailed discussion of paper in the section "Paper: Library and Archives Material" earlier in this chapter.

Blank sheets of paper are not common in collections of works of art, so it is also important to understand some of the other materials present, as they also have an impact on paper's longevity. Works of art on paper may contain inks, watercolors, pastel, charcoal, printing ink, oil paints, and adhesives.

### INKS

Ink is a colorant (pigment or dye) suspended in a vehicle. The earliest drawing inks were either carbon based or based on ground-earth pigments. Iron gall ink is found in manuscripts from as early as the first century BCE, and drawing inks were used from the Middle Ages onward. Carbon and ground-earth pigment inks tend to be stable, but iron gall ink is very unstable and can have deleterious effects on the paper substrate. More information about inks can be found in the section "Paper: Library and Archives Material" earlier in this chapter.

Printing ink is a complex medium, whose elements are combined to work in specific applications, whether that is on a printing press or in a modern ink jet printer. Printing ink is composed of colorants (pigments or dyes), a binder to hold it to the paper, a solvent carrier to give it viscosity, and additives to give it specific characteristics. Pigments and soluble dyes give ink its color. Pigments, which are insoluble, are either natural (usually mineral based) or synthetic. In general, pigment-based ink is more lightfast than dye-based inks. Dye-based inks saturate the paper more, giving deeper, richer colors, but it can be less lightfast than pigment-based inks.

### PASTELS, WATERCOLORS, CHARCOAL, GRAPHITE, AND OIL PAINTS

Pastels, watercolors, charcoal, graphite, and oil paints, like printing inks, consist of pigments or dyes for color, a binder, and a vehicle. Charcoal is a simple carbon powder mixed with a gum binder and compressed into a square stick. Charcoal needs to be fixed or it remains very friable. Pastels are a powdered pigment and a binder in stick form. Like charcoal, it needs to be fixed. Oil paints are composed of pigments in an oil-based vehicle that dries into a continuous film. Watercolors are finely powdered pigments in gum arabic applied with water. Of the watercolors, two in particular can be damaging to the paper substrate. Lead white, a warm white favored by artists, can darken to black. This is a relatively common result for artwork that has been stored in a location with high levels of sulfides in the air, which, in conjunction with the relative humidity, convert the white lead(II) carbonate to black lead(II) sulfide. Verdigris, a green pigment, is also fugitive and reacts with sulfides in the air. The sulfides degrade the basic copper acetate in verdigris, forming acetic acid that corrodes the paper or parchment substrate beneath.

## ADHESIVES

Adhesives are found in art collections in collage, Chine-collé prints, mounts, and wallpaper. The most stable and reversible adhesives are starch pastes and properly prepared gelatins. Problematic adhesives found in art collections include rubber cement, pressure sensitive tape, and irreversible synthetics. More information on adhesives can be found in the section "Paper: Library and Archives Material" earlier in this chapter.

## Purposes

Paper is the foundation for many works of art. Prints, drawings, watercolors, pastels, oil sketches, posters, and wallpaper are some of the most common examples.

## Dates in Use

Paper made from pulp was first developed in China. Archaeological remnants of paper made from hemp dating to the Han dynasty (estimated 100 BCE) have been excavated in Shannxi Province. For more information on the history of paper, refer to the section "Paper: Library and Archives Material" earlier in this chapter.

Paper quality varied in the handmade rag era, just as it does today. Many print and watercolor papers were made from the highest quality rags, and they remain strong and durable to this day. Sketch papers, conversely, were generally not as high in quality. With increased demand for paper came changes in processing and materials that had an impact on chemical stability. Details on some of these changes can be found in the section "Paper: Library and Archives Material" earlier in this chapter.

The development of wood-pulp papers was the principal response to the increased demand for paper. The high yield from wood pulp made it particularly appealing for many types of paper, as it brought the overall cost down. The pulp was not suitable, however, for fine art because of its high lignin content. Wood-pulp papers can be found in posters and wallpaper from approximately 1855 onward.

## Identification

Paper is the dispersion of cellulosic fibers that have been reduced to a pulp and formed into a sheet. Often, other materials in collections, such as papyrus, tapa, amatl, and pith paper, are incorrectly referred to as paper; they were not formed into a sheet from pulp but are strips of cellulosic fibers beaten into sheets. Parchment is the processed skin of animals (predominantly calf, sheep, or goat) and is not paper. All of these materials will be found in art collections, but only paper is noted in this section.

### ART ON PAPER

The most common works of art on paper found in collections are prints, drawings, and watercolors; less common are oil paintings on paper. Collages may be found in collections of more contemporary art and are similar to scrapbooks, noted in the section "Paper: Library and Archives Material" earlier in this chapter.

*Prints.* Three main processes were traditionally used to produce art prints: relief printing, intaglio printing, and lithography. Collections of more modern prints may also have prints created using photomechanical processes. Relief prints, including wood engravings, woodcuts, and linocuts, are created by inking the raised surfaces on the print block. Relief prints have a characteristic build-up of ink at the edges of the lines and, under magnification, the ink looks as if it is below the paper's surface. In intaglio printing only the recessed areas of the printing block hold the ink, requiring much greater pressure to force the paper into the channels containing the ink to form the image. Consequently, a press is always needed for intaglio printing, whereas relief printing can be done without a press. Intaglio prints can be identified, under magnification, by the raised ink on the paper surface and by a plate mark created by the pressure of the press. Intaglio includes the common processes of engraving and etching.

Woodcuts are commonly found in Western art between 1400 and 1600 CE and continue to be created today. Woodblocks were used to print text and images in East Asia from approximately 200 BCE, and they remained in common use for printing images until the 19th century in all parts of the world. Woodcuts are prepared on the plank side of the wood that runs parallel to the grain by removing the wood in spaces that are to be white on the finished image. Wood engravings, in common use from around 1800 to the 1950s, are cut perpendicular to the grain, rather than parallel, or on the end grain. If cut on the end grain, fine detail could be created and the blocks could sit type-high and be used in conjunction with moveable type. Linocuts, developed in 1905 and still used today, are similar to woodcuts but use linoleum rather than wood as the printing surface.

Engravings were in common use from 1450 CE through the mid-1800s and were made from metal plates, usually copper or steel. They are intaglio prints, so the ink is in the recesses of the plates rather than on the raised surface. Engraving allowed the artists to create their images directly on the plate, as if drawing. The process of etching was developed to create finer drawings and was in common use from the early 1500s through the mid-1800s. In etching, the artist uses a rounded needle to draw an image into the hard wax on a wax-coated metal plate, which then has acid poured onto it to etch the metal where the wax has been scratched off. The wax is then removed and the plate is inked, just as an engraving plate is inked.

Lithography, developed in 1796, uses a stone (lithographic limestone) or a metal plate with a smooth surface. The image is drawn on the stone with a grease or wax pencil and treated with acid. The stone is then wet and an oil-based ink applied, which is repelled by water and attracted to the grease or wax image. Chromolithography allowed for multicolor printing from 1837 on. Lithographs can be identified by their smooth, even tone, smooth edges, and ink that is level with the surface of the paper.

Photomechanical processes, such as offset printing and gravure, use a combination of photographic and lithographic processes to create an image. Offset images can be identified by the appearance of halftone dots, whereas gravure images can be identified by their grid pattern.

*Drawings.* Part of preserving drawings is understanding their composition. First, is the paper rag or wood pulp-based? Second, what type of drawing medium was used?

Ink drawings are usually composed of either black ink, wash, or brown ink with lead white highlights. Carbon black is the most common black ink found in drawings because it is lightfast and stable. It appears as deep, velvety black on the page, unless it has been diluted and used as a wash. Sometimes, inks that appear to be carbon black are actually blue-black dye inks. To know which it is, look under magnification at the edge of the ink. Carbon ink will be uniformly black, while the dye-based ink will show blue and black at the edge where it feathers into the paper.

Iron gall ink, bistre, and sepia are brown inks found in drawings, and it is often difficult to distinguish between them. Iron gall ink will tend to be brownish black and deteriorate as described in the section "Paper: Library and Archives Material" earlier in this chapter. Iron gall ink is the most common drawing ink. Bistre, in use from the 14th century, is an ink made from tarry chimney soot. Sepia is made from the ink sac of the cuttlefish and is the rarest of the three. All three brown inks are susceptible to fading from exposure to light.

Charcoal, chalk, and pastel drawings, produced for hundreds of years, are some of the most identifiable, but most fragile, of the artwork in collections. These friable drawing media are susceptible to abrasion, smudging, and flaking off the substrate. Storage of these drawings requires special care.

Graphite is a more recent addition to artists' options for drawing media, having been used since 1794 when bonded graphite was cased in a wooden cylinder. Graphite pencil drawings can be distinguished from charcoal by the slight metallic sheen caused by the alignment of the carbon particles. Heavy applications of graphite and softer compositions can be as fragile and easily smudged as charcoal, chalk, or pastels.

*Watercolors.* Watercolor paintings, being the foundation for cave paintings and manuscript illumination, have a long history. Watercolors are a finely ground pigment that is applied to the paper with water; they include a binder such as gum arabic. Watercolor as an artistic medium is generally considered to have been first used in the European Renaissance, in the work of Albrecht Dürer. Collections of works of art on paper will often contain watercolors and members of the watercolor family: gouache and tempera paintings. Watercolors, as we think of them now, can be identified by the thin, transparent wash that creates the image. Gouache looks like an opaque watercolor because of the white pigment added to give it extra body. Gouache will sit on the surface of the paper creating a matt surface, while watercolors are absorbed into the paper. Tempera, like gouache and watercolors, is a pigment in a water-soluble binder, often egg yolk. Tempera fell out of favor in the late Renaissance, when it was superseded by oil paints, but it regained popularity among 20th-century American artists.

It is often difficult to identify the difference between color prints and black-and-white prints that have been hand colored. Printed colors will be even on the surface of the paper and may not always be evenly registered. Hand-colored prints usually use watercolors or gouache, and the watercolor washes will appear transparent and show uneven pooling of color, especially at the edges.

*Oil and Acrylic Paintings on Paper.* Some works of art on paper may be found to have been painted with either oil or acrylic paints. Oil paint on paper can be identified by the way it sits on the surface of the paper, its matt appearance, and the potential for haloing around the paints caused by the incompatibility of the oil and the paper. Acrylic paints also sit on the surface of the paper, but they look more glossy because of the acrylic emulsion the pigments are suspended in.

*Collages.* Collage is an art form in which different materials are assembled and adhered to paper, board, canvas, or wood. A collage can include newspaper clippings, photographs, colored paper, ribbon, text, found objects, and just about anything else. Although the concept of collage can be traced back hundreds of years, the art form came into its own in the 20th century. Collages can be difficult to preserve because of the ephemeral nature of materials used and the frequently unstable nature of adhesives used, such as rubber cement. Collage pieces are similar to scrapbooks whose preservation is noted in the section "Paper: Library and Archives Material" earlier in this chapter.

*Posters.* The history of posters dates from the 18th century when printed broadsides were used to distribute information about community events, theatre productions, and advertising. Their history as an art form, however, begins in the 1870s when the process of chromolithography was developed to the extent that mass production of posters became possible. In the 1890s, established artists such as Henri de Toulouse-Lautrec, Alphonse Mucha, and Aubrey Beardsley used the poster in their artistic expression. America turned to the art poster for advertising after 1900, and the art form appealed to popular artists of the time. The poster, while always a popular means of advertising, became a very popular vehicle during the two World Wars for propaganda and political expression.

Most posters were not produced with a view to long-term storage in collections of art works. Consequently, most are printed on low-quality wood-pulp paper. Many posters were displayed in the open air and show evidence of water damage, mold, light, and pests. Many posters were distributed in folded form. If they have been stored folded, the folds will have become weak points in the paper where it will tear readily. Because of their size, posters are difficult to house and are often stored inappropriately, which results in damage.

*Wallpaper.* Wallpaper has a long history, beginning as simple, colored woodblock prints for religious devotion and to cover cracks in walls as well as large decorative pieces to hang on the walls as less expensive alternatives to tapestries in the 15th century. Repeating print papers have been dated to as early as the first decade of the 16th century in England and the 17th century in France. The 18th century was a period of rapid expansion in block-printed wallpapers throughout Europe, culminating in the development of the landscape or panoramic papers of the late 18th and early 19th centuries. The printing of wallpaper was mechanized in the 19th century, and little has changed in its production since then, apart from style and the use of vinyl-coated papers from the second half of the 20th century.

Until the 1830s, wallpaper was most commonly printed on several single sheets of paper from blocks and lined with canvas to create longer, repeating patterns. The images were created with blocks or stencils, or painted on with distemper, a type of tempera paint. Larger rolls of paper became more common after this time with the assistance of papermaking machines introduced at the turn of the century. These rolls were not generally lined with canvas but were filled with clay and sized with resin or flue. Rolls of filled and sized paper, and the introduction of cylinder printing machines, led to the use of faster drying printing inks, rather than distemper. Prior to the mid-1850s, the paper would have been rag-based and either hand or machine made. After this time, the paper would have been predominantly wood-pulp.

## Representation in Collections

Paper is the foundation for a large number of collection materials in many art collections, as well as in special collections in libraries. Depending on the type of institution and its collections, the focus could be on art (drawings, etchings, engravings, watercolors), ephemera (posters, wallpaper samples), or a variety of printed greeting, trade, or playing cards.

## Environment and Storage

### PREFERRED ENVIRONMENT

Managing the environment is one of the best ways to protect and preserve collections of works of art. For collections with a wide variety of materials and media, a single setting for temperature and relative humidity (RH) will not be safe or sufficient; different materials require different environments. Each institution must understand the varied needs of its collections.

For collections of works of art on paper, the preferred temperature for storage, exhibition, and research areas is below 75°F (24°C), ideally between 68 to 70°F (20 to 21°C) for the comfort of people and for the care of collections. In dedicated storage areas, the temperature can be lowered to 55 to 60°F (13 to 16°C). As a rule of thumb, for every increase of 10°C (18°F), the rate of deterioration doubles; if temperatures are lowered, the rate decreases proportionately. Regardless of the temperature settings, the relative humidity (RH) needs to be kept between 30 to 50 percent. For works of art on paper, it is important to minimize rapid changes in temperature or relative humidity to reduce the expansion and contraction of the paper substrate, which may have adverse effects on friable media such as pastels and charcoal or inflexible media such as oil or acrylic paints. For these reasons and others, spaces like attics, basements, and uncontrolled outbuildings should be avoided as storage spaces for works of art on paper.

RH levels that are too high can cause paper to cockle, activate iron gall ink corrosion, and encourage mold growth, while levels that are too low cause a loss of flexibility. High RH can also attract pests detrimental to collections.

Problems with temperature and relative humidity can be monitored and avoided by using thermohygrometers, data loggers, and alarms to give some warning of any rises in temperature or relative humidity to problematic levels.

Current research into environmentally sustainable conditions for storage environments is resulting in less rigid approaches to the ideal temperature and RH levels, as noted in chapter 5. Additional sources of information are listed in the "Further Readings" section of this chapter.

In addition to temperature and RH, light needs to be managed. The intensity and amount of light to which objects are exposed should be controlled. When works of art on paper are on exhibit, a maximum light level of 50 lux is recommended for very sensitive materials like watercolors and up to a maximum of 150 lux for less sensitive materials such as black-and-white prints. Ultraviolet (UV) radiation from windows, skylights, and lighting fixtures needs to be filtered, and objects should be protected from exposure to sunlight by closing curtains, blinds, or shutters. Light levels can be monitored with a UV meter, light meter, or Blue Wool Standard cards. More information can be found in the section "Paper: Library and Archives Material" earlier in this chapter.

Air quality also needs to be managed. Dust, volatile organic compounds (VOCs), and pollution affect the air quality and the rate of deterioration of collections, and it can be a direct cause of many types of damage. Airborne pollutants such as sulfur dioxide and nitrous oxides, by-products of burning fossil fuels, and ozone ($O_3$), a by-product of electrical equipment, are strong catalysts of chemical deterioration. These airborne pollutants, in conjunction with RH, react with chemicals in the paper, producing sulfuric acid and nitric acid and leading to embrittlement and discoloration. VOCs are produced by the gases given off by storage units, display cases, and framing materials made from woods, as well as paints, gaskets, adhesives, carpet, vinyl flooring, PVC and other plastics, and other materials. Careful selection of materials can reduce the production of VOCs, but when less-than-ideal materials must be used, allow sufficient time between their installation and their use for them to give off gases. More information can be found in the section "Paper: Library and Archives Material" earlier in this chapter.

## RECOMMENDATIONS FOR STORAGE

The method used for storing works of art will depend on their size as well as the media used in their creation. Works of art can be stored in a variety of methods, from framing or matting to folders and portfolios. Mats, folders, boxes, and other storage materials will be used most efficiently if a set of standard sizes is settled upon. Having four or five standard sizes will ensure safer storage of materials, more efficient preparation for exhibiting and more efficient processing, and cost savings from bulk purchasing of a few selected sizes.

Works of art are most commonly stored in mats. The matting package consists of a backing board and window mat, both made of chemically stable, museum-quality ragboard, with an interleaving sheet between the artwork and the window mat for an added layer of protection. This package allows the artwork to be handled safely, displayed aesthetically, easily framed for exhibit, and protected during storage.

Interleaving sheets should be acid-free, and preferably lignin-free and unbuffered, as some artwork is sensitive to buffering agents. The most suitable interleaving paper is acid-free glassine because of its smooth surface and translucency. Other papers that work well are Japanese tissues made from *gampi*, and any acid-free, lignin-free Western paper, although Western paper is not translucent, requiring the mat to be opened to see the image. Lighter-weight, clear polyester film can be used, but it is not preferred and should never be used with any friable or damaged media. Interleaving sheets that are acid-free will become acidic over time and should be replaced when they begin to show signs of deterioration. Remember that acid-free materials that are not also lignin-free and buffered will deteriorate more quickly if they are protecting an already acidic print rather than a chemically stable one.

Stable works of art that are not intended for exhibit can be stored in sturdy folders of acid-free, lignin-free, and buffered materials. These folders can also be used in small institutions that do not have the funds for matting. Items sensitive to buffers should be interleaved with acid-free glassine. Works that are on board or are particularly heavy and difficult to mat can be stored in four-flap portfolios that provide safe coverage of the entire item.

Folders and matted items can be stored in drop-front gallery boxes, Solander cases, and flat file cases. Boxes, like folders, should be acid-free, lignin-free, and buffered. Flat file cases should be made of powder-coated steel. Wooden flat files should not be used because of VOCs in wood that give off gas.

Framing works of art on paper is a safe option, especially for fragile works with friable media such as pastels and charcoals. Sound conservation framing techniques should be used, including window mats with museum-quality ragboard, chemically stable backing board, glazing (glass, not acrylic) to block UV, gasketed rabbets, and sealed backs.

Window mats are very important for works of art because they keep the artwork from direct contact with the glass, which can lead to mold growth. Framing fragile works will protect them from handling and from many environmental factors.

Framed works should be stored in vertical bins of different sizes to accommodate different-sized frames. The bottoms of the bins should be padded with carpet, Etha-foam, or Volara. Bins should be large enough to hold only four or five frames, so that disruption is minimized when accessing any one of those framed items. Frames should have spacers of cardboard or foam board larger than the frames to prevent damage. Framed items can also be hung on frame storage systems that are either stationary or on rails. Do not hang pastels, charcoals, or chalk drawings on storage frames that move, as the vibrations can damage the image. Framed items may be kicked or damaged by water if they are stored on the floor.

## Handling

Careless or inattentive handling and exhibition of works of art on paper can cause damage, resulting in the loss or shift in colors and requiring expensive treatments to restore the work. Most damage from handling occurs in the routine movement and study of the works. Training of staff and researchers is critical in minimizing damage.

### WHAT STAFF NEED TO KNOW

When moving works of art, always use some sort of support. For boxed, matted, or framed items, the support itself is sufficient. For items in folders or loose items, use a rigid support of corrugated cardboard or Coroplast that is larger than the item. If using a cart, ensure the box or item can sit flat and is supported on the cart. If not using a cart, use a rigid support. For framed items, a cart divided into bins similar to those used for storage is helpful. Any doors along the route must be wide enough for the materials being moved and must be propped open to prevent any accidental damage to the items as they pass through the doors.

### WHAT USERS NEED TO KNOW

Users must, first and foremost, be trained to handle items with clean, dry hands. Dirt and grime on hands will be transferred to the artwork or to the mat, disfiguring the item visually as well as leaving grit that could cause abrasion. For more information see "A Note on Wearing White Cotton Gloves" in the section "Paper: Library and Archives Material" earlier in this chapter. Handling of the actual artwork should be kept to a minimum. If it needs to be handled, it must be handled only at the edges, using supports, such as the mat or a folder, to turn the item over if the back must be viewed. Staff should always be on hand to assist researchers if they need to handle the actual work of art.

Researchers should be asked to register when using collections, and they should be trained in using the collections. Bags and coats should not be allowed near the works of art, and only pencils should be used for note taking. Clean, uncluttered work surfaces should be available for anyone handing and studying works, especially if they are not mounted and matted.

## Disaster Response

Few paper-based items cannot be salvaged after a disaster. The importance of a collection to your institution, and how much time and money you can invest in the salvage process, determine whether salvage is carried out. There are three options for the salvage of works of art on paper: air-drying, freezing, and vacuum freeze-drying. It is important to understand that no drying method restores artwork to its predamaged condition. However, if stabilization and recovery are achieved quickly, works of art on paper can often be dried and conserved at less cost than if they are left wet for long enough for colors to run, mold to grow, or to dry with tidelines.

Air-drying is the most common in-house method of dealing with small batches of damaged prints. The artwork should be removed carefully from the mat and dried image side up. Freezing is a good option for the stabilization of wet materials with bleeding inks or colors. Vacuum freeze-drying is the preferred method for large numbers of wet works and for materials with water-sensitive inks, as the whole item, including mats and interleaving, can be dried this way, minimizing the manipulation of wet, fragile artworks. Framed items should be removed from their frame prior to any attempt to dry them. If the image has adhered to the glass, leave it in the frame, dry glass side down, and seek the assistance of a conservator.

## Decay

Paper is always deteriorating. We cannot completely stop its deterioration, but we can slow it down by following the recommendations in the "Environment and Storage" section above.

Paper that is mostly cellulose will remain strong and flexible over time if stored and treated properly. Wood-pulp papers of the late 19th and 20th centuries are susceptible to yellowing and brittleness because of their lignin content. Paper is also susceptible to foxing when stored in high RH environments. Foxing usually occurs in machine-made paper of the late 18th and 19th centuries, and it is not completely understood. It is likely that its cause is fungal in nature. It will always be reddish-brown in color, will look like it is integral to the fibers of the paper, and will often appear in patchy locations on one page but not in the same patches on adjacent pages.

Paper can be discolored by substances other than lignin and foxing. Old adhesives, such as rubber cement, pressure-sensitive tape, and overcooked animal hide glue, as well as poor-quality framing materials, can also cause paper to discolor. Mat burn is the most common type of discoloration from poor framing materials, but dropped-out knotholes from wood-backed frames are also common.

Many inks and colored papers are susceptible to fading or darkening from exposure to light. To ensure the safety of the works, exposure to light should be kept to a minimum. Artwork should be stored in the dark, and when on exhibit, glazing with UV block should be used, with light levels kept below 150 lux and below 50 lux for watercolors and other light-sensitive materials.

Paper is vulnerable to attack by mold, especially works framed under glass with no mat. Mold will eat away at paper, especially if the temperature and RH remain high for an extended period of time. Paper is also susceptible to attack from rodents and pests, which can get into storage containers and frames and cause considerable damage to works of art.

Works of art on paper can become cockled from exposure to high RH, water incidents, and the misapplication of labels. Some cockling of paper occurs in the creation of prints, so before flattening a print, seek the advice of a conservator to prevent any damage to the original state of the work.

## Treatments

Some basic procedures that staff can be trained to perform in-house are tear repair and surface cleaning of prints. However, for works of art, extreme caution should be taken before in-house treatments on any collection item are started. Any treatment that requires the removal of tape or other stains, or has the potential to alter the image in any way, such as surface cleaning of anything other than prints or humidification of watercolors and ink drawings, should be left to a conservator.

# BOOKS (DAWN WALUS)

*Dates in use*: approximately the fourth millennium BCE to the present.
*Formats:* unique and mass-produced books mostly comprised of paper and parchment, proto-books, e-books.

## Material

A book is typically defined as a written or printed work consisting of pages glued or sewn together along one side and bound in covers. This definition is expanded here to include any portable, handheld device used for the transmission and storage of information, such as clay or wax tablets, rolls and scrolls, and e-books (electronic books). Books have undergone four transformations: from clay and wax tablets to rolls and scrolls, which evolved into the codex and then into e-books. The transformations were not abrupt but overlapped over decades or centuries. While clay and wooden tablets, scrolls, and rolls have fallen out of fashion, the codex and the e-book are currently in use.

## Purposes

Since its inception, the book has been used for the transmission and storage of textual and pictorial information. While most books are either for reference, entertainment, and pleasure, some are constructed merely for decorative purposes. Images, fine bindings, and artists' books, because of their content or because of the materials they are constructed from, or both, offer the book as decorative art. Fine bindings are often constructed from high-quality papers, sometimes handmade, and they are covered with beautiful materials, such as fine leather, and elaborately decorated with inlays and gold tooling. While some artists' books have stuck to the codex format, others present the book format in new and unusual ways, using myriad materials to create sculptural works of art, which reaches far beyond the idea of the bound codex.

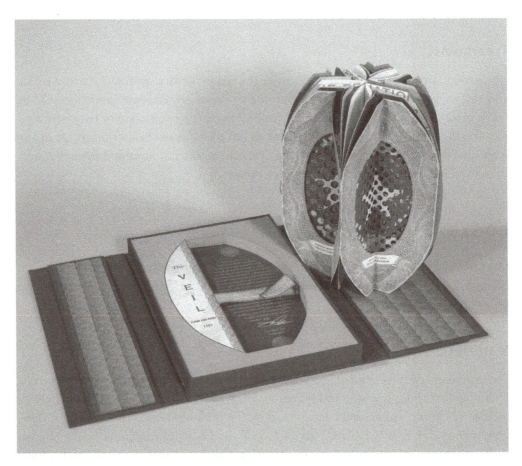

**FIGURE 8.3.** Artist's Book: Julie Chen, *The Veil* (Berkeley, CA: Flying Fish Press, 2002). Courtesy of the Boston Athenaeum

## Dates in Use

The earliest books (proto-books) can be traced as far back as the fourth millennium BCE when they took the form of clay or wax tablets. Some papyrus rolls and scrolls still in existence date from before the fourth century BCE, and there is evidence that papyrus was first manufactured in Egypt in the fourth millennium BCE. Writing on prepared animal skins such as parchment has a long history, David Diringer noting that "the first mention of Egyptian documents written on leather goes back to the 4th Dynasty c. 2550–2450 BC."[5] The most significant transformation has been from rolls and scrolls to codex, which began as early as the second century BCE. The codex remains the most common and recognizable form of the book to this day. Two factors led to the eventual replacement of parchment as text block material: the advent of printing with moveable type in 1450 CE, and the affordability and availability of paper. The e-book is the most recent form of the book, making its debut on the cusp of the 21st century.

## Identification

### CLAY AND WAX TABLETS

Clay tablets are considered the earliest form of the book, and they may be bound or unbound. Clay and wood are familiar materials and easy to identify, although identification of specific woods may be difficult without physical or microscopic examination. When wet, clay was inscribed with a tool, such as a reed. If what was inscribed on the clay tablet was to be kept it was either dried in the sun or fired in a kiln; if it was intended for reuse, it was left unbaked. Wax tablets were made by hollowing out wooden boards and filling the depression with wax. Once the wax was dry, information could be inscribed with a stylus. If the tablet was to be reused, the wax could be softened by heat and the inscription erased.

### ROLLS AND SCROLLS

The first rolls and scrolls were constructed from papyrus. Papyrus is made by cutting the pith of the papyrus plant into strips that are layered and pounded into flat sheets. The structure of papyrus sheets can be clearly seen when they are examined on a light table. (Papyrus is also noted in the section "Paper: Library and Archives Materials" earlier in this chapter.) Later, other materials such as parchment, bark, leather, and metal were used.

Parchment, vellum, and leather are made from animal hides, typically the skins of calves, sheep, and goats. The term *vellum* applies to calfskin only and is a high-quality material. The words *parchment* and *vellum* are often used interchangeably, with *parchment* commonly preferred. Parchment is made by soaking the skin in water and removing its hairs in a lime bath. The skin is washed again in water and then stretched and dried. (Parchment is also noted in the section "Paper: Library and Archives Materials" earlier in this chapter.) Leather is also made from animal hides and is produced through similar steps as parchment, but tannins are used instead of lime and the skins are not stretched to dry. Alum-tawed skin is similar in its manufacture to leather, but it uses aluminum salts instead of lime or tannins. Although there are many methods of tanning, vegetable-tanned and alum-tawed leathers are most often used in bookbinding. Vegetable tanning is an acidic process, and alum-tawing is an alkaline process that produces a more stable material. Under magnification, parchment and leather, both tanned and alum-tawed, can be identified by their hair follicle patterns. Generally, textual and pictorial information was inscribed on rolls and scrolls in ink or paint.

## THE CODEX

The book you are now holding is a codex in its most familiar form. Although the materials have changed over time, the codex remains a collection of single or folded sheets of papyrus, paper, parchment, wood, or other material secured at one edge. The collection of folded or single sheets is called the text block. It can be sewn, adhered, or held together with metal rings or leather ties, to name only some of the methods used. The collection of sheets may be bound in boards made from wood, laminated paper, or other material. The boards are most often covered in paper, leather, parchment, or textile. The pages may be printed upon or inscribed with various media, such as inks, paints, and graphite.

A codex comprises a text block and a binding, and so it is usually a composite of materials. As demand for paper and books increased and technologies in papermaking and bookbinding developed, especially following the advent of printing with moveable type around 1450, the structure of the codex was modified. Today, the codex is conventionally associated with early handwritten books, but the word can also be used to describe any bound book, inscribed or printed.

The text block is the core of the codex and can be made from a variety of materials. Before the invention of paper, it was often made of papyrus or parchment. Paper eventually became the most popular text block material. (For more information about the history of paper and its manufacture, see the section "Paper: Library and Archives Materials" earlier in this chapter.) The text block is constructed either by folding large sheets of paper, parchment or other material, or by stacking single sheets. When sheets are folded, they are folded to standard-size formats. The sections or single sheets are then sewn, adhered, or secured together in some fashion, either by hand or by machine.

The binding refers to the boards, covering material, and the board attachment. Common covering materials were tanned leather, alum-tawed skin, parchment, textile, and paper. Up until the early 18th century the covers were laced into the boards: that is, the boards were attached to the text block by lacing the support cords into the board. In the early part of the 18th century some papermaking and bookbinding processes became mechanized, and the text block was sewn and the boards were covered separately, and then the text block was cased into the boards. Merrill-Oldham and Parisi offer specifics on library bindings standards for circulating materials in their *Guide to*

*ANSI/NISO/LBI Library Binding Standard*,[6] which also provides illustrations of some book structures and binding techniques commonly applied to bound materials likely to be found in libraries.

Textiles are used for spine linings, hinging material, headbands, sewing, and cover material. The most common materials used are cotton, linen, and silk. Historically, silk is a common material for forming headbands and linen for sewing thread.

Other materials used in bookbinding are adhesives and media. The most common adhesives used in books are hide glue, wheat-starch paste, gelatin, isinglass, and modern polymer adhesives such as polyvinyl acetate (PVA). All except PVA are soluble in water. To determine whether an adhesive is water soluble, lightly dampen a small area with deionized water, then touch the area with your finger. If the adhesive is water soluble, the area will be sticky.

The media are the materials used to inscribe or print information, and they are water-based or oil-based. Traditional water-based inks were made by combining a carbon-based material, such as soot or lamp black, with water. Iron gall ink is a brown-black ink, made from iron salts and the tannic acids of tree galls, and it was in use from the 5th century until the 20th century CE. More modern inks contain pigments and/or dyes and can be combined with various solvents. Printing inks and paints are most often oil-based, although water-based inks are used. Both water- and oil-based paints are used for decorative and pictorial elements of books. Identification of specific paints requires microscopic analysis, which requires taking a sample and/or examination under ultra-violet radiation. (The section "Paper: Library and Archives Materials" earlier in this chapter provides more information about inks.)

## E-BOOKS

An e-book as an electronic version of a printed book that is read on a computer or on a handheld device. The texts can be a digital surrogate of a previously written book, or they may be first released in a digital format (born digital). The display device may be a computer, electronic reader (e-reader), tablet, mobile phone, or smartphone. Each of these devices is capable of holding a large quantity of e-books in the form of digital objects. The ephemeral nature of digital media makes it difficult to draw parallels between analog and digital formats, since digital information is essentially bits and bytes of data routed by the application of software programs through a device.

## Representation in Collections

Books are most often found in libraries and archives, but they may also be well represented in the collections of museums and historic houses. The type of institution will dictate the variety of formats held. A research library collection may have scrolls and codices but not clay tablets, whereas a museum may include many different formats, and a public library may only have codices and e-books. In addition, many libraries and archives are creating digital surrogates of written and printed materials that are becoming parts of collections.

## Environment and Storage

### PREFERRED ENVIRONMENT

Because books are composite objects made from a wide range of materials, there is a need for compromise in responding to the competing risks and benefits of different mechanisms of deterioration. The most important factors to control are sudden fluctuations in temperature and relative humidity (RH) and dew point (the point at which water in the air condenses).

The environment can be controlled using a heating, ventilation, and air-conditioning (HVAC) system and should be monitored over time with a data logger. If an HVAC system is too expensive for the institution, the environment can be controlled with a dehumidifier, air conditioning, and very careful monitoring with a data logger. Fluctuating RH is particularly harmful to sensitive items and can cause dimensional changes such as cracking, warping, and distortion. Environmental specifications should be in the form of targets and ranges. Ideally, 70°F (21°C) (±2°F [1°C]) and 50 percent (±5%) RH are good targets for objects and human comfort. In dedicated storage areas, the temperature can be lower. The RH should remain below 60 percent to prevent mechanical damage and to create an environment that is inhospitable to mold growth and pests. Good housekeeping, such as dusting, aids in preventing the germination of mold spores and pest nesting.

### RECOMMENDATIONS FOR STORAGE

Materials should be stored on metal shelving. Wooden shelves are not recommended because they may contain acidic lignin. Books on shelves should not extend past the shelf edge. This is especially important in compact shelving, where books that extend past the shelf may be damaged when the shelving unit is moved. Use bookends if shelves are not full. If bookends are not available, books placed on their sides can be used as bookends. Loose items should be tied up or placed in acid-free boxes if resources prohibit repair, rebinding, or purchasing a new copy. Special collection materials should be in secure storage with limited access. If items are in a display case, the interior environment must be monitored to avoid the possibility of creating an adverse microclimate.

## Handling

The book is a functional object and, for it to work properly, it needs to be handled in ways that prevent damage. Handling recommendations are essential for special collection material, and they are more easily enforced because patrons in the reading rooms of special collections can be monitored. Ideally, handling recommendations would also be applied to circulating material, especially given the ephemeral nature of some modern books.

## WHAT STAFF NEED TO KNOW

Staff needs to be trained in the safe storage, use, retrieval, and transport of material within the institution. Books should never be removed from the shelf by pulling at the head-caps of bindings. Instead, adjacent books should be pushed back so that the spine of the volume being removed from the shelf can be firmly grasped. Ideally, the safest transport for books is on a cart or book truck. If this is not possible, no more books should be carried than can be comfortably transported while safely navigating through the collection shelves and beyond. Whenever possible, a large book should be transported on a cart or book truck. If a cart or book truck is not available, the volume should be carried under the arm or in front with two hands.

## WHAT USERS NEED TO KNOW

If staff handles books with care, users are likely to follow their lead. First, hands should be clean. The wearing of white gloves should be discouraged as it often leads to the neglect of cleanliness. Although gloves are often thought to protect material handled, they actually place a bulky barrier between the hand and the book, which has the potential to damage the book. Every institution should provide clean areas for book viewing. The consumption of foods and beverages must be limited to specific areas of the library. Food and beverages must be prohibited in the reading rooms of special collections.

A book should never be opened flat. Book cradles or similar devices should be used to support the book and minimize damage to the spine. Often, the best way to handle a fragile book is to cradle it gently in one hand, supporting the spine, and to turn the pages with the other hand. Information about specific limitations of a particular book, such as fragile paper or joints and binding material, should be identified by staff and conveyed to users. Books should never be photocopied because this compromises book structure and limits further handling. When available, overhead copiers or copiers designed for books should be used. Digital imaging is a reliable and safer method of reproduction that can replace photocopying.

Metal paper clips, rubber bands, dog-earring, and marking pages must be prohibited. Staff should provide users with bookmarks made of acid-free paper.

## Disaster Response

This section assumes that the institution has a disaster or emergency plan, and it describes the recovery of book formats. Incidents involving water are a common occurrence in institutions, and items need to be controlled within twenty-four to forty-eight hours to stop or mitigate mold germination.

A small incident can be handled in house. Remove items from shelves to book trucks and transport them to a secure, safe area. Line tables, the floor, and other flat surfaces with plastic sheeting and paper towels, newsprint, or other absorbent material, such as Tek Wipe (an absorbent, fast-drying, reusable hydrospun polyester/cotton blend that can be purchased in rolls or sheets). This absorbent material is also used as interleaving material. Separate very wet items from slightly wet ones. Slightly wet items can be interleaved with absorbent materials and air-dried. Insert material every twenty pages and support the book to maximize drying. If the book was wet from above, stand it on its head, use absorbent material to remove excess water, and dry with fans, while simultaneously running a dehumidifier. Books that are thoroughly soaked, on coated paper, or contain leather or parchment should be frozen. To deal with larger incidents it will be necessary to contact a vendor who specializes in disaster recovery; up-to-date vendor information should be included in any disaster plan.

Water-damaged e-book reading devices should be completely dried out and then rebooted. If the reading or storage device is a computer, the hard drive can be extracted and installed on another computer. If this is not possible, the hard drive can be sent to a data recovery company. In the case of e-book readers, tablets, mobile phones, and smartphones, the manufacturer may need to be contacted for advice, or the device taken to a repair location.

## Decay

A properly controlled environment can slow down decay. For items that have been exposed to mechanisms of decay prior to accession or have survived years of neglect, the damage is done, but cultural heritage professionals can help in slowing down deterioration. Books are, most often, composite objects, and managing mechanisms of decay can be complicated as some materials can have a deleterious effect on others. The mechanisms of decay are threefold: chemical, biological, and mechanical.

### CHEMICAL CAUSES

As James Reilly notes, "Room temperature is too warm for safe storage of organic objects that are vulnerable to rapid chemical change."[7] Chemical reactions occur slowly, but fluctuations in temperature and humidity will accelerate reactions and lead to faster decay. High RH can accelerate metal corrosion; for example, iron gall ink, if not properly prepared, can oxidize in high RH and become unstable. Acids and lignin in ground wood-pulp paper deteriorate and embrittle paper if humidity and temperature levels are high. Lignin content in papyrus, wood, and some paper causes darkening when exposed to light. Heavily oil-laden formulations of printing ink can stain and deteriorate paper. Bleaches and sizing in rag paper and wood-pulp paper can also accelerate deterioration. Textiles, especially silk, are affected by light. PVA may give off acetic acid gas. Over time, hide glue can become brittle, and gelatin can cause discoloration. Plant-based adhesives, such as wheat-starch paste, and methyl cellulose seem to be stable adhesives, although further testing is required. Leather, especially vegetable-tanned leather, is susceptible to atmospheric pollutants, acid degradation, and is not stable in water.

## BIOLOGICAL CAUSES

Mold spores will germinate if the RH is above 60 percent and the temperature above 68°F (20°C). The optimum temperature for mold growth is 86°F (30°C). Pests are attracted to food, other pests, and warm, moist conditions. Keeping RH below 60 percent and summer dew points low will create an inhospitable environment for mold spores and pests.

## MECHANICAL CAUSES

Low and high RH can cause mechanical damage of hygroscopic materials. RH should not go below 20 percent or above 70 percent. Parchment, wood, vegetable-tanned leather, and textiles can become dimensionally unstable in conditions that are too moist and too dry. Books containing parchment need to be constrained either in bindings or in boxes.

E-books in the form of electronic media have unique issues. E-book reading devices can be dropped and made unusable, and digital files can be lost with the push of a button. Preserving digital files is noted in the section "Digital Files" in chapter 12.

## Treatments

Current treatment methodologies focus on stewardship, stabilization, and housing, as opposed to invasive, complex, single-item treatments. Single-item treatments are normally reserved for materials in special collections, and they aim to slow down decay, stabilize items for use, and maintain as much original material as possible. Financial constraints, curatorial discretion, and digitization projects will often dictate treatment.

The codex is the predominant format of the book in most collections. Book conservators are trained to address deterioration of these complex, composite objects. A book conservator can determine which treatments require specialist skills and which can be carried out by staff in-house. For example, the housing of clay and wooden tablets can be done in-house, but if more complex treatment is required, an objects conservator should be consulted. The abilities of in-house staff may vary and must be taken into consideration when delegating tasks. Enclosures, tying up unstable books, and minor tear repair are among the treatments that can be performed by staff in-house, with appropriate instruction and supervision.

Electronic devices will most likely need to be sent out for treatment. However, an in-house computer specialist can perform some treatments.

## Recommendations for Digitization

For digitization projects involving books of special significance, value, or fragility, a conservator should be consulted. The conservator can assess the stability of objects and make recommendations for handling during the imaging process, such as determining the angle of openings for a book. The conservator can also assist imaging staff in the handling of materials. Glass and Plexiglas give off static electric charges that may disturb fragile media, such as pastel, and should never be in direct contact with them; these materials should be imaged on a copy stand.


# STANDARDS AND FURTHER READING

## Standards

ANSI/NISO Z39.48-1992 (R2009). *Permanence of Paper for Publications and Documents in Libraries and Archives*. Bethesda, MD: NISO Press, 2010.
ANSI/NISO Z39.78-2000 (R2010). *Library Binding*. Bethesda, MD: NISO Press, 2011.

## Further Reading

American Institute for Conservation of Historic and Artistic Works (www.conservation-us.org).

Baker, Cathleen A. *From the Hand to the Machine: Nineteenth-Century American Paper and Mediums: Technologies, Materials, and Conservation*. Ann Arbor, MI: Legacy Press, 2010.

Baker, Cathleen A., and Randy Silverman. "Misperceptions about White Gloves." *International Preservation News* 37 (2005): 4–9. Accessed July 8, 2013. http://archive.ifla.org/VI/4/news/ipnn37.pdf.

Balloffet, Nelly, and Jenny Hille. *Preservation and Conservation for Libraries and Archives*. Chicago: American Library Association, 2004.

Benson, Richard. *The Printed Picture*. New York: Museum of Modern Art, 2008.

Forde, Helen, and Jonathan Rhys-Lewis. *Preserving Archives*. 2nd ed. London: Facet, 2013.

Gallo, Max. *The Poster in History*. New York: American Heritage Publishing Company, 1974.

Gascoigne, Bamber. *How to Identify Prints: A Complete Guide to Manual and Mechanical Processes from Woodcut to Ink Jet*. New York: Thames and Hudson, 1986.

Hatchfield, Pamela. *Pollutants in the Museum Environment*. London: Archetype Publications, 2007.

Heritage Preservation. *The Emergency Response and Salvage Wheel*. Washington, DC: Heritage Preservation, 2011.

Holben Ellis, Margaret. *The Care of Prints and Drawings*. Nashville, TN: AASLH Press, 1987.

Hoskins, Lesley. *The Papered Wall: History, Pattern, and Techniques*. New York: Abrams, 1994.

Hunter, Dard. *Papermaking: The History and Technique of an Ancient Craft*. New York: Dover, 1978.

Hutchins, Jane K. *First Aid for Art: Essential Salvage Techniques*. Stockbridge, MA: Hard Press Editions, 2006.

Image Permanence Institute website (www.imagepermanenceinstitute.org).

Image Permanence Institute. *IPI's Guide to Sustainable Preservation Practices for Managing Storage Environments*. Rochester, NY: IPI, 2012.

Kissel, Eléonore, and Erin Vigneau. *Architectural Photoreproductions: A Manual for Identification and Care*. New Castle, DE: Oak Knoll Press and the New York Botanical Garden, 2009.

Mecklenburg, Marion F. *Determining the Acceptable Ranges of Relative Humidity and Temperature in Museums and Galleries, Parts 1 and 2*. 2007. Accessed September 25, 2013. http://si-pddr .si.edu/dspace/handle/10088/7056 and http://si-pddr.si.edu/dspace/handle/10088/7055.

Merrill-Oldham, Jan, and Parisi, Paul. *Guide to the ANSI/NISO/LBI Library Binding Standard, ANSI/NISO/LBI Z39.78-2000*. Chicago: Preservation and Reformatting Section, Association for Library Collections and Technical Services, 2008.

Miller, Julia. *Books Will Speak Plain*. Ann Arbor, MI: Legacy Press, 2010.

Ogden, Sherelyn. *The Storage of Art on Paper: A Basic Guide for Institutions*. Champaign, IL: Graduate School of Library and Information Science, University of Illinois, 2001.

Price, Lois Olcott. *Line, Shade, and Shadow: The Fabrication and Preservation of Architectural Drawings*. New Castle, DE: Oak Knoll Press, 2010.

Ritzenthaler, Mary Lynn. *Preserving Archives and Manuscripts*. 2nd ed. Chicago: Society for American Archivists, 2010.

Tedone, Melissa, ed. *From Gray Areas to Green Areas: Developing Sustainable Practices in Preservation Environments, 2007, Symposium Proceedings*. Austin, TX: Kilgarlin Center for Preservation of the Cultural Record, 2008.

Teynac, Françoise, Pierre Nolot, and Jean-Denis Vivien. *Wallpaper: A History*. New York: Rizzoli, 1982.

Thompson, Jack C. *Manuscript Inks*. Portland, OR: Caber Press, 1996.

Valente, A. J. *Rag Paper Manufacture in the United States, 1801–1900*. Jefferson, NC: McFarland, 2010.

Wren, Diane J. *Books Gone Bad: Mold in Library Collections*. 2011. Accessed September 26, 2013. http://dianejwren.com/Mold%20Web%20Site/index.htm.

## NOTES

1. Cathleen A. Baker, *From the Hand to the Machine: Nineteenth-Century American Paper and Mediums: Technologies, Materials, and Conservation* (Ann Arbor, MI: Legacy Press, 2010), 91.

2. William K. Wilson, *Environmental Guide for the Storage of Paper Records* (NISO TR01-1995) (Bethesda, MD: NISO Press, 1995).

3. Mark A. Greene and Dennis Meissner, "More Product, Less Process: Pragmatically Revamping Traditional Processing Approaches to Deal With Late 20th-Century Collections," *American Archivist* 68 (2005): 208–63.

4. Nelly Balloffet and Jenny Hille, *Preservation and Conservation for Libraries and Archives* (Chicago: American Library Association, 2004).

5. David Diringer, *The Book Before Printing* (New York: Dover, 1982), 172.

6. Jan Merrill-Oldham and Paul Parisi, *Guide to the Library Binding Institute Standard for Library Binding ANSI/NISO/LBI Z39.78-2000* (Chicago: Preservation and Reformatting Section, Association for Library Collections and Technical Services, 2008).

7. James Reilly, "Specifying Storage Environments in Libraries and Archives," in *From Gray Areas to Green Areas: Developing Sustainable Practices in Preservation Environments, 2007*, Symposium Proceedings, ed. Melissa Tedone (Austin, TX: Kilgarlin Center for Preservation of the Cultural Record, 2008).

# CHAPTER 9

# Photographic Materials

Brenda Bernier, Ross Harvey

## PHOTOGRAPHS AND NEGATIVES (BRENDA BERNIER)

*Dates in use:* 1839 to the present.

*Processes and Formats*: *Cased photographs*: daguerreotypes, ambrotypes, tintypes; *Negatives*: paper negatives, glass-plate negatives, cellulose nitrate film, cellulose acetate film, polyester film; *Photographic prints*: albumen prints, cabinet cards, carbon prints, gelatin silver developed-out prints, salted paper prints, platinum prints, cyanotypes, "crayon portraits," chromogenic color prints, Polaroid SX70.

### Material

This chapter covers the identification and preservation of a range of the products of photographic processes and formats most commonly found in cultural heritage institutions.

### Purposes

From the introduction of photography in 1839 up to the present day, photographic images have been a powerful form of artistic expression and a key tool for documenting personal histories, scientific phenomena, and our cultural heritage. Photographers were keen to experiment and adapt techniques, resulting in an extraordinary array of photographic materials, processes, and formats. Photographic *materials* refer to the individual constituents making up the photograph; the term *process* refers to the techniques used to bring the materials together; and the term *format* refers to the presentation of the photograph, regardless of process.

## Dates in Use

Dates of most common usage are given here. Photographers routinely used processes well past typical end dates. Many 19th-century processes are practiced today.

Daguerreotypes: 1840s to 1860s
Ambrotypes: 1850s to 1860s
Tintypes: 1850s to 1870s
Paper negatives: 1840s to 1850s
Glass-plate negatives: mid-1850s to 1900s, later for scientific applications
Cellulose nitrate film: late 1890s to 1950s
Cellulose acetate film: 1930s to present
Polyester film: 1960s to present
Albumen prints: 1855 to 1890s
Collodion prints: 1860s to 1910s
Gelatin silver printed-out prints: 1890s to 1920s
Gelatin silver developed-out prints: 1890s to 1990s
Salted paper prints: 1840s to 1850s
Platinum prints: late 19th to early 20th centuries
Cyanotypes: late 19th to early 20th centuries
Autochromes: 1900s to 1930s
Carbro prints (pigment prints): 1920s to 1940s
Dye transfer prints: 1950s to 1960s
Cibachromes/Ilfochromes: 1960s to 1980s
Chromogenic color slides: 1935 to late 20th century
Chromogenic color negatives and prints: 1942 to present
Polaroid black and white instant prints: 1950s to 1970s
Polaroid SX70 instant prints: predominantly 1970s to 1990s

## Identification

For preservation purposes, identifying the type of photograph is helpful when making decisions about housing and storage, exhibition, and emergency response. Knowing the date a photograph was taken based on image and context can sometimes narrow down the type of photographic process, and vice versa. There are numerous resources for photograph identification, and it may be necessary to consult them for a more in-depth understanding of processes and materials. (See the section "Further Reading" at the end of this chapter.) Noted here are some of the most common identification questions, but the selection is by no means comprehensive.

### CASED PHOTOGRAPHS

French artist Louis Daguerre invented the first commercially viable photographic process in the late 1830s, but it was not announced to the world until 1839. Daguerreotypes were exposed directly in the camera, meaning there is no negative to make multiple copies. They are therefore unique, one-of-a-kind images. In American-cased daguerreotypes, the daguerreotype plate is covered with a decorative brass mat, then a piece of glass, which was usually bound at the edges with a paper tape and covered with a decorative framelike piece of brass called a preserver. The package was then inserted into a case usually made of wood, fabric, paper, and leather. They typically came in standard sizes, as presented in figure 9.1. (When measuring daguerreotypes in cases, note that the plate usually extends under the brass mat, so it is bigger than the displayed image; occasionally smaller plates are placed in cases designed for larger plates.) Daguerreotype images are capable of tremendous detail and clarity but, because they are on a silver-coated plate, they can be hard to see. If examined at a particular angle, a mirror reflection is seen. This is the most easily identifiable feature of daguerreotypes.

In the 1850s and 1860s, the popularity of daguerreotypes waned, as first ambrotypes, and then tintypes, were introduced as affordable alternatives. Both ambrotypes and tintypes have one-of-a-kind images, made up of fine silver particles suspended in a thin layer of collodion emulsion. For ambrotypes, the emulsion is on a piece of clear glass, or sometimes colored glass, the most common of which was red glass used in so-called ruby ambrotypes. Like daguerreotypes, ambrotypes were often housed in small cases. Since ambrotypes are made on glass, they can be somewhat reflective, but never to the extent of the mirrorlike quality of daguerreotypes. Ambrotypes and tintypes are easy to see from any angle, and it is not uncommon for tintypes to have a dull gray tonality to the highlights.

Tintypes were particularly popular during the American Civil War. They were not made on tin, as the name implies, but on a thin, blackened iron plate. For this reason they are also referred to as ferrotypes. As tintypes were fairly durable and easily obtainable, they were only occasionally placed in protective cases. They are often found mounted to a decorative paper mat.

## NEGATIVES

Shortly after the announcement of the daguerreotype process in 1839, Englishman William Henry Fox Talbot officially announced an alternative photographic process.

| Gem type | anything smaller than sixteenth plate |
| Sixteenth plate | $1\frac{3}{8}$ x $15\frac{5}{8}$ inches |
| Ninth plate | 2 x $2\frac{1}{2}$ inches |
| Sixth plate | $2\frac{3}{4}$ x $3\frac{1}{4}$ inches |
| Quarter plate | $3\frac{1}{4}$ x $4\frac{1}{4}$ inches |
| Half plate | $4\frac{1}{4}$ x $5\frac{1}{2}$ inches |
| Whole plate | $6\frac{1}{2}$ x $8\frac{1}{2}$ inches |
| Mammoth plate | anything larger than whole plate |

**FIGURE 9.1.** Daguerreotype Standard American Plate Sizes

Talbot's salted paper print process incorporated a negative image that could be used to print multiple copies of positive images on paper. The use of negatives to print multiple positives became the defining feature of photography in the 19th and 20th centuries.

Paper negatives are relatively rare in collections. They were generally in use between 1840 and the mid-1850s, until they were supplanted in popularity by negatives on glass supports, which gave a much sharper image. The image layer on a glass-plate negative consists of silver image particles suspended in an emulsion of albumen, collodion, or gelatin. Introduced in the 1870s, the "gelatin dry plate," as it is often called, was quickly embraced by photographers. Unlike collodion negatives, gelatin dry plates did not have to be made by hand immediately before use. They were commercially manufactured, making the process much easier for photographers and ensuring more reliable results. Gelatin dry plates remained the dominant form of negative until it was finally replaced by plastic film in the early 20th century. Because glass does not warp or shrink like film can, glass-plate negatives continued to be used by specialists, particularly in astronomy and the sciences, until the 1960s.

Cellulose nitrate film was introduced by George Eastman in the late 1890s as a significant improvement to glass-plate negatives. Flexible film-based negatives could be rolled, providing a lightweight, portable material. Cellulose nitrate proved to be very flammable so, starting in the 1930s, cellulose acetate was introduced as a safer alternative. By the 1950s, the use of nitrate film had been almost completely phased out in the United States. Because cellulose acetate and cellulose nitrate film can deteriorate quickly and pose a hazard to adjacent collections, it is useful to be able to identify them. The easiest identification tools for these materials are edge printing and deterioration characteristics. In general, acetate film tends to shrink and warp and give off a distinctive odor of vinegar. Nitrate film deterioration is characterized by amber, brown discoloration and image fading until the film becomes sticky. Eventually, nitrate film can become extremely brittle, even powdery. (See "Microform" later in this chapter.)

Both sheet and roll film may have printing by the manufacturer along the edge. An example of typical edge printing is "Kodak Safety Film." The word *safety* began to be used in 1950 to distinguish the film from more flammable cellulose nitrate film. Edge printing is mostly used to identify cellulose acetate film, but it could be used to identify polyester film. Nitrate film often does not have any edge printing.

Polyester film was introduced in the 1960s as a more stable alternative to cellulose acetate. Polarizing filters are used to identify polyester film. Polarizing film allows light to pass through it in a single direction. By sandwiching a negative between two pieces of polarizing film and looking through it in bright light, polyester film will appear brightly colored. It is not possible to distinguish between cellulose acetate and cellulose nitrate by this method, as both will appear dark. A simple holder can be made out of two pieces of archival board with windows cut out. Over each window, secure a piece of polarizing film, making sure that the pieces of film are at right angles to each other.

Regardless of the type of negative, it is useful to be able to distinguish the image-bearing side from the support side, as this has implications for handling, storing, and

**FIGURE 9.2.** Using Polarizing Filters to Identify Polyester Film (polyester on left, cellulose acetate on right)

printing negatives. Both sheet and roll film-based negatives are comprised of plastic coated with the image-bearing gelatin emulsion. Although there could be gelatin coatings on the other side of the plastic layer, the film usually looks duller on the emulsion side and shinier on the plastic side. Glass-plate negatives are very similar in that the dull side is the image-bearing side.

## PHOTOGRAPHIC PRINTS

When trying to identify photographic prints it is useful to consider four factors: context; color; fading; and what it looks like under magnification. The format and presentation of a photograph, the image depicted, and accompanying collection material all contribute to the context of the photograph and can help to roughly date it. The assumed date can help narrow down probable photographic processes.

In considering the second factor, color, questions to ask are: Is the photograph full color or monochromatic? If monochromatic, does it have the neutral gray tones of a typical "black-and-white" photograph, or is the tone blue, brown, purple, or sepia? (Further details about using tonality as a clue for process identification are found later in this chapter.)

**FIGURE 9.3.** Cellulose Acetate Negative with Severe Deterioration, Emulsion Side

The presence or absence of fading can be a clue to the type of process, particularly when distinguishing photomechanical prints from true photographs. Since photomechanical prints consist of ink on paper, they do not fade in the way photographs can. (See the section "Paper: Works of Art on Paper" in chapter 8 for more information about photomechanical prints.)

Looking at prints under magnification is an extremely useful identification technique. Using a handheld 30x magnifier, the visibility of paper fibers and emulsion layers can indicate features of the most common photographic processes. There are many good resources for identifying photographs, such as hands-on workshops, websites, and books (see the section "Further Reading" at the end of this chapter). Collection managers are encouraged to consult these resources to develop skills in photograph identification.

Albumen prints were the predominant photographic process of the 19th century, from roughly 1855 to 1895. They are best described as monochromatic, not "black-and-white." Bear in mind that albumen prints are made of a silver image (usually gold toned) suspended in an emulsion of egg white. As a result, the tones usually range from red-brown to purple, with the highlights yellowing as the albumen ages. Because albumen photographs are printed on very thin paper, they are almost always mounted on a support board such as a presentation board, album page, carte-de-visite, or cabinet card.

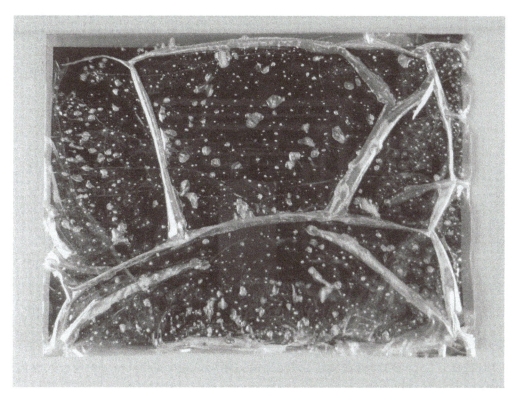

**FIGURE 9.4.** Same Negative on the Non-Emulsion or Base Side

Image fading, particularly along the edges, is extremely common. Under magnification, the paper fibers are clearly visible. The albumen emulsion may also be cracking, which will be most visible in the darker areas of the image.

The carte-de-visite and the cabinet card were extremely popular formats for portraiture in the 19th century. In these formats, a photograph, quite often an albumen print, was mounted onto a small card. Popular in the United States in the 1860s, the carte-de-visite was about the size of a calling card, usually about 4¼ x 2½ inches. By the early 1870s it had been largely replaced by the cabinet card, which remained popular until the beginning of the 20th century. American cabinet cards have decorative mounts measuring 6½ x 4½ inches. The products of a range of photographic processes are to be found in cabinet card collections, including glossy and matte collodion, gelatin printed-out prints, and platinum prints.

Collodion and gelatin printed-out prints, used predominantly in the 1870s through to the 1920s, are common in archival collections. These prints can appear reddish-brown, purple, or even gray, depending on the processing and toners used. There are two major types of collodion prints—glossy and matte. When viewed under direct light, particularly fluorescent light, glossy collodion prints can reflect back iridescent colors. Because they are toned with platinum, matte collodion prints appear very neutral gray and characteristically do not fade.

**FIGURE 9.5.** Cabinet Cards of Various Processes (left to right: platinum, glossy collodion, matte collodion, albumen)

A defining feature of printed-out prints is a white layer separating the image layer from the paper fibers. This layer of barium sulfate in gelatin is called the baryta layer and serves to make the image brighter and sharper, as it reflects light back to the viewer better than the paper fibers can. Under magnification, the baryta layer can sometimes be seen at the edge of the print or in areas of damage like tears or creases. Also under magnification, the image appears smooth, and the paper fibers will not be visible.

Carbon prints have a final image material of pigment, not silver, so an important characteristic is that they do not fade. The image tone can vary greatly, but, if it is in the same tonal range as albumen prints, look for the presence or absence of fading. Carbon prints are also slightly thicker in the dark areas of the image. If you look at the print in raking light (light held at the side of the photograph, very low to the surface), a carbon print should have a slightly three-dimensional topography.

Gelatin silver developed-out prints are the most prevalent and easily identifiable photographic process of the 20th century. Although there is a staggering variety of gloss, surface texture, and paper thickness, gelatin silver prints have a number of common features. The most basic feature is the black-and-white tonality, which is a consequence of the way the photographs are made. Unlike albumen prints and printed-out prints, which are made by exposing the paper in contact with the negative for a relatively long time to get an image, gelatin silver prints are exposed to the negative very briefly in a darkroom, resulting in a latent image. The latent image is invisible to the naked eye and must be brought out through chemical developing and fixing. The development process results in much larger silver particles than those in prints that were made by printing out in the sun. These larger silver particles make the print more stable to fading—although certainly not immune to it—and they give the print the characteristic neutral color tone. Because gelatin silver prints go through a development process, they are technically called gelatin silver developed-out prints or DOPs. Other names are silver gelatin prints, silver prints, or more rarely, gelatin prints.

The second most identifiable feature of gelatin silver prints is the presence of a white baryta layer. Although it is possible for a gelatin silver print not to have a baryta layer, particularly during the early 20th century, it is not common.

The emulsion and baryta layers were coated onto good-quality paper to minimize chemical interference. Prints are often described as being on fiber-based paper, or having a paper-based support. Photographs must be properly washed during original processing so that the paper fibers do not retain excess processing chemicals, causing fading and staining in the future. During the 1960s, resin-coated papers came into use. Resin-coated papers are coated on both sides with a layer of polyethylene. Because the polyethylene is water-resistant, chemicals are less likely to penetrate the paper, making the washing time much quicker. Resin-coated papers feel more like plastic than paper, and their slick surfaces make it difficult to write on the backs of photographic prints or to hinge them for exhibition.

One variation of the gelatin silver print is worth mentioning because it often causes confusion. Sometimes gelatin silver prints can be toned with a sulfur or sepia toner, resulting in a reddish-brown tonality. Sepia-toned prints appear to have been particularly popular for portrait photography during the 1920s, perhaps because of nostalgia for 19th-century prints. At first, the viewer might mistake the sepia tone as fading and yellowing of a standard black-and-white image. Sepia-toned prints are in fact not faded; their color should be quite even, rich, and beautiful. The toning process actually converts the silver to a more stable form, so that it will not fade as an untoned print can. If parts of the print are neutral gray and parts are reddish brown, it will not be a sepia-toned print but is more likely a gelatin silver print suffering from localized deterioration.

The products of some monochromatic photographic processes do not have the typical binder layer found on albumen or gelatin silver prints. Because the image material is embedded in the paper fibers, the prints usually have a very matte appearance. With no emulsion layer, paper fibers are clearly visible under 30x magnification. The most common of these single-layer photographs are salted paper prints, platinum prints, and cyanotypes. Salted paper prints typically have red-brown to almost purple tonality. Since they were mostly in use in the 1840s and 1850s, the images can be very similar to those found in albumen prints. In fact, some salted paper prints are found with glossy coatings, making them look very similar to albumen prints. Fading is very common, particularly along the edges, owing to the vulnerability of the image particles (silver, with or without gold toning). In contrast, platinum prints can be distinguished by a very neutral gray tonality and lack of fading due to the very stable platinum image. Platinum prints were most commonly used in the late 19th to early 20th centuries, especially for portrait photography. Gelatin silver prints without a baryta layer can be easily confused with salted paper or platinum prints. Cyanotypes are easily distinguished by their bright blue tonality. The iron-based process results in an image made of an insoluble blue dye (ferric ferrocyanide) known as Prussian blue. Photographers often used them in the late 19th and early 20th centuries as an easy and affordable process.

Around the turn of the 20th century, it was common to see hand-colored photographs, known as "crayon portraits." The photographic image, usually a salted paper print, is very thinly printed, and it is typically difficult to see beneath the media heavily applied to it. The portraits usually have a primitive quality. Occasionally the print is on a convex board, which leaves it very vulnerable once taken out of its frame.

**FIGURE 9.6.** Crayon Portrait Showing Extensive Hand-Coloring

There were many types of photographic processes for color photographs over the course of the 20th century, such as Autochromes (1904–1930s); carbro prints, also called pigment prints (predominantly 1920s–1940s); dye transfer prints (predominantly 1950s–1960s); and Cibachromes, later called Ilfochromes (predominantly1960s–1980s). By far the most commercially successful was the chromogenic process, as evidenced by the ubiquitous color snapshot and color slide. This process was used for negatives, prints, and transparencies. The first chromogenic transparency, Kodachrome, was introduced in 1935, and Kodacolor, the first chromogenic print, appeared in 1942. When identifying and dating chromogenic prints, the manufacturer's printing on the back of the print can give important clues. (See the section "Further Reading" at the end of this chapter.) The suffix *chrome* in Kodachrome and Ektachrome indicates transparencies with no corresponding negatives, while the suffix *color* in Kodacolor and Ektacolor indicates a print process using a negative. Chromogenic products have different dye formulations, resulting in varying color stability. For example, Kodachrome slides are well known for having much better dye stability than Ektachrome. Chromogenic negatives often appear orange because of the presence of masking dyes that aid printing.

Polaroid produced a series of products designed to eliminate traditional photo processing and to deliver instant photographs, in black-and-white and in color. The most popular was the SX70 instant color print, introduced in 1972. The SX70 is thicker than chromogenic prints because it contains all the chemical layers needed to produce the image. The overall dimension is usually 4¼ x 3½ inches, but the image itself is 3 inches square, surrounded by a white border that is significantly larger at the bottom, where the chemical pod had been located. While Polaroid was the pioneer in instant photography, it is possible to find other brands in collections, such as Kodak and Fujifilm, which is still in production today.

In the age of digital photography, digital files can still be converted into chromogenic prints, which are usually identified by the names Kodak or Fuji printed on the back. Those with no printing, or with names of computer printer companies, such as Epson, Canon, and others printed on them, are most likely inkjet prints. Inkjet prints are not chemically developed photographs but are ink on paper. Under magnification, they tend to look like discrete patches of color as opposed to the more diffuse blending of colors seen in chromogenic prints.

## Environment and Storage

### PREFERRED ENVIRONMENT

Ensuring proper storage and environment is arguably the most important preservation measure that can be taken for photograph collections. Photographic materials are inherently complex structures, making them physically and chemically vulnerable to poor conditions. Photographs are best kept in cool, dry conditions, with daily fluctuations kept to a minimum. The standard for archival storage of black-and-white photographic

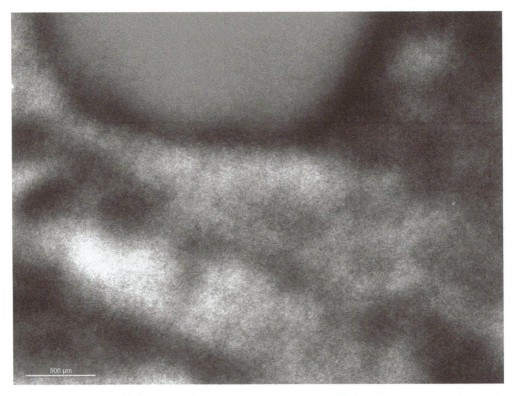

**FIGURE 9.7.** Chromogenic Print Shown under Magnification; Colors Are Finely Blended

prints, as set by the International Organization for Standardization (ISO 18920), is no greater than 65°F (18°C) and between 30 percent and 50 percent relative humidity (RH). Daily fluctuations should be kept below 5°F (2°C) and 5 percent RH.

Environmental pollutants can cause yellowing and fading of photographs. In regions with poor air quality, inadequately filtered outside air can result in exposure to pollutants such as sulfur dioxide, nitrogen oxides, and ozone. Other harmful pollutants can be generated from inside the building, from poorly sealed wood, paints, cleaning products, carpeting, construction material, and even photocopiers. Pollutants can be introduced from within the collection as well. Off-gassing from deteriorating cellulose acetate and cellulose nitrate film produces several harmful contaminates, including acetic and nitric acids.

Rates of chemical reactions are directly linked to temperature—the higher the temperature, the faster the chemical deterioration. Cold storage is an effective strategy for slowing down chemical deterioration. Cold or frozen storage is especially recommended for cellulose acetate, cellulose nitrate, and color photographic materials. It is generally not necessary to replace acidic enclosures with high-quality materials in preparation for cold storage as long as the enclosures are still functional. Again, the low temperatures will slow down chemical reactions, including interaction with poor-quality enclosures.

**FIGURE 9.8.** Inkjet Print under Magnification; Colors Appear as Discrete Shapes

Definitions for the terms *cool*, *cold*, and *frozen storage* are not universal. Generally, cool storage ranges from 50 to 65°F (10 to 18°C). Cold storage can be from 33 to 50°F (1 to 10°C), and frozen storage is anywhere below 32°F (0°C). Cold storage is sometimes generically used to describe both cold and frozen storage. There are generally two types of cold storage systems: cold storage vaults, in which the RH can be controlled, and stand-alone freezers that do not control for humidity. Freezers tend to have high levels of humidity, so photographs stored in them will need to be properly packaged.

Packaging can be achieved by double sealing in heavyweight, polyethylene zip-type bags (placing a bag within a bag), or double wrapping in 0.004-inch thick polyethylene (low-density polyethylene [LDPE] film). When wrapping a box, each seam must be completely taped with a polypropylene carton-sealing tape with acrylic adhesive, designed to withstand freezing temperatures as low as -30°F (-34°C). Commercially available barrier films have a combination of metallic and plastic layers, such as aluminized nylon and polyethylene. These barrier films are excellent for keeping out humidity and pollutants. However, since they are opaque or semiopaque, they are generally only used as the first wrapping layer.

Cobalt, salt-based humidity indicator cards are designed to show the approximate RH, as seen by the area of transition from pink to blue. These cards are not, however,

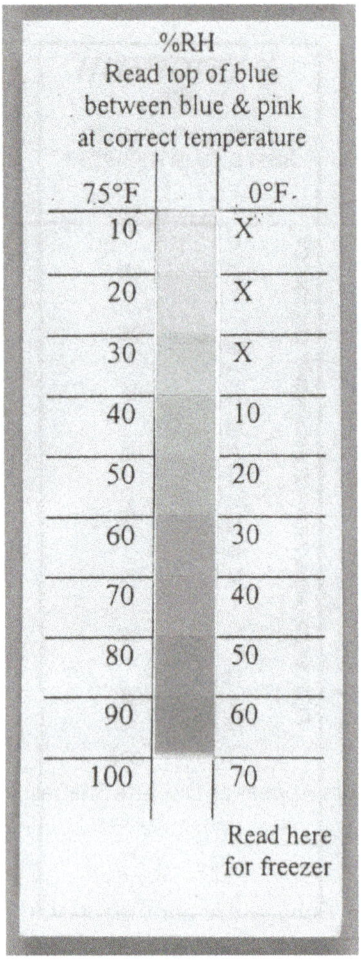

**FIGURE 9.9.** Humidity Indicator Card at Room Temperature Showing Approximately 35% RH

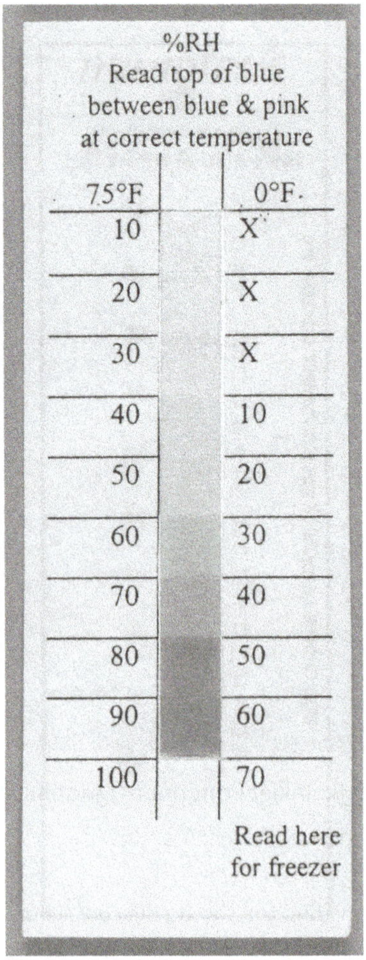

**FIGURE 9.10.** Humidity Indicator Card at Freezing Temperature Showing Approximately 35% RH

calibrated to work in freezing temperatures. In order to see the correct reading for packages in frozen storage, fabricate a new scale for use in low temperatures and affix them on the cards, showing the proper scales for reading at both room temperature and at 0°F (-18°C). For each box, two RH indicator cards should be placed in visible locations under each layer of the plastic for easy monitoring. The cards should be monitored on a regular basis, acclimating and rewrapping boxes when necessary. For more information on preparing materials for cold storage, see the National Park Service guidelines listed at the end of this chapter.

Even in a climate-controlled cold storage vault, items must be wrapped in plastic or in a sealed plastic bag before they leave cold storage, because when they are brought into warmer conditions, they can cross dew point, causing condensation to form on the surface in much the same way as condensation forms on a glass of ice water on a hot day. If the photographs are not protected by the plastic, they can become stuck or blocked to the enclosures. After use, items need to be rewrapped before placing back in cold storage.

Items do not need to be wrapped or bagged if they are stored in a climate-controlled cold vault with an adjacent acclimation chamber, designed to be slightly warmer than the cool storage but not so warm that the object crosses dew point. Unwrapped items can be brought into the acclimation chamber for a period of time before being brought out to room-temperature conditions. This system is usually efficient for large collections.

## RECOMMENDATIONS FOR STORAGE

Significant preservation gains can be made if appropriate storage materials for photograph collections are used. There is a dizzying array of options: paper or plastic enclosures; buffered or unbuffered materials; upright or flat boxes; keeping photos separate or grouping together; and so on. There is no single correct option, but some considerations in weighing options follow.

The type of sleeve used for archival photographs can depend on expectations of collection use. Transparent plastic sleeves are helpful for a collection likely to get frequent use, as they can protect against handling damage. They are also useful for photographs with labels that are poorly adhered to the back of the prints. If the labels do become detached, the information will stay with the correct photograph. Appropriate plastics include polyethylene, polypropylene, and polyester. Sleeves made of polyvinyl chloride (PVC) are to be avoided, as they can damage the photographs over time. For prints, look for sleeves welded on two adjacent sides in the shape of an L. Sleeves welded only on two opposite sides are problematic, as the photograph can easily fall out. Sleeves welded on three sides are also problematic, as a photograph can be easily damaged when it is slid in and out. It is best practice to be consistent in the orientation of the sleeve opening, which is usually to the top and right, in such a way that the seam weld is on the left and bottom, truly in the shape of an L.

Occasionally you may want to give a photograph extra protection by encapsulating it in transparent polyester film that is sealed on all four edges. The best encapsulations are made using an ultrasonic welder to seal the edges. The seams are inert, and the photograph can be easily cut out of the polyester at any time. Encapsulations using double-sided tape can be made if an ultrasonic welder is not available, but tape will invariably ooze adhesive over time, putting the photograph at risk. A better solution would be to use prefabricated sleeves with L-shaped seams, which if they are to be sealed only need to be taped on the two open sides. At least in this way, the photo can be placed close to the welded seam, leaving ample room around the tape.

The disadvantages of using plastic sleeves are their cost and weight, which can be serious considerations for large collections. In some collections, plastic sleeves might only be used strategically on those photographs that are at risk of loss or damage from handling, such as those with tears or loose labels. Plastic sleeves have static charge, so they are *not* for use as enclosures for photographs with a flaking image layer or with powdery hand coloring or inscriptions.

Cellulose acetate and cellulose nitrate negatives can deteriorate very quickly in plastic sleeves because acidic and oxidizing compounds are trapped and speed up the process. Plastic sleeves should only be used with vintage negatives if the film is in cold storage. Until placed in cold storage, the negatives *must be in paper sleeves*. Cut cellulose nitrate negatives appear not to have demonstrated the severe flammability of rolled cellulose nitrate motion picture film. Nevertheless, if you have cellulose nitrate in your collection, you should be aware of your local fire code regulations and institutional policies regarding that material. The guidelines for storage and handling of cellulose nitrate film most often followed are in NFPA 40: *Standard for the Storage and Handling of Cellulose Nitrate Film* (listed with other standards at the end of this section).

Paper enclosures for photographs can be sleeves that are sealed on three sides, or folders. The paper stock used to make enclosures should be made of high-quality materials, if used for long-term storage of photographs. The word *archival* is not a reliable indicator of quality since manufacturers and suppliers are not required to share a universal definition of the word. Instead, look specifically for materials that contain no lignin and have passed the Photographic Activity Test (PAT), which confirms that the paper

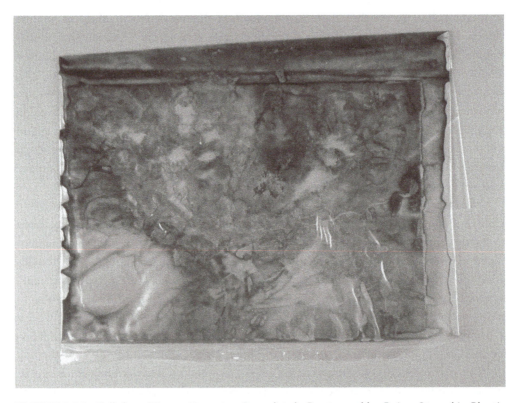

**FIGURE 9.11.** Cellulose Nitrate Negative Completely Destroyed by Being Stored in Plastic Sleeve

will not cause fading or staining of photographic materials over time. Suppliers of archival materials will usually indicate when enclosures, boxes, and matboard are lignin-free and have passed the PAT.

The term *acid-free* can mean that an enclosure is either neutral pH or alkaline. More helpful terms to look for are *buffered* and *unbuffered*. Buffered enclosures are more alkaline (have higher pH) than unbuffered, and they contain additives that will keep the enclosure from becoming acidic over a longer period of time. Cyanotypes and some types of color photographs can undergo color changes when exposed to an alkaline environment, particularly in the presence of moisture. Most institutions cannot adequately store and strategically deploy both buffered and unbuffered enclosures and folder stock for their photograph collections. For this reason, it has been customarily suggested that unbuffered storage materials be used with photographs. The problem with this familiar suggestion is that the vast majority of photographs *benefit* from long-term storage in alkaline materials. In order to provide superior preservation benefit to the largest number of photographs, the latest storage standard from the International Standards Organization (ISO)[1] *recommends the use of buffered storage materials for all photographs.* In theory, buffered enclosures need to be replaced less frequently than unbuffered ones, which may become acidic and brittle more quickly.

Traditionally the seams of paper sleeves have been areas of vulnerability, either from aging adhesive or as ingress for pollutants. It is common to see photographs and negatives that have stained or faded in areas corresponding to seams. To combat this tendency, make sure that the image side of a print or negative is placed against the smooth side and not the seam side of an enclosure. This also has the important benefit of keeping the vulnerable image away from the abrasive edges of the seam. When choosing paper sleeves, look for enclosures that have two seams placed to the side. If inadvertent scratching or staining occurs at the seams, it will at least occur away from the central part of the image in a sleeve with side seams. Sleeves with only one side seam are problematic for collections because they are more bulky along one edge, making a group of them become askew and not fit well in the box. Two side seams, also called balanced seams, alleviate this problem.

Undertaking a rehousing project for large photograph collections can be daunting if the original enclosures have extensive inscriptions that need to be transcribed, especially if they are in illegible handwriting, foreign languages, or are scientific notations. Photocopying the inscriptions onto new enclosures is usually not successful because the enclosures tend to get jammed in the machine. Inscriptions can, however, be copied using inexpensive inkjet or laser printers with copying and scanning functions. Usually the inscription on the old enclosure can be scanned directly onto the new enclosure, without having to save scanned files, in a very quick process. In some situations it might be preferable to scan an inscription, save it to a file, and then print onto the new enclosure. The cost of ink is a consideration that must be weighed against the cost of transcribing by hand and the importance of reducing transcription error. Printer designs can change from year to year, but the main characteristic to look for is a simple path for the paper feed to minimize jamming of the new enclosure as it is being printed. For inkjet printers, pigment-based inks tend to be more stable than dye-based inks. Any ink and enclosure combination must be tested for waterfastness to ensure that, in the event of a collection being subjected to water exposure, inscriptions that have washed off or have stained the photographs do not hamper its salvage.

When considering boxes, use the same criteria for selecting the material as for enclosures. Boxes should be made of board that is lignin-free, buffered, and passes the PAT.

Unframed fine art collections are usually housed horizontally, with each photograph in its own folder or window mat. This type of storage is not only safe for the photographs but also slows users down when they access the photographs, which results in less handling damage. Window mats are more expensive and take up more room than folders, but they enable safer handling and are more aesthetically pleasing. Photographs need to be secured in the window mats, preferably with photo corners or paper strips that require no adhesive to be directly placed on the photograph. If a photograph requires mounting with adhesive, consult with a professional museum matter and framer or photograph conservator. Mats, like other enclosures, should be of high-quality material.

Archival collections are usually stored upright or vertically. Photographs larger than 8 x 10 inches, which should be placed in folders and stored flat, are the exception. When storing photographs flat, try to group them by size whenever possible. If it is not possible, store the larger ones at the bottom, so they are not distorted by being draped over smaller photographs. For collections with minimal use, multiple photographs could be stored in the same folder. Interleaving is usually not recommended, as it can easily become crumpled and scratch the photographic images, causing more harm than good. If a collection is used frequently, consider using polyester sleeves to reduce handling damage.

For vertical storage, usually in document boxes, photographs that are all the same size can be housed in sleeves without the use of folders. If collections have slightly different sizes or items that need to be grouped for intellectual reasons, folders are recommended. The boxes need to be packed tightly enough so that the photographs do not slump in the box and become distorted. However, the boxes should not be so tight that it is difficult to get a photograph in and out of each box. The easiest way to get the right tension in the box is to use a spacer made of archival corrugated board, folded and placed at the back of the box and keeping light tension on the photographs during storage. The spacer is removed when the box is in use, so that the folders can be easily accessed.

There are pros and cons to storing mixed collections together and storing the photographs separately. Photographs are usually stored separately if they make sense intellectually without the accompanying documents, or if they require cold storage. For many collections, keeping the materials together is a better option, although it is necessary to be aware of acidic papers, staples, and paper clips in contact with photographs. Polyester sleeves are recommended for the photographs. Matboard supports might be necessary to protect photographs from distortions when adjacent materials are of different sizes.

Although it may be tempting to store prints with their corresponding negatives for organizational reasons, several preservation factors advise against this. Deteriorating acetate and nitrate negatives can give off products that can adversely affect accompanying prints. Cold storage is recommended for vintage negatives but, since cold storage is more expensive than regular storage, it may not be cost-effective to store an entire collection in low temperatures. Finally, for security reasons, it is recommended to store negatives and prints in different locations. If prints are damaged by fire or water, their negatives might still be safe, allowing the images to be retrieved.

Because of the high risk of flaking emulsion, glass-plate negatives are best stored in paper sleeves, since plastic sleeves can generate static charge and increase flaking. The most suitable sleeves are four-flap paper enclosures that fold open completely so that glass plates can be inserted and removed safely without risk of abrasion. Glass-plate negatives must be stored upright on edge. When stacked horizontally, they can easily crack under their own weight. Cracked and broken glass plates are usually housed flat in a custom sink mat, with small matboard spacers to keep the pieces from grinding against each other and causing image loss along the edges.

Photograph albums are best stored horizontally in order to protect both the mounted photographs and the album structure from the forces of gravity. This is especially true for photographs that are mounted with adhesive that is starting to fail. Boxing is recommended to give an album physical support, to keep all loose items together, to reduce exposure to dust and pollutants, to act as a buffer against sudden changes in relative humidity, and to provide some degree of protection during a water emergency. Use interleaving only sparingly, as it is a handling challenge for patrons, and too many sheets of interleaving can damage an album's binding. Interleaving is best used only where there is significant abrasion from adjacent materials, or where platinum-toned or platinum prints might interact with the facing page.

Panoramas are tricky to store and handle because of their length. Ideally, panoramas would be stored flat in archival folders in a flat file. When a panorama is too long for a flat file, it may be stored between archival boards. If using corrugated archival board, make sure either that the corrugations of the top and bottom boards run in opposite directions or that each board is double-walled. Single-walled boards whose corrugations run in the same direction are very easy to bend and will crease the photograph. If housing many panoramas, semicustom polyester sleeves can be made to order through plastic suppliers. The sleeves function much like a tri-lock sleeve, with a small locking flap along the bottom. The sleeves are welded to fit the most common height of panoramas but are sold in a long roll. Typical rolls would be 10½ or 17¼ inches high and 225 feet long, and a length can be cut to accommodate a panorama's length. A panorama can be stored with or without an archival support board, such as matboard, in the sleeve. The sleeves provide good protection for panoramas and easy handling and viewing by staff and researchers.

## Handling

### WHAT STAFF NEED TO KNOW

When handling photographs, staff should maintain a clean, uncluttered work area. Food and drink should not be allowed in the work area; if it must be allowed, photographs must be boxed or covered and placed on a cart or table separate from where food or drink is placed. Work surfaces must be cleaned of all crumbs, liquids, and grease. Working on a clean blotter is recommended because dirt from the collection will be visible and the blotter can be changed before the dirt transfers to other photographs.

When marking photographs with accession or identification numbers, staff can use a number of techniques to minimize risk of damage. As the location of the marking can make a difference, it is recommended that the back, or verso, of the photograph be marked in the lower right or lower left corner. Either corner is fine, as long as it is consistent for your institution. Marking the upper edge is not recommended for two reasons. First, in archival collections it can encourage mishandling, as researchers are tempted to peek at the numbers without removing folders from their boxes. Second, landscape and portrait photographs often have lighter image areas in the top part of the photograph. If a marking on the lower edge accidently showed through to the image side, it would be in the least visible and objectionable location.

When writing on the verso of a photograph, work on a smooth, hard surface, such as a piece of glass, so that the writing does not emboss the soft photograph. Soft drawing pencils, such as a 6B graphite pencil, are safe for use on photographs, including those on resin-coated papers. Use a white vinyl eraser to remove markings.

In order to avoid embossing, remove a photograph from its sleeve before writing on the sleeve. Pencil and water-insoluble ink are acceptable, but it is best practice not to have ink pens anywhere near uncovered photographs. For archival collections that will be stored upright, writing accession numbers along the top edge of sleeves will make their future retrieval from boxes easier.

The residue in fingerprints can etch permanently into the emulsion over time, even if a fingerprint is not obvious immediately. For this reason, staff should wear nitrile gloves when handling photographs and negatives. (Latex gloves are not recommended because they can induce allergic reactions in some people.) Wearing nitrile gloves for long periods can be uncomfortable. If this is the case, staff can be instructed to handle the photographs with bare hands, but with many caveats: hands must be washed often with pure, nonlotion soap; no sharp rings or nail polish are to be worn; no hand lotion or hand sanitizer are to be used, and if people touch their face, hair, or hands, they must wash their hands again. This requires discipline and practice, and it may not be feasible for all situations.

Although when one thinks of photograph collections one might think of white cotton gloves, their wearing is not recommended, as they decrease sensitivity and increase the risk of handling damage. This is especially true for glass-plate negatives, which can be slippery in cotton gloves. Cotton also draws perspiration from hands toward the photographs, and it can easily transfer dirt from one photograph to another.

In many institutions staff are required to wear identification cards. If an ID card is worn on a lanyard around the neck, it can easily swing and scratch photographs on a work table. If the card must be both visible and easily accessible, it is better to use a clip with retractable cord instead.

Unmounted photographs are very susceptible to developing crescent-shaped creases from poor handling that are often called handling creases, as they are caused by the pressure of a thumb on a print when it is held and manipulated with one hand. Mounted photographs are vulnerable to handling damage if their mounts become brittle, making them easy to break or tear. Both mounted and unmounted prints are vulnerable to corner breaks and tears. If a corner is folded, avoid the temptation to bend it back in place, as it will likely only snap off.

When picking up or turning over a photograph, use a microspatula or piece of card stock to lift one edge of the print, rather than grasp the edge or corner with your fingers. If clean blotter paper is used at the workstation, it can be lifted slightly and gently arched back to expose the corner of the print. Slip a support board under the print and place another board on the front. Grasp them firmly as you flip over the sandwiched print. A folder can also be used to sandwich the print. Gloved hands can be used instead of support boards for prints that are 8 x 10 inches or smaller. As the edge is lifted, slip your whole hand under the back of the print to support it and gently tilt it over, using your other hand to create a flat support for the front of the print. Then place it flat on the table, slipping out your support hand. Mounted prints in good condition can be handled gently at the edges.

Because of the layered structure of photographs, rolled panoramas are usually found rolled image-side in. Unfortunately, they are at high risk of cracking as they are unrolled. Normally these should be flagged for treatment, but it may be necessary to view the image of a rolled panorama in order to determine if the expense of treatment is warranted. If the print is flexible you may be able to roll up the outer edge as you examine it, allowing you to scroll through the image a few inches at a time.

## WHAT USERS NEED TO KNOW

Having good intellectual control of a photograph collection plays a key role in preservation, as it facilitates retrieval and minimizes excessive handling from browsing. Users must be made aware of pertinent reading room policies, such as: signing in or registering as a user; leaving bags and coats in designated areas; using only pencil or computer to take notes when collection materials are present; whether photography or scanning is permitted; and that their belongings will be checked upon exiting.

Users' workspaces should be clean, well lit, and large enough to accommodate the materials they are consulting. Users should be supplied with nitrile gloves and given basic instruction in how to safely handle and turn over the prints, as described above. Folders must be removed completely from boxes before looking through them. This is especially important for vertical storage, as users are often tempted to rifle through boxes, looking for particular photographs. In this respect, having well-labeled folders reduces handling.

Sometimes prints and negatives may be in individual sleeves that have unique and important identifying information. Users handling these should be instructed to have only one print or negative removed from its sleeve at any one time to avoid putting it back into the wrong enclosure and causing misidentification of the content for the staff or next researcher.

Photograph albums must be supported during use. Supports can be premade cradles, adjustable foam wedges, or simply rolled towels placed under the covers. They should keep the album open enough for viewing but not so far open that the binding is damaged. (See the "Books" section in chapter 8.)

## Exhibiting Photographs

Exhibiting photographs is a powerful way to illustrate historic or artistic narratives. Steps should be taken to mitigate physical and chemical risks to exhibited objects. Physical risks include handling damage during mounting, installation, and deinstallation, as well as deformation from inadequate mounts. Risk of theft can be reduced by restricting visitor access during installation and deinstallation and by using locked cases and security-bolted frames.

Photographs exposed to fluctuating RH can experience distortion. Low humidity can cause photographs to curl and even pop off hinges or album pages. High humidity can result in increased vulnerability to chemical changes and mold growth. Humidity should be monitored throughout the exhibition, either inside exhibit cases or in the gallery space, depending on the overall stability of the environment in the space. In exhibition spaces with poor humidity control, silica gel or some other humidity buffer should be placed in cases to maintain suitable conditions.

Maintaining stable temperature is less critical than maintaining stable humidity control. Nevertheless, keep in mind that higher temperatures speed chemical reactions such as fading and yellowing. The two major causes of chemical damage are pollutants and light. Pollutants can come either from the building environment or from the case components. Sulfur is a particularly damaging pollutant for photographic materials, as it can oxidize silver. Poor-quality case materials and rubber gaskets can be a source of pollutants. Other objects on display, if made of rubber or wool, may introduce enough sulfur into the case to put photographic images at risk.

Light damage is cumulative and irreparable. For this reason, it is advisable to keep records of each exhibited photograph. Damage may be caused by exposure to excessive visible light, or to ultraviolet (UV) light. Some photographic materials are more sensitive to light damage than others. In general, 19th-century photographs and most color photographs are considered light sensitive, while properly processed gelatin silver prints are considered less sensitive. In practice, it is more complicated. Sensitivity levels may change with improper original processing, prior exhibition history, and additional factors. Even daguerreotypes, long thought to be fairly stable to light, can undergo rapid and irreversible damage during exhibition. Sometimes the most light sensitive part of an object is not the photograph itself but the signature on the mat or the hand coloring.

Use a meter to measure visible and UV light levels in exhibition cases or the gallery environment. The meter should display light in lux and UV in microwatts per lumen. With proper lighting and UV filters, the UV level should be close to zero. For photographs, direct illumination should be in the range of 50 lux to 100 lux, depending on the type of photograph. What is important is the total light exposure over the period of exhibition, so the higher the lux, the shorter the period of display. For example, imagine you have a light level reading in an exhibition space of 100 lux. Lights are on from 8 a.m. to 10 p.m., seven days per week, for three months of exhibition. (Lights in an exhibition area are usually on for hours before and after the public exhibition hours each day.) The total light exposure would be 100 lux x (14 hours/day x 7 days/week x 12 weeks) or 117,600 lux hours. For a hand-colored albumen print, this amount of light exposure is considered excessive.[2] If light levels cannot be lowered, the time on display must be reduced, perhaps by rotating in a different print: 100 lux x (14 hours/day x 7 days/week x 6 weeks) = 58,800 lux hours. If light levels can reduced to 50 lux, then the exhibition time can be the full twelve weeks: 50 lux x (14 hours/day x 7 days/week x 12 weeks) or 58,800 lux hours.

Photographs should be properly mounted to physically withstand the rigors of exhibition. For matted photographs, use buffered, lignin-free matboard, and whenever possible, use photo corners, edge strips, or another nonadhesive technique to secure the photograph. If the photograph must be hinged into the mat, consult with a museum-quality matter and framer. For photographs that can be placed in an exhibition case without a mat, some support is still recommended. Each photograph could be simply cornered onto a backing board made of matboard, or supported with a "back and wrap" technique. Place the photograph on a matboard backing slightly larger than the photo (no more than ⅛ inch on each side). Wrap clear polyester film over the photograph and secure it to the back of the matboard with tape. This technique offers good protection, but it usually only looks acceptable with photographs smaller than 8 x 10 inches. Remove the photo from the wrap after exhibition before returning it to storage.

## Disaster Response

Whether it comes through leaky roofs, blocked storm drains, damaged pipes, or faulty sprinkler heads, water is the most probable cause of disaster to a collection. Immediate damage from water includes loss of inscriptions and hand coloring, staining, and detachment of labels. If left damp for too long, mold will grow, causing irreversible staining and potential health hazards. As photographs begin to dry, they warp and, even worse, block (stick to their enclosures or to each other). Blocking is a major risk to 20th-century photographs because most have gelatin image layers that are vulnerable to sticking.

Photographs must be dried face-up, with nothing touching the surface. An enormous amount of space is needed to dry even a single box of photographs. Air-drying will result in warping, but that can be reduced with treatment afterward. Alternatively, photographs can be dried in weighted stacks of blotter but must have spun polyester webbing, such as Hollytex, covering the image side, so that it will not stick to the blotter. Blotter stacks have the advantage of reducing warping during drying, but it requires a large amount of blotters and Hollytex, which can be awkward to keep on hand and may be difficult to secure quickly in an emergency.

Damp photographic surfaces are especially vulnerable to fingerprints and abrasion, so nitrile gloves must be worn during recovery procedures. If the photographs have been exposed to dirty or muddy water, they can be rinsed in clean distilled or deionized water before drying.

Because of the high risk of blocking, photographs must be kept damp and not allowed to partially dry. Wrap damp boxes in plastic, or enclose in garbage bags, until arrangements can be made to dry or freeze the material. Remember, mold growth can occur quickly, so material should not be kept damp for more than two days before drying or freezing. Freezing inhibits mold growth and will allow for some delay before drying. Frozen collection items can be thawed and dried as space and staffing allow.

Cased objects, especially daguerreotypes and ambrotypes and glass-plate negatives, should not be frozen, as more damage can occur. They should be given priority for air-drying. Freezing can also damage Polaroid prints and some digital prints. Framed prints should be disassembled to discourage mold growth and prevent the photograph from blocking to the glazing.

For some collections, it may be vitally important to preserve information written on accompanying enclosures. Sleeves can be placed under the corresponding photograph during air-drying. The key requirement is that nothing touches the image as it dries.

Vacuum freeze-drying of many types of photographs has been successful but has been known to cause blocking or surface damage. If you have large quantities of photographs that have been wet, consult with both photograph conservators and commercial emergency response vendors to come up with an appropriate solution for your particular collection.

Air-dried photographs can be quite distorted, hampering reboxing efforts. Contact a photograph conservator to arrange humidification and drying in blotter stacks, or with a low temperature drymount press.

If photographs become blocked, resist all temptation to pull them apart, because the image layer will separate in pieces. Conservators, using a variety of techniques such as humidity, steam, freezing, or bathing in aqueous solutions, can often successfully separate blocked photographs. The success rate of the conservators' techniques is lowered significantly if attempts have been made to pull the photographs apart when they were dry or partially dry.

As with other collection materials, prevention is the best defense for a water emergency. Photographic materials, including albums, should be stored in boxes. Evaluate risk factors in your storage area and keep emergency response plans up-to-date for a quicker, more efficient response.

# Decay

## PHYSICAL DAMAGE

Physical damage generally results from improper handling or storage and includes:

- Dirt and accretions
- Tears and losses
- Creases
- Breakage
- Cracking and flaking of the image layer
- Abrasion of the image layer
- Skinning or thinning of the paper layer
- Distortions such as warping or rolling
- Blocking or sticking
- Broken elements of cased photographs
- Detached elements, such as hinges, mounts, or labels

Surface dirt and accretions not only obscure the image but also can lead to abrasion of the image layer and, in some cases, chemical deterioration of the image. Tapes are a major concern. Tape is made up of an adhesive on a paper or plastic support layer, called a carrier. Tape may be water soluble, generally requiring to be moistened just prior to application, or pressure sensitive, known as self-stick. Pressure-sensitive tapes can have rubber-based or acrylic-based adhesives, both of which can cause both physical and chemical damage to photographs over time. Peeling off tape is a common cause of image loss or paper skinning (thinning of the paper layer). As these tapes age, the adhesive may ooze out of the carrier, causing a photograph to stick to adjacent materials. After further aging, the adhesive may begin to dry and fail, causing the carrier to fall off. Staining can be caused by the adhesive, particularly rubber-based adhesive. Pressure-sensitive labels can cause similar damage.

## CHEMICAL DETERIORATION

Chemical deterioration involves molecular change to the components of the photograph. Most typical are:

- Staining
- Yellowing
- Fading
- Color shifts
- Silver mirroring
- Metal and glass corrosion

Staining can occur as a result of poor original chemical processing. However, most staining is the effect of external sources, such as contact with acidic papers or boards, adhesives, water, mold, water-soluble inks, rusty paper clips, even insects and vermin. Yellowing is extremely common, particularly for albumen prints. In silver-based photographs, yellowing and fading typically occur together, as the silver particles break apart when exposed to poor environmental conditions or contaminants. Salted paper, albumen, and gelatin printed-out prints are especially vulnerable to fading. The deterioration may occur all over the prints or only in areas exposed to or in contact with the offending chemical. Nineteenth-century prints that are or have been mounted in albums often show fading along their edges, where air has got in.

Fading occurs in color prints, too, particularly in chromogenic prints. As one dye fades preferentially, a color shift in the image occurs. For example, the magenta dye in some chromogenic prints was especially prone to fading from light exposure, leaving the prints with an overall blue tonality. The cyan dye in some early chromogenic prints faded, even if the prints were kept in the dark, leaving the prints reddish-pink in color.

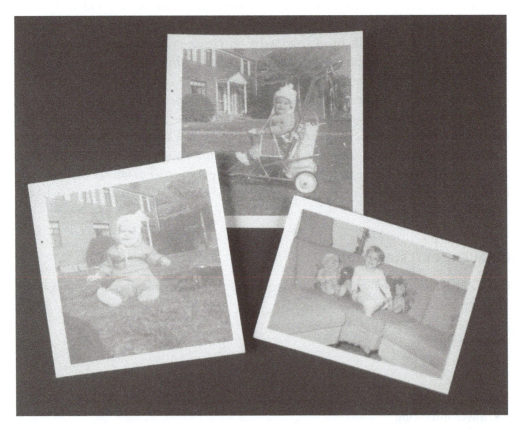

**FIGURE 9.12.** Chromogenic Prints Showing Light Fading on the Left and Dark Fading on the Right

Most commonly found on gelatin silver prints, silver mirroring appears as a reflective sheen in the dark areas of the silver-based image, which contain more silver than the lighter areas. If a photograph is exposed to high humidity, the gelatin emulsion layer may swell, exposing the silver to oxidation from acidic storage materials, pollutants, and other sources. The oxidized silver breaks away from the other silver molecules and travels through the swollen gelatin layer. The oxidized silver is eventually reduced back to metallic silver near the surface of the print. Consequently, some of the image is no longer in the same place and, therefore, it reflects light differently, giving a characteristic sheen. Silver mirroring does not improve once the photograph is in a stable storage environment, but it will not get worse either.

**FIGURE 9.13.** Gelatin Silver Print Showing Silver Mirroring in Dark Areas

Daguerreotypes are particularly vulnerable to metal and glass corrosion. Deterioration of the metal plate may first be visible as a blue or brown tarnish around the opening of the brass mat. As the metal corrosion progresses, the entire image may be obscured. Alkali salts tend to leach out of glass over time, particularly when enclosed in the daguerreotype package. This type of glass corrosion can appear either as droplets of liquid on the glass or as white crystalline deposits. In either case, the alkali salts can damage the image if they fall onto the daguerreotype plate. Glass supports for negatives and ambrotypes can also suffer from glass corrosion.

## Treatments

This section notes basic steps that can be taken to stabilize photographs and indicates when to call a conservator.

Photographs that are torn, cracked, or have detached labels should be placed into polyester sleeves, which will allow them to be viewed while providing physical support and keeping any detached elements together. Seek the services of a photograph conservator for tape removal or treatment of creases, tears, losses, and cracked or flaking emulsion.

Use clean pieces of soot-removal sponges, polyurethane sponges (also known as white cosmetic sponges), or white vinyl erasers to reduce surface dirt on mounts or on the back of photographs. Do not use pink or colored erasers. Be cautious of causing abrasion to the paper when using vinyl erasers, and stay clear of any inscriptions. Consult a conservator if the image area of a photograph needs cleaning, as photographic surfaces can be sensitive to abrasion.

Little can be done for fading, as chemical intensification of photographs is rarely practiced. Fading and color shifts are best addressed through scanning and digital restoration.

Photograph conservators must treat photographs that are blocked. They can very often be separated successfully, but treatment becomes much more complicated and less successful if part of the image layer has been pulled back, as happens when well-meaning, untrained people first come across the blocked photos and try to pull them apart. Likewise, conservators can remove photographs stuck to framing glass. To identify photographs blocked to glass, look for areas that seem darker and glossier than the surrounding image. If the image content of a photograph is more important than its historical or physical aspects, leave the photo in its frame and digitize it through the glass before treatment is attempted.

Rolled photographs should be humidified and flattened by a conservator. Unrolling photographs without humidification can easily cause them to crack and break, further complicating treatment.

During the first half of the 20th century, photo albums with black pages were very popular. Often these black pages have become exceedingly brittle and crumbly, making the album difficult to use, although they rarely cause chemical damage to photos in the album. Seek the advice of a conservator if you wish to repair the album to make it safe to use. If the physical presentation of the album is not significant to the historic or artifactual value of the photographs, stabilize the pages by removing them from the album and placing them in polyester sleeves.

Self-stick, or "magnetic" albums, were particularly popular in the 1970s and 1980s. The adhesive on these pages may cause staining of the photographs over time. If the plastic overlay is made of PVC, it may become blocked to the surface of the photographs. The adhesive might be very tenacious, so that the photographs cannot be easily removed, or it might have dried completely, so that the photographs are at risk of falling out of the album when pages are turned. If the album itself does not have historic, artistic, or artifactual value, the photographs may be removed, but consult a conservator if they do not come out easily.

Seek the advice of a photograph conservator when dealing with cased objects, particularly daguerreotypes. The exterior of the glass can be gently cleaned with a dry, lint-free cloth. Removing and unbinding the plate package is not recommended. The case can easily be broken when removing or inserting the daguerreotype plate package. As the images are extremely fragile, conservators experienced in working with daguerreotypes must clean them.

Lantern slides and the glass side only of gelatin dry plates can be gently wiped with a lint-free cloth. Be cautious of the labels and paper tape along the edges of lantern slides. Do not wipe the emulsion side of glass-plate negatives, and look out for any flaking. If a little moisture is needed to aid the cleaning, try the "huff and buff" technique of cleaning eyeglasses. Hold the glass close to your mouth and exhale quickly, causing a little fog on the glass, and wipe quickly with a lint-free cloth. If further cleaning is necessary, or if the glass-plate negatives are made with albumen or collodion emulsions, consult with a photograph conservator. Also consult with a conservator if they are cracked or flaking.

# MICROFORM (ROSS HARVEY)

*Dates in use*: 1930s to the present.
*Formats*: roll microfilm (16 and 35mm), microfiche, aperture cards, micro-opaques (also called microcards).

## Material

The term *microform* refers to "a highly reduced photographic copy of text and/or images stored on a translucent medium (microfiche or microfilm) or on an opaque medium such as card stock (micro-opaque or aperture card)."[3] The formats most heavily represented in collections are roll microfilm (16 and 35mm) and microfiche and aperture cards as flat sheets. A fourth format, micro-opaques or microcards, is similar to microfiche, but they are printed on card rather than photographic film.[4]

Microfilming (the process by which microforms are produced) was until the 1990s the most widely used method of preservation copying of analog materials. It was also used to provide access to analog materials that were determined to be at risk from frequent handling and materials for which there was a demand beyond the institution that held the originals. Digitizing has eclipsed microfilming as a method for providing access. Microfilming is now mainly used for the specialized purpose of long-term preservation of text-based information, although digitizing is rapidly replacing it for that purpose. Because microform still has a specialized role in an integrated life-cycle approach to preservation, digital files of textual information are being converted to microfilm using archive writer equipment.[5] Major libraries and archives throughout the world were in the past strongly committed to microfilming, so that microform is still heavily represented in collections. Currently many microform collections are being converted to digital formats because of the improved access and enhanced usability that digital versions provide.

The past popularity and ongoing use of microform is due to its longevity. When produced and stored to well-established standards for preservation microfilm, silver-gelatin PET films (films on a polyethylene terephthalate base) are stable, reliable information carriers that can store information securely for up to five hundred years, according to accelerated aging tests (ISO 18901:2010 Section 8.2).[6] Two other types of microfilm, diazo and vesicular, are also encountered in collections: these are used for making duplicate copies for use rather than for preservation purposes. A simple optical device is required to read microforms.

## Purposes

Microfilming was (and occasionally still is) used for making copies of physical documents, typically books, serials, newspapers, manuscripts, records on paper, and other text-based information on paper. It was commonly used to provide reformatted versions of objects of low artifactual value but also to make surrogates of objects with high artifactual value in order to protect those objects. It is best for black-and-white originals, and it does not capture gray tones well. (Color microfilm and continuous tone microfilm are briefly noted later in this chapter.) Many of the large-scale microfilming programs were a response to recognition that deteriorating paper was presenting major challenges for preservation; an example is the United States Newspaper Program (www.neh.gov/us-newspaper-program), funded by the National Endowment for the Humanities. Other large-scale microfilming programs were intended to provide improved access to inaccessible material, such as the Pacific Manuscripts Bureau (asiapacific.anu.edu.au/pambu), established in 1968 to locate and copy unpublished works relevant to the Pacific islands. The Bureau, sponsored by libraries in Australia, New Zealand, and Hawaii, carries out this task by locating relevant manuscripts and microfilming them.

In 1987 it was possible to write that "if the bulk of our materials are to remain available for the future, microfilming is currently our best preservation solution."[7] In addition to microform's primary applications of making long-lived preservation copies and improving access, other uses were for saving space (especially for serials, where the original object was discarded or moved to lower-cost storage after microfilming) and to provide a medium that could be cheaply and easily copied once a master had been produced. These characteristics of microform were significant in the past, in particular increased storage density (microform's ability to store large amounts of information in small containers) and the relative ease of duplicating copies, because they offered advantages over other methods of making surrogate versions. However, digitizing has largely superseded these advantages.

Microfilming is now predominantly used to provide a long-term preservation medium for copies of both physical and digital objects, in conjunction with digital copies to provide access. Another current use is to provide surrogates of damaged materials, such as brittle newspapers, that cannot be handled without significant loss of content. The materials are microfilmed, then the resulting microform is used to produce digital copies for access, while the microform master is stored for long-term preservation.

## Dates in Use

Microphotography was developed and available from 1839 but, apart from some isolated applications, it was not used consistently for library and archive purposes until a century later.[8] In the 1930s large projects commenced, such as the microfilming of deteriorating newspapers by the Library of Congress, the New York Public Library, and Harvard University's Foreign Newspaper Project, followed by microfilming of federal census records by the U.S. National Archives in the 1940s. In the 1950s and 1960s microfilming, especially of newspapers, was used increasingly in libraries and archives for preservation purposes and, in the 1970s, to save space. Major cooperative preservation microfilming programs, such as the United States Newspaper Program and its equivalents in other countries, proliferated in the 1980s and 1990s.

## Identification

Micro-opaques, also called microcards, are easily distinguished from other microforms because they are printed on card. Other microforms have a photographic film base.

### FILM BASES

Early microfilms used cellulose nitrate as the base. They are highly flammable, are subject to natural decomposition, and can release hazardous gases as they deteriorate. They were not produced after the early 1950s. Cellulose acetate film (also called safety base film), used from the 1920s until the 1990s, also degrades naturally over time but is not flammable. If not properly stored, cellulose acetate film degrades quickly. It is no longer considered acceptable as a preservation medium. Polyethylene (PET, polyethylene tere-phthalate), available from the 1980s, is the base material now used and specified in standards for preservation microfilming. It is stable and durable.

## FILM TYPES

Three types of microform are available: silver-gelatin, diazo, and vesicular. Silver-gelatin film that is carefully processed, housed, and handled to appropriate standards is used for archival master negatives for long-term retention. Because it is susceptible to damage from mechanical abrasion, working or use copies are more commonly diazo and vesicular, although they can be silver-gelatin. Diazo and vesicular film is less expensive and more scratch-resistant than silver-gelatin.

In *silver-gelatin* (or silver-halide) microforms the image is produced in the same way as black-and-white photographs. Light-sensitive silver compounds in an emulsion coating the base are exposed to light, and the resulting image is chemically developed, including—crucially—washing out potentially harmful chemicals during processing. If appropriately processed, stored, and handled, these silver-gelatin films are long lasting. Silver-gelatin microfilm is matte on one side and glossy on the other.

The image on *diazo* microforms is created by exposing diazonium salts in the coating layer to UV light. Film is exposed by contact printing from a master. Acids in the coating are neutralized by exposure to a strong alkali, allowing dyes to form in unexposed areas of the film. Diazo film may have an acetate or polyester base, although polyester is now more popular because it is more stable. Although diazo film is relatively stable, its image eventually fades, even if stored in the dark. It is less susceptible to abrasion because the image is embedded in the film and not on the film's surface as in silver-gelatin film. Exposure to strong light, such as the extended use of a film in a microfilm reader, speeds up the fading process of diazo microfilm. Diazo microfilm can be recognized by its glossy appearance on both sides of the film.

In *vesicular* microforms the diazonium salt coating is enclosed by two base layers. Applying heat to soften the base material develops the image and causes very small bubbles (vesicles) to form; these remain when the film cools. UV light fixes any residual photosensitive material. The areas with vesicles present appear dense when light is passed through them. The base must be polyester because acetate is not stable when heated. Vesicular film is susceptible to damage by mechanical pressure, which may collapse the vesicles, and to high temperatures which cause the gas in the vesicles to expand and rupture, appearing as clear patches on the film. Special care is necessary when vesicular film is used in a film reader. Vesicular microfilm can be recognized by its blue tinge.

Color microforms, although not common, are sometimes found in collections, particularly in Europe. Color microform has a lower life expectancy than preservation-quality silver-gelatin microform. Continuous-tone microfilm, used to reproduce gray-scale images, may also be encountered.

## Representation in Collections

Libraries and archives have traditionally produced or purchased 35mm microfilm because archival standards have been developed for this format. Also found in collections is 16mm microfilm, for which preservation microfilming standards have also been developed. Microfiche is also heavily represented, but it has typically been purchased as commercial products rather than produced in-house. Aperture cards, where a single frame of 35mm film is mounted in a card support, are no longer in common use.

Collections of preservation master microfilms are often encountered in the collections of libraries and archives. Microforms of newspapers are especially well represented in collections because of the many commercial filming programs and in-house and regional initiatives. Commercially produced microform collections, such as *Early English Books* and *Archives of the Communist Party of the Soviet State*, are widely held by larger libraries and archives; some of these collections were distributed on microfilm rolls and some on microfiche.

Roll film is most likely to be 35mm, the de facto library standard, with 16mm also well represented. Film cartridges containing either 8 and 16mm film are sometimes present. Microfiche was commonly used for commercial collections. Aperture cards are usually encountered in collections of engineering and architectural drawings and plans. The use of micro-opaques was principally for commercial collections, and they will be encountered in larger research libraries, which were the typical purchasers of these products. Because micro-opaques have a paper or card base rather than a film base, their preservation issues are not further noted in this section. (See the section "Paper: Library and Archives Material" in chapter 8 for information about paper preservation.)

The different reasons for the presence of microfilms in collections directly affect how their preservation should be managed. The highest priority is to preserve the preservation masters—the first-generation masters intended for long-term preservation. Second-generation masters (also called printing masters, copying masters, intermediates, or duplicate negatives), which also need to be given high priority, are printed from the first-generation master negative and are used to produce third-generation-use copies. The third-generation copies are intended for use in creating duplicates and for readers' end use. Use copies (also called service copies), including commercially distributed products, should have the lowest priority for preservation.

## Environment and Storage

### PREFERRED ENVIRONMENT

When considering the optimum storage environments for microform, it is necessary to distinguish between master negatives (including second-generation masters) and use copies. It is also essential to acknowledge that the processing of the film is of utmost importance in determining the archival life of a master negative. In the developing process the metallic silver image is fixed with a solution containing thiosulfate. If the fixing solution is not thoroughly washed off, the residual thiosulfate may result in staining and fading of the image. Tests to determine whether levels of residual chemicals are acceptable should be applied when master negatives are created.

*Storage Environment for Master Negatives.* To ensure as long a life as possible for master negatives, current standards must be followed. Key standards are ISO 18901:2010 and ANSI/AIIM MS23-2004, which prescribe a separate room or vault, define its fire resistance, and specify temperature and humidity levels. Maximum temperature in the vault is 65°F (18°C), with lower temperatures preferred, and the relative humidity should be kept at a level between 20 percent and 40 percent, with fluctuation ±5%. Ideally the vault should be at a separate physical location from the use copies, preferably in another geographic region. Appropriate storage facilities, likely to be too expensive for the individual institution to build and maintain, are available commercially and in some larger cultural heritage institutions, such as national libraries and archives. Cold storage of master negatives is ideal: the recommended levels are 40 to 50°F (4 to 10°C) and relative humidity 25 to 40 percent. Storage in temperatures below freezing point (32°F [0°C]) is also recommended.

Recommended practice is to make a second copy of the silver-gelatin master negative (a second-generation master) for duplicating purposes, again silver-gelatin. This is used when a copy of the negative is required, without causing damage to the master. It need not be stored in quite such stringent storage conditions as the master, although storing it at a physical location separate from the master negative is good risk-management practice.

If microforms are stored in temperatures that are different from reading room temperatures, they need to be conditioned (gradually warmed) if they are moved to warmer environments to avoid water condensation on the surface of the films. The recommended acclimatization period is twenty-four hours.

*Storage Environment for Use Copies.* As a general rule, the lower the temperature and the better controlled the relative humidity in the storage environment, the longer the expected life of the films, regardless of film type. Temperatures in which diazo and vesicular use copies are stored may be higher than those recommended for master negatives, but they should not exceed 70°F (21°C), relative humidity should not be higher than 50 percent, and fluctuations should be avoided. Diazo, vesicular, and silver-gelatin films should be separated and not stored in the same cabinet. Older vesicular films, in particular, should be stored separately, because they may produce hydrogen chloride gas as they deteriorate.

*Air Quality, Dehumidification, and Light.* Good-quality air is required for all areas where microforms are stored, but it is particularly important where masters are stored. Maintaining a positive air pressure in the storage area is recommended. Particulate air pollutants can scratch and abrade microfilm, especially silver-gelatin films, so mechanical filters should be used to filter out dust. Airborne contaminants, such as oxides of sulfur and nitrogen, paint fumes, ammonia, peroxides, ozone, and formaldehyde, can damage film bases and emulsions, for example, creating microblemishes on silver-gelatin films. To minimize these effects microforms should not be stored near photocopiers, which produce ozone, and they should be removed from any area being painted. Master microforms should not be stored where there are wooden shelves or cabinets.

Prefer refrigerant-based dehumidification systems over desiccant-based systems, which may generate fine dust particles that scratch film surfaces. If humidification is needed, the system must have a contaminant-free water source, as the corrosion inhibitors used in many large-scale systems can produce chemical and abrasive damage. Do not use trays of water or chemical solutions to humidify storage cabinets.

Light levels should be kept as low as possible, particularly levels of ultraviolet light.

Color microform is a special case. It has a shorter life expectancy than black-and-white film, largely because the dyes used are susceptible to fading and color change. Masters must be kept in the dark, and in very low temperatures (aim at 40°F [4°C]) and relative humidity kept less than 50 percent, with as little variation as possible.

## RECOMMENDATIONS FOR STORAGE

Roll film should be wound onto reels made from noncorrosive metal or inert plastic reels, and they should not be wound tightly on the reels. The containers in which the reels are stored should be of nonferrous metal, inert plastic, or paperboard with low lignin content and an alkaline reserve. To keep films from unrolling, use strips of alkaline paper with string ties; do not use rubber bands because they contain residual sulfur that reacts with the film. Relevant standards are ISO 18916:2007 *Imaging Materials—Processed Imaging Materials—Photographic Activity Test for Enclosure Materials* and ISO 18902:2013 *Imaging Materials—Processed Imaging Materials—Albums, Framing and Storage Materials.*

Steel cabinets with powder-coated finish are preferred. Microfilm should be stored vertically in them.

## Handling

### WHAT STAFF NEEDS TO KNOW

While all microform needs careful handling, the highest level of care in handling is essential for masters. Staff needs to be educated in the proper handling of microforms to ensure their longevity. Microform should be handled only by its edges in order to avoid obscuring the image by fingerprints depositing acidic oils on the surface. Roll film should never be pulled tight on the reel because this can cause abrasions. Threading film onto a microfilm reader is an activity in which it is easy to twist or scratch the film, so extra care is needed to avoid such damage.

Each film type has specific handling requirements. Silver-gelatin masters require special care because they are susceptible to damage from mechanical abrasion. Avoid touching the surface, and handle only using the leader (the piece of film at a beginning of a roll that precedes its image component). Gloves should always be worn by anyone handling master negatives. Controlling the use of different generations of microform is essential, in particular not allowing master negatives to be used as use copies and making duplicate copies only from second-generation masters.

Diazo film is damaged by exposure to light, so using it for long periods in a microfilm reader should be avoided. Vesicular film is susceptible to damage from mechanical pressure and high temperatures, so special care is necessary when it is used in a film reader. Because these film types are only used as use copies, copies can be replaced if damaged.

## WHAT USERS NEED TO KNOW

Users need to be made aware of the need for careful handling of microforms, especially when they are loading roll film onto a microfilm reader. The education of users regarding the need for proper handling and how to use microfilm readers is crucial.

## ONGOING MONITORING

Inspecting film on a regular basis to look for signs of blemish or deterioration and to identify and isolate unstable film (for example, cellulose acetate film) is important. Inspection every two years is optimum; in collections that hold very large numbers of films, random selection of film for inspection is advised. ANSI/AIIM MS45-1990 *Recommended Practice for Inspection of Stored Silver-Gelatin Microforms for Evidence of Deterioration* provides guidelines for inspecting silver-gelatin film.

## VIEWING EQUIPMENT

Reading equipment needs to be selected carefully, taking account of ease of use and of maintenance.

A frequent source of damage to microfilm is the difficulty some users have in threading microfilm onto reading equipment. This can be minimized by placing clear instructions on or near each microfilm reader. Microform reading machines should be turned off whenever a user leaves the equipment to avoid excess heat being generated and excessive light exposure if film is left in the reader.

Microform reading equipment must be well maintained so it does not damage the film. In particular, all parts of the equipment that come into contact with the microform must be thoroughly cleaned at frequent intervals, preferably daily. Responsibility for equipment maintenance should be assigned to a trained staff member. Dust covers should always be used to cover reading equipment when not in use. Glass flats and carriers should be cleaned daily to prevent the buildup of abrasive grime on the glass flats.

## Disaster Response

Microforms are highly susceptible to water damage, so the best strategy is to protect them in storage facilities that are free from any risk of flood, such as in metal cabinets located in areas away from water pipes. If a microform does become wet, it needs to be immersed in clean, cold water and kept wet until it is ready for drying, preferably by experts. It should be sent, as soon as possible, to a film processing laboratory for drying. It must be removed from enclosures (boxes, cans, or sleeves), and roll film must be unrolled for drying. Air-drying can be used, but for larger quantities a film processing laboratory can provide this service, so access to such services in the event of an emergency should be negotiated in advance. Microfiche can be dried flat, emulsion side up, in single layers or clipped to a line by an edge that does not bear an image. Everything possible should be done to prevent mold growth. If it occurs on silver-gelatin film, professional assistance must be sought. Mold on diazo and vesicular films may be removed with a slightly moistened, lint-free pad.

## Decay

On silver-gelatin film the gelatin layer is easily scratched, one major cause being use in readers that have not been adequately maintained. Silver-gelatin microforms are more sensitive to water and humidity damage than other film types. Where humidity levels are too high, fungus (mold, mildew) growth can attack the gelatin and destroy the image. Redox blemishes (microscopic red or orange spots and rings) caused by silver oxidation may develop, the risk of this increasing when relative humidity levels rise above 40 percent. (Polysulfide treatment of silver-gelatin microforms is often applied to reduce the risk of redox blemishes.) If the microform has not been correctly processed and residual chemicals are present, image loss can occur.

Diazo microforms are vulnerable to fungal attack when temperature and relative humidity levels of the storage environment are not controlled. Continuous exposure to light for more than three hours in readers causes damage.

Vesicular microforms are damaged when subjected to pressure, which causes the vesicles to collapse. Continuous elevated temperature can also deform the vesicles. They are, however, not vulnerable to fungal growth and do not develop redox blemishes.

Mechanical damage can affect all types of microform. Scratching can occur, and accidental tearing or bending of the microform can cause damage. As film ages it may become brittle, and in advanced cases of deterioration it may become severely decomposed to the extent that salvage is impossible.

Film on a nitrate base may sometimes be encountered, but it is now uncommon. Its irreversible chemical deterioration, exacerbated by high temperature and relative humidity levels, exhibits these symptoms:

- The film turns yellow and the image exhibits silver mirroring.
- The film becomes sticky and gives off a strong nitric acid odor.
- The film turns an amber color, and the silver image begins to fade.
- The film becomes soft and may adhere to adjacent materials, and the image becomes illegible.
- The film breaks down completely, turning into a brown powder.

When nitrate film is identified duplication onto stable film is recommended.

Acetate film is likely to be a significant risk. For film on a cellulose acetate base the symptoms of deterioration are:

- The film gives off a vinegar odor (due to acetic acid) and begins to become brittle and shrink.
- The film begins to curl and may have blue or pink staining.
- The film loses flexibility and warps.
- The film develops liquid-filled bubbles and crystalline deposits, sometimes obscuring the image.
- As the film base continues to shrink, the emulsion becomes separated from the base in some areas, known as channeling.

Cold or frozen storage slows deterioration. The use of A-D strips, which change color when acetic acid produced by degrading cellulose acetate film is detected, is recommended. Copying masters onto a polyester base is essential, perhaps also digitizing it at the same time if its level of use is high enough.

### Treatments

In-house staff can carry out some basic procedures. Splicing of masters, using splicing tape or silver polyester tape, should be carried out only by trained and experienced staff. Consider replacing damaged use copies rather than splicing them.

The specialist services of a film processing laboratory or a conservator knowledgeable about film should be sought to handle the drying of wet microforms.

## STANDARDS AND FURTHER READING

### Standards

ANSI/AIIM MS23-2004. *Recommended Practice—Production, Inspection, and Quality Assurance of First-Generation, Silver Microforms of Documents.*

ANSI/AIIM MS45-1990. *Recommended Practice for the Inspection of Stored Silver-Gelatin Microforms for Evidence of Deterioration.*

ANSI/AIIM MS48-1999. *Recommended Practice—Microfilming Public Records on Silver Halide Film.*

BS 1153:1992. *Recommendations for Processing and Storage of Silver-Gelatin-Type Microfilm.*

ISO 18901:2010. *Imaging Materials—Processed Silver-Gelatin-Type Black-and-White Films—Specifications for Stability.*

ISO 18902:2013. *Imaging Materials—Processed Imaging Materials—Albums, Framing and Storage Materials.*

ISO 18911:2010. *Imaging Materials—Processed Safety Photographic Films—Storage Practices.*

ISO 18916:2007. *Imaging Materials—Processed Imaging Materials—Photographic Activity Test for Enclosure Materials.*

ISO 18918:2000. *Imaging Materials—Processed Photographic Plates—Storage Practices.*
ISO 18920:2011. *Imaging Materials—Reflection Prints—Storage Practices.*
NFPA 40:2011. *Standard for the Storage and Handling of Cellulose Nitrate Film.*

## Further Reading

American Institute for Conservation of Historic and Artistic Works. "Find a Conservator." Accessed October 4, 2013. http://www.conservation-us.org/index.cfm?fuseaction=Page.view Page&pageId=495&parentID=472.

Barger, Susan M., and William B. White. *The Daguerreotype: Nineteenth-Century Technology and Modern Science.* Baltimore: Johns Hopkins University Press, 2000.

Brown, Heather. *Training in Preservation Microfilming: Physical Management and Storage of Micro-forms.* Canberra, ACT: National Library of Australia, 2003. Accessed September 27, 2013. http://www.nla.gov.au/sites/default/files/module9sc.pdf.

Brown, Heather, et al. "The Role of Microfilm in Digital Preservation." In *DCC Digital Curation Reference Manual.* Glasgow: HATII, 2011. Accessed March 1, 2013. http://www.dcc.ac.uk/sites/default/files/documents/Microfilm_2011_Final.pdf.

Dalton, Steve. "Microfilm and Microfiche." Andover, MA: Northeast Documentation Conservation Center, 2007. Accessed September 27, 2013. http://www.nedcc.org/free-resources/preservation-leaflets/6.-reformatting/6.1-microfilm-and-microfiche.

Elkington, Nancy E., ed. *RLG Archives Microfilming Manual.* Mountain View, CA: Research Libraries Group, 1994.

Elkington, Nancy E., ed. *RLG Preservation Microfilming Handbook.* Mountain View, CA: Research Libraries Group, 1992.

Fischer, Monique. "A Short Guide to Film Base Photographic Materials: Identification, Care, and Duplication." Andover, MA: Northeast Document Conservation Center, 2012. Accessed October 6, 2013. http://www.nedcc.org/free-resources/preservation-leaflets/5.-photographs/5.1-a-short-guide-to-film-base-photographic-materials-identification,-care,-and-duplication.

Fox, Lisa L., ed. *Preservation Microfilming: A Guide for Librarians and Archivists*, 2nd ed. Chicago: American Library Association, 1996.

George Eastman House. *Notes on Photographs.* Accessed October 4, 2013. http://noteson photographs.org.

Image Permanence Institute. *Graphics Atlas.* Accessed October 4, 2013. http://www.graphicsatlas.org.

Jürgens, Martin C. *The Digital Print: Identification and Preservation.* Los Angeles: Getty Conservation Institute, 2009.

Lavédrine, Bertrand. *Photographs of the Past: Process and Preservation.* Los Angeles: Getty Conservation Institute, 2007.

Lavédrine, Bertrand. *Preventive Conservation of Photograph Collections.* Los Angeles: Getty Conservation Institute, 2003.

National Park Service. "Cold Storage: A Long-Term Preservation Strategy for Film-Based Photographic Materials." Accessed November 5, 2013. http://www.nps.gov/history/museum/coldstorage/html/index.html.

Penichon, Sylvie. *Twentieth-Century Color Photographs: Identification and Care.* Los Angeles: Getty Conservation Institute, 2013.

Valverde, María Fernanda. *Photographic Negatives: Nature and Evolution of Processes*. 2nd ed. Rochester, NY: Advanced Residency Program in Photograph Conservation, 2005. Accessed October 4, 2013. https://www.imagepermanenceinstitute.org/webfm_send/302.

Von Waldthausen, Clara C. "Exhibition of Photographic Materials in Library and Archive Collections." *Topics in Photographic Preservation* 10 (2003): 178–90.

## NOTES

1. ISO 18902:2013. *Imaging Materials—Processed Photographic Films, Plates and Papers—Filing Enclosures and Storage Containers*.

2. For further information see Clara C. von Waldthausen, "Exhibition of Photographic Materials in Library and Archive Collections," in *Topics in Photographic Preservation* 10 (2003): 178–90.

3. Jean Reitz, *ODLIS: Online Dictionary for Library and Information Science*, ABC CLIO, accessed September 27, 2013, http://www.abc-clio.com/ODLIS/odlis_m.aspx.

4. William Saffady, *Micrographics: Technology for the 21st Century* (Prairie Village, KS: ARMA International, 2000), chapter 2, provides more details of the variety of microform formats.

5. Heather Brown et al., "The Role of Microfilm in Digital Preservation," in *DCC Digital Curation Reference Manual* (Glasgow: HATII, 2011), accessed September 27, 2013, http://www.dcc.ac.uk/sites/default/files/documents/Microfilm_2011_Final.pdf.

6. ISO 18901:2010, *Imaging Materials—Processed Silver-Gelatin-Type Black-and-White Films—Specifications for Stability* (London; Geneva: BSI; ISO, 2010), Section 8.2 Accelerated ageing test.

7. Nancy Gwinn, ed., *Preservation Microfilming* (Chicago: ALA, 1987), 4.

8. Paul Wilson, "Historical Perspective on the Use of Microfilm in Libraries and Archives," in *Preservation Microfilming: Does It Have a Future?: Proceedings of the First National Conference of the National Preservation Office, National Library of Australia*, 1994 (Canberra, ACT: National Library of Australia, 1995), 46–56.

# CHAPTER 10

# Sound Materials

· · · · · · · · · · · · · · · · · · · · · · · · · · · · · · · · · · · · · · · · · · · · · · · · · · · · · · · · · · · · · · · · · · · · · · · · · · ·

Elizabeth Walters, Bob Pymm, Matthew Davies

## SOUND MATERIALS: MAGNETIC MEDIA (ELIZABETH WALTERS)

*Dates in use*: mid-1930s to the present.

*Formats*: open-reel tape formats (notably ¼-inch audiotape); compact cassettes (more commonly referred to as audiocassettes); small-cassette formats such as minicassettes, microcassettes, and digital audio tape (DAT); other early cassette and cartridge formats; wire recordings; magnetic dictation belts and discs.

### Materials

Tape-based formats comprise by far the largest segment of the magnetic media group. Audio formats most commonly found in libraries and archives include a variety of open-reel tape formats (notably ¼-inch audiotape), compact cassettes (more commonly referred to as audiocassettes), and small-cassette formats such as minicassettes, microcassettes, and digital audiotape (DAT). Other magnetic recording formats include wire recordings, magnetic dictation belts and discs, and a host of early (and, in most cases, short-lived) cassette and cartridge formats.

Magnetic recording rapidly gained in popularity following the technology's introduction into the North American market in the late 1940s. Continual innovation and improvements in fidelity, functionality, portability, and pricing ensured that magnetic media remained the dominant presence in nearly every segment of the recording market (consumer, professional, educational, and industrial) for more than five decades. Today, virtually every magnetic sound recording format has been superseded, either by other types of physical media (for example, optical formats such as CDs) or by file-based digital recording technologies, for almost all applications. Nevertheless, content stored

· · · · · · · · · · · · · · · · · · · · · · · · · · · · · · · · · · · · · · · · · · · · · · · · · · · · · · · · · · · · · · · · · · · · · · · · · · ·

on magnetic media remains a significant and irreplaceable component of the holdings of most libraries, archives, and other cultural heritage institutions. The preservation of these legacy media poses formidable challenges, not only from the standpoint of physical deterioration of the carriers themselves (none of which was ever intended to last more than a few decades) but also in light of the obsolescence and dwindling availability both of the hardware required to access the content stored on these media and of the parts and technicians needed to service the equipment. Moreover, while it is often possible to slow the deterioration of audiovisual media by optimizing the storage environment and restricting handling and playback, the broad consensus within the audiovisual preservation community is that reformatting through digitization and continued migration is the only viable long-term strategy for preservation.[1]

## Purposes

Magnetic audiotape was introduced in Germany in 1935 by the BASF Corporation, after more than thirty years of experimentation and innovation with recording onto wire, metal bands, paper tape, and other materials.[2] The technology arrived in the United States immediately following World War II, and the first commercial magnetic tape products appeared on the market in 1947.[3] Adoption of the expensive new technology was initially limited to the recording and broadcasting industries, which quickly recognized the potential for use in studio mastering and prerecording programs for delayed broadcast.[4]

During the early years of the magnetic tape recording industry, the wire recorder, which previously had been used almost exclusively by the military, achieved a brief popularity for office, home, and field recording applications. Unlike the home recording discs of the time, wire recordings could be re-recorded repeatedly and offered much longer recording times. By the mid-1950s, however, the wire recorder had been supplanted by open-reel tape recorders thanks to the growing availability of affordable, portable, high-fidelity consumer models.[5] Thereafter, the use of open-reel audiotape recording quickly expanded beyond the professional arena to encompass fieldwork and scholarly research in virtually every academic discipline, as well as home recording, education and training applications, documentation, and commercial distribution of prerecorded music.

Numerous analog cassette and cartridge formats, most of which were extremely short-lived, emerged throughout the 1960s as manufacturers sought to develop a low-cost, portable, and easy-to-use alternative to open-reel tape for both prerecorded content and home recording use. Of these, the Philips Compact Cassette (more popularly known as the audiocassette), dominated the magnetic tape market for more than three decades following its introduction in 1963. Originally conceived as a simple and reliable office dictation format, the compact cassette quickly replaced the open-reel tape for most non-professional applications as rapid technological advances steadily improved its sound quality and performance.[6] For some thirty years the compact cassette remained one of the two main formats for dissemination of commercially recorded music, sharing this distinction first with the vinyl LP, and later with the compact disc, which took over as the dominant format in the commercial recording market in the early 2000s.

Several analog small-cassette formats, notably the minicassette and the microcassette, were introduced from the late 1960s. These durable, low-fidelity miniature cassettes were primarily used in office dictation and answering machines as well as in handheld personal recorders. In the early 1980s, a few manufacturers produced high-quality metal particle tapes in these formats for niche applications such as music recording and computer data storage. However, the high-grade tapes were not compatible with most conventional recorders, and they were largely unsuccessful due to the high cost and poor battery life of the special recorders they required. Analog small-cassette formats gradually disappeared in the early 1990s with the advent of the digital voice recorder.

Introduced by Sony in 1987, the Digital Audio Tape (known as R-DAT or DAT) was conceived as a replacement for the compact cassette. The DAT offered lossless encoding, making it a popular choice for studio and field recording, broadcasting, and archiving applications. However, the format failed to achieve similar success in the consumer market due in part to the high cost of recorders and the lack of commercial releases on the format.[7] DAT quickly became obsolete after Sony terminated the production of playback equipment in late 2005.

## Dates in Use

> Open-reel audiotape: mid-1930s to the present
> Wire recordings: 1930s to the mid-1950s
> Philips Compact Cassette (or audiocassette): 1963 to the mid-1990s
> Minicassettes: late 1960s to the early 1990s
> Microcassettes: late 1960s to the early 1990s
> Digital Audio Tape (R-DAT or DAT): 1987 to ca. 2005

## Identification

All magnetic tape is composed of at least two layers: (1) magnetic pigment or other magnetizable material that stores the recorded signal, and (2) a base layer, or basefilm, which serves as a structural support for the magnetic material (figure 10.1). In most cases, the magnetic particles are suspended in a polymer binder that disperses them evenly across the tape surface and bonds them to the base layer. In others (notably metal evaporate tapes), the magnetizable material is a thin, vapor-deposited layer of metal alloy that does not employ a binder. This mixture may also contain a variety of additives to improve the quality of the tape, including lubricants, plasticizers, surfactants, solvents, cleaning agents, and fungicides. Binders are notoriously proprietary, varying widely among manufacturers and even among individual product lines of a single manufacturer.[8] Since the late 1960s, most magnetic tape has also included a backcoating layer to improve tape wind and reduce curling and the buildup of static electricity, which can

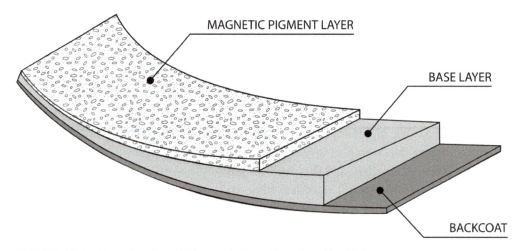

MAGNETIC PIGMENT LAYER

BASE LAYER

BACKCOAT

**FIGURE 10.1.** Cross Section of Magnetic Tape. Drawing, Eve Neiger

attract dust and cause dropouts. Each of these layers presents a different set of preservation challenges.

*Base Layer.* The base layer (also basefilm or substrate) is largely responsible for the tape's mechanical strength and stability. Historically, four different types of base layer have been used for audiotape: paper, used from the late 1940s to the early 1950s; cellulose acetate, manufactured from the mid-1930s until the mid-1960s; polyvinyl chloride (PVC), produced primarily in Germany from the early 1940s to around 1970; and polyester (polyethylene terephthalate, or PET), in use from the late 1950s to the present.[9] In addition to PET, polyethylene naphthalate (PEN) is used for some DAT tapes. Of the four types of base layer, polyester has demonstrated the greatest chemical stability.[10] Common trade names for polyester include Mylar (DuPont), Tenzar (Scotch/3M), and Estar (Kodak).

The base layer material of open-reel audiotape is easily identified. When held up to the light and viewed at an angle, a reel of acetate-base tape will appear translucent, while polyester and PVC tapes will appear opaque. Acetate tape is somewhat stiff and will break cleanly under sufficient tension, while polyester tape is comparatively supple and will stretch and curl before breaking.[11] Paper tape has a brown or white backing that looks and feels like paper and tears easily. All compact cassettes have a polyester base.

*Magnetic Pigment Layer.* The first widely used magnetic pigment was gamma ferric oxide ($\gamma Fe_2O_3$), used for all open-reel audiotape and IEC Type I (normal bias) compact cassettes[12] until the early 1960s. Although extremely stable, $\gamma Fe_2O_3$ offered only limited recording density. This prompted the development of chromium dioxide ($CrO_2$) and cobalt-doped ferric oxide (cobalt-doped $Fe_3O_4$) pigments in the late 1960s. These pigments, which achieved the greater concentrations of magnetic particles required to support higher recording densities, were mainly used for Type II (high-bias) compact cassettes.[13] Type III compact cassettes, which are rarely encountered, used a dual layer of both $\gamma Fe_2O_3$ and $CrO_2$. From the 1980s, two types of pure metal (nonoxide) pigments came into use: metal particle (MP), which contains pure iron particles treated with a protective coating to prevent oxidation; and metal evaporate (ME), comprised of a thin, homogeneous layer of metal alloy that is vapor-deposited onto the tape base.[14] Audio formats using metal pigments include Type IV compact cassettes and DAT.[15]

*Other*. Magnetic cassette formats almost always have identifying information such as format name, manufacturer, brand name, and maximum running time (in minutes) imprinted on the shell. The type of base layer and magnetic pigment layer may also be included. However, it should be remembered that commercial packaging materials such as blank labels, inserts, reels, and tape leader are frequently transferred from one AV object to another, and thus they may not always be a reliable indication of the media they contain.

Wire recordings are typically wound on metal or wooden reels of varying diameters, with 2¾-inch reels being the most common.[16]

## Representation in Collections

Magnetically recorded audio content has been an integral component of the collections of every type of cultural heritage institution since the technology became commercially available in the 1940s. Large concentrations of magnetic media may be found in academic, public, and corporate libraries, museums, archives, and historical societies, government and corporate entities, and private collections of all kinds. Content includes recordings of cultural, historical, scholarly, or institutional significance created by scholars, researchers, educators, artists, and performers as primary sources, works of art, and documentary records. The condition and quality of these media holdings varies widely, and they may include everything from professionally produced studio recordings on high-grade media to amateur recordings made in the field using handheld recorders on substandard media.

Magnetic media have played an especially important role in oral history, folklore, and ethnographic collections. Almost any magnetic format may be found in these collections, although ¼-inch open-reel audiotape, compact cassettes, miniature cassettes, and DAT are likely to be especially well represented. Recordings in such collections were often made at slow speeds on long-playing tapes, which have a very thin base layer and thus are more susceptible to mechanical damage.

Radio and television broadcasters were the earliest adopters of magnetic recording technologies, and they continued to embrace new formats as they became available. As a result, broadcast archives and collections typically contain a diverse range of magnetic audio formats, including wire recordings, open-reel audiotape, compact cassettes, and DAT.

As obsolescent formats were superseded by new ones, media content was repeatedly transferred to the newer formats to ensure continued access. It is not unusual for cultural heritage collections to hold the same content on several generations of copies in both magnetic and nonmagnetic formats.

Today, much of the content captured on these media is effectively inaccessible to users, in part because repositories often lack item-level control of the content and also because they no longer possess the specialized equipment or expertise required to play back the media. In addition, it is not unusual for media to be misidentified or poorly cared for because in-house staff lacks the resources and expertise to adequately process and preserve these materials.

## Environment and Storage

### PREFERRED ENVIRONMENT

Ensuring a clean, temperature- and humidity-controlled storage environment is the single best means of extending the life expectancy of magnetic media. An optimal environment cannot reverse or halt degradation, but it can go a long way toward slowing the progression.

Temperature and relative humidity have a major impact on the health and longevity of magnetic media. High humidity can promote binder hydrolysis, a chemical reaction in which the binder (typically polyurethane) absorbs ambient moisture and becomes soft and sticky. In moderate cases, this may cause the tape to chatter or squeal when played. In more severe cases, it may cause the magnetic layer to pull away from the tape base (a condition commonly referred to as "sticky shed syndrome") and clog playback equipment with a gummy residue that can lead to a significant loss of high frequencies.[17] Prolonged exposure to high levels of humidity (above 65 percent RH) can also encourage mold and other fungus growth, which can destroy the pigment layer of magnetic tape.[18] Fungus growth is more likely to be a problem with older tapes, as fungicides have been added to the binders of most modern tapes. High humidity and temperatures may also lead to curling, embrittlement, and shrinkage of the tape base, particularly in acetate-based tapes.[19] Wire recordings are subject to corrosion when exposed to high humidity, particularly in the case of early recordings, which may not be stainless steel.[20]

Temperature determines the speed of chemical reactions such as hydrolysis: reactions accelerate markedly as temperatures increase. Storage at elevated temperatures (greater than 75°F [24°C]) can also cause the tape pack to tighten, resulting in tape deformation and the increased likelihood of blocking (adhesion of successive tape layers) and print-through (the magnetization of one tape layer by an adjacent layer, creating an audible pre-echo or postecho).[21]

Excessively low temperatures and humidity can also be detrimental to magnetic media. Temperatures below 32°F (0°C) may cause binders to become brittle and even the most stable tape bases to stretch and shrink. Low humidity can cause a tape pack to loosen, leading to mechanical damage and static buildup during playback, and it may also promote loss of lubricant.[22]

Fluctuations in temperature and humidity, even within a fairly narrow range, can be even more damaging than any single extreme of temperature or humidity, particularly if they occur frequently. The magnetic pigment, binder, and base layer all expand and contract at different rates, and the resulting dimensional changes can permanently distort the tape base.[23] This distortion can impair head-to-tape contact, which is particularly problematic with high-density recordings.[24]

While recommendations for acceptable or optimal levels of temperature and relative humidity vary widely, nearly all of them call for low levels of both temperature and relative humidity and for minimal fluctuations in both these parameters. ISO standards offer recommendations regarding temperature and humidity levels for both medium-term (ten-plus years) and long-term (fifty-plus years) storage of magnetic media. The broadest range specifies temperatures of 46°F (8°C) to 74°F (23°C) and relative humidity of 15 percent to 50 percent with fluctuation of no more than 5°F (±2°C) and ±5 percent, respectively, over a twenty-four-hour period. The lower end of this range is preferable.

*Air Quality and Light.* Another critical environmental consideration for magnetic media is the presence of contaminants, such as pollution, dust, smoke, fingerprints, and hair. Contaminants hinder head-to-tape contact and may be dragged into the tape winds during playback, creating irreparable scratches or indentations in the magnetic layer that result in signal distortion or loss. Even minute debris can cause signal loss or drop-outs. Pollution may also cause corrosion of metal evaporate and metal particle tapes. A scrupulously clean storage and operating environment that includes clean, uncarpeted floors, good air filtration, and a smoke-free, food-free environment will help to minimize damaging dust and debris and will also discourage vermin.

Exposure to light, especially ultraviolet light, can be damaging to both the media and their enclosures, and it should therefore be kept to a minimum. Store media away from windows and fluorescent lighting, and use UV shields if necessary.

## RECOMMENDATIONS FOR STORAGE

All magnetic media should be oriented vertically in storage, resting on their spines or edges, to prevent tape pack deformation and edge damage. (The exception is wire recordings, which may be stored either vertically or horizontally.) Store media away from sources of both fluorescent and natural light, as well as from potential sources of water incursion such as windows, plumbing, and air-conditioning units. Tapes with a loose pack or uneven wind should be rewound before being placed in storage to avoid permanent deformation of the tape base. An even, well-tensioned wind will also help minimize damage to tapes in the event of a water disaster, as water and debris cannot easily penetrate the tape pack.[25]

Store media on sturdy shelves, preferably electrically grounded, that are capable of supporting the weight. Shelving should also allow for adequate air circulation. Use of dividers to keep media from leaning is also recommended. If using motorized compact shelving, keep media away from motors.

Popular myth to the contrary, accidental erasure of a magnetic tape recording by stray magnetic fields is a rare occurrence, owing both to the high coercivity (ability to resist demagnetization) of most magnetic tape and to the unlikelihood of exposure to a sufficiently strong magnetic field. (Analog audio recordings are somewhat more sensitive to stray fields than are later formats or digital recordings due to the lower coercivity of their magnetic pigments.) Nevertheless, it is advisable to store magnetic media at least four to six inches (ten to fifteen centimeters) away from anything that might generate a magnetic or electrical field (such as motors, generators, loudspeakers, and electrical transformers), as the magnetic fields emanating from these devices may also cause increased low-frequency noise or higher levels of print-through. Similar care should also be taken during shipping and transport. It should also be noted that many theft detection systems that use magnetized security strips emit strong magnetic fields that are not appropriate for use with magnetic media.[26]

If magnetic media are stored at temperature or humidity levels substantially lower than those of the use environment, they should be allowed to acclimatize in the use environment for up to twenty-four hours before attempting playback. Failure to allow for adequate acclimatization may lead to moisture condensation, mechanical damage, and mistracking during playback. Recommended acclimatization periods may differ markedly depending on such variables as tape thickness, enclosure type, and specific storage conditions. Acclimatization considerations and recommendations are discussed in standards AES-22:1997 (r2003) and ISO 18923:2000.

*Enclosures.* Enclosures should be made of durable, impact-resistant, chemically inert materials such as polypropylene, and should afford adequate protection from moisture, light, and heat as well as dust and other contaminants. Avoid cardboard, paper, or plastic slipcases, boxes, and other flexible containers that offer little protection from water or fire damage and may interact chemically with the media. Enclosures should latch securely and allow for proper orientation of the media in storage.

Loose paper or other items should not be stored inside the enclosure, as paper tends to generate dust, which is abrasive and can cause dropouts. Some paper may also contain harmful acids. Moreover, the added bulk created by inserts may exert damaging pressure or stress on the media, particularly if the inserts include paper clips, staples, or other sharp fasteners.

Open-reel tapes should be wound onto sturdy, unslotted reels made of noncorrosive metal or inert plastic and housed in enclosures with hubs that do not allow the reel's weight to rest on the flanges. The loose end of the tape should be secured to the outer side of the reel flange with hold-down tape made specifically for this purpose: do not use conventional pressure-sensitive tape, which may leave harmful, sticky residue. Protective paper collars may also be used. Small-cassette formats such as DAT and microcassettes should be grouped in larger containers to prevent damage or loss.

Use archival-quality labels that are nonacidic, adhere securely, and can otherwise be expected to last for the life of the media. Write on labels before affixing them to the media; do not write directly on media with pens or solvent-based markers. Do not use pressure-sensitive tape to attach labels or other documentation to reels, cassettes, or cartridges. In particular, do not adhere labels on or near the tape doors or in any other position that interferes with the tape transport. When feasible, labels should be attached to the enclosure rather than to the carrier itself. If media are rehoused, care should be taken to transfer all relevant descriptive information, including manufacturer and product information, to the new enclosure.

## Handling

### WHAT STAFF NEED TO KNOW

All magnetic media should be handled carefully; however, particular care must be taken with masters, fragile or deteriorating formats, and unique or irreplaceable items. Staff who deal with these materials must be trained in proper handling methods to prevent irrevocable loss of content.

Handle both media and playback equipment gently and as infrequently as possible. Keep hands clean and dry; consider wearing lint-free cotton gloves. Never touch the edges or recording surface of any magnetic media, as fingerprints may leave an oily residue. Handle tape reels by the center hub, taking care not to put pressure on the reel flanges, which could damage tape edges. Never pull on the loose end of a tape to tighten the wind, as this may cause the tape to stretch, crease, or break, and it may damage the magnetic layer. Magnetic media should not be dropped or subjected to sudden shock, which may cause reel or shell breakage, container damage, and tape pack distortion.

Magnetic media should never be forced into storage enclosures or playback equipment. Never eject a tape in the middle of a recording, or pause it for extended periods, as this may damage the tape or cause accidental erasure. Do not leave media sitting in playback equipment, where the tape may overheat and is in close proximity to recording and erase heads. For added security, engage the record-protection mechanism found on most cassette media. Cassettes should never be left in a partially wound state; always wind to one end before ejecting. Wind tapes at normal playback speeds; never fast-forward or rewind at high speed, which may cause uneven tension or wind. Return each tape to its enclosure immediately after use. Good housekeeping is essential; eating, drinking, and smoking should never be permitted in or near areas where magnetic media are stored or handled.

### WHAT USERS NEED TO KNOW

Ideally, users should not be allowed to handle or play back masters or any original recordings that contain unique or irreplaceable content. If users are to be permitted to play back media themselves, they should be trained in the same handling procedures as staff. Encourage all users to report any problems they may observe.

### OTHER HANDLING CONSIDERATIONS

Media should periodically be examined for signs of damage and deterioration, particularly after being subjected to sharp fluctuations in temperature or relative humidity.

Look for oxide shedding, tape pack problems, debris, enclosure deterioration, reel or shell damage, loose or detached pressure pads, and strong odors, which can indicate chemical deterioration. Any dust or debris should be wiped away using a lint-free cloth; solvents or other cleaning solutions should never be used to clean either the media themselves or their enclosures.[27]

## Playback Equipment

Playback on misaligned or poorly maintained equipment is a frequent cause of mechanical damage to magnetic media. Any playback equipment in frequent use should be professionally inspected, cleaned, and calibrated on a regular basis. Playback areas should be kept cool, dry, and free of dust and other contaminants, as dirt or debris anywhere in the tape transport can permanently scratch both the tape heads and the tape surface. When not in use, playback equipment should be turned off to prevent overheating; the use of dust covers is also recommended. Before attempting playback, carefully inspect all media for any signs of deterioration, including reel or shell damage, loose or missing pressure pads, and dirt or debris that could harm the media or the equipment during playback. Never attempt to play media on a machine not specifically designed for that format. Given the fragility and irreplaceability of both media and playback equipment, only trained personnel should be permitted to operate the equipment.

## Disaster Response

Nearly all magnetic media are extremely vulnerable to damage from water and fire. Salvage and remediation work is almost always an expensive and complex undertaking, with no guarantee of success. As such, the best strategy is to focus on preventive measures that include keeping media well protected from damage by housing them in appropriate protective enclosures and storing them far away from potential sources of heat, light, and water, including basements, attics, water pipes, sprinklers, air-conditioning vents, and windows. Media with content of enduring value should be digitized for preservation at the earliest opportunity.

### WATER DAMAGE

Most magnetic media are not in immediate danger from short-term exposure to clean water. However, extended exposure can cause irreparable damage, so recovery efforts should be considered time-sensitive.[28] Some magnetic media are extremely vulnerable to damage from even minimal exposure to water. These include older or deteriorating tapes, paper or acetate-based tapes, and metal particle or metal evaporate tapes such as DAT, which are highly susceptible to corrosion and may suffer permanent damage if immersed for any length of time. These media should be given top priority during a salvage effort.

Wet tapes should be kept cool (but not frozen) and treated as soon as possible to prevent fungal growth, which can occur in less than twenty-four hours. Magnetic media that have been exposed to rainwater, sewage, salt water, chlorinated water, or other contaminated water should be rinsed in cool, distilled water and not be permitted to dry out, as contaminants may adhere to the tape surface and be more difficult to remove later. Wire recordings should be rinsed if necessary and dried immediately to avoid possible corrosion.

Wet magnetic tape is easily stretched or torn and should be handled gently. Do not attempt to unwind or play back wet or contaminated media. Maintain wet media in the same orientation as found in order to avoid spreading contaminants. Prior to recovery, keep wet media in an area that is cool and well ventilated. If water-affected media must be separated from their enclosures and inserts to promote drying and prevent fungal growth, thorough documentation is essential in order to avoid disassociation of the media from their content information.

An experienced audiovisual disaster recovery vendor should be called in to handle large quantities of disaster-affected media, especially if very wet or contaminated by mold or debris. Uneven drying can cause irrevocable deformation of the tape base, as can recovery methods that use extreme heat or cold, such as freezing, vacuum thermal-drying, and vacuum freeze-drying.[29] Always consult with a specialist for guidance before attempting any in-house salvage or stabilization procedures.

## OTHER CONSIDERATIONS

Repository staff should be trained to quickly recognize the various types of magnetic media and other audiovisual materials in their collections *before* a disaster occurs to enable the timely identification and prioritization of high-risk formats during a time-sensitive disaster recovery effort. Securing sufficient quantities of media salvage supplies may be difficult in the wake of a disaster, so it is advisable to maintain an ample on-site cache of essential supplies such as distilled water, lint-free cloths, sturdy resealable plastic bags, and blotter paper.

## Decay

*Magnetic Layer.* The most serious and frequently encountered problem with the magnetic pigment layer is binder hydrolysis, a chemical reaction in which the long polymer molecules in the binder are broken down by the absorption of ambient moisture, causing the binder to become soft and sticky. The resulting loss of binder integrity can cause sticky-shed syndrome (described in "Environment and Storage" above). Hydrolysis also compromises the bond between the binder and the tape base, causing the magnetic layer to flake or peel away from the base.[30] Evidence of this degradation may include stickiness when the tape is unwound, oxide debris found in enclosures or on playback equipment, a squealing sound during playback, and a pungent odor often described as "dirty socks."[31] Binder hydrolysis occurs mainly in polyester-based back-coated tapes manufactured since the 1970s, when polyurethane binders came into widespread use, and it may be exacerbated by the presence of the chromium dioxide particles used in some magnetic pigments.[32] Binder degradation does not occur in metal evaporate tapes or wire recordings, which instead are subject to oxidation and corrosion.

Another type of binder-related degradation is the loss of lubricants added to the binder during the manufacturing process. Lubricants give the magnetic material a thin layer of protection that helps reduce wear and tear on both playback heads and the tape itself. This thin layer of lubricant wears off as the tape is used, but it is continually replenished as lubricant still embedded in the binder gradually migrates to the tape surface. Under normal conditions, lubricants added during the manufacturing process can be expected to last for the life of the tape. However, excessive use or prolonged exposure to poor environmental conditions can accelerate the depletion of lubricants through evaporation and hydrolysis, significantly shortening the tape's life expectancy.

Other problems that can adversely affect the magnetic layer include magnetic particle instabilities (such as diminished ability to retain the magnetic signal), flaking away of the metal layer in metal evaporate tapes, oxidation of some early metal particle tape coatings,[33] and print-through.

*Tape Base.* Acetate-based tapes may be subject to acid hydrolysis, a chemical reaction often referred to as "vinegar syndrome" owing to the characteristic odor of the acetic acid released during the reaction. The presence of acetic acid can also exacerbate binder hydrolysis. While vinegar syndrome has not been found to affect magnetic audiotape as severely as it does motion-picture film, acetate-based tapes should nevertheless be carefully monitored and segregated immediately at the first sign of this condition, which may infect healthy media. In addition to hydrolysis, acetate tapes may also become brittle and shrink dramatically with age due to plasticizer loss. Physical distortion of acetate-based tapes may include cupping (transverse curling), warped or ruffled edges, and mild to extreme polygonal distortion of the tape base. Acetate tapes are also more vulnerable to mold growth, particularly when subjected to high levels of temperature and relative humidity.

Polyester-based tapes are chemically stable and do not suffer the same binder degradation problems as acetate tapes. However, polyester tape also possesses a high tensile strength that causes it to stretch dramatically and deform rather than breaking cleanly as does acetate tape. Paper-based tapes have also proven to be chemically stable but are prone to tearing or breaking. PVC- and PEN-based tapes do not have any known degradation issues.[34]

Degradation of both binder and tape base is more frequently observed in open-reel tapes than in cartridge or cassette tapes.[35]

*Mechanical Damage.* All magnetic tape is subject to numerous types of mechanical deformation, including cupping, creasing, cinching, edge damage, scratches and abrasions, stretching, tearing, and breakage. Mechanical damage to wire recordings typically include tangles, kinking, and breaking. Mechanical damage can result from careless handling, inadequate storage conditions, poorly maintained playback equipment, and poor tape wind. All of these conditions are problematic because they compromise head-to-tape contact, resulting in dropouts, signal distortion, and mistracking during playback. Narrower and thinner tapes are more likely to suffer mechanical damage, as are tapes on reels.[36]

*Shell and Reel Damage.* Damage to cassette and cartridge shells may include cracks, breakage, and loose or missing pressure pads. Reel damage usually takes the form of bent, cracked, or broken flanges.

*Fungal Growth.* Mold and other fungus can feed on the binder polymer and additives, eventually destroying the magnetic pigment layer. Mold spores on the tape surface can cause dropouts and contaminate playback equipment.

### Treatments

Treatment methods for damaged or deteriorating magnetic media are highly complex and format-specific, and they should only be undertaken by a trained specialist; homegrown measures, however careful and well intended, may cause irreversible damage to already compromised media. Consulting a magnetic-media recovery expert before attempting any repairs or remediation work is strongly recommended.

Conducting a condition assessment survey of magnetic media holdings will provide essential information that can inform decisions about appropriate conservation actions.

## SOUND MATERIALS: MECHANICAL FORMATS (BOB PYMM)

*Dates in use*: 1870s to the present.
*Formats*: wax cylinders, 78rpm shellac discs, 16-inch transcription discs, 12-inch 33rpm vinyl LPs, 7-inch 45rpm single discs.

### Materials

This section covers the preservation of mechanical (or grooved media) sound recordings. Despite their virtual demise some years ago, they are enjoying a resurgence in production, ensuring they are more than just a historical format. More recent audio formats—magnetic, optical, and digital—are covered in the sections "Sound Materials: Magnetic Media" and "Sound Materials: Compact Discs" in this chapter. Digitization is seen as the long-term preservation and access solution for mechanical media, but the sheer volume of material held in major collections and archives around the world means that this is going to be a lengthy and costly process. In the meantime, collections of mechanical media have to be stored and handled appropriately in order to ensure their long-term survival and their ongoing accessibility to users.

For the purposes of this section, *formats* refers to grooved media that store sounds, recorded through the actions of a diaphragm responding to sound waves and moving a stylus. The stylus either records through inscribing onto a recording surface or replays through transmitting sound waves already inscribed on the surface. Edison's earliest recordings, of which a few survive today, were made on tin foil,[37] but the earliest formats commonly found in most library, archive, and museum collections are wax cylinders made from a variety of materials, most of which are brittle and easily broken. More widely familiar are discs of varying sizes, which quickly became the most popular format from around 1900. Standards settled by the 1920s, and the popularity of the 78rpm (revolutions per minute) shellac disc (usually 10- or 12-inch) meant that millions were produced worldwide from the 1920s to the 1940s. Sixteen-inch transcription discs became the preferred format for radio broadcast transmission, most holding episodes of the serials that were a mainstay of popular radio before television. From the late 1940s, 12-inch 33rpm vinyl LP (long play) discs, followed by the 7-inch 45rpm single, became the standard format for all forms of popular home entertainment until challenged by magnetic tape in the 1970s, and then by optical and digital media. Other disc formats exist on a variety of media, including aluminum, various lacquered surfaces, cardboard, and flexible vinyl, in a wide range of sizes, and even in shapes other than discs. In addition, original metal masters (both positive and negative) used for creating the stampers that produce the discs are found. While none of these are likely to figure prominently in any collection, they have their own unique collection management challenges.

The packaging of these media can also be of considerable value and needs to be appropriately stored and cared for. The playback technology for all formats is still readily available, or can be engineered with relative ease. More sophisticated archival turntables, with a wide range of styli capable of handling discs of almost any size and composition, can also be acquired.

### Purposes

Initially viewed as a dictating machine that would help "transform office work,"[38] the gramophone's potential as an entertainment medium, based on the sales of duplicated recordings, took some years to be realized. Once the price of machines began to fall and the production of popular recordings increased, the success of the technology became assured, with very large numbers of cylinders and discs, covering all musical genres, produced before the First World War and continuing to be produced today.

Discs were also used for recording dialogue to synchronize with early film prior to the incorporation of sound into film technologies. Vitaphone produced a considerable number of soundtracks to accompany shorts and feature films during the period 1926 to 1930[39] and discs for the distribution of broadcast material to radio stations from the 1930s to the 1960s.

Field recordings by anthropologists commenced prior to 1900, with home or amateur recordings to disc becoming popular from the 1920s. These direct recordings to disc continued well into the mid 20th century, when they were supplanted by tape recording.

The "instantaneous" recordings (often known as "acetates" because cellulose acetate was used early on for their coating) could be onto a variety of bases, but, from the 1930s on, most were on a nitrocellulose lacquer-coated disc that is susceptible to wear and tends to break away from its supporting substrate.[40] They were commonly used in radio for recording events and outside broadcasts, as well as by recording artists. Famous "live" recordings on disc include the loss of the *Hindenburg* in 1937,[41] and Elvis Presley's first recording for his mother's birthday, made in the Sun Studios in 1953.[42]

## Dates in Use

While there are earlier examples of sound being recorded, or made visible, through tracing sound waves onto a surface, it was not until 1877, when Edison recorded on tinfoil, that the technology really began to develop. Over the next decades wax cylinders (actually made of various materials) gradually evolved as effective sound carriers and were manufactured by Edison until 1929, although by then they had been long superseded by discs.[43] Emile Berliner introduced spiral-grooved discs and the gramophone in the late 1880s.[44] Early discs came in a variety of sizes, with varying playback speeds, although double-sided 10- or 12-inch 78rpm recordings became the standard by the 1920s for home use, with 16-inch transcription discs the most common format for radio transmission.

Improvements in disc-cutting techniques and the introduction of vinyl led to the launch of the 33⅓ rpm 12-inch LP and the 45rpm 7-inch single in the late 1940s. Within a decade, the market for 78rpm records had virtually disappeared in the West, although many were still produced elsewhere, including India, where early Beatles' recordings were released on 78rpm and have become highly collectable today.[45] For the next forty years, vinyl (and sometimes polystyrene) singles and vinyl LPs dominated the entertainment market, until they were quickly superseded by optical, digital media following the release of the first commercial CDs in 1982. The 12-inch vinyl LP has survived the move to digital recording, and small, specialist presses are continuing to produce LPs that sell steadily (well over five million in the United States alone in 2011);[46] playback technology (turntables and amplifiers with phono outputs) is still manufactured.

## Identification

Most audio formats are readily recognizable, although the material from which a cylinder or disc is made may not be so easily determined. For cylinders, the brand, information on the container, the color of the wax, and the shape of the cylinder help identify its type and the playback mechanism required to access the content. (It is now possible to access cylinder recordings using laser technology, which avoids any physical contact with the item.) Several websites provide detailed specifications for the composition of and identifying information for the various cylinders produced.[47]

Discs were also made from a variety of materials. Most produced before the 1940s were 10- and 12-inch discs made of a shellac compound, which is heavier and more brittle than the later vinyl discs. Vinyl discs are characterized by their light weight, flexibility, and durability, and they are practically unbreakable, although they are susceptible to heat. Most discs still have their identifying labels, which help in determining their age, playback speed, and other pertinent information. In addition, most discs, except for the very earliest, contain a matrix number cut into the "dead" area before the label. This identifying number indicates the pressing generation and often relates to the disc's catalog number. Many record companies, particularly in the early days, published catalogs of the recordings they had available, which can be a useful tool for identifying a disc.

## Representation in Collections

Many libraries made vinyl LP music collections available for lending or teaching purposes. However, with the advent of physically smaller, easier-to-handle formats such as compact discs, LP collections quickly vanished. Today, collections are generally found only in specialist music libraries, major collecting archives, state and national institutions with a focus on audiovisual materials, and in some museum collections (for example, in anthropology departments or popular culture collections).

Because of the popularity of many of the audio formats, and in later years their attractiveness to collectors, representative and comprehensive collections of all but the rarest recordings are not uncommon. Edison wax cylinders, particularly the later blue Amberol examples that were less fragile than their wax predecessors, survive in surprisingly large numbers, and there are major collections of them.[48] Early disc recordings, too, despite their fragility, are widely held, and the shellac 78rpm disc, produced in the millions, is likely to be central to any comprehensive collection. Instantaneous recordings, because of the nature of the material used, are far less likely to have survived intact and are not commonly found. Post–1950 vinyl discs are widely held, and copies of specific titles are generally not difficult to locate.

While most of these formats are readily found in collections, the condition of the objects may present challenges. Finding copies of earlier recordings, especially instantaneous recordings, in good condition can be difficult, and considerable effort may be required in order to achieve good audio reproduction from a broken, scratched, or mold-damaged cylinder or disc.

## Environment and Storage

### PREFERRED ENVIRONMENT

Like most audiovisual artifacts, discs and cylinders of all types are best stored in a relatively cool, dry environment. General recommendations are for a temperature range of 60 to 68°F (16 to 20°C) and relative humidity in the range of 40 to 45 percent. In these conditions mold growth is slowed or avoided, and paper packaging, such as sleeves and cylinder boxes, and the natural materials comprising the cylinder or disc, have sufficient humidity to maintain flexibility. Maintaining stability of conditions is important; fluctuations will stress materials and reduce longevity.[49] Good air quality, together with some form of filtration to remove dust particles, is desirable, and regular airflow through storage areas should be maintained. Exposure to light should be limited as much as possible. As with all materials, storage areas for discs and cylinders need to be regularly cleaned and maintained to limit their attractiveness for insect pests and rodents, which are attracted particularly to the paper packaging. These conditions are also suitable for storing the playback equipment associated with such collections.

Fixed metal shelving, with a suitable weight rating and regular shelf dividers, is necessary. Shellac discs, especially 16-inch transcription discs, are heavy and require short shelving spans constructed from appropriately rated steel.

Ideally, any collection will comprise multiple copies of each item. The copy in best condition is kept in the best storage conditions, separate from the other copies and with access severely limited.

Cylinders, discs, and their associated packaging stored in good conditions should remain reasonably stable. Periodic sampling of the collection for detailed examination, particularly of more vulnerable formats such as acetate discs, should be built into a regular collection management schedule.

## RECOMMENDATIONS FOR STORAGE

Preparation for storage is a key aspect of managing mechanical formats. Examination of all incoming items before they are placed in controlled storage is essential. Cleaning and examination for mold and mechanical damage is done at this stage, with items prioritized for any remedial conservation work that may be required.

Cylinders will be removed from their original containers, which are likely to be in poor condition, and stored in padded polypropylene or acid-free card boxes. Depending upon their condition and the objectives of the collecting institution, the original containers may be stored separately in metal drawers lined with acid-free card. Maintaining the link between the cylinder and its container should be done via the catalog.

Most 78rpm discs were issued in flimsy paper sleeves advertising the company and the recording artist. Some were retailer specific, advertising a particular record shop. Those that have survived are likely to be in poor condition; realistically, it may be better to keep only samples of the sleeves illustrating the range of labels, local shops, and other features, rather than aim to keep all of them. Sturdier cardboard sleeves were also produced, but it may also be appropriate to preserve only a sample. Sleeves should be placed between acid-free tissue, supported by card, and stored flat in metal cabinets. The discs are placed in a light, inert, polyethylene bag, then in a new acid-free card sleeve; the whole is stored inside a polyethylene or similar resealable bag, which can be labeled appropriately. Bags can then be stored upright on shelves, with regular dividers to ensure they stand supported at all times and do not lean. Alternatively, packaged discs can be stored in polypropylene boxes for further protection.

Vinyl records are packaged similarly. For LPs, with decorative and frequently informative sleeves, maintaining the sleeve and record together is usually desirable. For practical collection management purposes, it is useful to store the sleeve with the record in a resealable bag.

Storing different-sized discs together should be avoided. For extra large, broken, or otherwise damaged discs, it is best to package them as described above and lie them flat on shelving for storage. This method of storage can, however, introduce space utilization problems, and it raises the possibility that material will be placed on top of the disc, so it needs to be carefully planned.

The poor quality of some of the cardboard or paper used for sleeves and packaging can make their care and preservation challenging. Good storage conditions for paper (as described in the section "Paper: Library and Archives Materials" in chapter 8), which are not dissimilar to those required for the carriers themselves, and protection from exposure to light will help ensure longevity. If sleeves and other accompanying documentation are stored separately from the carrier, be sure that the link between the two is carefully recorded in the catalog record.

Turntables, cylinder players, and other equipment need to be protected from dirt and dust and stored in a cool, dry environment. Maintaining equipment in good working order is essential to ensure fragile materials are not damaged during playback.

## Handling

### WHAT STAFF NEED TO KNOW

The fragility of many nonvinyl discs and cylinders means they can easily be broken if handled incorrectly. The size of some discs makes them unwieldy and difficult to manage. All carriers should be handled individually—do not, for instance, pick up a stack of 78rpm discs unless they are enclosed in packaging of some sort—and care should be taken to make sure fingers do not come into contact with any playing surface. Cylinders should be removed from their packaging by placing two fingers of one hand inside the cylinder and pulling it out gently. Use the other hand to support the cylinder at the bottom, and always stand the cylinder upright, taking care it is not knocked over. Similarly, when handling discs, two hands should be used to hold the disc by the edge to avoid contact with the playing surface. Wearing latex gloves protects materials from dirt and oil on hands and allows for a firm grip.

### WHAT USERS NEED TO KNOW

Generally users will not be handling unique collection material but be given access to copies or, increasingly, digitized versions. In circumstances in which it is necessary to provide access to preservation material, users should be supervised and any listening handled by staff. All carriers should be cleaned prior to playback, dust being a major potential cause of damage to disc and cylinder recordings. For discs, vacuum cleaning turntable machines are available, and ultrasonic baths can be used to loosen stubborn dirt, but take care not to wet the label. The use of a lint-free, antistatic cloth, disc-cleaning brush, and, where necessary, distilled water, is usually sufficient for any of the formats.

## Playback Equipment

Having high-quality, professional-level playback equipment is essential. Poorly maintained equipment can damage any of the carriers. Traditionally, archival quality turntables with the ability to play discs of most sizes and hold a range of styli have been the predominant means of accessing archival disc collections. Different shapes and sizes of styli are required depending upon the disc; a vinyl microgroove LP will require a different stylus for playback than a shellac 78rpm disc. Styli should be checked for cleanliness and for wear prior to use. A worn stylus can damage a disc, so replace styli when necessary.

Original cylinder players need to be matched to the cylinder to be played; later machines should not be used to play earlier recordings.[50] Replaying cylinders will inevitably cause wear. In recent years noninvasive methods of capturing information from early recordings have been used with success. These methods include the use of lasers, optical microscopy, and digital mapping.[51]

## Disaster Response

Most pre-1940 formats are fragile and susceptible to catastrophic damage if dropped. In areas that are earthquake prone or subject to other instability, suitable shelving with lips or other retaining features are recommended, and consideration should be given to storing the most vulnerable material in fixed, closed storage containers.

In the event of flooding, most formats will survive a reasonable level of immersion if they are quickly set out to dry. Items need to be removed from their packaging and, if necessary, rinsed or more carefully cleaned with fresh water to remove dirt, then air-dried in an environment with good airflow to prevent mold growth. Wet labels are likely to be stained or lifting off, and they should be dried as well as possible with absorbent paper or towels. Paper packaging, sleeves, and the like will generally be unsalvageable once wet.

## Decay

Most commercially produced carriers are not susceptible to decay if housed in reasonable conditions. While the wax in early cylinders can separate and thus destroy the recording, accidental breakage is a far more likely cause of problems. Mold can grow on discs and cylinders in damp or humid conditions and, if it becomes embedded in them, can cause irreversible damage.

Shellac discs will become brittle over time, even if stored in good conditions, but a large number of variables affect the speed of the process;[52] most will remain playable for the long term.

Problems can arise with instantaneous recordings when the castor oil used as a plasticizer in the lacquer coating dries out, causing shrinkage, cracking, and separation from the surface of the platter. This is difficult to halt or reverse, and the only practical option is for conservation efforts to be focused on getting the disc into a playable condition so it can be copied.

For vinyl and shellac discs, warping can be a problem, but it may be possible to flatten them to make them playable. Successful flattening, however, requires a high level of specialist expertise and is not recommended for instantaneous discs.

### Treatments

Careful examination at the time of acquisition, clean packaging, careful handling, and a good storage environment are really the only practical methods that the nonspecialist can adopt to limit deterioration of all the mechanical formats. Piecing together broken carriers and reattaching lacquer pieces to their original base is work for the trained conservator with expertise in this area.

## SOUND MATERIALS: COMPACT DISCS (MATTHEW DAVIES)

*Dates in use*: 1982 to the present.
*Formats*: CD-A, CD-ROM, CD-I, CD-R, CD-RW, CD-V, CD-Extra, SACD.

### Materials

Compacts discs (CDs) were first introduced to the market in 1982, and they remain in use to the present day. Initially developed as a medium for publication of digital audio recordings, the format has been extended to a variety of other uses covering the gamut of digital media and data storage. All mass-produced (replicated) CDs are similar in their manufacture, materials, and properties, regardless of the type of data or media they contain.

The CD comprises transparent, polycarbonate discs of 1.2 mm thickness impressed with a spiral linear sequence of "pits" and "lands" of different length, injection molded from a negative metal stamper in a process referred to as "replication." The body of the CD is then covered with a reflective layer of aluminum or, sometimes, silver. This reflective layer is sealed by a protective lacquer on the label side on top of the disc. Data on the disc are read by laser light focused through the clear polycarbonate from underneath. Replicated CDs can easily be produced in large quantities, with typical minimum commercial production runs of five hundred units.

Since 1990, recordable forms of CDs have been available. These discs can carry the same range of data types as replicated CDs, but they are significantly different in their material and structure. Recordable discs (CD-R) and rewritable discs (CD-RW) are read by focused laser light, in the same way as replicated CDs. Laser light of higher intensity is used to write and erase these discs.

CD-R are a "write once read many times" medium; they have a polymer dye layer that is irreversibly modified by the heat of the laser during writing to mimic the pits and lands of a replicated CD. CD-RW are an erasable and rewritable medium, introduced to the market in 1997. The reflective layer in CD-RW discs is formed from a metallic alloy. The reflective properties of this alloy are modified by heat from the laser during recording to mimic the pits and lands of a replicated CD. The modification of reflectivity is reversible, allowing for erasure and re-recording.

Standard CDs are all 120 mm in diameter. Nonstandard variants include miniature discs of 80 mm or smaller diameter and even rectangular "business card" CDs.

## Purposes

*CD-As (CD-Audio)* are used for the publication and distribution of audio, including music and spoken word, in linear Pulse Code Modulation (PCM) format at 44.1 kHz sampling rate and 16-bit sample depth. In this format analog audio data are sampled or measured 44,100 times per second, with each measurement represented by a 16-bit digital integer. The sampled data are encoded as a continuous stream, with track-level access facilitated by a table of contents (TOC), referencing PQ codes embedded in the audio stream to facilitate track-by-track random access. P codes provide a simple indication of the pauses between tracks, while Q codes provide more detailed timing information and can contain Media Catalogue Number (MCN) or International Standard Recording Code (ISRC) information.

*CD-ROMs (CD Read-Only Memory)* are used for publication and distribution of software and multimedia content including text, audio, still images, and moving images. Data are structured in files and directories, according to the standards and conventions of common personal computer operating systems.

*CD-Is (CD-Interactive)* are used for publication of interactive multimedia content. The CD-I format depends on dedicated stand-alone multiformat CD players capable of integrating the interactive content supplied on CD-I into a typical home audiovisual system.

*CD-Extras* allow inclusion of some multimedia content in addition to a CD-A audio recording. The audio content can be played on any CD player; the multimedia content can be accessed with a suitable computer.

*CD-Digital Videos (also known as VCD)* carry up to eighty minutes of digital video encoded to the MPEG-1 standard. Stand-alone VCD/CD players are common in markets where VCD is popular. VCD has a significant presence in markets in the tropics where humidity is high and the optical disc format is more reliable than VHS tapes.

*CD-Rs (CD-Recordable)* can be recorded in any of the CD standards (except SACD) and are used for one-off and small publication runs. CD-R is popular for personal use as a data backup medium. CD-R production in short runs for publication and distribution is referred to as duplication, whereas replication refers only to the production of CDs by physically stamping the polycarbonate base before the disc is laminated.

*CD-RWs (CD-Rewritable)* can be recorded in any of the CD standards (except SACD) and are generally used for data backup.

*SACDs (Super Audio CD)* are used for publishing audiophile and multichannel recordings using Direct Streaming Digital (DSD) encoding.

## Dates in Use

CD-A: 1982 to the present
CD-ROM: 1985 to the present
CD-I: 1987–1998
CD-R: 1991 to the present
CD-RW: 1997 to the present
VCD and CD-Extra: 1995 to the present
SACD: 1999 to the present

## Identification

The initial approach in identifying CDs is to examine the information printed on the disc itself and on accompanying packaging. The majority of CDs display a standard logo on the label side of the disc indicating the specific type of CD. Other useful information, including title information, copyright, catalogue number, and system requirements, may be printed on the disc label. This information will often be duplicated on the CD packaging, which may include more detailed content and contextual information.

The use of logos has diminished as the CD has become ubiquitous, and many published audio CDs no longer have the logo. Some recordable discs have a plain white coating intended as a base for label printing, so they do not carry a printed logo. When there is no obvious logo, examine the fine printing around the center hole on the underside of the disc. (This may require magnification.) Text may include codes such as CD-R or CD-RW to identify the type of disc and may also include numerals indicating the recording capacity. For example, the text "CDR80" might appear on an eighty-minute recordable CD-R.

Recordable discs can also be identified by the blue or green hue of the underside of the disc. The disc color can be a guide to the type of dye used, but it is not definitive. Azo-based dyes typically result in a blue-colored disc, while cyanine or phthalocyanine dyes typically result in a green-colored disc.

Further information about the content of the disc can usually be obtained by mounting the disc in the optical drive of a suitable computer. This will enable direct interrogation of the CD table of contents (TOC) and/or file system. It should be noted that the .cda extension is used by both Windows and IOS operating systems to indicate tracks on an audio CD; these are not files, however, but merely place markers created from the TOC information, similar to though slightly different from shortcuts. An audio track cannot be copied from a CD by copying the .cda "nonfile"; the audio must first be extracted or "ripped" to the computer to make a valid copy.

Content information for audio CDs may be obtained by looking up external online databases such as Gracenote, which provide detailed track information. These databases are fairly reliable (with minor data-quality issues) for commercially published CDs, but they can sometimes give completely erroneous results if a disc and database information are incorrectly matched, which occurs especially in the case of unpublished material.

## Representation in Collections

CDs have become a significant publication medium for audio recordings, software, multimedia, and other data. They are often added to library and archive collections as the most convenient, cost-effective, and readily accessible format for reproduction of the recordings and other works they contain. CDs may be the only format in which some audio works are published. If a recording is available in alternative formats, they may be either obsolete, such as vinyl discs, or of lower quality, such as mp3 files, or both, such as audiocassettes. Audio books on CD represent a valuable resource for providing the print handicapped with access to information.

CD-ROMs will often represent information resources and/or creative works in a form that is unique to the CD-ROM format, even if elements of the content are available in other formats. CD-ROM versions of reference texts, such as encyclopedias, often include multimedia elements not available in their printed equivalents. Early examples of these kinds of publications are now largely superseded by the Internet and can therefore be regarded as interesting historical documents in their own right. CD-ROMs are also a cost-effective medium for the publication of information-dense resources such as technical databases, discographies, conference proceedings, and technical datasets. Duplicated CD-R data discs are similarly effective for very small-scale production (below one thousand units).

Software discs may serve a number of functions in an institution, from collection materials in their own right to tools for maintenance of current and/or obsolete software. This type of material is most likely to be governed by IT policy (except in a software library), and use would normally be confined to staff or other authorized persons.

CDs of all kinds may accompany printed publications. Audio CDs accompanying music publications are an obvious example. Even this small niche covers not only all genres of music but also a spectrum of uses from basic music tuition to interpretation of advanced experimental art and even to art practice.

For cultural heritage professionals, the most complex questions raised by CDs relate to collections of unique personal data that are the digital equivalent of manuscript collections. Managing these collections can require significant resources, and the volume of private data being produced currently far outweighs the ability of the memory institutions to ensure its ongoing accessibility. Careful assessment and prioritization are advised.

CD-ROMs, CD-Rs, CD-RWs, and CD-Digital Videos are commonly found in the collections of cultural heritage institutions, especially in libraries and archives. Less commonly found are CD-Extras and SACDs, while CD-Is are rare.

## Environment and Storage

### PREFERRED ENVIRONMENT

CDs were designed for use in normal home and office conditions, and in that context basic care and storage are all that is required to maintain them for a useful life span. Long-term preservation of CDs and the use of CDs as an archival medium are special cases requiring stable, cool, and dry conditions. Dark storage at 68°F (20°C) and 40 percent RH is optimal.

### RECOMMENDATIONS FOR STORAGE

The standard CD jewel case provides good protection and support for a CD and is the recommended storage container in most circumstances. Cases should be stored book style, with the spines vertical. In the typical case in which a replicated CD is supplied in a jewel case, any suitable-sized drawer, shelf, or box is adequate. A good scalable solution is to use slightly oversized archival card boxes for twenty to fifty CDs on fixed or compactus shelving.

To increase longevity of CDs supplied in cardboard envelopes or other suboptimal packaging, repackage the CD in a new jewel case, and repackage the jewel case and original packaging together in a resealable plastic bag. Repackaging to isolate CDs from all paper material in this manner should be considered when long-term preservation is a concern.

Additional precautions need to be taken for CD-Rs and CD-RWs, as they are far more fragile than replicated CDs and are more likely to fail in uncontrolled conditions. Exposure to the UV radiation in sunlight will quickly and reliably erase CD-Rs; although CD-RWs are less photosensitive, they are at risk of erasure at high temperatures. Opaque boxes, conditioned storage, and attention to separation from accompanying paper materials are recommended. Any investigation of unique discs should include the creation of backup copies as the first priority.

## Handling

### WHAT STAFF NEED TO KNOW

CDs need to be treated with care to maximize their useful life span. The label surface, consisting of a very thin layer of lacquer coated with ink that protects the underlying reflective material from the atmosphere, is the most vulnerable part of the CD. Any scratching or damage to the label side will allow airborne humidity to react with the reflective layer, eventually causing the disc to fail. CDs are vulnerable to damage from flexing, which can cause delamination and may also compromise the isolation of the reflective layer from airborne humidity. Scratching on the underside or playing side of the disc will cause increased error rates during reading; severe scratching of the playing side will cause mistracking or skipping. CD-Rs and CD-RWs are particularly fragile and much more sensitive to deterioration from exposure to sunlight and/or heat.

**WHAT USERS NEED TO KNOW**

Users should be informed of the following handling guidelines:

- Always keep a CD in its packaging when not in use.
- Store CDs in a cool, dry place and avoid extreme environments.
- To safely remove a CD from its package, press down with one thumb on the jewel case center support ("spider") and use the other hand to lift the CD out of the case while holding the disc by its outer edge.
- Always hold a CD by its outer edge, and never touch its playing surface.
- Never attach any adhesive product, such as sticky notes or adhesive tape, to a CD.

## Playback/Viewing Equipment

There are two different approaches to the reproduction of audio CDs: reproduction using stand-alone optical media players, and data extraction using a computer with a general purpose CD-ROM or DVD-ROM drive, commonly referred to as "ripping." Stand-alone players have error correction capabilities that are superior to data extraction methods, which gives them a significant advantage in copying discs for preservation, and have marginal benefits for normal auditioning.

Stand-alone media players, such as dedicated CD players, DVD players, and Blu-ray players, allow access to audio CDs using headphones or can be connected to an audio system for listening through loudspeakers. The most common consumer players have similar reproduction quality, but they differ in their functionality, connectivity, and durability. High-end audiophile CD players offer slight improvements in sound quality, which may be relevant for critical listening applications. Jukebox systems permit access to the content of a large number of CDs without user handling.

Dedicated hardware players are available for VCDs, some of which can also be played using DVD players. VCDs can also be played on a computer with an appropriately configured media player.

CD-ROMs are a data format and always require the use of a computer. They may be dependent on particular versions of software and operating systems for playback and viewing. Any deviation from the required software environment may result in limited or no functionality. Older CD-ROMs may not run in new computers. System specifications are normally indicated on the disc packaging.

SACDs can officially only be reproduced in a compatible media player; however, unauthorized software solutions that enable data extraction have been developed. Compatible players include dedicated CD-A/SACD players made by Sony, early generations of Sony PS3 PlayStation game consoles, and some high-end Blu-ray players.

Dedicated players are required for reproduction of CD-Is. As Philips only produced the players between 1987 and 1998, the format is considered obsolete.

CD players should be kept in a reasonably clean environment, free from dust and airborne contamination. They can be lightly cleaned with a lint-free cloth to minimize any potential contamination. Servicing should be carried out by qualified personnel, as there is little that anyone not qualified to work on electronic equipment can do in their maintenance. The use of cleaning discs is as likely to cause problems as to cure them and is not recommended.

## Disaster Response

Recovery of CDs from a disaster should be carried out in a way that avoids causing any more damage than what has already been inflicted by the disaster. Discs should be cleaned in a way that minimizes their scratching or flexing. Where paper packaging and other material has adhered to the discs, seek advice from a conservator before attempting to remove adhered materials as there is a risk of delaminating the disc.

Separate water-affected discs with nothing adhered to them from any paper packaging, attaching a temporary label (cardboard and string) to the discs for identification if they have no printed label. Wash the CDs with the cleanest available water as soon as possible, and dry them in a dust-free environment. Treat the separated packaging in the same way that water-affected paper is treated (See the section "Paper: Library and Archive Materials" in chapter 8).

Light brushing, or using compressed air or a light vacuum, is recommended for discs with loose particulate contamination; for example, from smoke. Any unique discs with important content should be stabilized, cleaned, and copied as a priority.

## Decay

Compact discs are designed to accommodate the inevitable presence of some data-read errors. They handle a moderate level of data-read errors through the use of data-correction systems, which introduce redundant data that is used to reconstruct the original recorded bitstream. Small read errors caused by vibration of the CD mechanism, dust, scratches, or minor reflective layer deterioration are corrected and go unnoticed by the user. Once the level of error exceeds the capability of the error-correction systems, read errors compromise the use of the disc. In the presence of uncorrectable errors, audio CDs may skip or freeze during replay, or in some cases will not play at all. Data CDs with uncorrectable errors may deliver corrupted data, or they may fail completely.

All CDs are vulnerable to corrosion of the reflective layer, which can lead to inability of data on the disc to be read. Corrosion will be accelerated if the seal on the label side of the disc is imperfectly manufactured or subsequently compromised; for example, by scratches or delamination. Initially corrosion will lead to an increase in error rate, which may be correctable, but eventually data errors reach a level at which the disc cannot be read.

Scratches on the underside of the disc cause data-read errors. Errors caused by small scratches may be correctable; large scratches may cause failure of the disc. Scratches that are concentric with the disc's circumference are most problematic, as they result in a long sequence of unreadable data. Radial scratches have less impact, as they result in a series of short error bursts that can be more easily recovered by the error-correction system.

CD-Rs are subject to dye fade—slow decay resulting from chemical deterioration of the polymer dye used to represent the data. This is greatly accelerated by exposure to UV radiation. Exposure to direct sunlight can completely erase data from a CD-R within days. CD-RWs can deteriorate if subjected to excessive heat, including by exposure to sunlight. Temperatures above 275°F (135°C) will result in significant deformation that renders the disc unusable.

## Treatments

As with any digital format, the inevitable failure of CDs is best mitigated by the availability of multiple redundant copies. Only when reliable redundant copies are held in a collection, or are readily available (for example, as currently available published music discs), can CDs safely be used for general access. Creation of backup copies should always be the first priority in any investigation of unique or irreplaceable discs.

Day-to-day maintenance of CDs is limited to good storage and basic cleaning. When cleaning discs, it is important to use techniques that minimize scratching. A soft brush or compressed air will remove loose particles. To remove sticky residues such as fingerprints, clean the underside of CDs using a soft cloth, wiping from the center to the outside of the disc to avoid concentric scratches.

A disc that will not read should be assessed for any obvious physical damage or deterioration. If no problems are observed, recovering the data or media can be attempted using an alternative player, possibly with assistance from IT support staff. Specialist assistance and/or advice should be obtained if significant physical damage or deterioration is noted, and in any case where important, unique content cannot be recovered using in-house resources. Specialized advice may be available from the relevant national and state audiovisual archives or from audiovisual archiving associations such as the International Association of Sound and Audiovisual Archives (IASA; www.iasa-web.org), the Southeast Asia-Pacific Audio Visual Archives Association (SEAPAVAA; archives.pia.gov.ph/seapavaa), and the Association of Moving Image Archivists (AMIA; www.amianet.org).

# STANDARDS AND FURTHER READING

## Standards

AES-11id-2006 (r2012). *AES Information Document for Preservation of Audio Recordings—Extended Term Storage Environment for Multiple Media Archives.*

AES-22:1997 (r2003). *AES Recommended Practice for Audio Preservation and Restoration—Storage of Polyester-Base Magnetic Tape.*

AES-49:2005 (r2010). *AES Standard for Audio Preservation and Restoration—Magnetic Tape— Care and Handling Practices for Extended Usage.*

AES28-1997 (r2008). *AES Standard for Audio Preservation and Restoration: Method for Estimating Life Expectancy of Compact Discs (CD-ROM), Based on Effects of Temperature and Relative Humidity.*

ANSI IT9.21-1996. *Life Expectancy of Compact Disks (CD-ROM): Method for Estimating, Based on Effects of Temperature and Relative Humidity.*

IEC 60908 (1999). *Audio Recording—Compact Disc Digital Audio System.* Ed. 2.0 (also known as "Red Book").

ISO 18921:2008. *Imaging Materials—Compact Discs (CD-ROM)—Method for Estimating the Life Expectancy Based on the Effects of Temperature and Relative Humidity.*

ISO 18923:2000. *Imaging Materials—Polyester-Base Magnetic Tape—Storage Practices.*

ISO 18933:2012. *Imaging Materials—Magnetic Tape—Care and Handling Practices for Extended Usage.*

ISO/IEC 10149-1995. *Information Technology—Data Interchange on Read-only 120mm Optical Data Disks (CD-ROM)* (also ECMA-130 and commonly referred to as "Yellow Book").

SMPTE RP-103. *Care, Storage, Operation, Handling and Shipping of Magnetic Recording Tape for Television.*

## Further Reading

Association of Research Libraries. *Sound Savings: Preserving Audio Collections.* Washington, DC: ARL, 2004. Accessed September 28, 2013. http://www.arl.org/storage/documents/publications/sound-savings.pdf.

Byers, Fred R. *Care and Handling of CDs and DVDs: A Guide for Librarians and Archivists.* Washington, DC: Council on Library and Information Resources, 2003. Accessed September 29, 2013. http://www.clir.org/pubs/abstract/reports/pub121.

Casey, Mike, Patrick Feaster, and Alan Burdette. *Media Preservation Survey: A Report.* Bloomington: Indiana University, 2009. Accessed October 4, 2013. http://www.indiana.edu/~medpres/documents/iub_media_preservation_survey_FINALwww.pdf.

Casey, Mike, and Bruce Gordon. *Sound Directions: Best Practice for Audio Preservation.* Bloomington: Indiana University; Cambridge, MA: Harvard University, 2007. Accessed September 28, 2013. http://www.dlib.indiana.edu/projects/sounddirections/papersPresent/sd_bp_07.pdf.

Cassaro, James P. *Planning and Caring for Library Audio Facilities.* Canton, MA: Music Library Association, 1989.

Daniel, Eric D., C. Denis Mee, and Mark H. Clark, eds. *Magnetic Recording: The First 100 Years.* New York: IEEE Press, 1999. http://www.indiana.edu/~medpres/documents/iub_media_preservation_survey_FINALwww.pdf.

International Association of Sound and Audiovisual Archives. *Guidelines on the Production and Preservation of Digital Audio Objects*. 2nd ed. Auckland Park: IASA, 2009. Accessed September 28, 2013. http://www.iasa-web.org/tc04/audio-preservation.

Iraci, Joe. *Disaster Recovery of Modern Information Carriers: Compact Discs, Magnetic Tapes and Magnetic Disks*. Technical Bulletin 25. Ottawa, ON: Canadian Conservation Institute, 2002.

Iraci, Joe. *Remedies for Deteriorated or Damaged Modern Information Carriers*. Technical Bulletin 27. Ottawa, ON: Canadian Conservation Institute, 2005.

Library of Congress National Recording Preservation Board. "Audio Preservation Bibliography." Accessed September 28, 2013. http://www.loc.gov/rr/record/nrpb/nrpb-presbib.html.

Library of Congress National Recording Preservation Board. *The Library of Congress National Recording Preservation Plan*. Washington, DC: Council on Library and Information Resources and Library of Congress, 2012. Accessed September 28, 2013. http://www.loc.gov/rr/record/nrpb/PLAN%20pdf.pdf.

Pohlmann, Ken C. *The Compact Disc: A Handbook of Theory and Use*. Madison, WI: A-R Editions, 1989.

Schüller, Dietrich. *Audio and Video Carriers: Recording Principles, Storage and Handling, Maintenance of Equipment, Format and Equipment Obsolescence*. Amsterdam: European Commission on Preservation and Access, 2007.

Van Bogart, John. *Magnetic Tape Storage and Handling: A Guide for Libraries and Archives*. Washington, DC: Commission on Preservation and Access, 1995.

## NOTES

1. Majella Breen et al., *Task Force to Establish Selection Criteria of Analogue and Digital Audio Contents for Transfer to Data Formats for Preservation Purposes* (Aarhus: International Association of Sound and Audiovisual Archives, 2004), 3.

2. For a comprehensive discussion of the evolution and development of the magnetic recording industry and technologies, see Eric D. Daniel, C. Denis Mee, and Mark H. Clark, eds., *Magnetic Recording: The First 100 Years* (New York: IEEE Press, 1999).

3. International Association of Sound and Audiovisual Archives, *Guidelines on the Production and Preservation of Digital Audio Objects*, 2nd ed. (Auckland Park: IASA, 2009), 5.4.1.2, accessed September 28, 2013, http://www.iasa-web.org/tc04/audio-preservation.

4. Dietrich Schüller, *Audio and Video Carriers: Recording Principles, Storage and Handling, Maintenance of Equipment, Format and Equipment Obsolescence*, edited by George Boston (Training for Audiovisual Preservation in Europe, 2008), 5, accessed October 4, 2013, http://www.tape-online.net/docs/audio_and_video_carriers.pdf.

5. David Morton, "Armour Research Foundation and the Wire Recorder: How Academic Entrepreneurs Fail," *Technology and Culture* 39 (1998): 233.

6. Daniel, Mee, and Clark, *Magnetic Recording*, 102–3.

7. Susan Eldridge, "Digital Audiotapes: Their Preservation and Conversion," 2010, 1, accessed October 4, 2013, http://siarchives.si.edu/sites/default/files/pdfs/digitalAudioTapesPreservation2010_0.pdf.

8. John Van Bogart, *Magnetic Tape Storage and Handling: A Guide for Libraries and Archives* (Washington, DC: Commission on Preservation and Access, 1995), 2–3.

9. IASA, *Guidelines*, 5.4.1.2.

10. Van Bogart, *Magnetic Tape Storage*, 6.

11. Gilles St-Laurent, "The Care and Handling of Recorded Sound Materials," January 1996, 7, accessed September 28, 2013, http://cool.conservation-us.org/byauth/st-laurent/care.html.

12. The International Electrotechnical Commission (IEC) classified compact cassettes into four groups based on magnetic pigment type: Type I (gamma ferric oxide), Type II (chromium dioxide or cobalt-modified gamma ferric oxide), Type III (ferrichrome), and Type IV (metal).

13. Schüller, *Audio and Video Carriers*, 5.

14. Denis Mee and Eric D. Daniel, eds., *Magnetic Storage Handbook*, 2nd ed. (New York: McGraw-Hill, 1996), 5.60, 7.27.

15. Schüller, *Audio and Video Carriers*, 5.

16. IASA, *Guidelines*, 5.4.14.

17. Van Bogart, *Magnetic Tape Storage*, 4.

18. George Boston, *Memory of the World: Safeguarding the Documentary Heritage, A Guide to Standards, Recommended Practices and Reference Literature Related to the Preservation of Documents of All Kinds* (Paris: UNESCO, 1998), 31, accessed October 4, 2013, http://unesdoc.unesco.org/images/0011/001126/112676eo.pdf.

19. Joe Iraci, *Remedies for Deteriorated or Damaged Modern Information Carriers*, Technical Bulletin 27 (Ottawa, ON: Canadian Conservation Institute, 2005), 11.

20. Mike Casey, *FACET: Format Characteristics and Preservation Problems* (Bloomington: Indiana University, 2007), 66, accessed October 4, 2013, http://www.dlib.indiana.edu/projects/sounddirections/facet/facet_formats.pdf.

21. Van Bogart, *Magnetic Tape Storage*, 14.

22. Van Bogart, *Magnetic Tape Storage*, 48.

23. Jim Farrington, "Preventive Maintenance for Audio Discs and Tapes," *MLA Notes* 48 (1991): 437–38.

24. Van Bogart, *Magnetic Tape Storage*, 6.

25. Joe Iraci, *Disaster Recovery of Modern Information Carriers: Compact Discs, Magnetic Tapes, and Magnetic Disks*, Technical Bulletin 25 (Ottawa, ON: Canadian Conservation Institute, 2002), 6.

26. Letitia Forgas, "The Preservation of Videotape: Review and Implications for Libraries and Archives," *Libri* 47 (1997): 47–48. Recommendations and restrictions regarding use with magnetic materials are usually addressed in the system user manual.

27. ISO 18933:2012, *Imaging Materials—Magnetic Tape—Care and Handling Practices for Extended Usage* and AES-49-2005 (r2010) *AES Standard for Audio Preservation and Restoration—Magnetic Tape—Care and Handling Practices for Extended Usage* describe a seven-step inspection process for magnetic tape.

28. Peter Brothers, "Magnetic Tapes Can Survive Flood Exposure," SPEC BROS, accessed October 5, 2013, http://www.specsbros.com/h_flood.htm.

29. Iraci, *Disaster Recovery*, 7.

30. St.-Laurent, "Care and Handling," 6.

31. Richard Hess, Joe Iraci, and Kimberley Flak, *The Digitization of Audio Tapes*, Technical Bulletin 30 (Ottawa, ON: Canadian Conservation Institute, 2013), 2–3.

32. St.-Laurent, "Care and Handling," 6.

33. Breen et al., *Task Force*, 6.

34. Richard Hess, "Tape Degradation Factors and Challenges in Predicting Tape Life," *ARSC Journal* 39 (2008): 249.

35. Hess, Iraci, and Flak, *Digitization*, 2–3.

36. Hess, Iraci, and Flak, *Digitization*, 3.

37. Smithsonian, "Early Sound Recording Collection and Sound Recovery Project," *Newsdesk*, December 14, 2011, accessed September 28, 2013, http://newsdesk.si.edu/factsheets/early-sound-recording-collection-and-sound-recovery-project.

38. Andre Millard, *America on Record: A History of Recorded Sound*, 2nd ed. (New York: Cambridge University Press, 2005), 37.

39. "The Vitaphone Project," accessed September 28, 2013, http://www.vitaphoneproject.com/.

40. Frank Hoffman, ed., *Encyclopedia of Recorded Sound, Volume 1. Instantaneous Recordings* (New York: Routledge, 2005), 519.

41. Seán Street, "Recording Technologies and Strategies for British Radio Transmission Before the 2nd World War," *Sound Journal*, accessed September 28, 2013, http://www.kent.ac.uk/arts/sound-journal/street002.html.

42. Sun Records, "Elvis Presley," accessed September 28, 2013, http://www.sunrecords.com/artists/elvis-presley.

43. Library of Congress, "The History of the Edison Cylinder Phonograph," accessed September 28, 2013, http://memory.loc.gov/ammem/edhtml/edcyldr.html.

44. Millard, *America on Record*, 32.

45. Frank Daniels, "Indian 78rpm Single Releases: Identification and Price Guide," accessed September 28, 2013, http://heroinc.hostingsiteforfree.com/btls/in/in78.htm.

46. Zach O'Malley Greenburg, "Vinyl Continues Unlikely Recovery, According to New Numbers," *Forbes,* January 18, 2012, accessed September 28, 2013, http://www.forbes.com/sites/zackomalleygreenburg/2012/01/18/vinyl-continues-unlikely-recovery-according-to-new-numbers.

47. Borri Audio Laboratories, "Cylinder Record Identification," accessed September 28, 2013, http://members.tripod.com/edison_1/id16.html.

48. The Library of Congress reported on its website in 2011 that it held over fifty thousand cylinders (www.loc.gov/preservation/resources/care/cyn.html).

49. UNESCO, "Mechanical Carriers," *Safeguarding our Documentary Heritage*, accessed September 28, 2013, http://webworld.unesco.org/safeguarding/en/all_meca.htm.

50. Borri Audio Laboratories, "Playing Cylinders," accessed September 28, 2013, http://members.tripod.com/edison_1/id7.html.

51. National Museum of American History, "Early Sound Recording Collection and Sound Recovery Project," accessed September 28, 2013, http://americanhistory.si.edu/press/fact-sheets/early-sound-recording-collection-and-sound-recovery-project.

52. St.-Laurent, "The Care and Handling of Recorded Sound Materials."

# CHAPTER 11

# Moving Image Materials

Liz Coffey, Elizabeth Walters

## MOVING IMAGE MATERIALS: MOTION PICTURE FILM (LIZ COFFEY)

*Dates in use*: 1891 to date.
*Formats*: most common are 8mm, Super 8, 16mm, 35mm, 70mm.

### Material

Motion picture film comes in many shapes and sizes. Only the most common are addressed in this section.

Motion picture film (hereafter "film") is a time-based medium, an analog optical format on which images are recorded on successive frames on a photographic emulsion-coated roll of pliable plastic. The film has perforations along one or both edges, which are engaged by a sprocket in a camera for recording and in a projector for playback.

Film comes on rolls (or reels); formats (gauges) are named according to the width of the film stock. The most common gauges in the United States are 8mm, 16mm, and 35mm. Less commonly encountered are 9.5mm, 28mm, and 70mm; even rarer formats (mostly pre-1930) are also encountered. The format that is by far the most commonly found in library and historical collections in the United States is 16mm. (The length of film is measured in feet in the United States and in meters in Europe.) Film encountered may contain positive or negative images, be in color or black-and-white, and may include a soundtrack.

Film is an excellent archival medium and will, if stored correctly, last for over a hundred years,[1] probably outlasting any surrogate including current video and digital formats. It requires specialized equipment for playback. Motion pictures on film are

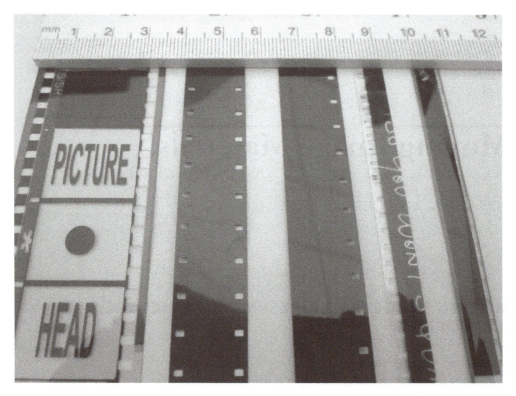

**FIGURE 11.1.** Formats (left to right: 35mm, 16mm silent stock, 16mm sound stock, 8mm, Super 8 with mag stripe)

still shot by filmmakers (both professional and amateur) and continue to be distributed to movie theatres, although they are being squeezed out by digital formats. Some film archives and other historical collections continue to use film as an archival medium because of its long-term viability.

## How Film Works: The Basic Facts

*Camera.* The raw (unprocessed) film stock is run through a camera (or otherwise exposed to light), with each frame held for a fraction of a second in the exposure gate. The film is then processed with photographic chemicals, and, depending on the film stock, the camera original is either a positive that can be projected or a negative from which a positive print can be made.

*Frame rates.* In the early days of cinema, hand-cranked cameras and projectors were used. The frame rates varied and could change during the film. Later cameras used springs; modern cameras use batteries. No matter how it was shot, a film needs to be projected at a minimum frame rate of 16 frames per second (fps). Anything slower will result in too much flicker in the projected image and some loss of the persistence of vision that is so important to enjoying a film. Modern (post 1927) sound film in 16mm and 35mm has a standardized frame rate of 24fps. Super 8 sound film is usually 18fps. Silent films' frame rates range from 16 to 20fps.

*Aspect ratio.* The aspect ratio of a film describes the image size as a ratio of the width to the height (described as 1) of the frame. For most 16mm and all 8mm and Super 8, this ratio is 1.37:1. Thirty-five millimeter film has a wider variety of aspect ratios, most of which are found only in feature films. It uses 1.33:1 (silent aperture), 1.37:1, as well as wide-screen formats such as 1.66:1, 1.85:1, 2.37:1, and more. Anamorphic films require a special lens to stretch the image during projection. If the proper lens is not used, these films appear quite distorted.

*Projection.* Prints or positive camera originals (reversal film stock) are played back through a projector at the same frame rate at which they were shot in the camera. Sprockets in the projector (as in the camera) engage with the perforations to move the film along and keep the frames in register. A mechanism in the machine (often a Maltese cross) keeps the frame in the gate of the projector (or camera) for a certain length of time. This speed is the "frame rate" described above. A shutter moves in conjunction with the Maltese cross to ensure each frame is illuminated and interrupted regularly, allowing for the persistence of vision that characterizes motion pictures.

## Purposes

As one of the main media forms of the 20th century, motion picture film was originally primarily used for entertainment ("the movies"), and it quickly became used for a wide variety of purposes, including education, documentary, and art.

### THEATRICAL USE

Early film formats differ widely in width, perforations, and frame rates. By 1909, four-perf (four perforations per frame) 35mm film had become the international standard. This standard has persisted to the present.

Until the second decade of the 21st century, 35mm film was the international standard for the presentation of feature films in cinemas. From early in the 21st century, 35mm projection in mainstream theatres was phased out, as the industry began to switch to digital presentation. As 35mm film prints have declined in their availability, independent theatres have been forced to adopt digital presentation.

Until 1952, the vast majority of 35mm film, used in cameras and for print stock, was cellulose nitrate. Although safety stocks were invented early in the history of cinema, they did not stand up to the wear and tear of theatrical presentation.[2] Nitrate was used for theatrical releases because the prints were shown hundreds of times and the arc lamps in projectors subjected the film to a lot of heat. The heat, which was not intense enough to ignite the nitrate, could cause the safety stocks to buckle and warp. When tri-acetate was developed, the major problems of theatrical presentation of safety film were solved. The United States ceased production of nitrate film in 1951. Thirty-five millimeter film stock produced after 1952 is known as "safety" stock. From 1952 to the mid-1990s, the base was usually cellulose tri-acetate and generally polyester-based after the mid-1990s.

## NONTHEATRICAL USE

The dangers of nitrate film were always well known, and serious fires involving nitrate film were not uncommon. Film storage depots and projection booths were common sites of fires brought on by the ignition of nitrate film stocks. Strict fire-safety codes written with regard to the storage and projection of nitrate film are still in use to this day. Experiments in creating safety film stocks were being conducted as early as 1909.[3]

In the interest of public safety, nitrate film was not marketed to the amateur and nontheatrical market. Safety-film stocks were produced in widths smaller than 35mm to avoid the possibility of confusion. The first nontheatrical format was 28mm, which was only used from 1911 to about 1930,[4] by which time 16mm film, invented in 1923, had become popular because it was easy to use and relatively inexpensive. One of the reasons 16mm was chosen as the width of this new film was to prevent 35mm nitrate film from being slit economically to make 16mm film, thus ensuring that 16mm film was made of nonflammable materials.

Sixteen millimeter film was the standard for nontheatrical presentation until VHS came into common use in the 1980s; it was shown in a wide variety of nontheatrical venues, including schools, churches, military bases, airplanes, and on television. TV news reporters, ethnographers, documentary filmmakers, amateur filmmakers, and artists embraced the 16mm format.

## AMATEUR AND HOME USE

Amateur formats include 8mm, Super 8, 9.5mm (primarily in Europe), 16mm, and 28mm, which was, as noted above, the first nontheatrical format. Home film formats were used for reduction prints of theatrical features and shorts for sale to the general public and were sold as raw film stock for amateur filmmakers. The camera stock most commonly used for amateur film (home movies), as well as for prints of films that could be purchased and viewed in the home, was 16mm. These included copies of theatrical films sold for home use, short animated titles, and, of course, pornography (available on all film formats). Sixteen millimeter amateur film, as with successive amateur formats, was a reversal product, which means the film that ran through the camera was processed as a positive and then run through the projector. As there was no negative in this process, camera original reversal films are usually unique.

By 1932, home filmmaking had been made even more affordable following the introduction of 8mm film, which was shot in a 16mm width in the camera but only exposed on one half of the film. Once the roll of film had come to an end, it was flipped and run through the camera again, exposing the second side of the film. At the lab, the film was processed and slit down the center. The two pieces of film were spliced together and returned to the customer. Since the 8mm frame is smaller than the 16mm frame, the film stock has similar but more numerous perforations. There is one perforation per frame in 16mm and 8mm.

Super 8 brought a revolution in amateur film stocks in 1965. It had two major advantages: it was sold in a cartridge, which made loading the camera extremely simple; and it had a larger image area than 8mm. Like its older siblings, 8mm and 16mm, it uses one perforation per frame, but the area needed for the perforations is much smaller for Super 8, making extra space available for the image. In 1973 Kodak introduced the Ektasound System, which paired a new camera with a magnetic soundtrack Super 8 cartridge, allowing for synchronized sound to be recorded with the picture. The film had a second magnetic strip, which served the dual purpose of creating a balance stripe so the film would sit flat on a reel and providing a second soundtrack, which could be recorded on when the film was projected.

Amateur film stocks are still in production, but they have been losing popularity since the small, inexpensive camcorders hit the market in the 1990s. Super 8 sound has been discontinued, and stocks of all kinds are now less readily available than they were at the height of amateur filmmaking.

## TELEVISION

*Kinescope.* Early television was performed in and broadcast live from a studio and not initially recorded for posterity. Programs that survive from this era were recorded on black-and-white 16mm film directly from a video monitor during a live broadcast. Prints of programs recorded this way are called Kinescopes and were made so the program could be broadcast again later. Sixteen millimeter film was commonly used to gather material from outside the studio for broadcast. In the case of narrative programming, the television program would often contain a mix of footage shot in the field on 16mm and in the studio on video. These programs were generally edited to 16mm, but the source material is obvious to the trained eye.

*Film at 11.* News reporters in the field used 16mm film, gathering color and black-and-white for TV news broadcasts into the 1980s. A variety of cameras made for a variety of content quality. Newsfilm was often shot without sound, and the anchorman would talk over the film from the studio as it ran live. These live soundtracks were rarely recorded. Sometimes film was shot in the field with synchronous sound, either as optical tracks or on magnetic stripes along the edge of the film. After being shot in the film, they would be brought back to the studio for processing, quickly edited if needed, and shown hours or moments later on the evening news. The phrase "film at 11," commonly heard on the evening news in the TV newsfilm era, refers to a film that was not ready for broadcast for the evening news but would be shown on the late-night news. TV stations regularly retained the films shot for the news. They are commonly found wound up in small spools ("donuts"), labeled with a piece of tape, and shelved. Sometimes logs are available, with brief descriptions of the story. When camcorders came into vogue in the 1980s, news gatherers no longer used 16mm film. The videotape method was much less expensive, did not require processing, and the tapes could be recorded over again and again. There is often a better archive of local TV news history available (from those studios that did not junk their 16mm film) from the era before the adoption of the video camera than there is of more recent TV news coverage.

*TV Prints.* Feature films were frequently shown on television. Those in the public domain were the least expensive for the stations to show and, therefore, they were popular with content programmers. TV prints of feature films are common. They are 16mm, often black-and-white, and sometimes have sections of opaque leader ("slugs") spliced into them to indicate commercial breaks. The content of some of these films was edited for television broadcasting. Films that were distributed in widescreen for theatres were cropped to the 4:3 format of television in these 16mm prints.

## EDUCATIONAL

The projection of 16mm films was familiar in venues such as schools, churches, and military bases. Educational films were produced on 16mm from the time of its invention in 1923 through the mid-1980s. The topics for these films are as diverse as the topics found in books; most schools in the United States had films in their libraries. Mostly they were shown in the classroom, although they were sometimes available as circulating material. Large educational distribution companies made films available for schools to rent or purchase. Universities produced and distributed educational films, and sometimes films sponsored by for-profit companies found their way into the classroom in the guise of education.

Educational film was used in the classroom with the youngest primary grade students (primarily nonverbal films and adaptations of children's books) through the university level. Millions, if not billions, of feet of film have been produced in the name of education. When 16mm film fell out of vogue and projectors ceased to be operated regularly, many schools and libraries junked their film collections to free up much-needed space in their buildings, thus jettisoning a history of the use of film in education in the process.

## Dates in Use

Motion picture film was developed in the early 1890s, and the 35mm format was internationally standardized by 1909. Motion picture film is still in wide use, both by professionals and amateurs, but its use is declining. Some important dates are:

1891–1951: nitrate film in use
1909 to date: 35mm gauge used as the standard
1909–ca. 1948: diacetate film in use (early safety stock)
1922 to date: 9.5mm gauge in use
1923 to date: 16mm gauge in use

1930s–1948: other acetate safety stocks in use

1932 to date: 8mm gauge in use

1948 to date: triacetate film in use

1952: discontinuation of nitrate film production in the United States

ca. 1960 to date: polyester film in use

1965 to date: Super 8 film in use

## Identification

When opening a film can for the first time, try to open it away from your face to avoid breathing in fumes produced if the film is decomposing. Nitrate film decomposition or a rusty interior could release dust from the can when it is opened.

Labels on film cans are not always reliable. A film cannot be truly identified unless it has been wound through on rewinds, and in some cases the sound must also be listened to for proper identification.

The running time of a film may be determined by measuring its footage. If a footage counter is not available, there are several methods of approximation. Many film reels show the footage along one flange. A film ruler is available for films that are on cores. The least accurate method is to judge by the size of the can the film fits into.

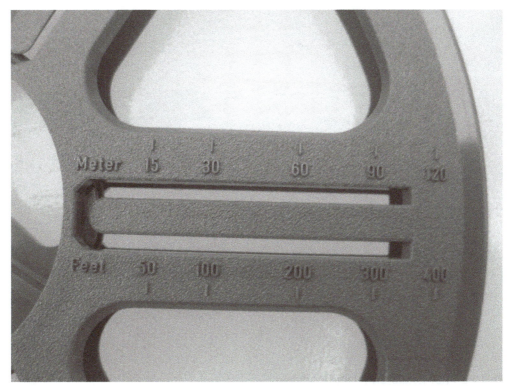

**FIGURE 11.2.** Gepe Reel Showing Footage Flange

## GAUGE IDENTIFICATION

Measure the width of the film. Keep in mind that it may have shrunken laterally.

The size of the perforations of 8mm film differs from those of Super 8 film.

## DATE IDENTIFICATION

Many companies have produced film during the past century. Most manufacturers marked their film stocks along the edge, in the area outside the perforations. Some company names are widely known, such as Kodak and Fuji; other common names are Dupont, 3M, Agfa and Agfa-Gevaert, Pathé, Ansco, and ORWO.

Some film stocks have a date code in between the perforations. This date marks the year the film stock was made by the manufacturer, although it may not have been actually run through a camera until years later. Kodak has used date codes since 1916.[5] Fuji and Dupont also used date codes in their film stocks, although not as consistently as Kodak.

Using a loupe, examine the area on the outside edge of the perforations. Date code charts are available online. For Kodak, there will be a shape or series of shapes after some text, which will ensure you are reading the order of the shapes correctly.[6]

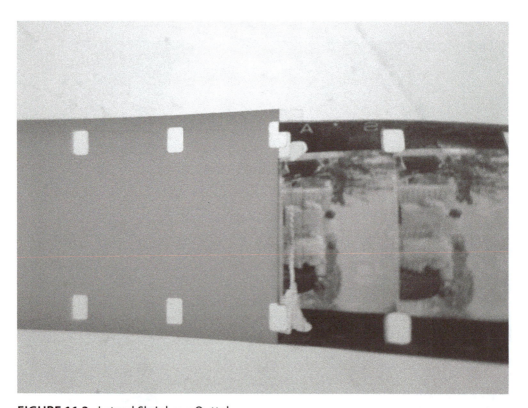

**FIGURE 11.3.** Lateral Shrinkage Outtakes

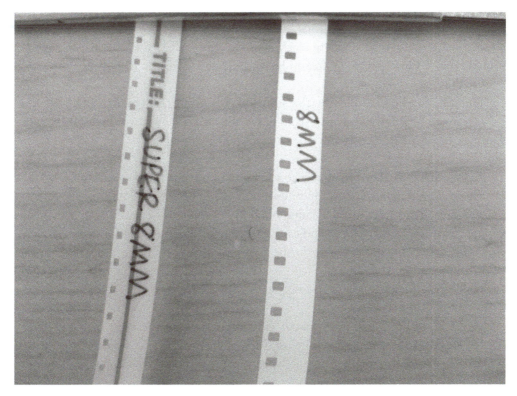

**FIGURE 11.4.** 8mm and Super 8

**FIGURE 11.5.** Kodak Date Code

## BASE IDENTIFICATION

All film made after 1952 is safety stock, and the word "SAFETY" will probably be printed outside the perforation area in black. Nitrate-based film usually has the word "NITRATE" printed in black.

The base can be identified by the sniff test. Begin gingerly by keeping your face away from the film and using your hand to fan the air above it toward you. If the odor is strong, do *not* inhale deeply.

- Photographic chemical smell is inconclusive, but healthy film is indicated.
- Vinegar smell indicates decomposing acetate base.
- Sweet smell indicates nitrate (35mm only).
- Camphor (moth balls) smell indicates diacetate or older acetate film that has been stored with a slice of camphor in the film can, as was common practice from the 1920s to the 1940s.
- Vomit or similar smell indicates early safety stock (pre-1949).

Most nitrate bases will be marked "NITRATE" along the edge in black lettering. If "NITRATE" appears as white on black along the edge, it indicates a print has been made from a nitrate negative (the word is print-through, from an optical copying

**FIGURE 11.6.** Camphor in Can

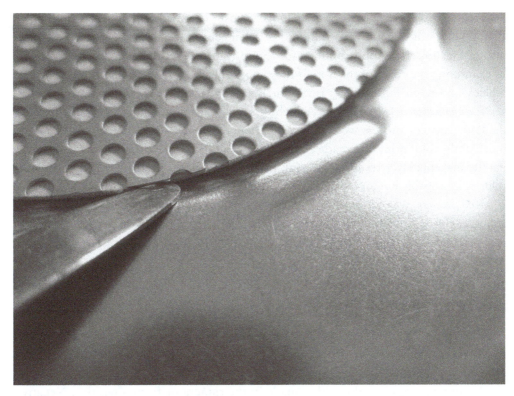

**FIGURE 11.7.** Closeup of Camphor Slice with Pointer

process). Nitrate was only produced in 35mm (and in some early, rare, nonstandard for-mats) in the United States.

Safety (non-nitrate) stocks are usually marked "SAFETY" along the edge in black lettering.

## REVERSAL STOCK

Reversal stock can readily be identified if the area outside of the image, extending to the edge of the film and between the perforations, is solid black. Reversal stock can be a camera original or a print made from a positive image. Kodachrome, Ektachrome, and black-and-white are common reversal film stocks.

## COLOR

Film may be black-and-white, black-and-white tinted, black-and-white toned, or color.

Although tinting and toning of 35mm film, relatively common in the silent movie era, went out with the advent of sound, 16mm tinting remained relatively common in silent prints through 1939.

*Technicolor* was an additive process that employed a black-and-white negative and dye-imbibition printing on black-and-white stock. This color system is extremely stable, but because it is very expensive it is no longer in use. Technicolor is not very common in 16mm, but it was sometimes used for industrial or commercial films, as well as reduction prints of features. It is most common for 35mm features. Technicolor may be identified by examining the edges of the film. If they appear black-and-white, and the soundtrack is black-and-white but the color is vibrant, then it is probably a Technicolor print.

*Eastmancolor*, released in 1950, was the first color negative system. Prints made using the Eastmancolor process were subject to dramatic color fade within just a few years; much of the color print film made between 1950 and 1985 has faded, with most losing all but the magenta layer resulting in "pink prints." If a print from these decades has good color, it is probably not an Eastmancolor print.

*Kodachrome* was an extremely successful color reversal stock (1935–2010) used almost exclusively in amateur filmmaking. The color dyes, except those used in the first few years of production, proved remarkably stable. Kodachrome films are marked as such along the edge of the film.

## ELEMENTS

*Print*: a print is a positive film that has been made from a negative or, if on reversal stock, made from another positive. Prints were, by and large, made to be projected. Prints are copies, not originals.

*Negative*: a negative film, either made in the camera or from a positive. Negative film is meant to be handled only by filmmakers and film lab technicians.

*Sound only*: This can be an optical track or a magnetic track. Fullcoat mag, which is brown and looks like audiotape although it is on film stock, is common. Fullcoat mag often suffers from extreme vinegar syndrome.

*Double system*: In this format, seen often in workprint and student works, the image is on one reel and a magnetic soundtrack is on a second reel. The two reels are synchronized for projection.

*A/B rolls*: A/B rolls can be a positive or negative silent image. A/B rolling is a method of editing in which one shot is on reel A while on reel B there is the same number of frames of leader. The next shot is on reel B, with reel A having the leader, and so on. This method is used to avoid having jumpy frames at the splices in prints. If you are handling A/B rolls, it is important not to remove any leader from between images.

*Camera original*: may be positive (on reversal stock) or negative. This is the film that was originally exposed in the camera. Many cameras leave coded marks in between the perforations, which are a good indicator that something is a camera original.[7] Camera original reversal is often unique footage and should be treated carefully.

## Representation in Collections

Film is common in the collections of cultural heritage institutions. The nature of a film is commonly indicated by format, as summarized here:

35mm: feature films, theatrically released shorts, including newsreels, cartoons, trailers, and advertising.

16mm: anything, including, but not limited to, home movies, nontheatrical film, television news, reduction prints of feature and other 35mm films, reduction prints of shorts, including cartoons and newsreels.

8mm: home movies, reduction prints of feature films (usually abridged), reduction prints of shorts, including cartoons and newsreels.

Pornography, commonly found in film collections, was made on all film formats.

## Environment and Storage

### PREFERRED ENVIRONMENT

Film can last for over one hundred years if stored properly. Films made in the 19th century still exist in good condition in archives. The basic key is to keep it cool and dry. Ideal conditions are 40°F (4°C) and 35 percent relative humidity; the Image Permanence Institute's preservation calculator assists with determining and maintaining suitable storage conditions.[8] Good air circulation is also recommended.

Perfect temperature and humidity are, of course, not always attainable. Keep the above ideals in mind when storing film and get as close to them as possible. Do not store film near radiators or heat sources, and never store it on the floor. Store it in a cool, clean space, away from water, avoiding pipes and windows.

Film can in theory be damaged by exposure to too much light, but it does not have the same light-sensitivity problems in its use in motion pictures as it does in still photography because the film is wound on a reel, keeping it effectively in the dark most of the time. Dark rooms, however, do tend to stay cooler.

Film is heavy, and this should be taken into account when choosing storage shelving. A film stored on a metal reel in a metal container may double or triple the total weight of the film.

Nitrate motion picture film requires very specialized storage because of its flammability.[9] Currently, there are five repositories for nitrate film in the United States: Library of Congress; Museum of Modern Art; George Eastman House; University of California Los Angeles; and the University of South Carolina.[10] Guidance is available in NFPA 40: *Standard for the Storage and Handling of Cellulose Nitrate Film*. If nitrate film is found in a collection, a film archivist should be consulted as soon as possible. Questionable reels of 35mm film also require consultation if they were made before 1952.

Decaying acetate film should be sequestered from healthy film, as it may be a contagious issue and could infect nearby films. It should not be stored in an area often shared with people or animals.

Film with vinegar syndrome may be frozen in a frost-free freezer in five simple steps:

- Seal film can with tape.
- Label the can so it may be read easily without opening the bag.
- Removing as much air as possible, seal the can inside a clear, thick (three milliliter or more) resealable bag.
- Double bag the film.
- Place the can in the freezer, keeping in mind the horizontal vs. vertical rules (see next section).

To thaw your film, remove it from the freezer but leave it in its bags. Let it come to room temperature overnight in a cool space to avoid water condensing inside the can or bags. Wait for at least twenty-four hours before you open the can.[11]

Polyester film, while more stable than nitrate or acetate, still has an organic layer (the emulsion) and should also be kept cool and dry.

## RECOMMENDATIONS FOR STORAGE

Film needs to be protected from trauma and possible water events, so it should ideally be stored in a proper film can, not a paperboard enclosure. Archival film cans provide some ventilation, which is recommended. Film should not be left on the floor; if stored on lower shelves, it should be a few inches off the floor.

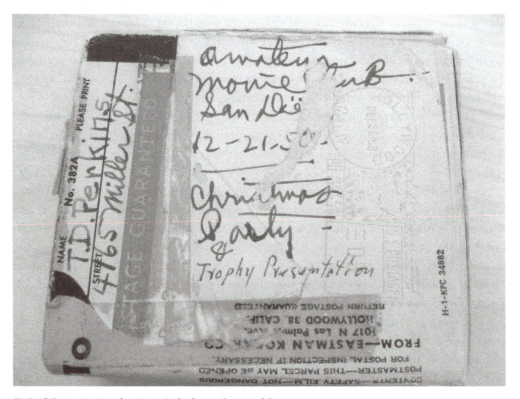

**FIGURE 11.8.** Handwritten Labels on Original Box

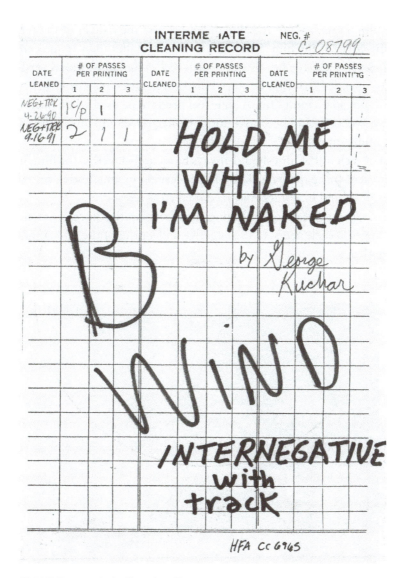

**FIGURE 11.9.** Lab Cleaning Report

Retaining the original container is advised. Information that may not always be evident to the archivist or librarian may be inherent in original enclosures. This is especially true for containers with any kind of handwritten labels, laboratory papers, or brand-identifying film cans. Rusting cans should be disposed of; they may be recycled with other metal recycling.

Cans in which films are stored should be the correct size so the films have very little space to move about within their cans. Ideally, only one reel should be stored in each film can, but this is not always practical. Although it is not recommended, if two layers of 16mm film are stored in a 35mm film can, an inert disc should be inserted to create a stable barrier between the two layers.

Storing film on reels is not recommended because the flanges of the reel can cause damage to the edges of the film. Small-gauge films (smaller than 16mm) are, however, generally stored on reels. If a film is stored on a reel, it should be stored vertically.

It is recommended that film be stored on a core. Three-inch or larger cores should be used for 16mm and 35mm film. A split reel needs to be used when putting film onto a core. Film on cores should be stored horizontally and should always be handled very carefully and fully supported.

The end of each roll of film should always be securely taped to the film, using a two-inch length of acid-free paper tape. Use a fresh piece every time, and never reuse it. Film that becomes unwound in storage may be damaged as a result.

Storage in separate locations, including an off-site location, is recommended for rare items. Two copies of such items, or the negative and a print of the same film, should not be stored together.

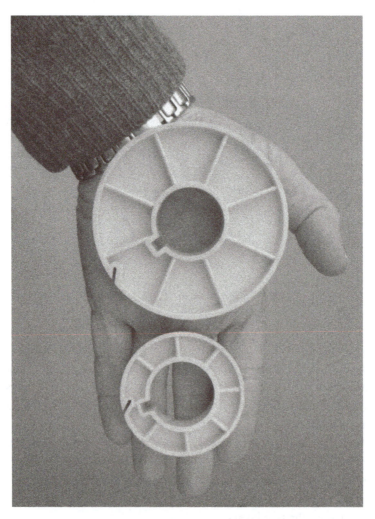

**FIGURE 11.10.** 3-Inch and 2-Inch Cores

**FIGURE 11.11.** Split Reel and Core

## Handling

### WHAT STAFF NEED TO KNOW

Handling motion picture film requires expertise and specialized equipment. Proceed with caution. Inexperienced staff should not handle film.

Like photographs, film can be damaged through improper handling. The oils in our skin can adversely affect the emulsion. Gloves should be worn if the image area could be touched. Nitrile gloves allow for dexterity and easy handling; cotton gloves should be used cautiously, as perforation damage or loose splices could turn into tears if the edge catches on a glove. Film on a core (as opposed to a reel) should be handled gingerly. Support the entire roll from below, being careful not to let the core drop from the center.

Unless the film has been carefully inspected and repaired, film should not be run through a projector. The projector can easily damage film if care is not taken. Shrunken or otherwise damaged film should not be projected. All splices should be checked for sturdiness prior to projection. Leader should be added to the beginning and end (head and tail) if there is none or only a small amount. Evidence of damage to perforations may be an indication of shrinkage. Use a shrinkage gauge, pins on a splicer, or a fresh piece of film to test for shrinkage. Shrunken film should not be run through anything with a sprocket.

Film needs to be wound carefully and evenly so edges do not pop out from the sides, as this could cause damage.

**FIGURE 11.12.** Shrunken Vinegar Syndrome Film with Spoking

Basic equipment and supplies needed for handling film are:

- Film rewinds
- Split reels
- Splicers (for all available formats, cement or tape)
- Splicing tape or cement (as needed)
- Footage counter
- Fresh leader to add to head and tail (beginning and end) of reel, as needed
- Loupe
- Tabletop viewer

### WHAT USERS NEED TO KNOW

Users should not be handling film. If the institution is able to provide access to film prints on a viewer such as a Steenbeck editing table, staff should be handling the film.

Users should be shown how to stop viewing equipment and be encouraged to stop the playback if anything appears to be going awry.

If viewing of films is not possible, patrons are frequently given access to digitized versions. A vendor specializing in handling delicate film should be used for digitization.

## Playback/Viewing Equipment

Film, like any time-based medium, is relatively useless without playback equipment. For the most part, each gauge requires its own size equipment. Projectors and other equipment need to be kept clean, lubricated, and in good working order. Although film projection equipment is still produced, it is, like film, an endangered species.

Exceptionally rare or unique film should not be projected. Copies should be made for use.

## Disaster Response

Avoiding a disaster is, of course, always preferable to cleaning up after one. Make sure your film is stored away from obvious sources of water. Disasters do happen, so it is very important to have a plan for dealing with their aftermath.

Fire is a danger when storing nitrate film stock, which must be stored away from people and animals. Because nitrate film creates its own oxygen source as it burns, fires cannot be extinguished. In case of nitrate fire, get people to safety.

Water is most likely to be the cause of disasters associated with films in cultural heritage collections. Be prepared by following these guidelines:

- Store film in durable, archival polypropylene film cans whenever possible. New, powder-coated steel cans (the standard for nitrate film storage) are also acceptable. A sturdy film can will protect its contents from water and physical trauma.
- Do not store film on the floor at any time; if stored on lower shelves, make sure it is a few inches off the floor.
- Label film clearly; use waterproof labeling on the film leader and film cans. If you use barcodes, place them on the outside of the film can. Waterproof labeling on the film leader and film cans is essential. Test ahead of time to find out what happens if your labeling does get wet.
- Keep supplies on hand. A source for distilled water will be helpful. Buckets with tight-fitting lids may also come in handy.
- Know your collection. In case of emergency, be able to retrieve your most valuable items.
- Talk to local film archivists and film laboratories ahead of time. These relationships will be invaluable in dire circumstances.

Water can cause irretrievable emulsion damage and foster mold growth. Some types of mold will eat away at the organic layers of the emulsion.

Steps to take if you have wet film are:

- Treat the film with care, as wet film is delicate.
- Keep the film moist.
- Call a film laboratory or film archive and ask their advice. The film may need to be rewashed in a properly equipped laboratory.
- Depending on the quality of the water the film has been in contact with, you may have to immerse it in a bucket of clean water, preferably distilled.
- If there is a lot of wet film to be treated, prioritize it.
- Place film in a thick (three millimeter) resealable bag with a sprinkle of clean water to stop the film from drying out before it gets to the laboratory.
- If you need to wait for some days or a week before you can ship the films to a laboratory, refrigerate them in their bags.
- Determine whether disaster recovery vendors with appropriate expertise in treating film are able to assist.

## Decay

### NITRATE FILM

Decomposing nitrate film is dangerous, and decomposition can accelerate unpredictably. The odor of decomposing has been likened to that of rotting bananas or stinky feet. The following five stages of nitrate decomposition are a descriptive standard recognized internationally:

Stage 1: Film has an amber discoloration (not to be confused with a tint) with fading of the image. There will be a faint, noxious odor. A rust ring may form on the inside of metal film cans. Although a rust ring is not an indicator for identifying nitrate film, as it may occur with other bases, it is an indication of decay if the film has already been identified as nitrate.

Stage 2: Emulsion becomes adhesive and the film tends to stick together during unrolling. There will be a faint, noxious odor.

Stage 3: Portions of the film are soft, contain gas bubbles, and emit a noxious odor.

Stage 4: The entire film is soft and welded into a single mass, the surface may be covered with viscous froth, and a strong, noxious odor is given off.

Stage 5: Film mass degenerates partially or entirely into a shock-sensitive, brownish acrid powder.

### ACETATE BASES

The decomposition of acetate-based film is called "vinegar syndrome" because during the process of decomposition, acetic acid, the main component of vinegar, is emitted from the base. The typical pattern for acetate decay is:

1. Vinegar odor.
2. Shrinkage.
3. Cupping: the film retains a curve. It will not lie flat, but instead appears wavy.
4. Crazing: the emulsion cracks and the image appears as a crazy mosaic.
5. Appearance of white powder on edges (from binder deterioration, this is the plasticizer separating from the film).
6. Film becomes square on reel.
7. Film is no longer flexible, and the emulsion flakes off from the base.[12]

A-D strips (dye-coated paper strips that detect and measure the severity of acetate film deterioration) may be used to determine the level of acetate decay. Films registering a level higher than 1.5 should be moved away from "healthy" film, as vinegar syndrome may be contagious. See the "Environment and Storage" section earlier in this chapter.

## Treatments

Film is both sturdy and easily damaged. Treated correctly, it can last for decades. If you have no experience with handling motion picture film, you should consult with a professional film archivist or vendor.

**FIGURE 11.13.** Reel with Level 3 Indicated on A-D Strip

Simple repairs and joins may be made using a film splicer. Cement splices may be used on acetate- and nitrated-based films, but not with polyester-based films. Tape splices may be used with all bases, but they are not recommended for nitrate.

# MOVING IMAGE MATERIALS: MAGNETIC MEDIA (ELIZABETH WALTERS)

*Dates in use*: mid-1950s to the present.
*Formats*: analog open-reel formats such as 2-inch Quaduplex, 1-inch SMPTE Type C, and ½-inch EIAJ Type; and analog and digital cassette formats such as U-Matic, VHS, Betacam SP, Digital Betacam, Hi8, and MiniDV.

## Material

Tape-based formats comprise by far the largest segment of the magnetic media group. The most prevalent videotape formats include analog open-reel formats such as 2-inch Quaduplex, 1-inch SMPTE Type C, and ½-inch EIAJ Type 1, as well as analog and digital cassette formats such as U-Matic, VHS, Betacam SP, Digital Betacam, Hi8, and MiniDV.

Magnetic recording rapidly gained in popularity following the technology's introduction into the North American market in the late 1940s. Continual innovation and improvements in fidelity, functionality, portability, and pricing ensured that magnetic media remained the dominant presence in nearly every segment of the recording market (consumer, professional, educational, and industrial) for more than five decades. Today, virtually every magnetic video recording format has been superseded, either by other types of physical media (for example, optical formats such as DVDs) or by file-based digital recording technologies, for almost all applications. Nevertheless, content stored on magnetic media remains a significant and irreplaceable component of the holdings of most libraries, archives, and other cultural heritage institutions. The preservation of these legacy media poses formidable challenges, not only from the standpoint of physical deterioration of the carriers themselves (none of which was ever intended to last more than a few decades) but also in light of the obsolescence and dwindling availability both of the hardware required to access the content stored on these media and of the parts and technicians needed to service the equipment. Moreover, while it is often possible to slow the deterioration of audiovisual media by optimizing the storage environment or restricting handling and playback, the broad consensus within the audiovisual preservation community is that reformatting through digitization and continued migration is the only viable long-term strategy for preservation.[13]

## Purposes

Ampex Corporation introduced the first commercial videotape recorder in 1956. The Quadruplex (or "Quad"), which recorded onto 2-inch open-reel magnetic tape, was quickly adopted by television broadcasters to record live programs for delayed rebroadcast in multiple time zones.[14] It remained in use until the early 1980s, when it was largely replaced by the SMPTE Type C, a 1-inch open-reel professional-use format introduced by Ampex and Sony in 1978 based on standards formulated by the Society of Motion Picture and Television Engineers (SMPTE). Type C was used until the late 1990s, often as an archival preservation master format.[15]

Several ½-inch open-reel video formats emerged in the 1960s. The most common of these, EIAJ Type 1, was introduced in 1969 based on a standard developed by the Electronic Industries Association of Japan.[16] The first standardized, nonprofessional video format, EIAJ-1 was widely used throughout the 1970s for industrial, educational, and consumer applications thanks in part to the affordability of the recorders, which included Portapak, the first portable videotape recorder, marketed in 1964.[17]

The first commercial videocassette format, ¾-inch U-Matic, was launched by Sony in 1971. Portable U-Matic recorders, which used the somewhat smaller U-Matic SP cassettes, became available in the mid-1970s, ushering in the era of electronic newsgathering. In addition to professional broadcasters, U-Matic also won favor with artists, community organizations, academic institutions, and libraries. U-Matic SP, a professional-grade variant of the standard U-Matic developed in the mid-1980s, was used primarily by broadcasters. Both U-Matic and U-Matic SP remained in use until well into the 1990s.[18]

The consumer market for videocassette recording took off with Sony's U.S. launch of the Betamax ½-inch videocassette in 1975. Despite its technical superiority, Betamax was quickly edged out of the market by VHS, a competing ½-inch format that offered multiple recording speeds and longer playing times, introduced in 1976. VHS remained the dominant consumer video format throughout the 1980s, and it was the format of choice for commercial releases of films and educational materials, as well as for home recording of television programs. S-VHS, a high-grade format variant marketed in the late 1980s, found favor with both consumer and institutional users. VHS-C (1982), a small-cassette variant for camcorder use, could be played back in standard VHS machines with the use of an adapter.[19]

Betacam, an analog ½-inch professional-use format launched in 1982, was followed by Betacam SP (Superior Performance), which debuted in 1986. Both variants came in large and small cassette versions and were developed for broadcast, educational, and professional applications. Betacam SP was widely used for electronic newsgathering as well as for edit mastering by producers and artists, and it was a popular choice for the creation of preservation masters from the early 1990s into the early 2000s. Digital Betacam (or "Digibeta"), introduced in 1993, was the first digital format variant in the Betacam family. Intended to replace Betacam SP, Digibeta also became a popular preservation format and was used extensively into the late 2000s.[20] Other Betacam format variants include Betacam SX (1996), HDCAM (1997), MPEG IMX (2001), and HDCAM SR (2003).

The emergence of the portable, handheld videocamera-recorder (or camcorder) in the early 1980s further expanded the range of both consumer and professional out-of-studio applications thanks to greater portability, longer recording times, and increasingly accessible pricing. Video8, an 8mm consumer-use format introduced in 1984, was followed in 1989 by Hi8, a high-grade variant targeting the consumer, industrial, and educational markets. Hi8 was especially popular with artists and educational institutions. MiniDV, a ¼-inch small-cassette format that took over much of the market for Video8 and Hi8 from the mid-1990s, quickly permeated all but the very high-end professional applications. Format variants include DVCAM and DVCPro.[21]

D1, the first digital video format, reached market in 1987, and it was soon followed by a number of other digital formats including D2, D3, D5, D6, and the aforementioned Digital Betacam. All of these formats require different and incompatible playback equipment.[22]

With the exception of VHS, which was widely used for the distribution of prerecorded content such as commercial films and educational materials, most of the formats discussed above can be assumed to hold mostly rare or unique content.

## Dates in Use

Quadruplex: 1956 to the early 1980s
EIAJ Type 1: 1969 to the late 1970s
SMPTE Type C: 1978 to the late 1990s
U-Matic: 1971 to the late 1990s
U-Matic SP: 1986 to the late 1990s
Betamax: 1975 to the late 1980s
VHS: 1976 to the mid-2000s
S-VHS: 1987 to the mid-2000s
Betacam: 1982 to the mid-2000s
Betacam SP: 1986 to the mid-2000s
Digital Betacam: 1993 to the late 2000s
Video8: 1984 to the 2000s
Hi8: 1989 to the 2000s
MiniDV, DVCAM, DVCPro: mid-1990s to the present

## Identification

All magnetic tape is composed of at least two layers: (1) magnetic pigment or other magnetizable material that stores the recorded signal, and (2) a base layer, or basefilm, which serves as a structural support for the magnetic material (see figure 11.14). In most cases, the magnetic particles are suspended in a polymer binder that disperses them evenly across the tape surface and bonds them to the base layer. In others (notably metal evaporate tapes), the magnetizable material is a thin, vapor-deposited layer of metal alloy that does not use a binder. This mixture may also contain a variety of additives to improve the quality of the tape, including lubricants, plasticizers, surfactants, solvents, cleaning agents, and fungicides. Binders are notoriously proprietary, varying widely among

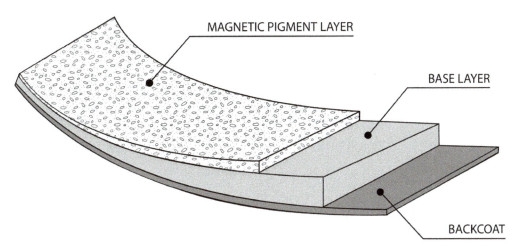

MAGNETIC PIGMENT LAYER

BASE LAYER

BACKCOAT

**FIGURE 11.14.** Cross Section of Magnetic Tape. Drawing, Eve Neiger

manufacturers and even among individual product lines of a single manufacturer.[23] Since the late 1960s, most magnetic tape has also included a backcoating layer to improve tape wind and to reduce curling and the buildup of static electricity, which can attract dust and cause dropouts. Each of these layers presents a different set of preservation challenges.

## BASE LAYER

The base layer (also basefilm or substrate) is largely responsible for the tape's mechanical strength and stability. Polyester, usually polyethylene terephthalate (PET), is the base layer used for all videotape. In addition to PET, polyethylene naphthalate (PEN) is used for some long-play and thin digital videotape formats. Common trade names for polyester include Mylar (DuPont), Tenzar (Scotch/3M), and Estar (Kodak).

## MAGNETIC PIGMENT LAYER

The first widely used magnetic pigment was gamma ferric oxide ($Fe_2O_3$), used for early open-reel videotape until the early 1960s. Although extremely stable, $Fe_2O_3$ offered only limited recording density. This prompted the development of chromium dioxide ($CrO_2$) and cobalt-doped ferric oxide (cobalt-doped $Fe_3O_4$) pigments in the late 1960s. These pigments, which achieved the greater concentrations of magnetic particles required to support higher recording densities, were mainly used for analog videocassettes and high-bias audiocassettes.[24] From the late 1980s, two types of pure metal (nonoxide) pigments came into use for videotape: metal particle (MP), which contains pure iron particles treated with a protective coating to prevent oxidation, and metal evaporate (ME), comprised of a thin, homogeneous layer of metal alloy that is vapor deposited onto the tape base.[25] Formats using metal pigments include Video8 and Hi8, Betacam SP, and digital videocassettes.[26]

## OTHER

Magnetic cassette formats almost always have identifying information such as format name, manufacturer, brand name, and maximum running time (in minutes) imprinted on the shell. The type of base layer and magnetic pigment layer may also be identified. However, it should be remembered that commercial packaging materials such as blank labels, inserts, reels, and tape leader are frequently transferred from one audiovisual object to another, and thus it may not always be a reliable indication of the media they contain.

## Representation in Collections

Magnetically recorded video content has been an integral component of the collections of every type of cultural heritage institution since the technology became commercially available. Large concentrations of magnetic media may be found in academic, public, and corporate libraries; museums, archives, and historical societies; government and corporate entities; and private collections of all kinds. Content includes recordings of cultural, historical, scholarly, or institutional significance created by scholars, researchers, educators, artists, and performers as primary sources, works of art, and documentary records. The condition and quality of these media holdings varies widely, and they may include everything from professionally produced studio recordings on high-grade media to amateur recordings made in the field using handheld recorders on substandard media.

Magnetic media have played an especially important role in ethnographic collections, in which small-format videocassettes are likely to be especially well represented. Small-format cassette tapes generally have a very thin base layer and thus are more susceptible to mechanical damage.

Sizable collections of VHS videocassettes, consisting mainly of educational materials and commercial titles produced in the 1980s and 1990s, may still be found in both the general and special collections of academic and public libraries, though these holdings have declined markedly over the past decade or so as videocassettes are replaced by DVDs. Such collections typically have been heavily used and stored under less than optimal conditions.

Museum collections frequently include video artworks and multimedia installations, often in the early 1-inch and ½-inch open-reel formats favored by many pioneering video artists. More recently, archival masters may be found on Betacam SP or on digital video formats such as DVCAM, which has also been a popular reference and exhibition format. Museum holdings may also comprise educational and promotional materials as well as documentary recordings of lectures, classes, performances, interviews, openings, and other events. Such content is often recorded on small-cassette video formats such as Video8 and MiniDV.

Radio and television broadcasters were the earliest adopters of magnetic recording technologies, and they continued to embrace new formats as they became available. As a result, broadcast archives and collections typically contain a large and diverse range of video formats. Especially common are: 2-inch Quadruplex (the first broadcast video format); ½-inch and 1-inch open-reel videotape formats; analog cassette formats such as U-Matic, VHS, Betacam, Betacam SP (often used as a preservation master format in the late 1980s and early 1990s), and Hi8; as well as a plethora of digital video formats including D2, D3, Digital Betacam, DVCAM, and DVCPro.

As new formats superseded obsolete ones, media content was repeatedly transferred to the newer formats to ensure continued access. It thus is not unusual for cultural heritage collections to hold the same content on several generations of copies in both magnetic and nonmagnetic formats. For example, an original motion-picture film may be retained along with one-off use copies of the same content transferred to U-Matic, VHS, MiniDV, and most recently DVD. In most cases, these copies (which in a sense are themselves originals) were created solely for access purposes, and thus they seldom met current standards for preservation-quality transfer.

Today, much of the content captured on these media is effectively inaccessible to users, in part because repositories often lack item-level control of the content and also because they no longer possess the specialized equipment or expertise required to play back the media. In addition, it is not unusual for media to be misidentified or poorly cared for because in-house staff lacks the resources and expertise to adequately process and preserve these materials.

## Environment and Storage

### PREFERRED ENVIRONMENT

Ensuring a clean, temperature- and humidity-controlled storage environment is the single best means of extending the life expectancy of magnetic media. An optimal environment cannot reverse or halt degradation, but it can go a long way toward slowing the progression.

Temperature and relative humidity have a major impact on the health and longevity of magnetic media. High humidity can promote binder hydrolysis, a chemical reaction in which the binder (typically polyurethane) absorbs ambient moisture and becomes soft and sticky, causing the magnetic layer to pull away from the tape base (a condition commonly referred to as "sticky shed syndrome") and clog playback equipment with a gummy residue that can lead to signal dropouts.[27] Prolonged exposure to high levels of humidity (above 65 percent RH) can also encourage mold and other fungus growth, which can destroy the pigment layer of magnetic tape.[28] Fungus growth is more likely to be a problem with older tapes, as fungicides have been added to the binders of most modern tapes. High humidity and temperatures may also lead to curling, embrittlement, and shrinkage of the tape base.[29]

Temperature determines the speed of chemical reactions such as hydrolysis: reactions accelerate markedly as temperatures increase. Storage at elevated temperatures (greater than 75°F/23°C) can also cause the tape pack to tighten, resulting in tape deformation and the increased likelihood of blocking (adhesion of successive tape layers) and print-through (the magnetization of one tape layer by an adjacent layer, creating increased noise with analog video and increased errors in digital video). Excessively low temperatures and humidity can also be detrimental to magnetic media. Temperatures below 32°F (0°C) may cause binders to become brittle and cause even the most stable tape bases to stretch and shrink. Low humidity can cause a tape pack to loosen, leading to mechanical damage and static buildup during playback, and it may also promote the loss of lubricant.[30]

Fluctuations in temperature and humidity, even within a fairly narrow range, can be even more damaging than any single extreme of temperature or humidity, particularly if they occur frequently. The magnetic pigment, binder, and base layer all expand and contract at different rates, and the resulting dimensional changes can permanently distort the tape base.[31] This distortion can impair head-to-tape contact, which is particularly problematic with high-density recordings.[32]

While recommendations for acceptable or optimal levels of temperature and relative humidity vary widely, nearly all of them call for low levels of both temperature and relative humidity and for minimal fluctuations in both these parameters. ISO standards listed at the end of this chapter offer recommendations regarding temperature and humidity levels for both medium-term (ten-plus years) and long-term (fifty-plus years) storage of magnetic media. The broadest range specifies temperatures of 46°F (8°C) to 74°F (23°C) and relative humidity of 15 percent to 50 percent, with fluctuation of no more than 5°F (±2°C) and ±5 percent, respectively, over a twenty-four-hour period. The lower end of this range is preferable.

*Air Quality and Light.* Another critical environmental consideration for magnetic media is the presence of contaminants such as pollution, dust, smoke, fingerprints, and hair. Contaminants hinder head-to-tape contact and may be dragged into the tape winds during playback, creating irreparable scratches or indentations in the magnetic layer that result in signal distortion or loss. Even minute debris can cause signal loss or dropouts, especially in the case of videotapes, which generally have a thinner base layer. Pollution may also cause corrosion of metal evaporate and metal particle tapes. A scrupulously clean storage and operating environment that includes clean, uncarpeted floors, good air filtration, and a smoke-free, food-free environment will help to minimize damaging dust and debris and will also discourage vermin.[33]

Exposure to light, especially ultraviolet light, can be damaging to both the media and their enclosures, and it should therefore be kept to a minimum. Store media away from windows and fluorescent lighting, and use UV shields if necessary.

## RECOMMENDATIONS FOR STORAGE

All magnetic media should be oriented vertically in storage, resting on their spines or edges, to prevent tape pack deformation and edge damage. Store media away from sources of both fluorescent and natural light, as well as from potential sources of water incursion such as windows, plumbing, and air-conditioning units. Tapes with a loose pack or uneven wind should be rewound before being placed in storage to avoid permanent deformation of the tape base. An even, well-tensioned wind will also help minimize damage to tapes in the event of a water disaster, as water and debris cannot easily penetrate the tape pack.[34]

Store media on sturdy shelves, preferably electrically grounded, that are capable of supporting the weight. Shelving should also allow for adequate air circulation. Use of dividers to keep media from leaning is also recommended. If using motorized compact shelving, keep media away from motors.

Popular myth to the contrary, accidental erasure of a magnetic tape recording by stray magnetic fields is a rare occurrence, owing both to the high coercivity (ability to resist demagnetization) of most magnetic tape and to the unlikelihood of exposure to a sufficiently strong magnetic field. (Early videotape formats such as Quadruplex and U-Matic are somewhat more sensitive to stray fields than are later analog video formats or digital recordings due to the lower coercivity of their magnetic pigments.) Nevertheless, it is advisable to store magnetic media at least four to six inches (ten to fifteen centimeters) away from anything that might generate a magnetic or electrical field (such as motors, generators, loudspeakers, and electrical transformers), as the magnetic fields emanating from these devices may also cause increased low-frequency noise or higher levels of print-through. Similar care should also be taken during shipping and transport. It should also be noted that many theft detection systems that use magnetized security strips emit strong magnetic fields that are not appropriate for use with magnetic media.[35]

If magnetic media are stored at temperature or humidity levels substantially lower than those of the use environment, they should be allowed to acclimatize in the use environment for up to twenty-four hours before attempting playback. Failure to allow for adequate acclimatization may lead to moisture condensation, mechanical damage, and mistracking during playback. Recommended acclimatization periods may differ markedly depending on such variables as tape thickness, enclosure type, and specific storage conditions. Acclimatization considerations and recommendations are discussed in standards AES-22:1997 (r2003) and ISO 18923:2000.

*Enclosures.* Enclosures should be made of durable, impact-resistant, chemically inert materials such as polypropylene, and they should afford adequate protection from moisture, light, and heat, as well as from dust and other contaminants. Avoid cardboard, paper, or plastic slipcases, boxes, and other flexible containers that offer little protection from water or fire damage and may interact chemically with the media. Enclosures should latch securely and allow for proper orientation of the media in storage.

Loose paper or other items should not be stored inside the enclosure, as paper tends to generate dust, which is abrasive and can cause dropouts. Some paper may also contain harmful acids. Moreover, the added bulk created by inserts may exert damaging pressure or stress on the media, particularly if the inserts include paper clips, staples, or other sharp fasteners.

Open-reel tapes should be wound onto sturdy, unslotted reels made of noncorrosive metal or inert plastic and housed in enclosures with hubs that do not allow the reel's weight to rest on the flanges. The loose end of the tape should be secured to the outer side of the reel flange with hold-down tape made specifically for this purpose: do not use conventional pressure-sensitive tape, which may leave harmful, sticky residue. Protective paper collars may also be used. Small-cassette formats such as MiniDV and Hi8 should be grouped in larger containers to prevent damage or loss.

Use archival-quality labels that are nonacidic, adhere securely, and can otherwise be expected to last for the life of the media. Write on labels before affixing them to the media; do not write directly on media with pens or solvent-based markers. Do not use pressure-sensitive tape to attach labels or other documentation to reels or cassette shells. In particular, do not adhere labels on or near the tape doors or in any other position that interferes with the tape transport. When feasible, labels should be attached to the enclosure rather than to the carrier itself. If media are rehoused, care should be taken to transfer all relevant descriptive information, including manufacturer and product information, to the new enclosure.

## Handling

### WHAT STAFF NEED TO KNOW

All magnetic media should be handled carefully; however, particular care must be taken with masters, fragile or deteriorating formats, and unique or irreplaceable items. Staff who deal with these materials must be trained in proper handling methods to prevent irrevocable loss of content.

Handle both media and playback equipment gently and as infrequently as possible. Keep hands clean and dry; consider wearing lint-free cotton gloves. Never touch the edges or recording surface of any magnetic media, as fingerprints may leave an oily residue. Handle tape reels by the center hub, taking care not to put pressure on the reel flanges, which could damage tape edges. Never pull on the loose end of a tape to tighten the wind, as this may cause the tape to stretch, crease, or break, and it may damage the magnetic layer. Magnetic media should not be dropped or subjected to sudden shock, which may cause reel or shell breakage, container damage, and tape pack distortion.

Magnetic media should never be forced into storage enclosures or playback equipment. Never eject a tape in the middle of a recording, or pause it for extended periods, as this may damage the tape or cause accidental erasure. Do not leave media sitting in playback equipment, where the tape may overheat and is in close proximity to recording and erase heads. For added security, engage the record-protection mechanism found on most cassette media.[36] Cassettes should never be left in a partially wound state; always wind to one end before ejecting. Wind tapes at normal playback speeds; never fast-forward or rewind at high speed, which may cause uneven tension or wind. Return each tape to its enclosure immediately after use. Good housekeeping is essential; eating, drinking, and smoking should never be permitted in or near areas where magnetic media are stored or handled.

## WHAT USERS NEED TO KNOW

Ideally, users should not be allowed to handle or play back masters or any original recordings that contain unique or irreplaceable content. If users are to be permitted to play back media themselves, they should be trained in the same handling procedures as staff. Encourage all users to report any problems they may observe.

## OTHER HANDLING CONSIDERATIONS

Media should periodically be examined for signs of damage or deterioration, particularly after being subjected to sharp fluctuations in temperature or relative humidity. Look for oxide shedding, tape pack problems, debris, enclosure deterioration, reel or shell damage, and strong odors, which can indicate chemical deterioration. Any dust or debris should be wiped away using a lint-free cloth; solvents or other cleaning solutions should never be used to clean either the media themselves or their enclosures.[37]

## Playback/Viewing Equipment

Playback on misaligned or poorly maintained equipment is a frequent cause of mechanical damage to magnetic media. Any playback equipment in frequent use should be professionally inspected, cleaned, and calibrated on a regular basis. Playback areas should be kept cool, dry, and free of dust and other contaminants, as dirt or debris anywhere in the tape transport can permanently scratch both the tape heads and the tape surface. When not in use, playback equipment should be turned off to prevent overheating; the use of dust covers is also recommended. Before attempting playback, carefully inspect all media for any signs of deterioration, including reel or shell damage and dirt or debris that could harm the media or the equipment during playback. Never attempt to play media on a machine not specifically designed for that format. Given the fragility and irreplaceability of both media and playback equipment, only trained personnel should be permitted to operate the equipment.

## Disaster Response

Nearly all magnetic media are extremely vulnerable to damage from water and fire. Salvage and remediation work is almost always an expensive and complex undertaking, with no guarantee of success. As such, the best strategy is to focus on preventive measures that include keeping media well protected from damage by housing them in appropriate protective enclosures and storing them far away from potential sources of heat, light, and water, including basements, attics, water pipes, sprinklers, air-conditioning vents, and windows. Media with content of enduring value should be digitized for preservation at the earliest opportunity.

## WATER DAMAGE

Most magnetic media are not in immediate danger from short-term exposure to clean water. However, extended exposure can cause irrevocable damage, so recovery efforts should be considered time-sensitive.[38] Some magnetic media are extremely vulnerable to damage from even minimal exposure to water. These include older or deteriorating tapes and metal particle or metal evaporate tapes such as MiniDV, which are highly susceptible to corrosion and may suffer permanent damage if immersed for any length of time. These media should be given top priority during a salvage effort.

Wet tapes should be kept cool (but not frozen) and treated as soon as possible to prevent fungal growth, which can occur in less than twenty-four hours. Magnetic media that have been exposed to rainwater, sewage, salt water, chlorinated water, or other contaminated water should be rinsed in cool, distilled water and not be permitted to dry out, as contaminants may adhere to the tape surface and be more difficult to remove later.

Wet magnetic tape is easily stretched or torn and should be handled gently. Do not attempt to unwind or view wet or contaminated media. Maintain wet media in the same orientation as found in order to avoid spreading contaminants. Prior to recovery, keep wet media in an area that is cool and well ventilated. If water-affected media must be separated from their enclosures and inserts to promote drying and prevent fungal growth, thorough documentation is essential in order to avoid disassociation of the media from their content information.

An experienced audiovisual disaster recovery vendor should handle large quantities of disaster-affected media, especially if the media is very wet or contaminated by mold or debris. Uneven drying can cause irrevocable deformation of the tape base, as can recovery methods that use extreme heat or cold, such as freezing, vacuum thermal-drying, and vacuum freeze-drying.[39] Always consult with a specialist for guidance before attempting any in-house salvage or stabilization procedures.

## OTHER CONSIDERATIONS

Repository staff should be trained to quickly recognize the various types of magnetic media and other audiovisual materials in their collections *before* a disaster occurs to enable the timely identification and prioritization of high-risk formats during a time-sensitive disaster recovery effort. Securing sufficient quantities of media salvage supplies may be difficult in the wake of a disaster, so it is advisable to maintain an ample on-site cache of essential supplies such as distilled water, lint-free cloths, sturdy resealable plastic bags, and blotter paper.

## Decay

### MAGNETIC LAYER

The most serious and frequently encountered problem with the magnetic pigment layer is binder hydrolysis, a chemical reaction in which the long polymer molecules in the binder are broken down by the absorption of ambient moisture, causing the binder to become soft and sticky. The resulting loss of binder integrity can cause sticky-shed syndrome (described in "Environment and Storage" earlier in this chapter). Hydrolysis also compromises the bond between the binder and the tape base, causing the magnetic layer to flake or peel away from the base.[40] Evidence of this degradation may include stickiness when the tape is unwound, oxide debris found in enclosures or on playback equipment, a squealing sound during playback, and a pungent odor often described as "dirty socks."[41] Binder hydrolysis occurs mainly in polyester-based backcoated tapes manufactured since the 1970s, when polyurethane binders came into widespread use, and it may be exacerbated by the presence of the chromium dioxide particles used in some magnetic pigments.[42] Binder degradation does not occur in metal evaporate tapes, which instead are subject to oxidation and corrosion.

Another type of binder-related degradation is the loss of lubricants added to the binder during the manufacturing process. Lubricants give the magnetic material a thin layer of protection that helps reduce wear and tear on both playback heads and the tape itself. This thin layer of lubricant wears off as the tape is used, but it is continually replenished as lubricant still embedded in the binder gradually migrates to the tape surface. Under normal conditions, lubricants added during the manufacturing process can be expected to last for the life of the tape. However, excessive use or prolonged exposure to poor environmental conditions can accelerate the depletion of lubricants through evaporation and hydrolysis, significantly shortening the tape's life expectancy.

Other problems that can adversely affect the magnetic layer include magnetic particle instabilities (such as diminished ability to retain the magnetic signal), flaking away of the metal layer in metal evaporate tapes, oxidation of some early metal particle tape coatings,[43] and print-through.

## TAPE BASE

Polyester-based tapes are chemically stable. However, PET tape also possesses a high tensile strength that causes it to stretch dramatically and deform, rather than breaking cleanly as does acetate tape. PVC- and PEN-based tapes do not have any known degradation issues.[44]

## MECHANICAL DAMAGE

All magnetic tape is subject to numerous types of mechanical deformation, including cupping (transverse curvature), creasing, cinching, edge damage, scratches and abrasions, stretching, tearing, or breakage. Mechanical damage can result from careless handling, inadequate storage conditions, poorly maintained playback equipment, and poor tape wind. All of these conditions are problematic because they compromise head-to-tape contact, resulting in dropouts, signal distortion, and mistracking during playback. Narrower and thinner tapes are more likely to suffer mechanical damage, as are tapes on reels.[45]

## SHELL AND REEL DAMAGE

Damage to cassette and cartridge shells may include cracks, breakage, and loose or missing pressure pads. Reel damage usually takes the form of bent, cracked, or broken flanges.

## FUNGAL GROWTH

Mold and other fungus can feed on the binder polymer and additives, eventually destroying the magnetic pigment layer. Mold spores on the tape surface can cause dropouts and contaminate playback equipment.

## Treatments

Treatment methods for damaged or deteriorating magnetic media are highly complex and format specific, and they should only be undertaken by a trained specialist; homegrown measures, however careful and well-intended, may cause irreversible damage to already compromised media. Consulting a magnetic media recovery expert before attempting any repairs or remediation work is strongly recommended.

Conducting a condition assessment survey of magnetic media holdings will provide essential information that can help inform decisions about appropriate conservation actions.

# STANDARDS AND FURTHER READING

## Standards

For a list of ISO standards for film, see the ISO *Standards Catalogue* at http://www.iso.org/iso/products/standards/catalogue_ics_browse.htm?ICS1=37&ICS2=060&ICS3=20&.

For the Society of Motion Picture and Television Engineers' standards for film, see their listing of standards at http://standards.smpte.org.

ISO 18923:2000. *Imaging Materials—Polyester-Base Magnetic Tape—Storage Practices.*

ISO 18933:2012. *Imaging Materials—Magnetic Tape—Care and Handling Practices for Extended Usage.*

NFPA 40:2011. *Standard for the Storage and Handling of Cellulose Nitrate Film.* Accessed October 4, 2013. http://www.nfpa.org/codes-and-standards/document-information-pages?mode=code&code=40.

SMPTE RP-103:1995. *Care, Storage, Operation, Handling and Shipping of Magnetic Recording Tape for Television.*

## FURTHER READING

Association of Moving Image Archivists. "Videotape Preservation Fact Sheets." http://www.ami-anet.org/resources-and-publications/documents-publications (available only to members).

Bigourdan, Jean-Louis, Liz Coffey, and Dwight Swanson. *Film Forever: the Home Film Preservation Guide.* Accessed October 12, 2013. http://www.filmforever.org.

Casey, Mike, Patrick Feaster, and Alan Burdette. *Media Preservation Survey: A Report*. Bloomington: Indiana University, 2009. Accessed October 5, 2013. http://www.indiana.edu/~medpres/documents/iub_media_preservation_survey_FINALwww.pdf.

Daniel, Eric D., C. Denis Mee, and Mark H. Clark, eds. *Magnetic Recording: The First 100 Years*. New York: IEEE Press, 1999.

Eastman Kodak Company. *The Book of Film Care*. 2nd ed. Rochester, NY: Motion Picture and Television Imaging, Eastman Kodak Company, 1992.

Iraci, Joe. *Disaster Recovery of Modern Information Carriers: Compact Discs, Magnetic Tapes and Magnetic Disks*. Technical Bulletin 25. Ottawa, ON: Canadian Conservation Institute, 2002.

Iraci, Joe. *Remedies for Deteriorated or Damaged Modern Information Carriers*. Technical Bulletin 27. Ottawa, ON: Canadian Conservation Institute, 2005.

Jimenez, Mona, and Liss Platt. *Videotape Identification and Assessment Guide*. Austin: Texas Commission on the Arts, 2004. Accessed October 5, 2013. http://www.arts.state.tx.us/video/pdf/video.pdf.

Kattelle, Alan D. *Home Movies: A History of the American Industry, 1897–1979*. Nashua, NH: Transition Publishing, 2000.

Kodak. "Broadening the Impact of Pictures." 2009. Accessed October 12, 2013. http://www.kodak.com/country/US/en/corp/kodakHistory/impactOfPictures.shtml.

Kodak. "Chronology of Motion Picture Films." Accessed October 12, 2013. http://motion.kodak.com/motion/About/Chronology_Of_Film/index.htm.

Kodak. "Storage and Handling of Processed Nitrate Film." Accessed October 12, 2013. http://motion.kodak.com/motion/Support/Technical_Information/Storage/storage_nitrate.htm.

National Film Preservation Foundation. *The Film Preservation Guide: The Basics for Archives, Libraries and Museums*. San Francisco, CA, 2004. Accessed October 12, 2013. http://www.filmpreservation.org/preservation-basics/the-film-preservation-guide.

Schüller, Dietrich. *Audio and Video Carriers: Recording Principles, Storage and Handling, Maintenance of Equipment, Format and Equipment Obsolescence*. Amsterdam: European Commission on Preservation and Access, 2007.

Van Bogart, John. *Magnetic Tape Storage and Handling: A Guide for Libraries and Archives*. Washington, DC: Commission on Preservation and Access, 1995.

The websites of the following organizations and institutions are invaluable sources of further information:

Association of Moving Image Archivists (www.amianet.org)
Independent Media Arts Preservation (www.imappreserve.org)
National Film and Sound Archive (Australia) (www.nfsa.gov.au/preservation)
Video Aids to Film Preservation (www.folkstreams.net/vafp)

## NOTES

1. James M. Reilly, *IPI Storage Guide for Acetate Film* (Rochester, NY: Image Permanence Institute, 1993), 5.

2. Anthony Slide, *Nitrate Won't Wait* (Jefferson, NC: McFarland, 1992), 4.

3. Slide, *Nitrate Won't Wait*, 3.

4. Anke Mebold and Charles Tepperman, "Resurrecting the Lost History of 28mm Film in North America," *Film History* 15 (2003): 148.

5. Brian R. Pritchard, "Date Codes," accessed October 12, 2013, http://www.brianpritchard.com/Date%20Codes.htm.

6. Robin Williams, "Kodak Edge Codes," in *Film Forever: The Home Film Preservation Guide* by Jean-Louis Bigourdan et al., accessed October 12, 2013, http://www.filmforever.org/Edgecodes.pdf.

7. Alan D. Kattelle, *Home Movies: A History of the American Industry, 1897–1979* (Nashua, NH: Transition Publishing, 2000), 367.

8. Image Permanence Institute, "Calculators," accessed October 12, 2013, https://www.imagepermanenceinstitute.org/resources/calculators.

9. Kodak, "Storage and Handling of Processed Nitrate Film," accessed October 12, 2013, http://motion.kodak.com/motion/Support/Technical_Information/Storage/storage_nitrate.htm.

10. Association of Moving Image Archivists Nitrate Film Interest Group, *Identifying and Handling Nitrate Film*, 2008, accessed October 12, 2013, http://www.amianet.org/groups/committees/nitrate/documents/NitrateIGNov08.pdf.

11. "Home Storage," in *Film Forever: The Home Film Preservation Guide* by Jean-Louis Bigourdan et al., accessed October 12, 2013, http://www.filmforever.org.

12. "Know Your Enemy: Damage and Decomposition," in *Film Forever: the Home Film Preservation Guide* by Jean-Louis Bigourdan et al., accessed October 12, 2013, http://www.filmforever.org.

13. Majella Breen et al., *Task Force to Establish Selection Criteria of Analogue and Digital Audio Contents for Transfer to Data Formats for Preservation Purposes* (Aarhus: International Association of Sound and Audiovisual Archives, 2004), 3.

14. Eugene Marlow and Eugene Secunda, *Shifting Time and Space: The Story of Videotape* (New York: Praeger, 1991), 16–17.

15. Mike Casey, Patrick Feaster, and Alan Burdette, *Media Preservation Survey: A Report* (Bloomington: Indiana University, 2009), 51, accessed October 5, 2013, http://www.indiana.edu/~medpres/documents/iub_media_preservation_survey_FINALwww.pdf. Other 1-inch open-reel video formats include SMPTE Type A, SMPTE Type B, and IVC. For further information on the identification of these and other videotape formats, see Mona Jimenez and Liss Platt, *Videotape Identification and Assessment Guide* (Austin: Texas Commission on the Arts, 2004), accessed October 5, 2013, http://www.arts.texas.gov/wp-content/uploads/2012/04/video.pdf, and *The Little Reference Guide for Small Videotape Collections* (Amsterdam: Little Archives of the World Foundation/ECPA, 2008), accessed October 5, 2013, http://www.little-archives.net/guide/content/home.html.

16. Two other ½-inch video formats, CV (1965) and Shibaden (late 1960s–1970s), appear identical to EIAJ-1 but are not interoperable.

17. Jim Wheeler, *Videotape Preservation Handbook* (2002), 3, accessed October 5, 2013, http://www.media-matters.net/docs/resources/Traditional%20Audiovisual%20Preservation/WheelerVideo.pdf.

18. Jimenez and Platt, *Videotape Identification*, 11.

19. Jimenez and Platt, *Videotape Identification*, 15–16.

20. Casey et al., *Media Preservation Survey*, 56.

21. Casey et al., *Media Preservation Survey*, 57.

22. Letitia Forgas, "The Preservation of Videotape: Review and Implications for Libraries and Archives," *Libri* 47 (1997): 47.

23. John Van Bogart, *Magnetic Tape Storage and Handling: A Guide for Libraries and Archives* (Washington, DC: Commission on Preservation and Access, 1995), 2–3.

24. Dietrich Schüller, *Audio and Video Carriers: Recording Principles, Storage and Handling, Maintenance of Equipment, Format and Equipment Obsolescence*, edited by George Boston (Training for

Audiovisual Preservation in Europe, 2008), 5, accessed October 4, 2013, http://www.tape-online .net/docs/audio_and_video_carriers.pdf.

25. C. Denis Mee and Eric D. Daniel, eds., *Magnetic Storage Handbook*, 2nd ed. (New York: McGraw-Hill, 1996), 5.60, 7.27.

26. Schüller, *Audio and Video Carriers*, 5.

27. Van Bogart, *Magnetic Tape Storage*, 4.

28. George Boston, *Memory of the World Programme: Safeguarding the Documentary Heritage, A Guide to Standards, Recommended Practices and Reference Literature Related to the Preservation of Documents of All Kinds* (Paris: UNESCO, 1998), 31, accessed October 4, 2013, http://unesdoc .unesco.org/images/0011/001126/112676eo.pdf.

29. Joe Iraci, *Remedies for Deteriorated or Damaged Modern Information Carriers*, Technical Bulletin 27 (Ottawa, ON: Canadian Conservation Institute, 2005), 11.

30. Forgas, "Preservation of Videotape," 47–48.

31. Jim Farrington, "Preventive Maintenance for Audio Discs and Tapes," *MLA Notes* 48 (1991): 437–38.

32. Van Bogart, *Magnetic Tape Storage*, 6.

33. J. Dumont, J. Johansen, and G. Kilander, "Handling and Storage of Recorded Videotape," *EBU Technical Review* 254 (Winter 1992): 43–44.

34. Joe Iraci, *Disaster Recovery of Modern Information Carriers: Compact Discs, Magnetic Tapes, and Magnetic Disks.* Technical Bulletin 25 (Ottawa, ON: Canadian Conservation Institute, 2002), 6.

35. Forgas, "Preservation of Videotape," 47–48. Recommendations and restrictions regarding use with magnetic materials are usually addressed in the system user manual.

36. Jimenez and Platt, *Videotape Identification*, gives excellent guidance on locating the record protection mechanism for the most common types of videocassette.

37. ISO 18933:2012 *Imaging Materials—Magnetic Tape—Care and Handling Practices for Extended Usage* and AES-49:2005 (r2010) *AES Standard for Audio Preservation and Restoration— Magnetic Tape—Care and Handling Practices for Extended Usage* describe a seven-step inspection process for magnetic tape.

38. Peter Brothers, "Magnetic Tapes Can Survive Flood Exposure," SPECS BROS, accessed October 5, 2013, http://www.specsbros.com/h_flood.htm.

39. Iraci, *Disaster Recovery*, 7.

40. Gilles St.-Laurent, "The Care and Handling of Recorded Sound Materials," January 1996, 6, accessed September 28, 2013, http://cool.conservation-us.org/byauth/st-laurent/care.html.

41. Richard Hess, Joe Iraci, and Kimberley Flak, *The Digitization of Audio Tapes*, Technical Bulletin 30 (Ottawa, ON: Canadian Conservation Institute, 2013), 2–3.

42. St.-Laurent, "Care and Handling," 6.

43. Majella Breen et al., *Task Force*, 6.

44. Richard Hess, "Tape Degradation Factors and Challenges in Predicting Tape Life," *ARSC Journal* 39 (2008): 249.

45. Hess, Iraci, and Flak, *Digitization*, 3.

CHAPTER 12

# Digital Storage Media and Files

Leslie Johnston, Ross Harvey

## DIGITAL STORAGE MEDIA: MAGNETIC FORMATS

*Dates in Use*: 1956 to the present.
*Formats*: Hard disc drives; SyQuest, Bernoulli, Zip, Jaz discs); floppy discs (8-inch, 5¼-inch, 3½-inch, SyQuest); magnetic tape (DAT, DLT, LTO).

### Material

This section notes preservation activities for magnetic formats in the collections of cultural heritage institutions. It also describes briefly the variety of formats in use over time, with special note of both analog and digital encoding on magnetic media.

Magnetic storage refers to the storage of data on a magnetized medium. Magnetic storage uses different patterns of magnetization on magnetized media to store data. The information is accessed using one or more read/write heads designed to decode the magnetic patterns. This is the most common form of media used to store audio, video, and data files. The data may be written in digital form, recorded by writing negative or positive polarity bits, or analog form, recorded by altering the polarity of the magnetic medium to encode waveforms of vibrations (audio) or intensities of color and brightness (video) on analog magnetic tape. Magnetic storage media can be classified as either sequential access memory (data read in sequence), or random access memory (data read in appropriately ordered, but random, locations).

*Hard disc drives* consist of one or more rigid ("hard") rapidly rotating discs, with magnetic heads arranged on a mechanical actuator arm to read and write data to the surfaces. The storage media and the mechanism to read it are encased in the same physical enclosure.

*Floppy discs* are flexible, circular film coated in a magnetic oxide (iron oxide, cobalt-doped iron oxide, or barium ferrite), housed within a rigid or semirigid casing.

*Magnetic tape* encompasses a range of media that use a magnetic recording layer on a flexible substrate. The various formats of magnetic tape currently in use are all housed within cartridges (which have one spool) or cassettes (which have two spools).

## Purposes

Digital storage media in magnetic formats are used for commercial distribution of data, software, audio, or video content, for personal and institutional primary storage, and backup storage of any formats of files.

## Dates in Use

Hard disc drives: 1956 to present
8-inch floppy discs: 1971–1985
5¼-inch floppy discs: 1976–1995
3½-inch floppy discs: 1984 to present
SyQuest discs: 1982–2009
Bernoulli discs: 1983–1995
Zip discs: 1994–2002
Jaz discs: 1995–2002
DAT Tape: 1987–2010
DLT Tape: 1984 to present
LTO Tape: 2000 to present

## Identification

*Hard disc drives* can range from weighing a ton and being comparable in size to that of a washing machine (dating to the 1950s or 1960s) to the more common 2½-inch or 3½-inch drives found in current laptop or desktop computers. A typical hard disc drive consists of a spindle that holds flat circular disks (platters), which are made from a nonmagnetic material (aluminum alloy, glass, or ceramic) coated with a thin layer of ferromagnetic material. The platter, read-write head(s) and actuator, and motor(s) are housed in a metal enclosure with interface connector cables. There are both internal hard disc drives, meant for mounting inside a machine or storage array, and external hard disc drives, meant for connection to a machine through an external port. Such external drives often have a plastic or more rugged case, as they are portable and must be able to be handled more often, possibly roughly.

*8-inch floppy discs* (eight inches square in size) are housed in a flexible, fabric-lined plastic shell, with a capacity of 70 KB.

*5¼-inch floppy discs* (5¼ inches square in size) are housed in a flexible, fabric-lined plastic shell, with capacities of 360 KB to 1.2 MB.

*3½-inch floppy discs* (3½ inches square in size) are housed in a hard cartridge, with capacities of 400 KB to 1.44 MB.

*SyQuest discs* were available as both 5¼ inches and 3½ inches square in size, housed in a translucent, hard cartridge. The 5¼-inch version was available in capacities of 44 MB, 88 MB, and 200 MB. The many 3½-inch versions ranged in capacity from 5 MB to 4.7 GB.

*Bernoulli discs* are made from two discs made of stretched polyethylene terephthalate (PET) film, encased in a hard cartridge. The original Bernoulli discs came in capacities of 5, 10, and 20 MB, and they were roughly 8¼ inches by 10¾ inches. Later Bernoulli discs were the size and form of a 3½-inch floppy disc, with a capacity of 230 MB.

*Zip discs* are 3½ inches square in size, housed in a rugged, hard cartridge with capacities of 100, 250, and 750 MB.

*Jaz discs* are 3½ inches square in size, housed in a rugged, hard cartridge, with capacities of 1 GB and 2 GB.

*Magnetic tapes* use a magnetic recording layer on a flexible substrate, typically polyethylene naphthalate, housed in a hard cartridge. The various formats of magnetic tape currently in use are all housed within cartridges (which have one spool) or cassettes (which have two spools).

*Digital Audio Tape (DAT)* is a dual reel 4mm tape, identical in format to a consumer audiocassette, used for data storage in capacities of 1.3 to 80 GB on 60- to 180-meter tapes.

*Digital Linear Tape (DLT)*, called CompacTape in an early version, is a single-reel ½-inch tape available in capacities of 100 MB to 160 GB.

*Linear Tape Open (LTO)* is a single-reel ½-inch tape available in capacities of 100 GB to 2.5 TB. LTO tapes are still in active development for increased capacity.

## Representation in Collections

Every collection that has digital items will contain at least one of these media types.

## Environment and Storage

No digital storage media are stable enough for preservation purposes, so files should be migrated off all media as soon as possible after acquisition. The following recommendations relate to storage of the media in the interim period when they await migration.

### PREFERRED ENVIRONMENT

Keep storage areas free of smoke, dust, dirt, and other contaminants, and maintain proper ventilation and air circulation to prevent the formation of microclimates. Store away from direct sunlight. Store at a constant temperature between 62°F (17°C) and 70°F (21°C) and at a constant relative humidity between 30 percent and 45 percent. Store the media away from any magnetic field, including fluorescent lights and electrical equipment.

## RECOMMENDATIONS FOR STORAGE

Store media vertically on well-supported shelving. Enclose media in a sleeve or box made of archival-quality materials such as acid-free paper, paperboard, paperboard-plastic laminate, or inert plastics such as polyethylene, polyester, or polycarbonate. Do not pack the media tightly.

## Handling

### WHAT STAFF NEED TO KNOW

No digital storage media are stable enough for preservation purposes, so files should be migrated off all media using digital forensic tools and disc imaging best practices as soon as possible after acquisition. Never discard the original media; retain it in the collection, as it is likely to include hidden data that might be invaluable for researchers. The labeling on the original media may also be of value, as is the organization of files, which is why it is important to document the media and make authentic forensic disc images to retain the intended content organization. The best practices for handling magnetic media are:

- Clean and dry hands before handling any media.
- Avoid sudden shocks or vibrations.
- Avoid sudden temperature changes.
- Do not touch the magnetic recording surface. Keep the media away from any magnetic field, including fluorescent lights and electrical equipment.
- Never read media without a write blocker in place to disable the possible alteration of the media contents. Set write-protect tabs, if available.
- Magnetic tape cartridges must not be opened, nor the tape surface touched. Prior to use, tapes should be subject to a full forward and rewind cycle to equalize tape tension and, after writing, the tape should be fully rewound. Tape cartridges should also be retensioned annually by performing a full forward and rewind cycle.
- Never leave the media in a drive after use.

### WHAT USERS NEED TO KNOW

The best practices for handling magnetic media are:

- Clean and dry hands before handling any media.
- Do not touch the magnetic recording surface. Keep the media away from any magnetic field, including fluorescent lights and electrical equipment.
- Never read media without a write blocker in place to disable possible alteration of the media contents. Set write-protect tabs, if available.
- Magnetic tape cartridges must not be opened, nor the tape surface touched. Prior to use, tapes should be subject to a full forward and rewind cycle to equalize tape

tension and, after writing, the tape should be fully rewound. Tape cartridges should also be retensioned annually by performing a full forward and rewind cycle.

- Never leave the media in a drive after use.

## Playback/Viewing Equipment

Only use the recommended hardware and appropriate operating system identified for the type of media. While physical media might be used across many environments, the writing of data to the media can vary depending upon the type and version of operating system; for example, DOS, Linux, Windows, or Mac. You may only have one opportunity to read the media.

There are forensic tools for working with older forms of magnetic media. Specialist advice is required before using these tools. Among hardware tools to be considered for use are:

- Write Blockers (www.forensicswiki.org/wiki/Write_Blockers)
- FRED (www.digitalintelligence.com/products/fred) or any computer with a reader for 3½-inch and 5¼-inch discs, the ability to connect additional disc controllers, a USB drive enclosure for IDE, SCSI, and SATA drives, plus multiple USB and FireWire ports
- FC5025 disc controller (www.deviceside.com/fc5025.html)
- Kryoflux disc controller (www.kryoflux.com/)
- Catweasel disc controller (www.jschoenfeld.com/products/catweasel_e.htm)

Among software tools to be considered for use are:

- BitCurator (www.bitcurator.net/software-2)
- MagicDisc (www.magiciso.com/tutorials/miso-magicdisc-history.htm)
- FTK Imager (accessdata.com/support/adownloads#FTKImager)
- MD5summer (download.cnet.com/MD5summer/3000-2248_4-10050856.html)

## Disaster Response

For magnetic storage media, damage done by smoke and dry debris is not as time sensitive as water damage. Do not attempt to play back wet media: water compromises the physical structure of magnetic media, making it highly susceptible to stretching, tearing, and edge damage. If the media is already wet, keep it wet and do not attempt to dry it out. Rinse it as soon as possible with clean, distilled water to remove contaminants from the water. If the media is wet and dirty, rinse it as soon as possible in clean, distilled water to remove solid contaminants. Do not rub.

In-house drying is best done by exposing the media to an environment of cool, dry air, but attempts to do this without the supervision of experienced specialists may result in deformation of the media and/or media sticking to the inside of the cartridge. Freeze-drying wet media is not recommended.

Copy the dried media to new media as soon as possible. Coatings on media may be unstable and may continue to deteriorate. Get the media to a digital media preservation and data recovery specialist as soon as possible. Keep the media cool to prevent mold growth. If mold has already started to grow, wear a respirator. If the media is dry and soiled, leave it alone and send it to a digital media preservation and data recovery specialist.

Cartridges are not watertight. If there is moisture on the exterior, then there is likely to be interior moisture. Cartridges are not airtight either, so exterior debris usually indicates that there will be interior debris.

Guard against exposing magnetic media to magnetic fields and static electricity. Bag or wrap them in antistatic plastic.

### Decay

Decay can be summarized as an unreadable media. The media cannot be "mounted" (read) by the hardware used, or the files on the media cannot be seen or recognized by the system in use.

### Treatments

Unreadable magnetic media require specialist expertise to recover data from them, which will not always be possible. Do not attempt to recover the data yourself. Data recovery should only be attempted by a preservation professional specializing in the treatment of magnetic media, or an archivist who specializes in data recovery from magnetic media using forensic tools.

## DIGITAL STORAGE MEDIA: OPTICAL AND MAGNETO-OPTICAL FORMATS (LESLIE JOHNSTON)

*Dates in Use*: 1978 to the present.
*Formats*: CD-ROM, DVD, CD-R, DVD-R, CD-RW, DVD-RW, BD-R, magneto-optical discs.

### Material

This section notes preservation activities for optical and magneto-optical formats in the collections of cultural heritage institutions. It also briefly describes the variety of formats in use over time, with special note of both analog and digital encoding on magnetic media.

An optical disc is a flat, usually circular disc that encodes binary data in the form of pits (binary value of 0 or off, due to lack of reflection when read) and lands (binary value of 1 or on, due to a reflection when read) on one of its flat surfaces. The encoding pattern follows a continuous, spiral path covering the entire disc surface and extending from the innermost track to the outermost track. A magneto-optical disc is a hybrid variant in which the physical encoding is accompanied by differences in magnetic polarity.

*Compact Disc-Read Only Memory* (CD-ROM) is a type of optical disc capable of storing large amounts of data—up to 1 GB—although the most common size is 650 MB. A single CD-ROM has the storage capacity of seven hundred floppy discs with enough memory to store about three hundred thousand text pages.

*Digital Versatile Disc* or *Digital Video Disc* (DVD) is a type of optical disc technology similar to the CD-ROM. A DVD holds a minimum of 4.7 GB of data with enough memory for a full-length movie.

*CD-R* (CD-Recordable) and *DVD-R* (DVD-Recordable) are optical discs on which data can be recorded once, after which the disc becomes read-only. CD-R and DVD-R discs should be used only for storing temporary records. They provide protection for records against tampering or loss of data.

*CD-RW* (CD Rewritable) and *DVD-RW* (DVD Rewritable) are optical discs that can be written to multiple times. The film layer on RW discs degrades at a faster rate than the dye used in CD-R and DVD-R discs, especially with frequent recording and rewriting.

*Blu-ray discs* (BD-R) use a more precise type of laser (blue/violet in color) to store much greater amounts of data on an optical disc. The disc surface is also more resistant to scratching than that of most CD or DVD media.

*Magneto-optical discs* are a hybrid, in which a laser encodes data on a plastic-coated magnetic disc. Although optical, they appear as hard disc drives to the operating system and do not require a special file system. The storage media and the mechanism to read it are encased in the same physical enclosure.

## Purposes

Optical discs have been used for two main purposes: commercial distribution of data, software, audio, or video content; and personal and institutional primary and backup storage of any formats of files. Some are in common use for specific purposes; for example, DVDs are commonly used as a medium for digital representation of movies and other multimedia presentations that combine sound with graphics.

## Dates in Use

Magneto-optical: 1985–2012
Floptical magneto-optical: 1991–2002
CDs: 1988 to the present
DVDs: 1995 to the present
Blu-ray: 2000 to the present

## Identification

*Magneto-optical discs* came in two sizes. The 130mm media looks similar to a CD-ROM enclosed in a caddy, while 90mm media is approximately the size of a 3½-inch floppy disc, but twice the thickness. The disc consists of a ferromagnetic material sealed beneath a plastic coating. Magneto-optical discs were initially WORM (write once, read many) drives, but later read/write magneto-optical drives became available. The "floptical" disc was meant as a replacement for floppy discs, using magneto-optical technology in the form of a floppy disc; the most common is the SuperDisk.

*CDs, DVDs, and Blu-ray discs* are made of polycarbonate plastic, laminated together with a thin layer of aluminum or, more rarely, gold, making it reflective. A film of lacquer, normally spin-coated directly on the reflective layer, protects the metal. From the center outward, the components are: the center spindle hole; the first-transition area (clamping ring); the clamping area (stacking ring); the second-transition area (mirror band); the program (data) area; and the rim. Standard CDs and DVDs have a diameter of 120mm (4.7 inches). Mini CDs and DVDs have a variety of diameters ranging from 60 to 80mm (2.4 to 3.1 inches).

Visually distinguishing the different formats of optical discs is possible because of differences in the manufacturing of the disc data layers:

CD-R: greenish tint
CD-ROM: silver or gold
DVD-R 5: purple
DVD-R 9: bluish-purple
Blu-ray: dark gold/brown

## Representation in Collections

Every collection that has digital items will contain at least one of these media types.

## Environment and Storage

No digital storage media are stable enough for preservation purposes, so files should be migrated off all media as soon as possible after acquisition. The following recommendations relate to storage of the media in the interim period when they await migration.

### PREFERRED ENVIRONMENT

Store optical and magneto-optical formats in cool, dry storage that is free of large temperature fluctuations. Useful life will be increased by storing discs at a low temperature and low relative humidity, since chemical degradation is inhibited in these conditions. If possible, store at 62 to 70°F (17 to 21°C) and 35 to 50 percent relative humidity.

Fluctuations in the storage area should not exceed ±2°F (1°C) temperature and ±5 percent relative humidity, as high humidity may cause oxidation of the reflective layer. Do not store media near heat or ultraviolet light sources. Light cannot affect the media, but heat (including from ultraviolet light) can cause the different layers of the media to delaminate or can cause birefringence, the double bending of light. This optical effect leads to reduced signal strength and disc errors or failure.

## RECOMMENDATIONS FOR STORAGE

Discs are best stored upright in rigid cases that are designed specifically for disc media. Remove any accompanying label inserts or booklets from inside the case and store them separately. The paper can attract moisture and produce higher moisture content in the case, or spread moisture by contact with the disc. Paper inserts may become acidic over time, so contact with the media should be avoided.

## Handling

### WHAT STAFF NEED TO KNOW

No digital storage media are stable enough for preservation purposes, so files should be migrated off all media using digital forensic tools and disc imaging best practices as soon as possible after acquisition. Never discard the original media; retain it in the collection, as it is likely to include hidden data that might be invaluable for researchers. The labeling on the original media may also be of value, as is the organization of files, which is why it is important to document the media and make authentic forensic disc images to retain the intended content organization.

The best practices for handling optical media are:

- Clean and dry hands before handling any media.
- Handle discs only by the outer edge or the center hole, never by touching the surface.
- Fingerprints, smudges, dirt, or dust on the laser reading side of the disc can disrupt laser focus on the data even more than a scratch can.
- Do not touch the writeable side of the disc or the label side of the discs unnecessarily.
- Don't pull pressure-sensitive tape or labels off media because this may lead to delamination.
- To eliminate risk of deterioration of the thin protective lacquer coating, it is recommended that only solvent-free, water-based markers be used for labeling. Never use a ballpoint, fine point, or rolling ball marker; a felt-tip marker will minimize the risk of scratching or denting. For risk-free labeling of any disc, it is best to mark the clear inner hub or the so-called mirror band of the disc, where there are no data.
- Never leave the media in a drive after use.
- Check media for delamination and information loss at regular intervals, perhaps as often as annually.

## WHAT USERS NEED TO KNOW

The best practices for users handling optical media are:

- Clean and dry hands before handling any media.
- Handle discs only by the outer edge or the center hole, never by touching the surface. Fingerprints, smudges, dirt, or dust on the laser reading side of the disc can disrupt laser focus on the data even more than a scratch can.
- Do not touch the writeable (bottom) side of the disc or the label (top) side of the discs unnecessarily.
- Never leave the media in a drive after use.

## Playback/Viewing Equipment

Only use the recommended hardware and appropriate operating system identified for the type of media. While physical media might be used across many environments, the writing of data to the media can vary depending upon the type and version of operating system; for example, DOS, Linux, Windows, or Mac. You may only have one opportunity to read the media.

There are forensic tools for working with older forms of optical media. Specialist advice is required before using these tools. Hardware tools and software tools for forensic purposes are listed in the "Playback/Viewing Equipment" section in "Digital Storage Media: Formats" earlier in this chapter.

## Disaster Response

In any response to disasters involving optical discs, be careful not to scratch the disc, especially the shiny, nonlabel side, or data may be lost.

Rinse dirty discs in clean, distilled water. If the dirt will not come off with rinsing, soak the disc in mild detergent solution, then rinse. Air dry the label edge up in racks, or label side down on a sheet of clean wax paper.

Dust and smudges can be cleaned with a soft, lint-free cloth using light strokes only from the outside edge toward the center of the disc.

Copy the affected disc to new media as soon as possible. The lamination of the media layers may be unstable and may continue to deteriorate.

## Decay

The first signs of media degradation of optical discs are often imperceptible because any abnormalities are handled by the error detection and correction system built into media players. With further decay, a user will be able to pick up jitters and other errors, which means the error coding system is losing its ability to function. The more errors that subsequently arise, the closer the disc is to being ineffective for use.

Degradation can occur for any number of reasons. Some degradation occurs when the metal layer oxidizes and reduces the layer's shine. Without the shine, there is less reflectivity, which translates to a laser's inability to properly read reflected data. There may be physical damage to the media, such as scratches or breaks in the internal layers brought on by excessive flexing of the media, often when removing the media from hub-style media storage.

The labeling of discs can cause degradation. The thin, protective lacquer coating can deteriorate from contact with certain solvents in markers. The metal layer in the media is particularly susceptible to damage by surface marking, such as from a ballpoint, fine point, or rolling ball marker.

## Treatments

Clean optical media only when absolutely necessary. Use compressed air for cleaning. If compressed air does not work, dampen a cloth with distilled water and brush the media to the outer edge from the center of the disc. Never use solvents. Do not rub optical discs, because you may embed dirt in them. Do not brush media in a circular movement, because it may cause data errors.

It is often less expensive to transfer the data from a damaged disc onto a new one than to try to restore the problem disc.

# DIGITAL STORAGE MEDIA: FLASH STORAGE (LESLIE JOHNSTON)

*Dates in Use*: 1983 to the present.
*Formats*: SSD drives, USB flash drives, memory cards.

## Material

This section notes preservation activities for flash storage in the collections of cultural heritage institutions. In flash storage devices, data are stored in memory chips that are modified electronically.

*Solid-state disc (SSD)* drives, also known as "electronic discs," offer the large storage capacity of magnetic hard disc drives, but they are more durable because there are no moving parts that can fail or be damaged. Solid-state storage devices use flash memory. Storage capacities offered are in the range 512 MB to 128 GB. A drawback with flash memory is that it degrades with repeated use. Because the archival properties of solid-state media are not well understood, they should not be used for long-term storage.

*USB flash drives*, also known as "thumb drives," or "jump drives," are very portable and compatible with virtually all computers via USB port connections. USB flash drives are flash memory chips with an embedded USB port, usually in an extremely small form factor. They draw power directly from the USB connection. At the time of writing, the maximum available capacity is 256 GB, although 1 TB drives have been announced. In terms of longevity, some are specified for up to one hundred thousand write/erase cycles and a ten-year shelf life. Some flash drives come with write-protect switches.

*Memory cards*, also known as "flash cards," are used most often in digital cameras or other portable devices for convenient, temporary storage of data intended for later transfer to a PC or other device. Examples include the CompactFlash (43 x 33 mm in size), SmartMedia (45 x 37 mm in size), PCMCIA (86 x 54 mm), Secure Digital/SD (32 x 24 mm), Multimedia (32 x 24 mm), Mini SD (22 x 20 mm), and Micro SD (15 x 11 mm) cards.

## Purposes

Flash storage is used for personal and institutional primary storage, backup storage of any formats of files, and direct capture of data in portable devices.

## Dates in Use

RAM-based solid-state drives: 1983–2009
Flash-based solid-state drives: 1994 to the present
USB flash drives: 2000 to the present
Memory cards: 1994 to the present

## Identification

RAM-based and flash-based *solid-state drives* may look physically similar to magnetic hard drives or optical drives. What distinguishes them is that they have no disc or mechanical components, such as read/write heads. Their shape could be virtually anything because they are not limited to the shape of rotating media drives. In appearance they can simply be circuit boards without cases, or they may be enclosed in cases designed for installing into rack systems. They may or may not have labeling that identifies them as solid-state drives.

On a *USB flash drive*, one end is fitted with a single USB plug. Inside the plastic casing is a small, printed circuit board, which has some power circuitry and integrated circuits. Typically, one of these circuits provides the interface between the USB connector and the onboard memory, while the other is the actual flash memory. They may also have jumpers for testing and LEDs to signal that they are in operation. They are most often small, rectangular objects with a removable cover on the visible USB connector, but they may also be shaped like keys or more extreme novelty shapes, from cartoon characters to food.

*Memory cards* are very small circuit boards in rigid plastic cases, almost always labeled with the manufacturer's name and storage capacity. Some may have visible external connector circuitry. At the time of writing, Secure Digital/SD cards have become the most prevalent memory cards on the market due to the increase in hardware manufacturers providing SD card readers in desktop and laptop machines.

## Representation in Collections

Every collection that has digital items will probably contain at least one of these media types, most often so-called USB thumb drives.

## Environment and Storage

### PREFERRED ENVIRONMENT

Keep storage areas free of smoke, dust, dirt, and other contaminants, and maintain proper ventilation and air circulation to prevent the formation of microclimates. Store at a constant temperature between 62°F (17°C) and 70°F (21°C) and at a constant relative humidity between 30 percent and 45 percent.

### RECOMMENDATIONS FOR STORAGE

Drives should be stored flat, not on their edges. Drives should not be stored uncovered; they should be boxed up to provide protection from dust and some cushioning in case of a fall. Flash drives should always be stored with their accompanying covers on their USB connectors.

## Handling

### WHAT STAFF NEED TO KNOW

No digital storage media are stable enough for preservation purposes, so files should be migrated off all media using digital forensic tools and disc imaging best practices as soon as possible after acquisition. Specialist advice is required before using these tools. Never discard the original media; retain it in the collection, as it is likely to include hidden data that might be invaluable for researchers. The labeling on the original media may also be of value, as is the organization of files, which is why it is important to document the media and make authentic forensic disc images to retain the intended content organization.

The best practices for handling flash storage media are:

- Never read media without a write blocker in place to disable the possible alteration of the media contents.
- Never leave a drive attached to a machine after use.
- Never remove a flash drive from the USB port while it is still in operation. Close all files and exit all programs viewing the files. Use the "Eject" command to eject a flash drive before removing it from a computer.
- When not using a flash drive, be sure to cover the USB connector with a cap to prevent the accumulation of dusts and contaminants on the contacts.

## WHAT USERS NEED TO KNOW

The best practices for handling such media are:

- Never read media without a write blocker in place to disable possible alteration of the media contents.
- Never leave a drive attached to a machine after use.
- Never remove a flash drive from the USB port while it is still in operation. Close all files and exit all programs viewing the files. "Eject" the drive before removing it from a computer.

### Playback/Viewing Equipment

Solid-state drives use the same I/O (Input/Output) interfaces as hard drives, and they can often be swapped with conventional magnetic drives to be read.

USB-based devices can in theory be connected to and read by any machines with a USB port on any operating system. USB flash drives generally have their drivers stored on board in their circuitry, and those drivers will automatically install when the drive is plugged into the machine.

Memory cards require a port or reader that is an exact match to the size of the card or they will not function. Some machines come with on-board hardware readers. Generic USB-based card readers with multiple card size adaptors are available.

### Disaster Response

Damage caused by smoke and dry debris is not as time sensitive as water damage.

In-house drying is best done by exposing the flash storage media to an environment of cool, dry air, but attempts to do this without the supervision of experienced specialists may result in the deformation of the media and/or media sticking to the inside of the enclosure.

Enclosures are not watertight. If you see moisture on the exterior, there is likely to be interior moisture. Enclosures are not airtight. Exterior debris is usually an indicator of interior debris.

Copy affected flash storage media to new media as soon as possible. Use the services of a digital media preservation and data recovery specialist.

### Decay

Flash drives are meant for temporary storage, not for long-term or archival storage. Flash storage is volatile and will fail much more quickly than other media. They are engineered to fail after a certain number of read-writes. The specifications are for ten thousand to one hundred thousand read-writes, but content should be copied off flash drives as soon as feasible. The consumer market is flooded with cheap flash drives that do not contain Grade A memory and were not manufactured in ISO-9001:2008 certified factories.

Decay has occurred when, in attempts to read the media, the media cannot be "mounted" (read) by the hardware used and/or the files on the media cannot be seen or recognized by the system in use.

## Treatments

Always call a preservation professional specializing in the treatment of storage media; do not attempt any treatment yourself. Data recovery should only be attempted by a preservation professional specializing in the treatment of digital storage media, or an archivist who specializes in data recovery from digital storage media using forensic tools.

# DIGITAL FILES (ROSS HARVEY)

*Dates in use*: 1940s to the present.
*Formats*: potentially, any of the myriad file formats can be found in cultural heritage collections. File formats created by applications in common use such as office productivity software, image files, audio files, video files, and HTML, are most likely to be encountered.

## Material

Digital files are a block of information in the form of a sequence of bytes (data in binary form) used by a computer program, which interprets the binary data as appropriate (for example, as text characters or image pixels). The file is structured in a standard way; this structuring is the file format, which specifies how the bytes are encoded, and it may be either proprietary or open source.

The sections on "Digital Storage Media" earlier in this chapter note: "No digital storage media are stable enough for preservation purposes, so files should be migrated off all media . . . as soon as possible after acquisition." This cannot be emphasized strongly enough. As noted in many places in this book, the life span of digital media is counted in a small number of years. *There are no exceptions*. Harvey notes this in more detail, with examples.[1] In addition, digital storage media have little, if any, value as artifacts, because nothing about their physical form demonstrates "the originality, faithfulness (or authenticity), fixity, and stability of the content" that are the reasons we value artifacts.[2]

This section describes how to preserve digital files once they have been migrated off the storage media described in this chapter. Briefly summarized, best practice is to commit digital files to a managed environment, typically a digital repository that has the primary aim of keeping digital objects over long periods of time, as quickly as possible after they have been created. By themselves digital files are not very useful. To manage them and enable them to be usable and understandable in the future we also need metadata, including information about the files' context and about what is needed to render them. In preserving digital files, what we are really managing and preserving is a digital *object*, made up of a file (or files) plus metadata. (Chapter 6 notes metadata and its importance in more detail.)

## Purposes

Digital files are used to represent information of all kinds. As more information is created in digital form, either born digital or digitized from analog objects, the number and content of digital files is massively increasing. File formats most likely to be encountered in cultural heritage collections are those created by software applications in common use such as office productivity software, image files, audio files, video files, and HTML. Specialist collections are likely to have specialized file formats well represented in them.

## Dates in Use

The earliest files were created in the 1940s, when fully electronic computers (as distinct from earlier electromechanical computers) were first used. Computers were available commercially in the 1950s. Data archives were among the earliest repositories of digital files, early examples being established in the 1960s to preserve social science datasets. Mass-produced minicomputers were available from the 1960s, and personal computers from the mid-1970s.[3] All of these produced digital files. Digital files are now ubiquitous.

## Identification

Digital files exist in a bewildering variety of formats. It is necessary to know what those formats are before the files can be preserved, but identifying them can be time-consuming and not always successful.

Files are not always true to label. We are now familiar with the file extension (the three characters following the period in a file name, such as .doc, .pdf, etc.) representing the software application in which a file was created and can be opened, but this is a relatively recent convention. Older files may have an arbitrary file extension, or one that does not represent an application, or no file extension at all. Even if the file extension correctly represents the application, that application may not open the file because the application lacks backward compatibility—that is, it does not recognize files created in earlier versions of it.

To identify files, first make a copy of the file, and work *only* on the copy and not on the original. Try opening the file with software applications commonly in use in your organization, or applications that have been developed to handle a wide range of file formats, such as Open Office (www.openoffice.org) or Libre Office (www.libreoffice .org) for files created using common office productivity software. If this approach does not identify the format, try to open it in a text editor, such as Notepad or TextEdit, or a hex editor, to see if there is eye-readable information at the start of the file that helps identify it. Another approach, to be taken after common applications have been tried, is to search for the file extension appearing in the file name on the Web; the results are often useful, but this needs to be approached with caution because files are not always true to label and file extensions can represent more than one format. If files are not identifiable after taking these steps, the advice of an expert is probably needed.

## Representation in Collections

The ubiquity of digital files and their bewildering variety means that, potentially, any kind of file may be encountered in cultural heritage collections. File formats most commonly encountered in collections are likely to be created using common software applications, such as word-processing applications (Office, especially Microsoft Office, and earlier ones such as WordPerfect and WordStar) and common database applications. They may be in formats that can be used in more than one application, such as spreadsheets, PDF, image files (TIFF, JPEG), audio files (MP3, FLAC), and so on. If an institution hosts specialist collections, file formats common to a specific environment or discipline may be well represented, such as CAD (Computer Aided Design) formats in architecture collections.

## Environment and Storage

Unlike the other object types noted in chapters 8 to 14 of this book, storage of digital files in controlled environments is not crucial for preservation, except as an interim action for short periods. Emphasis on high quality of the media on which the files are stored does *not* constitute preservation of digital files, although interim storage of the media in the hopefully brief period before files are taken off them should be as good as possible. (See the earlier sections on "Digital Storage Media" in this chapter for further information.) A statement made earlier is worth repeating: "No digital storage media are stable enough for preservation purposes, so files should be migrated off all media . . . as soon as possible after acquisition."

Digital files have to be preserved in a *managed* environment. Their management starts, ideally, from the moment they are created, and it continues until the files are determined to be no longer of use. Their management must be constant, as any interruptions will mean that there is no collection left to manage—failure to pay an electricity bill is an example. For these reasons, a life-cycle management approach is taken. The managed environment necessary for digital preservation comprises many activities, designed to "maintain access to digital materials beyond the limits of media failure or technological change."[4]

## PREFERRED ENVIRONMENT

If the digital files are on digital storage media, as a preliminary and strictly interim step the tangible objects (such as the diskettes, flash drives, or hard drives) need to be kept in optimal conditions, awaiting transferring of the files to the managed environment for their preservation. (See the recommendations in the sections on "Digital Storage Media" earlier in this chapter, covering optical and magneto-optical formats, magnetic formats, and flash storage.)

The characteristics of a managed environment for preserving digital files are explained in considerable detail in the Open Archival Information System (OAIS) Reference Model (ISO 14721:2012)[5] (noted in more detail in chapter 5). The OAIS model defines the functions that a digital archive needs to perform in order to preserve the digital objects committed to it. The objects being preserved are "information packages" consisting of the bitstream, information that tells us what we did to preserve that bitstream, information about its attributes, information about how to render (or re-present) the bitstream in the future so it can be understood, and more. The characteristics of a preservation-focused digital repository include:

- It is OAIS compliant—this is mandatory.
- It has the primary aim of keeping the material it houses for the long term (rather than a primary aim of making an institution's intellectual output or digital holdings discoverable).
- It is open source, not proprietary (there are exceptions).
- It stores files in high-quality storage at multiple locations.
- It handles a range of metadata standards, including preservation metadata standards.
- It performs a range of preservation-related processes: assigning a persistent identifier for each object; creating a checksum (a numeric value, computed for a block of data, that is as unique as possible) to monitor changes in the data; using the checksums created at the ingest stage in ongoing monitoring of file integrity.
- It restricts the number of file formats it supports, undertaking to manage those formats for the long term; this may require the conversion of files in formats that it does not support to those formats that it does support.

This selected list of characteristics is by no means the full list of requirements, which are given in ISO 16363:2012 *Space Data and Information Transfer Systems—Audit and Certification of Trustworthy Digital Repositories*. (Chapter 5 notes Trusted Digital Repositories in more detail.) These requirements are difficult to achieve and are almost certainly unattainable for smaller institutions. For this reason many institutions collaborate to share resources and expertise. Two examples of collaboration, LOCKSS and MetaArchive, are described next. There are many other collaborative programs in digital preservation, and it is well worth investigating what is available locally and considering participating.

LOCKSS (Lots of Copies Keep Stuff Safe; lockss.stanford.edu) was developed initially for preserving electronic journals, but its use has expanded significantly. LOCKSS uses basic technology: open source software; access to the Internet; and standard personal computers. Three sets of actions underlie its operation: keeping multiple copies of files in distributed locations to safeguard against loss; regularly comparing copies of files to identify errors; and automatically repairing errors in files from a clean copy held by another participant in the cooperative. Members of a LOCKSS-based cooperative submit digital material that is copied to other computers in the cooperative, stores files from other members, and run the LOCKSS software to continuously check the files for errors. The LOCKSS software is used widely as the basis of Private LOCKSS Networks (PLNs). These have been established as regional networks (for example, the Council of Prairie and Pacific University Libraries PLN (http://www.coppul.ca/), and the DFG-Projekt: LuKII (LOCKSS und KOPAL Infrastruktur und Interoperabilität, www.lukii.hu-berlin.de) and on the basis of type of content (for example, Synergies (Canadian Social Science and Humanities), www.synergiescanada.org/).

An example of a collaboration that uses LOCKSS software is the MetaArchive Cooperative (MetaArchive.org), a coalition of libraries, archives, and other cultural heritage institutions from four countries, which has developed and operates a preservation infrastructure for their digital materials. Members of MetaArchive share expertise and infrastructure, and in return they can store their digital materials in a high-quality digital archive.

## RECOMMENDATIONS FOR STORAGE

Once they have been extracted from their interim storage media, digital files, together with associated metadata, need the highest possible quality storage. David Rosenthal identifies the basic requirements for storage:

- The more copies, the safer
- The more independent the copies, the safer ("independent" refers to different storage technologies)
- The more frequently the copies are audited, the safer[6]

The characteristics of high-quality storage defined in the TDR standard ISO 16363:2012 are very difficult to achieve by smaller institutions, which should consider participating in a cooperative whose aim is to provide high-quality digital preservation. Before that, though, there are some basic actions that can be taken by all institutions.

## Guidelines

Providing a high-quality environment for digital files can be translated into a set of basic steps for all cultural heritage institutions, but particularly institutions that cannot afford to establish their own high-quality digital preservation program or participate in a cooperative to implement. These steps are based on three principles:

- Selection is necessary.
- Action is possible now, even if we do not have all the answers.
- Take action now, doing what you can, and then reconsider what is possible.

These steps begin the process of preserving digital files and will position the institution well to participate effectively in digital preservation in the future.

Initial steps:

- Quarantine files (especially files coming in to the institution from another source): run up-to-date virus-checking software on them, put them in storage and leave them for four to six weeks, then rerun the virus-checking software.
- Identify where your digital files are stored: it is common for files to be located in many different places in an institution, including on staff personal computers.
- Decide which files are most important to your institution. If there are multiple versions of an important file, decide whether to save drafts and earlier copies, datasets and the visualizations derived from it, and other versions, as well as a final version. Consider sorting your files into three categories: short term (for a specific short period); medium term (access beyond a technology change); long term (indefinite access). This will help to determine the kinds of preservation actions and resources that are needed: short term requires managed backups; medium term requires more complex migration; and long term requires a fully managed environment.
- Create a directory/folder structure on your computer to hold the files you are saving. Document the directory structure.
- Make a copy of the files you intend to keep, store the original, and work only with the copy.

Preparing the files:

- Assign file names, according to a file-naming system that provides a unique name.[7]
- Run checksums and record them.
- Assign other metadata as relevant.

Managing the files:

- Make at least two copies of the files and associated metadata and store them in different locations on different servers.
- Back up all files regularly. This can be done using automated backup software. Verify that the backups have been successful.

- Check your files on a regular schedule. Run checksums on the files and compare them with the checksum generated initially to determine if the files have changed. Make random checks to see if readability of the files has been compromised.

Where possible and relevant:

- Encourage the creators of the digital files you will be managing in your institution to create them in preservation-friendly file formats and to assign metadata. (Chapter 6 provides guidance on creating preservation-friendly digital files.)
- Decide on a limited number of file formats that your preservation program will support, and convert files not in those formats to the supported formats.

Seek expert advice when setting up a preservation program for digital files. For example, expert advice will help you identify which steps can be automated (one is generating and checking checksums). Make sure you keep a watching brief on this fast-changing field. Applications that may be useful for your digital preservation and for nonspecialists are being developed and may suit your institution's requirements; an example is Archivematica (www.archivematica.org).

## Handling

### WHAT STAFF NEED TO KNOW

Digital files should be migrated from their storage media using digital forensic tools and disc imaging best practices as soon as possible after acquisition. (The "Digital Storage Media" sections earlier in this chapter provide more information about migrating files from storage media.) Never work with an original file: always make a copy, and work with the copy.

### WHAT USERS NEED TO KNOW

Users should only have access to copies that have been made for use. Because one of the attributes of digital files is the ease with which they can be copied, damaged, or lost (perhaps through accidental erasure), this attribute needs to be managed by providing the user with exact copies for their use.

## Disaster Response

Incidents such as catastrophic failure of a storage device can be recovered from if best practice for digital preservation has been followed. Best practice includes storing multiple copies of files in distributed locations, so the data lost in the disc failure can be reinstated from another location. Other incidents, such as virus infestation, power failure, or loss of a computer facility (perhaps through fire or flood) can also be recovered from if digital preservation best practice has been followed; quarantining files when they are ingested into a digital archive and reinstating files from copies located elsewhere are examples.

### Decay

Digital files may deteriorate over time, usually because of failure of a storage device or because the processes of copying, refreshing, or migrating files are faulty.

### Treatments

Failure of a storage device is addressed by replacing the storage device and restoring the files from backup copies.

Deterioration resulting from faulty copying, refreshing, or migrating files is also addressed by restoring the files from backup copies. In addition, the processes applied to copy, refresh, or migrate need to be investigated to determine where the fault occurs and changed to address the problem identified. Specialized expertise may be required to identify where the problem lies.


## STANDARDS AND FURTHER READING

### Standards

Consultative Committee for Space Data Systems. *Reference Model for an Open Archival Information System (OAIS): Recommended Practice, CCSDS 650.0-M-2*. Washington, DC: CCSDS, 2012. Accessed September 16, 2013. http://public.ccsds.org/publications/archive/650x0m2.

Digital Curation Centre. "DCC Curation Lifecycle Model." Accessed September 16, 2013. http://www.dcc.ac.uk/resources/curation-lifecycle-model.

METS: Metadata & Encoding Standard, http://www.loc.gov/standards/mets/

PREMIS Data Dictionary for Preservation Metadata, http://www.loc.gov/standards/premis/

### Further Reading

Adelstein, Peter Z. *IPI Media Storage Quick Reference*, 2nd ed. Rochester, NY: Image Permanence Institute, 2009. Accessed October 9, 2013. https://www.imagepermanenceinstitute.org/webfm_send/301.

Brown, Adrian. *Care, Handling and Storage of Removable Media*. Digital Preservation Guidance Note 3. London: The National Archives, 2008. Accessed October 9, 2013. http://www.nationalarchives.gov.uk/documents/information-management/removable-media-care.pdf.

Brown, Adrian. *Practical Digital Preservation: A How-to Guide for Organizations of Any Size*. London: Facet, 2013.

Byers, Fred R. *Care and Handling of CDs and DVDs: A Guide for Librarians and Archivists*. Washington, DC: Council on Library and Information Resources, 2003. Accessed September 29, 2013. http://www.clir.org/pubs/abstract/reports/pub121.

Digital Preservation Coalition. *Preservation Management of Digital Materials: The Handbook*. York: DPC, 2008. Accessed October 8, 2013. http://www.dpconline.org/pages/handbook.

*Forensics Wiki*. Accessed October 9, 2013. http://www.forensicswiki.org/wiki/Main_Page.

Harvey, Ross. *Digital Curation: A How-to-Do-It Manual*. New York: Neal-Schuman, 2010.

Harvey, Ross. *Preserving Digital Materials*. 2nd ed. Berlin: De Gruyter Saur, 2012.

Iraci, Joe. "Relative Stabilities of Optical Disc Formats." *Restaurator* 26 (2005): 134–50.

National Park Service. "Digital Storage Media." *Conserve O Gram* 22/5 (2010). Accessed September 30, 2013. http://www.nps.gov/history/museum/publications/conserveogram/22-05.pdf.

Paradigm Project. *Workbook on Digital Private Papers*. Accessed September 24, 2013. http://www.paradigm.ac.uk/workbook.

*The Signal: Digital Preservation* (blog). Accessed October 9, 2013. http://blogs.loc.gov/digitalpreservation/.

Swanson, Marianne, et al. *Contingency Planning Guide for Federal Information Systems*. Washington, DC: National Institute of Standards and Technology, 2010. Accessed November 5, 2013. http://csrc.nist.gov/publications/nistpubs/800-34-rev1/sp800-34-rev1_errata-Nov11-2010.pdf.

Van Bogart, John. *Magnetic Tape Storage and Handling: A Guide for Libraries and Archives*. Washington, DC: Commission on Preservation and Access, 1995.

## NOTES

1. Ross Harvey, *Preserving Digital Materials*, 2nd ed. (Berlin: De Gruyter Saur, 2012), chapter 3.

2. Task Force on the Artifact in Library Collections, *The Evidence in Hand: Report of the Task Force on the Artifact in Library Collections* (Washington, DC: Council on Library and Information Resources, 2001), vi, accessed October 9, 2013, http://www.clir.org/pubs/abstract//reports/pub103.

3. "Timeline: Digital Technology and Preservation," accessed October 9, 2013, http://www.dpworkshop.org/dpm-eng/timeline/viewall.html.

4. Digital Preservation Coalition, *Preservation Management of Digital Materials: The Handbook* (York: DPC, 2008), 24, accessed October 8, 2013, http://www.dpconline.org/pages/handbook/docs/DPCHandbook.pdf.

5. Consultative Committee for Space Data Systems, *Reference Model for an Open Archival Information System (OAIS): Recommended Practice, CCSDS 650.0-M-2* (Washington, DC: CCSDS, 2012), accessed September 16, 2013, http://public.ccsds.org/publications/archive/650x0m2.pdf.

6. David S. H. Rosenthal, "Keeping Bits Safe: How Hard Can It Be?" *Communications of the ACM* 53 (11) (2010): 47–55, accessed October 9, 2013, http://cacm.acm.org/magazines/2010/11/100620-keeping-bits-safe-how-hard-can-it-be/fulltext.

7. There is an abundance of guidance on the Internet: an example is the University of Oregon Libraries' "File Naming & Tracking Changes (Version Control)" page (library.uoregon.edu/data-management/filenaming.html).

# CHAPTER 13

# Textiles

...............................................................................

Frances Lennard

*Dates in use*: from prehistory to the present day.
*Formats*: historic dress, accessories and shoes, tapestries, flags and banners, samplers and embroideries, rugs and carpets, household textiles.

## Material

Textile collections encompass many different categories, including historic dress, accessories and shoes, tapestries, flags and banners, samplers and embroideries, rugs and carpets, and household textiles. Textiles have traditionally been made mainly of natural fibers, but 20th-century developments in regenerated and synthetic fibers have greatly expanded the range of materials used and provide new challenges to conservators and curators. Although research is ongoing, to date we do not have a good understanding of their manufacture and degradation pathways. Textiles are found in combination with a wide range of other materials—costumes may include metal fasteners, glass beads, plastic sequins, fur, feathers and leather, to name a few—so an understanding of a wide range of materials is a necessary component of caring for textiles. Other classes of material, for example, paper dresses, barkcloth, and plastic dress accessories, while not actually made of textile, are usually included with textile collections, and they come under the care of the textile conservator or curator.

## Purposes

Textiles are among the earliest of man-made objects: carbon dating has established that textiles found in a Peruvian cave date to around 12,000 BCE, demonstrating that the occupation of the Andes had begun by this date and that sophisticated plant processing and artifact construction were carried out in South America soon after the retreat of the glaciers.[1] Textiles are fundamental to human existence, providing clothing and shelter—the nomadic peoples of Central Asia used wool felt to make tent walls for thousands of years—and functioning as vital components of sacred ritual.

## Dates in Use

Textiles are among the earliest of man-made objects, their use dating from prehistory to the present day.

## Identification

For millennia textiles have been made primarily of animal products (silk, wool, and other animal hairs) or plant products (cotton, linen, and other bast fibers such as hemp and jute). A broad identification can be made by look and feel, underpinned by an understanding of local context, but in a mixed collection it is not possible to identify fibers confidently and accurately by these means alone. Unless a more scientific method is used, when cataloging textiles it is advisable to make it clear that fiber identification is made on appearance alone.

Specialists identify textile fibers in various ways. Many textile fibers can be identified by their characteristic appearance under magnification using a microscope (see the Fiber Reference Image Library),[2] although it can be hard to distinguish bast fibers and synthetic fibers from each other in this way. The morphology of a fiber in cross section is also characteristic and can be used to identify similar fibers. Stain tests, burn tests, and solvency tests have also traditionally been used to help identify specific fibers, though today analytical equipment, such as Fourier Transform Infrared (FTIR) spectroscopy or Near-Infrared (NIR) spectroscopy, which compares the spectrum derived from a fiber with reference spectra, may be used.[3]

## Representation in Collections

The great majority of museums have some textiles, and larger museums may have significant collections. Most local history museums are repositories for costume and other textiles associated with local people. Textiles may also be found in archive and library collections, for example, as book covers or seal ribbons.

## Environment and Storage

### PREFERRED ENVIRONMENT

Textiles are easily damaged and vulnerable to degradation from physical and chemical forces caused by light, inappropriate temperature and humidity, insect pests, dust and atmospheric pollution, as well as by handling and inappropriate storage.

Light, in particular, is a significant cause of deterioration in textiles, causing physical damage to the material as well as dye fading. Lighting should be carefully controlled for displayed textiles. Damage occurs in direct relationship to both the amount of light present and the length of time of exposure, so both need to be controlled, with light completely excluded outside opening hours. Traditionally a level of 50 lux was given as the maximum recommended for the display of sensitive material such as textiles, but it is now more common for exposure to be expressed as lux-hours per year, giving some flexibility in the degree of light used. A maximum of 150,000 lux-hours per year is usually recommended for mixed collections;[4] this could be calculated as 1,500 hours of display at 100 lux, or 3,000 hours at 50 lux, for example. Ultraviolet (UV) radiation has more energy than visible light and is more damaging, but it can be totally excluded, as it is not needed to view textiles. This is achieved by excluding daylight or fitting UV-screening film to windows and selecting appropriate light sources that do not emit UV. The light source should not cause heating of displayed objects. A wide range of light sources is available, and good lighting design can make the most of low light levels. The use of motion-sensitive light sensors or providing curtains to be drawn back by visitors in order to view the objects (which can add to the sense that the textiles are precious, vulnerable objects) are good ways of minimizing overall light exposure.

As organic materials, textiles should be stored in stable environmental conditions, avoiding extremes of temperature and relative humidity (RH). High temperature can accelerate degradation reactions; low temperature can make objects more brittle and more vulnerable to physical damage. Temperature control is also necessary for its effect on RH levels, as these can have an even more significant effect on textiles. High RH is a particular problem as it provides appropriate conditions for mold growth and also for insect pests, as well as risking the movement of dyes and the corrosion of metal components. Low RH causes desiccation and loss of flexibility. Fluctuations of temperature and RH should also be avoided, as these cause organic materials to expand and contract as water vapor is absorbed and desorbed to the atmosphere. This is particularly important when textile materials are restrained; for example, silk embroideries nailed to wooden stretcher frames are often found to have cracked where the silk fabric has become too brittle to enable repeated expansion and contraction. As textile collections are usually made of mixed materials, it is generally recommended that RH is kept within the band of 50 to 65 percent.[5]

Where possible, textiles should be displayed in display cases to protect them from dust and atmospheric pollutant gases, to buffer them from changes in RH, and to provide a first-line (though not impenetrable) defense against insect pests. Display cases also provide security and protection from handling. Safe, inert display materials should be selected to avoid introducing harmful chemicals into display cases; some woods, paints, and even fabrics can off-gas to produce acetic acid vapors and other damaging gases. Where it is necessary to use open display methods—in historic houses for example—or for large textiles such as tapestries, it is important to ensure that visitors do not touch textiles. Although there is a huge temptation for visitors to touch textiles, the cumulative effect is devastating. Sample fabrics provided for visitors to handle, such as in the Conservation Gallery of the Ashmolean Museum, Oxford, provide a good demonstration of the effects—silk fabrics disintegrate within weeks. Considerable research has been carried out into dust deposition. This is best avoided, as far as possible, by the careful positioning of objects in relation to the route visitors take through an exhibit, as repeated cleaning is also damaging to textiles.

## RECOMMENDATIONS FOR STORAGE

Textiles are vulnerable to the effects of poor storage conditions. Overfilling boxes with folded textiles will cause permanent creases, which will eventually split, especially in the case of silk textiles. Storage materials should be good quality, made of inert or acid-free materials.

Textiles should be stored flat if they are small, interleaved with acid-free tissue paper, and layered in acid-free boxes. Larger textiles should be rolled and covered with tissue paper, Tyvek, or washed white fabric. Melinex film is also good for covering rollers, as the textile can be seen without needing to unwrap it. Costume items are often best stored hanging, on suitably padded hangers, although very heavy or embellished costumes should be stored flat in acid-free boxes. Three-dimensional objects should be carefully padded with acid-free tissue paper to provide support and to prevent crushing. Objects such as shoes should also be given internal supports to prevent deformation; they can range from shaped tissue-paper padding to bespoke mounts suitable for both display and storage.

Insect pests, in particular carpet beetles and moths (case-bearing clothes moths and webbing clothes moths), are a major cause of damage to textiles, while other pests such as rodents may also cause damage. The widely used, integrated pest-management approach favors noninvasive and preventive measures, rather than relying on toxic pesticide treatments to kill pests. Good building maintenance is the first line of defense to prevent pests entering the building. For example, putting mesh over chimneys to prevent bird nesting avoids a potential host site for pests, while avoiding high RH levels minimizes the risk from silverfish, which can damage textiles and paper.

Good housekeeping methods are also vital. Storage and display cases should be kept clean—accumulated dust in the dead space beneath display cases is a perfect food source for pests, and food debris from visitors and staff is a major pest attractant. It is wise to inspect parts of the collection particularly at risk. Textile pests feed on the protein keratin, present in wool, horsehair, fur, and feathers; larvae will eat through other materials to reach these sources of keratin. All textiles entering the museum should be put into a quarantine space until it is confirmed that they are not affected. A pest-monitoring program should be set up, using blunder (sticky) traps to give early warning of insects; the program should encompass the whole building and not just storage and display areas. The traps should be inspected every three months and the results recorded to build up a history. Training of all staff, including cleaning and security staff, is an important element of preventive conservation, particularly in avoiding pest damage.

## Handling

### WHAT STAFF NEED TO KNOW

Textiles are particularly vulnerable to poor handling. Physical damage can easily occur when damaged and fragile textiles are lifted or moved incautiously, and chemical damage can be accelerated by grease and salt residues on skin. Unnecessary handling can be avoided by clearly labeling boxes and other storage containers with lists of contents and images of individual objects so that the correct textile can easily be retrieved. Any object should be unpacked onto a clear space on a clean tabletop covered with tissue, fabric, or Melinex. Large or fragile textiles require two people to lift them safely; it is advisable to use sheets of tissue or Melinex to provide support. It is often recommended that cotton or nitrile gloves be worn to handle textiles, which is good advice as long as they are replaced or cleaned frequently; sometimes it is safer to handle very fragile textiles without gloves, although hands must be washed and dried frequently.

### WHAT USERS NEED TO KNOW

Users should also be asked to wear gloves if they are to handle any textiles. It may, however, be more appropriate if visitors do not handle the textiles themselves but consult them in the presence of staff who can turn them or open them out. No food or drink should be allowed in the vicinity of any textile, as even water can cause major harm if accidentally spilled. When textiles are examined, no ink pens should be used to make records—only pencils should be used. Textiles should be covered with acid-free tissue, clean fabric, or Tyvek when they are not being examined to protect them from light and dust.

## Disaster Response

Textiles may be seriously and permanently damaged by flooding or fire, as well as by pests and by mold. An emergency plan should be in place to mitigate against these potential disasters and to aid prompt action if a real emergency occurs. It is also recommended to keep a stock of materials, such as sheets of acid-free blotting paper and rolls of polyethylene, to use in an emergency.

It may be necessary to clean smoke-damaged textiles, and the specialist advice of a textile conservator should be sought.

If textiles are damaged by water, prompt action can prevent further damage. Textiles should be carefully moved if they are wet. Because they will be heavy, and consequently at risk of physical damage, they should be supported on sheets of Melinex or polyethylene when they are lifted. Dye bleeding and transfer of dye from one area or textile to another is a major risk, and it can easily lead to permanent staining. If textiles are flooded by relatively clean water, they can be given first-aid treatment to dry them. The best method is to spread textiles out flat on top of acid-free blotting paper and blot them dry with more absorbent paper. If possible, use a cool fan or dehumidifier to dry out textiles gradually; hot-air dryers should not be used. Areas where the dye is obviously bleeding should be padded underneath with absorbent material so that the dye is drawn into that rather than allowed to spread into surrounding areas. In most cases they should also be blotted gently from the top, though particularly vulnerable areas such as painted surfaces should not be touched. Use acid-free blotting paper, and then Melinex or polyethylene, to separate bleeding areas from layers above and below. Monitor the condition of the textiles frequently. Do not attempt any treatments without seeking the advice of a textile conservator. Textiles flooded with dirty water should be kept wet by interleaving with Melinex or polyethylene until they can be wet-cleaned by a textile conservator.

Mold infestation may also occur on textiles in conditions of high relative humidity, such as the aftermath of water damage in a disaster. Treatment of mold is noted in the "Treatments" section.

## Decay

Textiles are mainly made from organic materials and are subject to a range of chemical and physical forces of decay. Oxidation is an aging process that causes weakening of all textiles and has visible results on cellulose fabrics, such as cotton and linen, which gradually become yellower with age as their chemical structure changes. Two other chemical reactions are significant—hydrolysis and cross-linking. Hydrolysis is a reaction caused by the absorption of water, resulting in the breakage of bonds within the molecular structure and the weakening of textiles. Cross-linking causes the formation of new chemical bonds, with the result that textiles become stiffer and more brittle. Photodegradation is a significant cause of damage to textiles; the energy from absorbed light causes molecular bonds to break and cross-link, so that light causes major structural damage (as seen in curtains and their linings) as well as the visible fading of dyes. Silk is particularly vulnerable to light damage, and early synthetic fibers are also often badly affected.

All these reactions are interconnected. As light, oxygen, and acidic or alkaline conditions can speed up the rate of other deteriorative reactions, controlling the light falling on textile objects has a significant effect in preventing damage. It is generally not practical to exclude oxygen from textile storage, although exceptionally significant textiles such as the Shroud of Turin are kept in temperature- and humidity-controlled cases filled with argon. The presence of moisture and pollutants can accelerate damage to textiles; wool degrades ten times faster in humid conditions than in dry conditions.[6] It is now recognized, for example, that the RH behind a heavy textile hanging may be significantly raised, and this can cause degradation on the reverse of the hanging's textile, even though the reverse may be protected from light. Textiles are also damaged by physical forces; the repeated expansion and contraction of fibers caused by fluctuating RH causes strain, and wear and stress of their own weight on hanging textiles may also result in damage.

Thus, textiles exhibit many different forms of damage. Chemical deterioration leads to textiles becoming weak, discolored, and faded, while the application of physical forces can result in tears and splits. Insect damage is apparent in holes and loss of pile, while soiling and staining can cause both chemical and physical damage. Some parts of textiles break down as a result of the manufacturing processes; dark-brown-dyed components are often particularly weak because the dye used was very acidic, while white- and cream-colored areas that may have been bleached can exhibit particularly obvious damage. Some historical processes, such as the weighting of silk with metal salts, mainly in the 19th century, have caused major deterioration.

## Treatments

Interventive conservation treatment falls into three broad categories: cleaning, support treatment, and mounting. Specialist textile conservators should undertake them all. It is very easy to cause further damage if the long-term effects of the intervention are not understood; for example, a repair to one area of a textile very often initiates further damage in the surrounding areas as the strain is transferred from one part to another, and wet cleaning can cause irrevocable damage. The aim of treatment is to stabilize the condition of the textile to enhance its long-term preservation and also perhaps to improve its appearance for display. It is important that conservators discuss with curators and other stakeholders the role of any object and have a clear understanding of the treatment goals in order to make informed decisions about treatment options. For example, in some contexts cleaning may not be appropriate if it would remove soiling or creasing that provides significant evidence of use, whereas in others the removal of soiling may significantly improve the condition of a textile.

If cleaning is undertaken, it often begins with surface cleaning, using low-powered vacuum suction to remove surface dust and particulate soiling—if not removed the dust and soiling can be attached more firmly by further treatments such as wet cleaning. Surface cleaning is often the only form of cleaning that can be undertaken, but in some cases it may be possible and desirable to carry out solvent or wet cleaning. The method selected depends on the materials and condition of the object and the type of soiling.

Weak and damaged textiles are usually given support in the form of patches or complete supports of new fabric. These are often dyed to tone in with the original so that they provide a visual infill in missing areas and the textile appears more complete; however, this may not always be desirable. Overlays of semitransparent fabrics are also often used to protect fragile surfaces. Stitching techniques in fine threads are often used to apply textiles to new supports, but in some cases in which textiles are too fragile or brittle to stitch, support fabrics are adhered by the controlled application of specially prepared adhesive films.

Mounting is an important part of textile conservation. Samplers and embroideries are often displayed on fabric-covered boards made of acid-free or inert materials that provide support across the whole surface. Textiles may be stitched onto such boards, but they are more frequently laid onto slightly sloping padded and fabric-covered surfaces for display, which is a less permanent measure. It is important that a historic garment is fully supported on an appropriately shaped mannequin or display form, which avoids stress and strain while creating the correct historic silhouette. Bespoke mounts, which function as both storage and display mounts, can be created for smaller items, such as shoes. The provision of an appropriate mount does much to avoid further damage to a fragile object on display and in storage.

Pest attack results initially in small holes or grazing of textile surfaces where pest larvae have hatched. If undetected, major damage can occur very quickly. Moth cases and the "woolly bear" cases of carpet beetle larvae, together with accumulations of gritty insect frass, are indications of pest damage. Affected objects should be isolated, the area should be thoroughly cleaned, and a course of treatment should be decided on. The use of insecticides should be avoided where possible, as they can cause damage to textiles, though they may be necessary for large areas, such as carpets. Insect frass and cases should be removed from textiles following an infestation so that any new outbreak can be detected if it occurs in the future. Clean textiles are less attractive to insect pests.

Common treatments include freezing, the use of high temperatures, and the exclusion of oxygen to kill insects at all stages of their life cycle: eggs, larvae, and adult. Most objects can be exposed to low temperatures in a freezer, so long as they do not include glass. Objects should be wrapped in acid-free tissue paper and sealed in polyethylene to exclude air. Freezing at a temperature of below −22°F (−30°C) for three days (colder than a domestic freezer) or 0°F (−18°C) for two weeks is sufficient to kill pests. The objects should not be unwrapped until they have thawed after freezing to avoid damage from condensation. The Thermo Lignum process, available in Europe, uses a temperature of 125°F (52°C) to kill insect pests in textiles, and even on furniture and paintings. The temperature and humidity are controlled in a special chamber to avoid damage caused by decreasing humidity that would usually occur during the rise in temperature. The anoxia technique displaces oxygen with another gas, either nitrogen or carbon dioxide, in a sealed environment. Placing objects in a nitrogen chamber for three to five weeks will kill pests, while single objects can be successfully treated by sealing them in an envelope made from a barrier film under vacuum, with an oxygen scavenger such as Ageless. A good low-tech treatment in hot countries is the "black-bag" treatment, using solar energy to raise the temperature to the point at which pests are killed.

Mold infestation may occur on textiles in conditions of high relative humidity. Mold spores are always present in the air, so the only way to avoid mold growth on textiles and other objects is to keep the RH below 65 percent while avoiding high temperatures and maintaining good ventilation. If a mold outbreak is noticed, measures should be taken to isolate the affected textile, sealing it in a polyethylene bag until it can be treated by a textile conservator. In severe cases, the bag should be placed in a freezer to inhibit further mold growth. Mold can be removed from textiles with low-powered vacuum suction. In the very early stages, the mold can be removed before it causes staining. However, as mold is a health hazard, it is necessary to take health and safety precautions, including wearing an appropriate mask. All equipment must be cleaned thoroughly afterward. It is important to establish the cause of the mold outbreak and to make any necessary improvements to prevent it from reoccurring.

## STANDARDS AND FURTHER READING

### Standard

Museums, Libraries, and Archives Council. *Standards in the Museum Care of Costume and Textiles Collections*. London, 1998.

### Further Reading

American Institute for Conservation of Historic and Artistic Works. "Caring for Your Treasures: Textiles." Accessed September 12, 2013. http://www.conservation-us.org/index.cfm?fuseaction=Page.viewPage&pageId=634&parentID=497.

Canadian Conservation Institute website (www.cci-icc.gc.ca).

Collections Trust. Collections Link website (www.collectionslink.org.uk).

Integrated Pest Management Working Group. *MuseumPests.net*. Accessed September 27, 2013. http://www.museumpests.net.

National Trust. *Manual of Housekeeping*. Oxford, UK: Butterworth-Heinemann, 2006.

Rendell, Caroline. "Preventive Conservation Solutions for Textile Collections." In *Textile Conservation: Advances in Practice*, edited by Frances Lennard and Patricia Ewer, 210–20. Oxford, UK: Elsevier, 2010.

Robinson, Jane, and Tuula Pardoe. *An Illustrated Guide to the Care of Costume and Textile Collections*. London: Council for Museums, Archives and Libraries, 2000.

Silence, Patricia. "Preventive Conservation at the Colonial Williamsburg Foundation." In *Textile Conservation: Advances in Practice*, edited by Frances Lennard and Patricia Ewer, 204–10. Oxford, UK: Elsevier, 2010.

## NOTES

1. Edward A. Jolie et al., "Cordage, Textiles, and the Late Pleistocene Peopling of the Andes," *Current Anthropology* 52, no. 2 (2011): 285–96.

2. "Fiber Reference Image Library," accessed September 27, 2013, https://fril.osu.edu.

3. Barbara H. Stuart, *Analytical Techniques in Materials Conservation* (Chichester, UK; Hoboken, NJ: John Wiley & Sons, 2007).

4. The National Trust, *Manual of Housekeeping* (Oxford, UK: Butterworth-Heinemann, 2006), 96.

5. National Trust, *Manual of Housekeeping*, 106.

6. Ágnes Tímár-Balázsy and Dinah Eastop, *Chemical Principles of Textile Conservation* (Oxford, UK: Butterworth-Heinemann, 1998), 51.

# CHAPTER 14

# Paintings

······································································································

Heather Hole

*Dates in use*: from the start of recorded history to the present.
*Formats*: works of art, framed or unframed, created with oil, acrylic, tempera, or other paint, often on a canvas or wooden support.

## Material

This section describes the preservation, documentation, handling, and storage of paintings in cultural heritage collections. The term *painting* encompasses a variety of materials, but it usually refers to a primarily two-dimensional work of art created with oil, acrylic, tempera, or other paint, on a canvas or wooden support. Because many paintings are framed, the care and preservation of frames is also noted.

## Purposes

As a fine art object, much of a painting's value is aesthetic in nature. Important information can be derived from close analysis of the material object itself, including brushstroke and impasto (thickly textured paint). Often this information cannot be gleaned from photographs or other copies of the work. This means that the physical condition of a painting is of primary importance and that paintings are treated with the highest level of care.

## Identification

In order to store and preserve a painting, it is important to identify its physical makeup as precisely as possible, although in some cases complete certainty may be impossible without expert scientific testing. Artists use a variety of paints and supports, each with its own special set of considerations. A frame is an ancillary component of

······································································································

most paintings, though it may or may not have been an original part of the work. Characteristics that identify different materials and specific recommendations for preservation follow.

## PAINTS

Four elements can comprise the image layer of a painting: paint, sizing, primer or ground, and varnish. Only paint is present in all works; the other three components are used at the discretion of the artist. Descriptions of oil, acrylic, and other types of paint follow. (Watercolor is used on paper and is noted in the section "Paper: Works of Art on Paper" in chapter 8). Sizing is a thin layer of gelatin, similar to diluted glue, applied directly to a canvas support to make it less absorbent. Gesso, a mixture of glue and chalk, is a common sizing material. A base coat of neutral primer or ground is often applied to many different kinds of support materials, providing an even surface for the paint. Varnish creates a transparent, protective layer over the paint surface.[1]

*Oil.* Though antecedents can be found as early as the 12th century, oil was widely adopted by painters as the medium of choice in the 15th and 16th centuries. Flemish painter Jan van Eyck is often credited with popularizing oil paint through his exquisite use of the material.[2] Oil paint consists of a pigment, which has been ground into a powder and suspended in an oil-based medium or binder. This medium is usually a drying oil like linseed oil. Many, but not all, oil paintings are coated with a layer of natural-resin varnish. Varnish has been used for centuries to protect the paint surface and often to enhance the work's appearance with a glossy finish. Varnish tends to yellow over time, and some paintings have been varnished repeatedly over the years, while others have at some point had their original varnish removed and a new layer added. If a painting shows a noticeably glossy or reflective surface, it may be varnished, although not all varnishes create this appearance. If an older painting seems to have a yellow cast and/or darkened appearance, this is an indication that aged or deteriorating varnish might be present.

*Acrylic.* Acrylic paint is a synthetic substance first introduced in the 1950s. It can be impossible to distinguish from oil with the naked eye, so this information should be gathered from the artist if possible. Traditional protective natural-resin varnishes used with oil paintings are not recommended for acrylic paintings because of potentially destructive chemical interactions. Synthetic varnishes suitable for acrylic paintings have been manufactured, though they tend to be used less frequently. If a painting appears to be varnished, it is less likely to be acrylic.[3] Acrylic has somewhat different properties from oil. Most important for preservation is the fact that acrylic surfaces are softer, making it more difficult to remove dust and dirt once they have settled. Because they also usually lack the protection of a layer of varnish, it is doubly important to prevent the accumulation of dust on acrylic paintings.[4]

*Other Paints.* Other types of paints may occasionally be encountered. These consist of pigment suspended in different, less frequently used media, including encaustic (wax), fresco (lime plaster, usually part of the surface of a plaster wall), gouache (gum arabic), casein (milk protein glue), tempera (egg yolk), and glair (egg white).[5] Basic guidelines for the care of these works are similar to those for oil and acrylic paintings, but preservation, treatment, and extensive movement such as shipping should be undertaken according to the advice of a conservator. Sometimes unusual materials, such as house paints and automobile lacquers, are found in 20th-century and contemporary paintings. Objects created with such paints frequently age in unpredictable ways and are often more inherently fragile and difficult to treat. A qualified professional should individually assess them, and they should be stored, handled, and conserved according to their recommendation.

## SUPPORT

A painting's support can include multiple elements. First, there is the surface onto which the paint was applied, usually canvas or a wood panel. A stretcher or strainer almost always supports a canvas; cradles sometimes support wood panels. Many paintings are also framed, although frames are not usually considered part of the artwork proper and are often not original.

*Canvas and Stretcher.* The term *canvas* generally refers to any textile upon which an artist paints. Although artists usually work on linen or cotton fabric, it is possible to find examples of the use of almost any type of cloth at some moment in history. Canvas supports are usually readily identified by looking at the back of a painting, where the fabric is often visible. A canvas is a textile like any other, and it becomes weaker and less flexible as it ages or is exposed to detrimental environmental conditions. Bare canvas is particularly sensitive.[6] A painting that includes significant areas of exposed raw cloth should be treated according to the guidelines for textiles rather than paintings (see "Textiles," chapter 13).

A canvas is almost always affixed at each edge with tacks or staples to a rigid framework that holds it flat and taut. This is usually a stretcher, a wooden rectangle that may or may not have additional horizontal stretcher bars at midpoints to provide extra support. Although the term *stretcher* is commonly used to refer to any such wooden framework, there are in fact two types: strainer and stretcher. A strainer has securely attached joints and no mechanism by which to adjust its dimensions. A stretcher, however, has open joints and keys, or flat triangular wedges, at each corner. These keys can be used to expand the stretcher and tighten the canvas.[7]

*Wood Panel and Cradle.* The other common support used is a wooden panel. Paint behaves much the same way on a panel as it does on a canvas. Panel paintings differ from canvases primarily in their patterns of expansion and contraction and in their capacity for warping.[8] Paintings on panel generally can be stored and handled in much the same way as a canvas painting. Some panels are backed by a cradle, or wooden support grid. Cradles are intended to secure the painting and prevent warping, though at times a very tight cradle can cause cracking by restraining the normal expansion and contraction of the wood.[9]

*Glass, Metal, and Other Supports.* Artists have at times used a variety of other supports. Some folk artists and modernists regularly painted on glass, while other artists used various metals such as copper, particularly in Europe and Latin America. Miniaturists often painted on ivory. Contemporary artists have been known to paint on a wide range of materials. These unusual objects should generally be treated the same way as paintings on canvas or panel, but with an awareness that they may be particularly fragile. If damage occurs and treatment is necessary, or shipping or other special handling is anticipated, seek the advice of a qualified conservator.

*Frames.* Frames occupy an odd hybrid position between collection object and exhibition mount. They are in some ways independent artworks in their own right. Many frames are the product of exquisite craftsmanship, and some can be quite valuable. They are not merely one part of another art object; the same frame may be used on many different paintings over time, as paintings are often reframed for aesthetic and practical reasons. Frames also serve a protective function and are intended to sustain bumps and scrapes that might otherwise damage the painting inside. They are often resized to fit various artworks, refitted with new hanging hardware that requires additional screw holes, and marked on the back with stamps or labels. Thus, they are not always treated in the same way one would treat a designated object of cultural heritage in an institutional collection.

Frames are mixed media objects, usually consisting of a wooden base coated with paint, gilding, gesso (a mixture of glue and chalk), compo (a composite material with a plaster base), or other substances. Each of these components will become more fragile with time.[10] General recommendations for preserving wooden objects also apply to frames.

Adding a backing board to a frame can provide an extra layer of protection to paintings on canvas. A backing board is a sturdy piece of acid-free cardboard attached to the back of the stretcher or strainer to cover the vulnerable canvas.[11] Some frames have a rabbet, or strip of molding that covers the far edge of each side of the painting. Sometimes the area of the image protected from light and other damage by the rabbet is in much better shape than the rest of the painting and can offer valuable information about the original condition and color palate of the work.

Because frames can transform the look of a painting, the selection of an appropriate frame can be an important curatorial decision. As a general rule, many professionals look for frames appropriate to the period in which the object was created and consistent with frames the artist is known to have used.

More and more frequently, institutions are adding protective sheets of glass or Plexiglas to painting frames (called glazing). Glazing shields paint surfaces from visitor and environmental damage; ultraviolet-filtered glass or Plexiglas can prevent degradation from light exposure. The problems this poses for works with original or period frames often call for difficult compromises. Retrofitting a frame so that it can support glass will alter its look and proportions, so the process often leads to replacement with a less historically appropriate frame. Glazing can also interfere with the visual experience of a painting by causing glare and making it more difficult to see small details like brushstrokes.

Frames should be cataloged separately from paintings as auxiliary objects (sometimes referred to as apparatus). If a frame is original to a painting, this is important information that must be documented when cataloging both frame and painting. Never remove an original frame (or a frame you suspect is original) without recording its relationship to the work inside.

## DOCUMENTATION

The documentation of a painting is in many ways similar to that of other objects of cultural heritage, noted in chapter 6. However, when cataloging a painting, certain categories of information assume particular importance and may be treated in a specific way. Chief among them are condition and provenance.

Upon acquisition, a painting should be cataloged using a standardized cataloging sheet. This sheet should be completed when the object is thoroughly and carefully examined (observing all guidelines noted in the "Handling" section in this chapter). The sheet then remains in the object file, and the data it contains becomes the basis for the database or other electronic record of the object.

The cataloging sheet should at minimum include these fields: artist/maker; title; date; accession number; dimensions; materials; object type; brief description; any signature or other distinctive marking (historic or contemporary); artist's nationality and cultural or ethnic group; object's place of origin; provenance and history; date and method of acquisition; credit line; location; and insurance value. Not all information will be available for each object, and the completion of some fields requires additional research.[12] Exhaustive documentation of a work of fine art also includes an exhibition history and a publication history. A list of all exhibitions in which the artwork has appeared and of publications in which it is reproduced should be appended to the cataloging sheet. Clippings from any publications should also be kept in the object file.

A painting's state of preservation is documented through a condition report. It is standard practice in most museums to produce a baseline condition report upon the acquisition of a work, usually at the time the painting is cataloged. Then, a new condition report is created both before and after any exhibition, loan, or shipment; when any damage occurs; and during periodic conservation surveys. By documenting changes in the painting over time, the accumulation of reports provides invaluable information for any conservator treating the painting at a later date. A review of an artwork's condition report can alert staff to potential problems prior to handling. The practice also ensures the careful examination of an artwork before and after the periods of greatest risk to the object, increasing the likelihood that any damage or deterioration will be noticed and addressed quickly.

A condition report traditionally consists of a written description of the overall condition of the artwork, front and back, and a diagram marking the location and type of any localized damage. Digital photographs are commonly used to supplement the report. A trained staff member can create a standard collections-management condition report; only a fully qualified conservator can create the type of detailed condition report needed to plan and document a conservation treatment.[13]

Provenance (or history of ownership) is another important element of the full documentation of a painting. A complete provenance includes the following: name, location, nationality, and cultural or ethnic group of each owner including the artist; dates of ownership; location and method of transfer including, if applicable, sale and price information; and any import or export of the object from one nation to another. Establishing clear provenance for a painting can be crucial. For example, a documented chain of ownership back to the original artist constitutes powerful proof of its authenticity. An object's provenance is also essential for determining its rightful owner. When presented with a request for the return of an artwork (usually the repatriation of an object of cultural patrimony or restitution of an artwork transferred under the Nazi regime), an institution must look to the object's provenance to ascertain the validity of the claim.[14] Never acquire a work without performing enough provenance research to be certain the seller or donor has legal title.

Provenance information for a specific object can be gleaned from many sources. Labels or stamps on the back of a painting may document a past owner or exhibition. Auction, exhibition, and estate records are also useful places to look. Published reproductions of artworks often credit the then-current owner or collection, so press coverage or scholarship on the painting can also be invaluable.[15]

In addition to identifying its physical components, as discussed above, it is important to determine a painting's authenticity and attribution. If there is any doubt about either, this can be resolved by seeking an expert opinion. Ideally this would come from a scholar in the relevant field, but in practice it often comes from a more accessible (and less expensive) appraiser or dealer. This expert should be able to offer a written opinion on the artist or school they believe created the work, and whether the work is authentic or not.

## Representation in Collections

Paintings are widely held in all kinds of cultural heritage collections. They frequently constitute the core of an art museum's collection. However, they are also represented in many libraries, historical societies, archives, and other institutions, often in the form of portraits of historical figures.

## Environment and Storage

### PREFERRED ENVIRONMENT

Over time, canvas becomes less flexible, paint becomes more brittle, and varnish darkens and discolors. High light levels and extremes or rapid fluctuations in temperature and humidity accelerate all of these changes. Paintings are particularly prone to environmental damage because they are comprised of many different materials, each with its own characteristic reaction to temperature, humidity, and light. A change in any one component places additional stress on the others. For example, when shifts in humidity cause a canvas to contract, the paint layer above is also necessarily compressed. The paint can then crack or, in extreme cases, begin to lift off the canvas entirely.[16]

The broad recommendations for collections environments discussed in chapter 5 apply to paintings. Temperature and relative humidity in a painting's storage environment should meet the general museum standards of 70°F (21°C) ±2°F (1°C), and 50 percent ± 5 percent. Rapid change in any aspect of the environment can be damaging, and it should be carefully avoided.[17] Placing a painting in a box or other enclosure can provide some protection from extreme shifts in humidity levels.[18] Dust, pollutants, and other contaminants should be minimized through air filtration systems, and pests should be eliminated through an integrated pest management (IPM) system.[19]

Light, particularly ultraviolet (UV) light, will permanently damage a painting by accelerating the degradation of its materials. For the purpose of determining appropriate light levels, paintings are classified as moderately sensitive materials, carrying a recommendation of no more than 50 lux or 5 footcandles at any time.[20] In addition to the general guidelines for minimizing UV light in storage and galleries discussed in chapter 6, paintings can be further protected by glazing with UV filtered glass, as noted in the discussion of frames.

## RECOMMENDATIONS FOR STORAGE

Paintings should be kept in a secure, dedicated storage area. Whenever possible, paintings should be stored vertically, in the orientation in which they are displayed. If a painting has any areas of loose or flaking paint, however, it should be stored horizontally with the paint surface up.

Framed paintings can be hung on a storage screen or placed on a storage shelf. Screens, the preferred method for storing framed paintings, are large, vertical panels consisting of an open metal latticework. Paintings are hung on the screen using moveable two-sided metal hooks that fit inside the gaps of the lattice and suspend the painting from its existing hanging hardware. Painting storage shelves (sometimes called bins) consist of narrow vertical compartments, in which paintings can be housed upright and slightly tilted, leaning from one corner of a compartment to another corner. Paintings stored in this manner should be face up, so the paint surface does not come into contact with the shelving.

Stacking paintings, either on storage shelves or against a wall, is not recommended. However, limitations of space or equipment may make this unavoidable. To stack framed paintings, lean them on top of one another against a wall or other secure vertical surface. They should not rest directly on the floor, where they are likely to slide and are more exposed to dust, flooding, and other dangers. Instead, paintings should be stacked on two or more sturdy, padded, skid-proof blocks. The blocks should be placed near the wall and far enough apart to stably support all the paintings you plan to store. Always select an interior wall (to minimize environmental fluctuations and potential vibrations) far away from any commonly used paths of travel. Stacked paintings should be positioned as vertically as possible without any danger they might topple over. Stack only similarly sized paintings together. Lean them face-to-face and back-to-back with a piece of sturdy, acid-free cardboard between each work. Be sure that each frame is large enough to overlap with the next. A painting with a frame that is too small to cross that of its neighbor can cause damage if it leans directly into the painted surface of that other work.[21]

Unframed paintings should be stored on shelves much the way a framed painting would be. They should either rest flat on the shelf or lean image-side up against a secure, vertical surface. Unframed paintings should never be stacked under any circumstances because their paint surface is completely unprotected.

## Recommendations for Exhibition Display

The best way to protect a painting on display from accidental damage by visitors is to hang it in an open area away from heavy foot traffic. Study the potential flow of movement through the exhibition, and avoid places where visitors are more likely to accidentally bump into the work. These include bottlenecks, narrow areas like hallways, and spots where visitors turn a blind corner. Always hang a painting well away from doors, furniture, or other objects that might come into contact with it. If a painting must be hung in a high-risk location or is likely to attract a crowd, a stanchion, guardrail, or rope can keep visitors at a safe distance.[22] Security guards, gallery attendants, "don't touch" signs, and alarms can help prevent intentional damage or theft.

Environmental conditions in an exhibition should meet the same standards as storage areas. Paintings on display should be hung away from any heat source (like vents or radiators) and out of direct sunlight. Once the gallery has been lit, light levels on each individual painting should be measured to ensure they do not exceed the recommended maximum (50 lux or 5 footcandles).

Installing a painting requires great care. It should be hung from secure hanging hardware on well-anchored hooks that have been driven into a wall stud or other sturdy support. Adding a bracket under the frame can also support a particularly heavy painting from below. Check hooks, hanging hardware, and all other forms of support regularly throughout the exhibition. Hanging hardware (usually some combination of hooks, eye screws, d-rings, and painting wire) should be securely attached to the back of the painting's frame. Though not recommended, many paintings are still hung from a wire attached to eye screws or d-rings screwed into the wood on either side. Paintings can be hung without wire from hooks or d-rings that fit directly onto complementary hooks on the wall. This hanging method lessens the potential for the movement or swinging sometimes seen with wire and eliminates the possibility that excess wire will come into contact with the back of the painting.

In the activity and energy that often surrounds an exhibition installation, it can be particularly easy to rush or become distracted when placing or rearranging objects. This is one reason the risk of damage to an artwork during this time is so high. Any movement of an artwork during installation should be done deliberately, with careful planning and forethought. Resist the temptation to hurry, and remember to follow all the guidelines for handling.

## Handling

### WHAT STAFF NEED TO KNOW

Because so much of the value of a painting is inseparable from it as a material object, paintings should be handled with great care. Important information lies in the tiniest brushstroke, and that information is easily lost with a small bump or scrape. Even minute areas of damage detract from the aesthetic experience of viewing a painting. Photographs cannot capture the three-dimensional nature of a paint surface and are not an adequate substitute for viewing the work itself. A painting's physical condition is therefore of the highest importance.

Only thoroughly trained staff members should touch or move paintings. Visitors and untrained staff should never handle them.

Paintings, like other works of art, should be moved as infrequently as possible. No matter how carefully a work is handled, the risk of damage is exponentially higher during transit or installation than it is in storage. Before handling a painting, make a thorough visual inspection. Check for any areas of flaking paint that might be dislodged by movement. If it is framed, look for any loose or broken frame pieces that might compromise your grip, and make sure no painting wire or other hanging hardware is in a position to bump against the front or back of the artwork.[23]

Before you pick up a painting, know where you are going and how you will get there. Plan your route and make sure you have a clear path to your destination. Always move slowly and deliberately; never hurry. Paintings should be carried with two hands at all times. Because both hands will always be occupied, moving a painting any substantial distance often requires an additional person, who should be the one to open doors, clear a pathway through visitors in an open gallery, operate elevators, and so forth. Make sure they are present to assist you before you begin your move.

*Framed Paintings.* Always carry a framed painting vertically in front of you using both hands. One hand should support the painting from below at all times, and the other hand should grasp the painting from the side. If the frame is unstable, or you lose your grip, a painting held only from the top or sides will fall to the ground.[24] When possible, use cotton gloves. If gloves are not available, wash your hands before touching the painting.

Slowly lift the painting with a firm (but not clenched or damaging) grip. Hold it by the frame only. Be sure no part of your hand touches the front or back of the painted surface. Never grasp the painting by its stretcher or stretcher bar. If you are lifting a painting that is low to the ground, keep your back straight and bend at the knees as you rise while holding the painting out in front of you.

Large or heavy paintings often need to be moved by two or more people. If two people are holding a painting, one should stand at each end with one hand supporting the painting from below and the other holding it from the side. These individuals should clearly communicate any intended movement to each other in advance and work in careful unison.

When possible, use a padded A-frame when moving a painting any substantial distance and when moving more than one painting. An A-frame is a long, wheeled cart specially designed for moving framed paintings. It consists of two padded shelves running lengthwise on either side, behind which are two vertical surfaces tilted at an angle greater than 90° to form two sides of a triangle (creating the shape of a capital A). Paintings are placed on the shelves face-out and leaned against the tilted sides. They are then gently secured using a broad, cloth strap tied to either end of the cart. If an A-frame is not available, other types of carts may also be used. A suitable cart would have a flat bottom and two or more secure vertical sides. Framed paintings can then be stacked as they would be against a wall, using the method described in the "Environment and Storage" section in this chapter.

*Unframed Paintings.* Without a frame, a painting has little protection, and it must be handled very gently and with great care. It is impossible to avoid touching an unframed painting's supports (such as canvas and stretcher), even if only briefly and on the back or side. Always wear gloves to protect these fragile elements from fingerprint oils and other contaminants. Latex or other smooth gloves are preferable to cotton, which can snag on delicate areas of impasto.

To move an unframed painting by hand, hold it as lightly as possible by the edges. Avoid closing your fingers around the object, thereby touching the paint surface. Carry it vertically in front of you as you would a framed painting, with one hand below and one at the side. When moving an unframed painting a short distance, another option is to place it flat on a larger piece of sturdy, acid-free cardboard, then carry it horizontally by grasping the cardboard rather than the painting itself. The cardboard must be kept very level, so the painting cannot slide off.[25]

*Shipment.* The shipment of paintings is a complex and specialized process that can involve a wide range of procedures, including constructing custom crates and mounts, arranging for an art courier to accompany the object in transit, and booking specialized forms of travel. It is recommended that experienced professionals manage the process.[26]

## Disaster Response

### WATER

Wet paintings can be helped greatly by immediate action. Damage continues to occur throughout the drying process, so time is of the essence. Call a conservator at once, and have them examine and treat the paintings right away. In the meantime, take the following first-aid steps:

1. Remove frames (but not stretchers) if you can do so safely.
2. Remove excess water by gently tilting each painting to let water run off the surface and to keep it from pooling around the stretcher.
3. Set up a work area where there is no risk of further damage.
4. Lay all wet paintings horizontally with the image side up in the work area. Those with any flaking paint should not be touched again.
5. Place fans and dehumidifiers around the work area to accelerate drying. Maintain a higher-than-normal relative humidity of 60 percent to 70 percent to avoid overdrying.[27]

As water can cause enormous damage, it is essential that conservators treat wet paintings immediately. Wood swells when wet, creating significant problems both for paintings on wood panels and for canvases on wooden stretchers. Wet canvas expands and shrinks as it absorbs water and dries, although the order in which it does so depends on the materials with which it has been treated.[28] Water can also dissolve sizing, separating paint from its support. Treatment by a qualified paintings conservator is crucial.

## FIRE

Paintings damaged by fire are not subject to the same kind of ongoing destructive process as a wet and drying painting. Therefore, there is less need for urgent action and more time for careful planning and consideration. Immediately after a fire, make sure no paintings are in a precarious position that could lead to further damage. Then contact a trained conservator, and don't touch anything until he or she arrives and is able to advise you.

Fire damage generally falls into two categories: soot and blistering. A conservator may be able to remove soot from a painting through surface cleaning, particularly if it is varnished. Blistering is far more difficult and sometimes impossible to repair.[29]

## ACCIDENT

Despite all precautions, accidents can happen in storage. Paintings can be dropped, and canvases can be accidentally torn. After an accident, once there is no further risk to the painting, the best course of action is to leave the object where it is. Clear the area around the accident site. Hurried action can create more damage; people walking in the vicinity can unintentionally step on paint fragments, or other pieces of the artwork, that have flown far from the object. Take your time, call a conservator, and carefully begin to document the accident as described below.

## DAMAGE ASSESSMENT AND RECORDKEEPING

Once a disaster is over and there is no further risk to the object, the next tasks are assessment and documentation. A conservator should carry out the assessment, create a treatment plan to repair damage, and advise on the storage of affected objects.

Before moving damaged artworks, search carefully the entire area for any object fragments that may have scattered. Record their location, bag and label them, and keep them with the painting from which they came. Create a complete record of the disaster or accident. This includes a thorough, written description of the event, a detailed condition report on the object (see the "Documentation" section in this chapter), and multiple photographs of the damaged artwork, accident location, and method of damage. The goal is to create as complete a record of the event as possible, which will help conservators present and future to understand what happened to the object and to decide how to treat it.

## Decay

Common signs of aging in paintings are the discoloration of varnish, cracking of paint, and sometimes the tearing of canvas in areas subject to particular stress (such as the fold over a stretcher). Varnish naturally yellows as it ages, and both paints and canvases become more brittle over time. These signs of aging can be addressed and sometimes prevented through treatment by a fully qualified conservator, as described below.

## Treatments

First, do no harm. This is the guiding principle of paintings treatment. Never try to treat a painting yourself, and never take it to anyone other than a fully qualified paintings conservator. The only action that should ever be undertaken by anyone but an expert conservator is the occasional light dusting of a painting's surface with a clean, soft artist's brush.

Inexpert conservation of paintings is very likely to cause damage, leaving the object in worse condition than before. For example, unqualified conservators can easily overclean paint surfaces, removing irreplaceable layers of pigment. Irresponsible conservators can overvarnish, sometimes in an effort to create a bright, shiny, colorful appearance, regardless of the artist's original intention. Mistakes like these are usually difficult or impossible to undo, and they will compromise an object that was previously reparable if put in the right hands.

Always call a conservator if you notice active changes in a painting, like cracking or flaking of paint, warping of the wood panel or stretcher, or the appearance of white or milky areas in the varnish. A conservator should also examine any damage to a painting.

Expert conservators can perform a wide range of treatments that will significantly improve a painting's condition and prevent future deterioration. These include cleaning, repair of tears, consolidation of flaking paint, inpainting of lost areas, addition of a protective lining, and other procedures. Fully trained professional conservators usually strive to preserve as closely as possible the artist's intention and to minimize distractions that interfere with the experience of the work.

## STANDARDS AND FURTHER READING

### Standards

American Alliance of Museums. "Standards Regarding Collections Stewardship." Accessed September 29, 2013. http://www.aam-us.org/resources/ethics-standards-and-best-practices/collections-stewardship.

Buck, Rebecca A., and Jean Allman Gilmore, eds. *MRM5: Museum Registration Methods*, 5th ed. Washington, DC: AAM Press, 2010.

### Further Reading

American Institute for Conservation of Historic and Artistic Works. "Code of Ethics and Guidelines for Practice." Accessed September 29, 2013. http://www.conservation-us.org/index.cfm?fuseaction=page.viewPage&PageID=858&E.

Appelbaum, Barbara. *Guide to Environmental Protection of Collections*. Madison, CT: Sound View Press, 1991.

Edson, Gary, and David Dean. *The Handbook for Museums*. London and New York: Routledge, 1994.

International Foundation for Arts Research. "Provenance Guide." Accessed September 29, 2013. http://www.ifar.org/provenance_guide.php.

Keck, Caroline K. *A Handbook on the Care of Paintings*. Nashville, TN: American Association for State and Local History, 1965.

Keck, Caroline K. *How to Take Care of Your Paintings*. New York: Scribner, 1978.

Matassa, Freda. *Museum Collections Management: A Handbook*. London: Facet, 2011.

National Park Service. "Appendix L: Curatorial Care of Easel Paintings." In *Museum Handbook*, Part I. Washington, DC: National Park Service, Museum Management Program, 2000. Accessed September 29, 2013. http://www.nps.gov/history/museum/publications/MHI/AppendL.pdf.

Smithsonian Museum Conservation Institute. "Care of Acrylic Paintings." Accessed September 29, 2013. http://www.si.edu/mci/english/learn_more/taking_care/acrylic_paintings.html.

Smithsonian Museum Conservation Institute. "Caring for Your Paintings." Accessed September 29, 2013. http://www.si.edu/mci/english/learn_more/taking_care/care_painting.html.

Smithsonian Museum Conservation Institute. "Painting Conservation Glossary of Terms." Accessed September 29, 2013. http://www.si.edu/mci/english/learn_more/taking_care/painting_glossary.html.

Smithsonian Museum Conservation Institute. "What Is a Painting?" Accessed September 29, 2013. http://www.si.edu/mci/english/learn_more/taking_care/what_painting.html.

Thomson, Garry. *The Museum Environment*, 2nd ed. London: Butterworths-Heinemann, 1986.

Yeide, N., A. Walsh, and K. Akinsha. *The AAM Guide to Provenance Research*. Washington, DC: American Association of Museums, 2001.

# NOTES

1. Smithsonian Museum Conservation Institute, "What Is a Painting?" accessed September 29, 2013, http://www.si.edu/mci/english/learn_more/taking_care/what_painting.html.

2. Helen Gardner and Fred S. Kleiner, *Gardner's Art through the Ages: A Global History*, 13th ed. (Australia: Wadsworth/Cengage Learning, 2010), 522.

3. Smithsonian Museum Conservation Institute, "Care of Acrylic Paintings," accessed September 29, 2013, http://www.si.edu/mci/english/learn_more/taking_care/acrylic_paintings.html.

4. Smithsonian, "Care of Acrylic Paintings."

5. Caroline K. Keck, *A Handbook on the Care of Paintings* (Nashville, TN: American Association for State and Local History, 1965), 30.

6. Barbara Appelbaum, *Guide to Environmental Protection of Collections* (Madison, CT: Sound View Press, 1991), 211.

7. National Park Service, "Appendix L: Curatorial Care of Easel Paintings," in *Museum Handbook,* Part I (Washington, DC: National Park Service, Museum Management Program, 2000), L:3–L:4, accessed September 29, 2013, http://www.nps.gov/history/museum/publications/MHI/AppendL.pdf.

8. Appelbaum, *Guide to Environmental Protection*, 215.

9. National Park Service, "Appendix L," L:4.

10. Appelbaum, *Guide to Environmental Protection*, 216–17.

11. National Park Service, "Appendix L," L:11.

12. Freda Matassa, *Museum Collections Management: A Handbook* (London: Facet, 2011), 77–80.

13. For a detailed description of condition reporting, vocabulary of terms, and sample condition report forms, see Marie Demeroukas, "Condition Reporting," in *MRM5: Museum Registration Methods*, 5th ed., eds. Rebecca A. Buck and Jean Allman Gilmore (Washington, DC: AAM Press, 2010), 223–32; for a glossary of condition reporting terms, see Smithsonian Museum Conservation Institute, "Painting Conservation Glossary of Terms," accessed September 29, 2013, http://www.si.edu/mci/english/learn_more/taking_care/painting_glossary.html.

14. For the American Alliance of Museums' standards and best practices regarding ownership of ancient art and the restitution of objects transferred during the Nazi era, see their "Standards Regarding Collections Stewardship," accessed September 29, 2013, http://www.aam-us.org/resources/ethics-standards-and-best-practices/collections-stewardship.

15. For more on uncovering provenance, see "Provenance Research in Museum Collections," in *MRM5: Museum Registration Methods*, eds. Buck and Gilmore, 62–77.

16. Appelbaum, *Guide to Environmental Protection*, 211–15.

17. Genevieve Fisher, "Preventive Care," in *MRM5: Museum Registration Methods*, eds. Buck and Gilmore, 287; for discussion of recent debates over these standards, see Fisher, "Preventive Care," 288–89.

18. Appelbaum, *Guide to Environmental Protection*, 213.

19. Fisher, "Preventive Care," 290–91.

20. Fisher, "Preventive Care," 290.

21. National Park Service, "Appendix L," L:11–L:12.

22. National Park Service, "Appendix L," L:14.

23. Dixie Nelson, "Object Handling," in *MRM5: Museum Registration Methods*, eds. Buck and Gilmore, 210.

24. Nelson, "Object Handling," 212.

25. Nelson, "Object Handling," 213.

26. For more information, see "Packing and Crating" and "Shipping by Land, Air, and Sea," in *MRM5: Museum Registration Methods*, eds. Buck and Gilmore, 223–32 and 322–31.

27. Adapted from the recommendations in National Park Service, "Appendix L," L:17.

28. Caroline K. Keck, *How to Take Care of Your Paintings* (New York: Scribner, 1978), 60–63.

29. National Park Service, "Appendix L," L:17–L:18.

# Bibliography

Adcock, Edward P., ed. *IFLA Principles for the Care and Handling of Library Material*. International Federation of Library Associations and Institutions Core Programme on Preservation and Conservation, 1998. Accessed September 16, 2013. http://archive.ifla.org/VI/4/news/pchlm.pdf.

Adelstein, Peter Z. *IPI Media Storage Quick Reference*, 2nd edition. Rochester, NY: Image Permanence Institute, 2009. Accessed October 9, 2013. https://www.imagepermanenceinstitute.org/webfm_send/301.

"ALA's Third Resolution on Permanent Paper." *Abbey Newsletter* 14, no. 1 (1990): 2.

Altenhöner, Reinhard. "Preservation and Conservation as an Integrated Process in the German National Library: Status Quo and Outlook." Paper presented at IFLA WLIC 2013, Singapore, July 30, 2013. Accessed September 28, 2013. http://library.ifla.org/247/1/146-altenhoener-en.pdf.

"Amateur Restoration Botches Jesus Fresco in Spain." *PRI's The World*, August 23, 2012. Accessed September 17, 2013. http://www.theworld.org/2012/08/amateur-restoration-botches-jesus-fresco-in-spain/.

American Institute for Conservation of Historic and Artistic Works. "Caring for Your Treasures: Textiles." Accessed September 12, 2013. http://www.conservation-us.org/index.cfm?fuseaction=Page.viewPage&pageId=634&parentID=497.

American Institute for Conservation of Historic and Artistic Works. "Code of Ethics and Guidelines for Practice." Accessed September 17, 2013. http://www.conservation-us.org/index.cfm?fuseaction=page.viewPage&PageID=858&E.

American Institute for Conservation of Historic and Artistic Works. *Defining the Conservator: Essential Competencies*. 2003. Accessed October 1, 2013. http://www.conservation-us.org/docs/default-source/governance/definingcon.pdf?sfvrsn=2.

American Institute for Conservation of Historic and Artistic Works. "Definitions of Conservation Terminology." Accessed October 1, 2013. http://www.conservation-us.org/index.cfm?fuseaction=page.viewpage&pageid=620.

American Institute for Conservation of Historic and Artistic Works. "Find a Conservator." Accessed October 4, 2013. http://www.conservation-us.org/index.cfm?fuseaction=Page.viewPage&pageId=495&parentID=472.

American Institute for Conservation of Historic and Artistic Works. "Position Paper on Conservation and Preservation in Collecting Institutions." Accessed September 16, 2013. http://www.conservation-us.org/index.cfm?fuseaction=Page.viewPage&pageId=619.

American Institute for Conservation of Historic and Artistic Works. *Requisite Competencies for Conservation Technicians and Collections Care Specialists*. June 2005. Accessed October 1, 2013. http://www.conservation-us.org/docs/default-source/governance/competencies.pdf?sfvrsn=2.

American Library Association. *ALA's Core Competences of Librarianship*. Chicago, 2009. Accessed October 1, 2013. http://www.ala.org/educationcareers/sites/ala.org.educationcareers/files/content/careers/corecomp/corecompetences/finalcorecompstat09.pdf.

American Library Association. "Preservation Policy, Revised 2001." Accessed September 17, 2013. http://www.ala.org/alcts/resources/preserv/01alaprespolicy.

Anderson, Hazel, and John E. McIntyre. *Planning Manual for Disaster Control in Scottish Libraries and Record Offices*. Edinburgh: National Library of Scotland, 1985.

Anderson, Ian. "Archival Digitisation: Breaking Out of the Strong Box." In *Record Keeping in a Hybrid Environment: Managing the Creation, Use, Preservation and Disposal of Unpublished Information Objects in Context*, edited by Alistair Tough and Michael Moss, 203–25. Oxford, UK: Chandos, 2006.

Appelbaum, Barbara. *Guide to Environmental Protection of Collections*. Madison, CT: Sound View Press, 1991.

Association for Library Collections and Technical Services. *Minimum Digitization Capture Recommendations*. June 2013. Accessed September 24, 2013. http://www.ala.org/alcts/resources/preserv/minimum-digitization-capture-recommendations.

Association of College and Research Libraries. "Guidelines: Competencies for Special Collections Professionals, approved by the ACRL Board, July 1, 2008." Accessed October 1, 2013. http://www.ala.org/acrl/standards/comp4specollect#preservation.

Association of Moving Image Archivists. "Videotape Preservation Fact Sheets." http://www.amianet.org/resources-and-publications/documents-publications (available only to members).

Association of Research Libraries. *Sound Savings: Preserving Audio Collections*. Washington, DC: ARL, 2004. Accessed September 28, 2013. http://www.arl.org/storage/documents/publications/sound-savings.pdf.

Baker, Cathleen A. *From the Hand to the Machine: Nineteenth-Century American Paper and Mediums: Technologies, Materials, and Conservation*. Ann Arbor, MI: Legacy Press, 2010.

Baker, Cathleen A., and Randy Silverman. "Misperceptions about White Gloves." *International Preservation News* 37 (2005): 4–9. Accessed July 8, 2013. http://archive.ifla.org/VI/4/news/ipnn37.pdf.

Baker, Paul R., and Daniel J. Benny. *The Complete Guide to Physical Security*. Boca Raton, FL: Auerbach Publications, 2012.

Balloffet, Nelly, and Jenny Hille. *Preservation and Conservation for Libraries and Archives*. Chicago: American Library Association, 2004.

Bansa, Helmut. "The Conservation of Library Collections in Tropical and Sub-Tropical Conditions." *IFLA Journal* 7 (1981): 264–67.

Barger, Susan M., and William B. White. *The Daguerreotype: Nineteenth-Century Technology and Modern Science*. Baltimore: Johns Hopkins University Press, 2000.

Barrow, W. J. *The Manufacture and Testing of Durable Book Papers*. Richmond: Virginia State Library, 1960.

Bastian, Jeannette, Michèle Cloonan, and Ross Harvey. "From Teacher to Learner to User: Developing a Digital Stewardship Pedagogy." *Library Trends* 59 (2011): 607–22.

Batterham, Ian. *The Office Copying Revolution*. Canberra, ACT: National Archives of Australia, 2008.

Battin, Patricia. "From Preservation to Access: Paradigm for the Nineties." *IFLA Journal* 19 (1993): 367–73. doi: 10.1177/034003529301900406.

Baynes-Cope, A. D. *Caring for Books and Documents*. 2nd ed. London: British Library, 1989.

Benny, Daniel J. *Cultural Property Security: Protecting Museums, Historic Sites, Archives, and Libraries*. Boca Raton, FL: CRC Press, 2012.

Benson, Richard. *The Printed Picture*. New York: Museum of Modern Art, 2008.

Besser, Howard. "Archiving Media from the Occupy Movement: Trying to Involve Participants in Making Their Creations More Preservable." Paper presented at the American Library Association Conference, Seattle, WA, January 26, 2013. Accessed September 24, 2013. http://besser.tsoa.nyu.edu/howard/Talks/12ala-occupy-seattle-outreach.pdf.

Bigourdan, Jean-Louis, Liz Coffey, and Dwight Swanson. *Film Forever: The Home Film Preservation Guide*. Accessed October 12, 2013. http://www.filmforever.org.

Blades, Nigel, Tadj Oreszczyn, Bill Bordass, and May Cassar. *Guidelines on Pollution Control in Heritage Buildings*. London: Council for Museums, Archives and Libraries, 2000. Accessed October 7, 2013. http://discovery.ucl.ac.uk/2443/1/2443.pdf.

Blue Ribbon Task Force on Sustainable Digital Preservation and Access. *Sustainable Economics for a Digital Planet: Ensuring Long-Term Access to Digital Information*. San Diego, CA: Task Force, 2010. Accessed September 24, 2013. http://brtf.sdsc.edu/biblio/BRTF_Final_Report.pdf.

Borri Audio Laboratories. "Cylinder Record Identification." Accessed September 28, 2013. http://members.tripod.com/edison_1/id16.html.

Borri Audio Laboratories. "Playing, Recording and Shaving Cylinders." Accessed September 28, 2013. http://members.tripod.com/edison_1/id7.html.

Boston, George. *Memory of the World: Safeguarding the Documentary Heritage, A Guide to Standards, Recommended Practices and Reference Literature Related to the Preservation of Documents of All Kinds*. Paris: UNESCO, 1998. Accessed October 4, 2013. http://unesdoc.unesco.org/images/0011/001126/112676eo.pdf.

Botticelli, Peter, Bruce Fulton, Richard Pearce-Moses, Christine Szuter, and Pete Watters. "Educating Digital Curators: Challenges and Opportunities." *International Journal of Digital Curation* 6 (2011): 146–64.

Breen, Majella, Gila Flam, Isabelle Giannattasio, Per Holst, Pio Pellizzari, and Dietrich Schüller. *Task Force to Establish Selection Criteria for Analogue and Digital Audio Contents for Transfer to Data Formats for Preservation Purposes*. Aarhus: International Association of Sound and Audiovisual Archives, 2004. Accessed October 4, 2013. http://www.iasa-web.org/sites/default/files/downloads/publications/taskforce.pdf.

British Library Preservation Advisory Centre. *National Library of Ireland: Preservation Assessment Survey Case Study*. Accessed October 1, 2013. http://www.bl.uk/blpac/pdf/nli.pdf.

Brothers, Peter. "Magnetic Tapes Can Survive Flood Exposure." SPECS BROS. Accessed October 5, 2013. http://www.specsbros.com/h_flood.htm.

Brown, Adrian. *Care, Handling and Storage of Removable Media*. Digital Preservation Guidance Note 3. London: National Archives, 2008. Accessed October 9, 2013. http://www.nationalarchives.gov.uk/documents/information-management/removable-media-care.pdf.

Brown, Adrian. *Practical Digital Preservation: A How-to Guide for Organizations of Any Size*. London: Facet, 2013.

Brown, Adrian, *Selecting File Formats for Long-Term Preservation*. Digital Preservation Guidance Note 1. London: National Archives, 2008. Accessed September 24, 2013. http://www.nationalarchives.gov.uk/documents/selecting-file-formats.pdf.

Brown, Heather. *Training in Preservation Microfilming: Physical Management and Storage of Micro-forms*. Canberra, ACT: National Library of Australia, 2003. Accessed September 27, 2013, 2013. http://www.nla.gov.au/sites/default/files/module9sc.pdf.

Brown, Heather, et al. "The Role of Microfilm in Digital Preservation." In *DCC Digital Curation Reference Manual*. Glasgow: HATII, 2011. Accessed March 1, 2013. http://www.dcc.ac.uk/sites/default/files/documents/Microfilm_2011_Final.pdf.

Buck, Rebecca A., and Jean Allman Gilmore, eds. *MRM5: Museum Registration Methods*. 5th ed. Washington, DC: AAM Press, 2010.

Byers, Fred R. *Care and Handling of CDs and DVDs: A Guide for Librarians and Archivists*. Washington, DC: Council on Library and Information Resources, 2003. Accessed September 29, 2013. http://www.clir.org/pubs/abstract/reports/pub121.

Caplan, Priscilla. "At the Nexus of Analog and Digital: A Symposium for Preservation Educators, School of Information, University of Michigan, June 5–7, 2011, Panel 1: Definitions." *Preservation, Digital Technology and Culture*, forthcoming.

Carden, Michael. "Digital Archiving at the National Archives of Australia: Putting Principles into Practice." Paper presented at the International Council on Archives Congress, Brisbane, August 20–24, 2012. Accessed September 17, 2013. http://www.naa.gov.au/about-us/partnerships/conferences/michael-carden-digital-archiving.aspx.

Carr, David. *The Promise of Cultural Institutions*. Walnut Creek, MD: AltaMira Press, 2003.

Casey, Mike. *FACET: Format Characteristics and Preservation Problems*. Bloomington: Indiana University, 2007. Accessed October 4, 2013. http://www.dlib.indiana.edu/projects/sound directions/facet/facet_formats.pdf.

Casey, Mike, Patrick Feaster, and Alan Burdette. *Media Preservation Survey: A Report*. Bloomington: Indiana University, 2009. Accessed October 4, 2013. http://www.indiana.edu/~medpres/documents/iub_media_preservation_survey_FINALwww.pdf.

Casey, Mike, and Bruce Gordon. *Sound Directions: Best Practice for Audio Preservation*. Bloomington: Indiana University; Cambridge, MA: Harvard University, 2007. Accessed September 28, 2013. http://www.dlib.indiana.edu/projects/sounddirections/papersPresent/sd_bp_07.pdf.

Cassaro, James P. *Planning and Caring for Library Audio Facilities*. Canton, MA: Music Library Association, 1989.

Chancellor, Gordon, John van Wyhe, and Kees Rookmaaker. "Darwin's *Beagle* Field Notebooks (1831–1836)." *Darwin Online*. Accessed September 24, 2013. http://darwin-online.org.uk/EditorialIntroductions/Chancellor_fieldNotebooks.html.

Checkley-Scott, Caroline, and Dave Thompson. *Wellcome Library Preservation Policy for Materials Held in Collections*. London: Wellcome Library, 2007. Accessed October 1, 2013. http://wellcomelibrary.org/content/documents/policy-documents/preservation-policy.

Churchill College, Cambridge. "Preservation Policy." Updated 2011. Accessed October 2, 2013. http://www.chu.cam.ac.uk/archives/about/preservation.php.

Clemens, Raymond, and Timothy Graham. *Introduction to Manuscript Studies*. Ithaca, NY: Cornell University Press, 2007.

Clifton, Gerard. "Risk and the Preservation Management of Digital Collections." *International Preservation News* 36 (2005): 21–23. Accessed September 17, 2013. http://archive.ifla.org/VI/4/news/ipnn36.pdf.

Cloonan, Michèle Valerie. "The Preservation of Knowledge." *Library Trends* 41 (1993): 594–605.

Commission on Preservation and Access. *Annual Report, July 1, 1989–June 30, 1990*. Washington, DC: CPA, 1990.

Consultative Committee for Space Data Systems. *Reference Model for an Open Archival Information System (OAIS): Recommended Practice, CCSDS 650.0-M-2.* Washington, DC: CCSDS, 2012. Accessed September 16, 2013. http://public.ccsds.org/publications/archive/650x0m2.pdf.

Conway, Paul. "The Relevance of Preservation in a Digital World." Andover, MA: Northeast Document Conservation Center, 2007. Accessed September 16, 2013. http://www.nedcc.org/free-resources/preservation-leaflets/6.-reformatting/6.4-the-relevance-of-preservation-in-a-digital-world.

Dalton, Steve. "Microfilm and Microfiche." Andover, MA: Northeast Documentation Conservation Center, 2007. Accessed September 27, 2013. http://www.nedcc.org/free-resources/preservation-leaflets/6.-reformatting/6.1-microfilm-and-microfiche.

Daniel, Eric D., C. Denis Mee, and Mark H. Clark, eds. *Magnetic Recording: The First 100 Years.* New York: IEEE Press, 1999.

Daniels, Frank. "Indian 78rpm Single Releases: Identification and Price Guide." Accessed September 28, 2013. http://heroinc.hostingsiteforfree.com/btls/in/in78.htm.

"Design Is Selected for *Times* Capsule." *New York Times*, December 2, 1999. Accessed September 24, 2013. http://www.nytimes.com/1999/12/02/arts/design-is-selected-for-times-capsule.html.

Digital Curation Centre. "DCC Curation Lifecycle Model." Accessed September 16, 2013. http://www.dcc.ac.uk/resources/curation-lifecycle-model.

Digital Curation Centre. "List of Standards." Accessed September 24, 2013. http://www.dcc.ac.uk/resources/metadata-standards/list.

Digital Preservation Coalition. *Preservation Management of Digital Materials: The Handbook.* York: DPC, 2008. Accessed October 8, 2013. http://www.dpconline.org/pages/handbook.

Diringer, David. *The Book Before Printing.* New York: Dover, 1982.

Dumont, J., J. Johansen, and G. Kilander. "Handling and Storage of Recorded Videotape." *EBU Technical Review*, 254 (1992): 41–50.

Eastman Kodak Company. The Book of Film Care. 2nd ed. Rochester, NY: Motion Picture and Television Imaging, Eastman Kodak Company, 1992.

Edson, Gary, and David Dean. *The Handbook for Museums.* London and New York: Routledge, 1994.

Eldridge, Susan. "Digital Audiotapes: Their Preservation and Conversion." 2010. Accessed October 4, 2013. http://siarchives.si.edu/sites/default/files/pdfs/digitalAudioTapesPreservation2010_0.pdf.

Elford, Douglas, Lisa Jeong-Reuss, Somaya Langley, and Melanie Wilkinson. "Getting the Whole Picture: Finding a Common Language Between Digital Preservation and Conservation." National Library of Australia Staff Papers 2012. Accessed September 17, 2013. http://www.nla.gov.au/openpublish/index.php/nlasp/article/viewArticle/2458.

Elkington, Nancy E., ed. *RLG Archives Microfilming Manual.* Mountain View, CA: Research Libraries Group, 1994.

Elkington, Nancy E., ed. *RLG Preservation Microfilming Handbook.* Mountain View, CA: Research Libraries Group, 1992.

Erway, Ricky. *Swatting the Long Tail of Digital Media: A Call for Collaboration.* Dublin, OH: OCLC Research, 2012. Accessed September 17, 2013. http://www.oclc.org/content/dam/research/publications/library/2012/2012-08.pdf.

European Confederation of Conservator-Restorers' Organisations. "E.C.C.O. Professional Guidelines." Adopted March 1, 2002. Accessed September 17, 2013. http://www.ecco-eu.org/about-e.c.c.o./professional-guidelines.html, Article 6.

*Facsimiles of the Declaration of Independence and the Treaty of Waitangi*. Wellington, New Zealand: Government Printer, 1976.

Farrington, Jim. "Preventive Maintenance for Audio Discs and Tapes." *MLA Notes* 48 (1991): 437–38.

Federal Agencies Digital Guidelines Initiative. *Guidelines*. Accessed September 24, 2013. http://www.digitizationguidelines.gov/guidelines/.

"Fiber Reference Image Library." Accessed September 27, 2013. https://fril.osu.edu.

Fischer, Monique. "A Short Guide to Film Base Photographic Materials: Identification, Care, and Duplication." Andover, MA: Northeast Document Conservation Center, 2012. Accessed October 6, 2013. http://www.nedcc.org/free-resources/preservation-leaflets/5.-photographs/5.1-a-short-guide-to-film-base-photographic-materials-identification,-care,-and-duplication.

Foot, Mirjam M. *Building a Preservation Policy*. London: British Library Preservation Advisory Centre, 2013. Accessed October 1, 2013. http://www.bl.uk/blpac/pdf/blocks.pdf.

Foot, Mirjam M. "Towards a Preservation Policy for European Research Libraries." *Liber Quarterly* 9 (1999): 323–26.

Forde, Helen. "Preservation Policies—Who Needs Them?" *Journal of the Society of Archivists* 18 (1997): 165–73.

Forde, Helen, and Jonathan Rhys-Lewis. *Preserving Archives*. 2nd ed. London: Facet, 2013.

*Forensics Wiki*. Accessed October 9, 2013. http://www.forensicswiki.org/wiki/Main_Page.

Forgas, Letitia. "The Preservation of Videotape: Review and Implications for Libraries and Archives." *Libri* 47 (1997): 43–56.

Fox, Lisa L., ed. *Preservation Microfilming: A Guide for Librarians and Archivists*. 2nd ed. Chicago: American Library Association, 1996.

Gallo, Max. *The Poster in History*. New York: American Heritage Publishing Company, 1974.

Gardner, Helen, and Fred S. Kleiner. *Gardner's Art through the Ages: A Global History*. 13th ed. Australia; United States: Wadsworth/Cengage Learning, 2010.

Gascoigne, Bamber. *How to Identify Prints: A Complete Guide to Manual and Mechanical Processes from Woodcut to Ink Jet*. New York: Thames and Hudson, 1986.

George Eastman House. *Notes on Photographs*. Accessed October 4, 2013. http://notesonphotographs.org.

Gertz, Janet. "Preservation and Selection for Digitization." Andover, MA: Northeast Document Conservation Center, 2007. Accessed September 17, 2013. http://www.nedcc.org/free-resources/preservation-leaflets/6.-reformatting/6.6-preservation-and-selection-for-digitization.

Gill, Tony, Anne J. Gilliland, Maureen Whalen, and Mary S. Woodley. *Introduction to Metadata*, Version 3.0. Los Angeles, CA: Getty Research Institute, 2008. Accessed September 24, 2013. http://www.getty.edu/research/publications/electronic_publications/intrometadata/index.html.

"Good Resolutions." *Abbey Newsletter* 12, no. 2 (1988): 29–31.

Greenburg, Zach O'Malley. "Vinyl Continues Unlikely Recovery, According to New Numbers." *Forbes*, January 18, 2012. Accessed September 28, 2013. http://www.forbes.com/sites/zackomalleygreenburg/2012/01/18/vinyl-continues-unlikely-recovery-according-to-new-numbers.

Greene, Mark A., and Dennis Meissner. "More Product, Less Process." *American Archivist* 68 (2005): 208–63.

Griffith, Anna. "Learning from the Holdings Protection Team at the National Archives and Records Administration (NARA), USA." *Australian Library Journal* 62 (2013): 148–57.

Gwinn, Nancy, ed. *Preservation Microfilming*. Chicago: ALA, 1987.

Harvey, Ross. *Digital Curation: A How-to-Do-It Manual.* New York: Neal-Schuman, 2010.

Harvey, Ross. "Instalment on 'Appraisal and Selection,' January 2007." In *DCC Curation Reference Manual.* Accessed September 17, 2013. http://www.dcc.ac.uk/webfm_send/121.

Harvey, Ross. *Preservation in Libraries: Principles, Strategies, and Practices for Librarians.* London: Bowker-Saur, 1993.

Harvey, Ross. *Preserving Digital Materials.* München: K. G. Saur, 2005.

Harvey, Ross. *Preserving Digital Materials.* 2nd ed. Berlin: De Gruyter Saur, 2012.

Harvey, Ross, and Martha Mahard. "Mapping the Preservation Landscape for the Twenty-First Century." *Preservation, Digital Technology and Culture* 42 (2013): 5–16. doi: 10.1515/pdtc-2013-0002.

Hatchfield, Pamela. *Pollutants in the Museum Environment.* London: Archetype Publications, 2007.

Heckman, Heather. "Burn After Viewing, or, Fire in the Vaults: Nitrate Decomposition and Combustibility." *American Archivist* 73 (2010): 483–506.

Henderson, Jane. *Environment.* London: British Library Preservation Advisory Centre, 2013. Accessed October 7, 2013. http://www.bl.uk/blpac/pdf/environment.pdf.

Heritage Preservation. *The Emergency Response and Salvage Wheel.* Washington, DC: Heritage Preservation, 2011.

Hess, Richard. "Tape Degradation Factors and Challenges in Predicting Tape Life." *ARSC Journal* 39 (2008): 240–74.

Hess, Richard, Joe Iraci, and Kimberley Flak. *The Digitization of Audio Tapes.* Technical Bulletin 30. Ottawa, ON: Canadian Conservation Institute, 2013.

Higginbotham, Barbra Buckner. *Our Past Preserved: A History of American Library Preservation 1876–1910.* Boston: G. K. Hall, 1990.

Hodell, Chuck. *ISD from the Ground Up: A No-Nonsense Approach to Instructional Design*, 3rd ed. Alexandria, VA: ASTD Press, 2011.

Hoeven, Hans van der, and Joan van Albada. *Lost Memory: Libraries and Archives Destroyed in the Twentieth Century.* Paris: UNESCO, 1996. Accessed October 6, 2013. http://unesdoc.unesco.org/images/0010/001055/105557e.pdf.

Hoffman, Frank, ed. *Encyclopedia of Recorded Sound, Volume 1. Instantaneous Recordings.* New York: Routledge, 2005.

Hofman, Hans. "Rethinking the Archival Function in the Digital Era." Paper presented at the International Council on Archives Congress, Brisbane, August 20–24, 2012, accessed January 29, 2014, http://ica2012.ica.org/files/pdf/Full%20papers%20upload/ica12final00187.pdf.

Holben Ellis, Margaret. *The Care of Prints and Drawings.* Nashville, TN: AASLH Press, 1987.

Hoskins, Lesley. *The Papered Wall: History, Pattern, and Techniques.* New York: Abrams, 1994.

Hunter, Dard. *Papermaking: The History and Technique of an Ancient Craft.* New York: Dover, 1978.

Hutchins, Jane K. *First Aid for Art: Essential Salvage Techniques.* Stockbridge, MA: Hard Press Editions, 2006.

"IFLA Permanent Paper Resolutions." *Conservation Administration News* 40 (1990): 22.

Image Permanence Institute. "Calculators." Accessed October 12, 2013. https://www.imagepermanenceinstitute.org/resources/calculators.

Image Permanence Institute. *Graphics Atlas.* Accessed October 4, 2013. http://www.graphicsatlas.org.

Image Permanence Institute. *IPI's Guide to Sustainable Preservation Practices for Managing Storage Environments.* Rochester, NY: IPI, 2012.

Indiana University Bloomington Media Preservation Initiative Task Force. *Meeting the Challenge of Media Preservation: Strategies and Solutions.* Bloomington, 2011. Accessed October 1, 2013. http://www.indiana.edu/~medpres/documents/iu_mpi_report_public.pdf.

Integrated Pest Management Working Group. *MuseumPests.net*. Accessed September 27, 2013. http://www.museumpests.net.

International Association of Sound and Audiovisual Archives. *Guidelines on the Production and Preservation of Digital Audio Objects*. 2nd ed. Auckland Park: IASA, 2009. Accessed September 28, 2013. http://www.iasa-web.org/tc04/audio-preservation.

International Council of Museums Committee on the Training of Professionals. "ICOM Curricula Guidelines for Museum Professional Development." Accessed October 1, 2013. http://museumstudies.si.edu/ICOM-ICTOP/comp.htm.

International Foundation for Arts Research. "Provenance Guide." Accessed September 29, 2013. http://www.ifar.org/provenance_guide.php.

InterPARES 2 Project. *Creator Guidelines: Making and Maintaining Digital Materials: Guidelines for Individuals*. Accessed September 24, 2013. http://www.interpares.org/ip2/display_file .cfm?doc=ip2(pub)creator_guidelines_booklet.pdf.

Iraci, Joe. *Disaster Recovery of Modern Information Carriers: Compact Discs, Magnetic Tapes and Magnetic Disks*. Technical Bulletin 25. Ottawa, ON: Canadian Conservation Institute, 2002.

Iraci, Joe. "Relative Stabilities of Optical Disc Formats." *Restaurator* 26 (2005): 134–50.

Iraci, Joe. *Remedies for Deteriorated or Damaged Modern Information Carriers*. Technical Bulletin 27. Ottawa, ON: Canadian Conservation Institute, 2005.

"'Irreplaceable' Nazi-era Documents Stolen from Danish Archives." *Telegraph*, October 25, 2012. Accessed September 30, 2013. http://www.telegraph.co.uk/history/world-war-two/9634459/Irreplaceable-Nazi-era-documents-stolen-from-Danish-archives.html.

Jimenez, Mona, and Liss Platt. *Videotape Identification and Assessment Guide*. Austin: Texas Commission on the Arts, 2004. Accessed October 5, 2013. http://www.arts.texas.gov/wp-content/uploads/2012/04/video.pdf.

JISC. "Digital Preservation Briefing Paper." November 20, 2006. Accessed September 16, 2013. http://www.jisc.ac.uk/publications/briefingpapers/2006/pub_digipreservationbp.aspx.

JISC Digital Media. *An Introduction to Metadata*. Accessed September 24, 2013. http://www .jiscdigitalmedia.ac.uk/guide/an-introduction-to-metadata.

Jolie, Edward A., Thomas F. Lynch, Phil R. Geib, and J. M. Adovasio. "Cordage, Textiles, and the Late Pleistocene Peopling of the Andes." *Current Anthropology* 52 (2011): 285–96.

Jürgens, Martin C. *The Digital Print: Identification and Preservation*. Los Angeles: Getty Conservation Institute, 2009.

Karasti, H., K. S. Baker, and E. Halkola. "Enriching the Notion of Data Curation in E-Science: Data Managing and Information Infrastructuring in the Long Term Ecological Research (LTER) Network." *Computer Supported Cooperative Work* 15 (2006): 321–58.

Kattelle, Alan D. *Home Movies: A History of the American Industry, 1897–1979*. Nashua, NH: Transition Publishing, 2000.

Keck, Caroline K. *A Handbook on the Care of Paintings*. Nashville, TN: American Association for State and Local History, 1965.

Keck, Caroline K. *How to Take Care of Your Paintings*. New York: Scribner, 1978.

Kenney, Anne R., Oya Y. Rieger, and Richard Entlich. *Moving Theory into Practice: Digital Imaging Tutorial*. Ithaca, NY: Cornell University Library Research Department, 2000–2003. Accessed September 24, 2013. http://www.library.cornell.edu/preservation/tutorial/contents.html.

Kissel, Eléonore, and Erin Vigneau. *Architectural Photoreproductions: A Manual for Identification and Care*. New Castle, DE: Oak Knoll Press and the New York Botanical Garden, 2009.

Knight, Barry. "Multi-Spectral Imaging for the Codex Sinaiticus." Accessed September 16, 2013. http://codexsinaiticus.org/en/project/conservation_msi.aspx.

Kodak. "Broadening the Impact of Pictures." 2009. Accessed October 12, 2013. http://www.kodak
.com/country/US/en/corp/kodakHistory/impactOfPictures.shtml.

Kodak. "Chronology of Motion Picture Films." Accessed October 12, 2013. http://motion.kodak
.com/motion/About/Chronology_Of_Film/index.htm.

Kodak. "Storage and Handling of Processed Nitrate Film." Accessed October 12, 2013. http://
motion.kodak.com/motion/Support/Technical_Information/Storage/storage_nitrate.htm.

Krtalic, Maja, and Damir Hasenay. "Exploring a Framework for Comprehensive and Successful
Preservation Management in Libraries." *Journal of Documentation* 68 (2012): 353–77.

Lavédrine, Bertrand. *Photographs of the Past: Process and Preservation*. Los Angeles: Getty Conservation Institute, 2007.

Lavédrine, Bertrand. *Preventive Conservation of Photograph Collections*. Los Angeles: Getty Conservation Institute, 2003.

Lewis, Paul. "Preservation Takes Rare Manuscripts from the Public." *New York Times*, January
25, 1987. Accessed October 1, 2013. http://www.nytimes.com/1987/01/25/books/preservation
-takes-rare-manuscripts-from-the-public.html.

Library of Congress. "Frequently Asked Questions: Audio Recording and Moving Image Media."
Accessed September 17, 2013. http://www.loc.gov/preservation/about/faqs/audio.html.

Library of Congress. "The History of the Edison Cylinder Phonograph." Accessed September 28,
2013. http://memory.loc.gov/ammem/edhtml/edcyldr.html.

Library of Congress. "Standards at the Library of Congress." Accessed September 24, 2013.
http://www.loc.gov/standards.

Library of Congress National Recording Preservation Board. "Audio Preservation Bibliography." Accessed September 28, 2013. http://www.loc.gov/rr/record/nrpb/nrpb-presbib
.html.

Library of Congress National Recording Preservation Board. *The Library of Congress National
Recording Preservation Plan*. Washington, DC: Council on Library and Information
Resources and Library of Congress, 2012. Accessed September 28, 2013. http://www.loc.gov/
rr/record/nrpb/PLAN%20pdf.pdf.

Ling, Ted. *Solid, Safe, Secure: Building Archive Repositories in Australia*. Canberra, ACT: National
Archives of Australia, 1998.

*The Little Reference Guide for Small Videotape Collections*. Amsterdam: Little Archives of the
World Foundation/ECPA, 2008. Accessed October 5, 2013. http://www.little-archives.net/
guide/content/home.html.

LOCKSS. "Preservation Principles." Accessed September 17, 2013. http://www.lockss.org/about/
principles/.

Mannon, Melissa. *Cultural Heritage Collaborators: A Manual for Community Documentation*. Bedford, NH: ArchivesInfo Press, 2010.

Marlow, Eugene, and Eugene Secunda. *Shifting Time and Space: The Story of Videotape*. New
York: Praeger, 1991.

Matassa, Freda. *Museum Collections Management: A Handbook*. London: Facet, 2011.

Mayfield, Kendra. "How to Preserve Digital Art." *Wired*, July 23, 2002. Accessed September 24,
2013. http://www.wired.com/culture/lifestyle/news/2002/07/53712.

Mebold, Anke, and Charles Tepperman. "Resurrecting the Lost History of 28mm Film in North
America." *Film History* 15 (2003): 137–51.

Mecklenburg, Marion F. *Determining the Acceptable Ranges of Relative Humidity and Temperature in Museums and Galleries, Parts 1 and 2*. 2007. Accessed September 25, 2013. http://www
.si.edu/mci/downloads/reports/mecklenburg-part1-RH.pdf.

Mee, C. Denis, and Eric D. Daniel, eds., *Magnetic Storage Handbook*, 2nd ed. New York: McGraw-Hill, 1996.

Merrill-Oldham, Jan, and Paul Parisi. *Guide to the ANSI/NISO/LBI Library Binding Standard, ANSI/NISO/LBI Z39.78-2000*. Chicago: Preservation and Reformatting Section, Association for Library Collections and Technical Services, 2008.

Meyer, Rebecca, Shannon Struble, and Phyllis Catsikis. "Sustainability: A Literature Review." In *Preserving Our Heritage: Perspectives from Antiquity to the Digital Age*, edited by Michèle Cloonan. Chicago: ALA Neal Schuman, 2014.

Millard, Andre. *America on Record: A History of Recorded Sound*, 2nd ed. New York: Cambridge University Press, 2005.

Miller, Julia. *Books Will Speak Plain*. Ann Arbor, MI: Legacy Press, 2010.

Moore, Michelle. "Conservation Documentation and the Implications of Digitisation." *Journal of Conservation and Museum Studies* 7 (2001): 1–19.

Morton, David. "Armour Research Foundation and the Wire Recorder: How Academic Entrepreneurs Fail." *Technology and Culture* 39 (1998): 213–44.

Museums and Galleries Commission. *Standards in the Museum Care of Costume and Textiles Collections*. London, 1998.

"NARA Returns Landau Docs." *History News Network*, May 14, 2013. Accessed September 30, 2013. http://hnn.us/articles/nara-returns-landau-docs.

The National Archives. *Preservation Policy*. London, 2009. Accessed October 1, 2013. http://www.nationalarchives.gov.uk/documents/tna-corporate-preservation-policy-2009-website-version.pdf.

National Archives and Records Administration. *National Archives Gift Collection Acquisition Policy: Motion Pictures and Sound and Video Recordings* (General Information Leaflet 34). Washington, DC: 1990. Accessed October 1, 2013. http://www.archives.gov/publications/general-info-leaflets/34-media.html.

National Archives and Records Administration. *Preserving the Past to Protect the Future: the Strategic Plan of the National Archives and Records Administration, 2006–2016*. Revised 2009. Washington, DC, 2009. Accessed October 1, 2013. http://www.archives.gov/about/plans-reports/strategic-plan/2009/nara-strategic-plan-2006-2016-final.pdf.

National Archives and Records Administration. "Recover Lost and Stolen Documents." Accessed September 30, 2013. http://www.archives.gov/research/recover/.

National Archives and Records Administration, Office of the Federal Register. *Code of Federal Regulations Title 36: Parks, Forests, and Public Property, Part 1254. Using Records and Donated Historical Materials*. Washington, DC, 2012. Accessed September 30, 2013. http://www.gpo.gov/fdsys/pkg/CFR-2012-title36-vol3/xml/CFR-2012-title36-vol3-part1254.xml.

National Film Preservation Foundation. *The Film Preservation Guide: The Basics for Archives, Libraries and Museums*. San Francisco, CA, 2004. Accessed October 12, 2013. http://www.filmpreservation.org/preservation-basics/the-film-preservation-guide.

National Library of Australia. *Guidelines for the Preservation of Digital Heritage*. Paris: UNESCO Information Society Division, 2003. Accessed September 18, 2013. http://unesdoc.unesco.org/images/0013/001300/130071e.pdf.

National Library of Australia. *Preservation Copying of Collection Materials Policy*, June 2007. Accessed September 18, 2013. http://www.nla.gov.au/policy-and-planning/preservation-copying.

National Library of Australia. "Preservation Policy." Reviewed 2009. Accessed October 2, 2013. http://www.nla.gov.au/policy-and-planning/preservation-policy.

National Museum Directors' Council. "NMDC Guiding Principles for Reducing Museums' Carbon Footprint." 2009. Accessed October 7, 2013. http://www.nationalmuseums.org.uk/media/documents/what_we_do_documents/guiding_principles_reducing_carbon_footprint.pdf.

National Museum of American History. "Early Sound Recording Collection and Sound Recovery Project." Accessed September 28, 2013. http://americanhistory.si.edu/press/fact-sheets/early-sound-recording-collection-and-sound-recovery-project.

National Park Service. "Appendix L: Curatorial Care of Easel Paintings." In *Museum Handbook*, Part I. Washington, DC: National Park Service, Museum Management Program, 2000. Accessed September 29, 2013. http://www.nps.gov/history/museum/publications/MHI/AppendL.pdf.

National Park Service. "Care and Security of Rare Books." *Conserve O Gram* 19/2 (1993). Accessed September 30, 2013. http://www.nps.gov/history/museum/publications/conserveogram/cons_toc.html.

National Park Service. "Cold Storage: A Long-Term Preservation Strategy for Film-Based Photographic Materials." Accessed November 5, 2013. http://www.nps.gov/history/museum/coldstorage/html/index.html.

National Park Service. "Digital Storage Media." *Conserve O Gram* 22/5 (2010). Accessed September 30, 2013. http://www.nps.gov/history/museum/publications/conserveogram/22-05.pdf.

National Park Service. "Museum Management: Archivist Track: Essential Competencies." Accessed October 1, 2013. http://www.nps.gov/training/npsonly/rsc/archivst.htm.

National Trust. *Manual of Housekeeping*. Oxford, UK: Butterworth-Heinemann, 2006.

Netz, Reviel, and William Noel. *The Archimedes Codex: How a Medieval Prayer Book Is Revealing the True Genius of Antiquity's Greatest Scientist*. Boston: Da Capo Press, 2007.

New York Public Library. "The Medieval and Renaissance Western Manuscripts of the New York Public Library." Accessed October 2, 2013. http://www.nypl.org/locations/tid/36/node/29598.

NISO. *Understanding Metadata*. Bethesda, MD: NISO Press, 2004. Accessed September 24, 2013. http://www.niso.org/publications/press/UnderstandingMetadata.pdf.

Ogden, Sherelyn. *Preservation Planning: Guidelines for Writing a Long-Range Plan*. Washington, DC: American Association of Museums and the Northeast Document Conservation Center, 1997.

Ogden, Sherelyn. *The Storage of Art on Paper: A Basic Guide for Institutions*. Champaign-Urbana, IL: Graduate School of Library and Information Science, University of Illinois, 2001.

Paradigm Project. *Workbook on Digital Private Papers*. Accessed September 24, 2013. http://www.paradigm.ac.uk/workbook.

Pearse-Moses, Richard. *A Glossary of Archival and Records Terminology*. Chicago: Society of American Archivists. Accessed September 17, 2013. http://www2.archivists.org/glossary.

Pearson, David. "Preserve or Preserve Not, There is No Try: Some Dilemmas Relating to Personal Digital Archiving." Presentation at DigCCurr 2009: Digital Curation Practice, Promise and Prospects, April 1–3, 2009, Chapel Hill, NC. Accessed September 17, 2013. http://www.ils.unc.edu/digccurr2009/6a-pearson.pdf.

Penichon, Sylvie. *Twentieth-Century Color Photographs: Identification and Care*. Los Angeles: Getty Conservation Institute, 2013.

Phillips, Jessica. "Educating the Community: Preserving Tomorrow's Treasures Today." In *Preserving Local Writers, Genealogy, Photographs, Newspapers, and Related Materials*, edited by Carol Smallwood and Elaine Williams, 296–304. Lanham, MD: Scarecrow Press, 2012.

Pohlmann, Ken C. *The Compact Disc: A Handbook of Theory and Use*. Madison, WI: A-R Editions, 1989.

PrestoSpace. "Deliverable D14.1 Preservation Guide: General Guide to Audiovisual Preservation (Web Report)." 2006. Accessed October 1, 2013. http://prestospace.org/project/deliverables/D14-1.pdf.

Price, Lois Olcott. *Line, Shade, and Shadow: The Fabrication and Preservation of Architectural Drawings*. New Castle, DE: Oak Knoll Press.

Pritchard, Brian R. "Date Codes." Accessed October 12, 2013. http://www.brianpritchard.com/Date%20Codes.htm.

Rankin, Frank. "Implementing EDRMS and Shaping the Record." In *Record Keeping in a Hybrid Environment: Managing the Creation, Use, Preservation and Disposal of Unpublished Information Objects in Context*, edited by Alistair Tough and Michael Moss, 27–45. Oxford, UK: Chandos, 2006.

Reilly, James M. *IPI Storage Guide for Acetate Film*. Rochester, NY: Image Permanence Institute, 1993. Accessed October 12, 2013. https://www.imagepermanenceinstitute.org/webfm_send/299.

Reilly, James M. "Measuring Environmental Quality in Preservation." *Journal of Library Administration* 38 (2003): 135–40.

Reilly, James M. "Specifying Storage Environments in Libraries and Archives." In *From Gray Areas to Green Areas: Developing Sustainable Practices in Preservation Environments*, 2007, Symposium Proceedings, edited by Melissa Tedone. Austin, TX: Kilgarlin Center for Preservation of the Cultural Record, 2008.

Reitz, Joan. *ODLIS: Online Dictionary for Library and Information Science*. ABC CLIO. Accessed September 27, 2013. http://www.abc-clio.com/ODLIS/odlis_m.aspx.

Rendell, Caroline. "Preventive Conservation Solutions for Textile Collections." In *Textile Conservation: Advances in Practice*, edited by Frances Lennard and Patricia Ewer, 210–20. Oxford, UK: Elsevier, 2010.

Research Libraries Group. *RLG Preservation Manual*. 2nd ed. Stanford, CA, 1986.

Ritzenthaler, Mary Lynn. *Preserving Archives and Manuscripts*. 2nd ed. Chicago: Society for American Archivists, 2010.

RLG-NARA Task Force on Digital Repository Certification. *Trustworthy Repositories Audit & Certification: Criteria and Checklist*. Chicago: Center for Research Libraries, 2007. Accessed October 7, 2013. http://www.crl.edu/sites/default/files/attachments/pages/trac_0.pdf.

RLG/OCLC Working Group on Digital Archive Attributes. *Trusted Digital Repositories: Attributes and Responsibilities*. Mountain View, CA: Research Libraries Group, 2002.

Robinson, Jane, and Tuula Pardoe. *An Illustrated Guide to the Care of Costume and Textile Collections*. London: Council for Museums, Archives and Libraries, 2000.

Roland, Lena, and David Bawden. "The Future of History: Investigating the Preservation of Information in the Digital Age." *Library & Information History* 28 (2012): 220–36.

Rosenthal, David S. H. "Keeping Bits Safe: How Hard Can It Be?" *Communications of the ACM* 53 (11) (2010): 47–55. Accessed October 9, 2013. http://cacm.acm.org/magazines/2010/11/100620-keeping-bits-safe-how-hard-can-it-be/fulltext.

Saffady, William. *Micrographics: Technology for the 21st Century*. Prairie Village, KS: ARMA International, 2000.

Schüller, Dietrich. *Audio and Video Carriers: Recording Principles, Storage and Handling, Maintenance of Equipment, Format and Equipment Obsolescence*. Amsterdam: European Commission on Preservation and Access, 2007.

Schüller, Dietrich. *Audio and Video Carriers: Recording Principles, Storage and Handling, Maintenance of Equipment, Format and Equipment Obsolescence*, edited by George Boston. Training for Audiovisual Preservation in Europe, 2008. Accessed October 4, 2013. http://www.tape-online.net/docs/audio_and_video_carriers.pdf.

"Security in Museums and Galleries: Access to Collections: A Practical Guide." London: Arts Council England; Collections Trust, 2013. Accessed September 30, 2013. http://www.collectionslink.org.uk/media/com_form2content/documents/c1/a842/f6/PracticalGuide_Access_to_Collections_01.pdf.

"Security in Museums and Galleries: CCTV Systems: A Practical Guide." London: Arts Council England; Collections Trust, 2013. Accessed September 30, 2013. http://www.collectionslink.org.uk/media/com_form2content/documents/c1/a844/f6/PracticalGuide_CCTVsystems_02.pdf.

Shaw, Naomi L., Seth Shaw, Nancy Deromedi, Michael Shawcross, Cynthia Ghering, Lisa Schmidt, Michelle Belden, Jackie R. Esposito, Ben Goldman, and Tim Pyatt. *Managing Born-Digital Special Collections and Archival Materials* (SPEC Kit 329). Washington, DC: Association of Research Libraries, 2012.

Silence, Patricia. "Preventive Conservation at the Colonial Williamsburg Foundation." In *Textile Conservation: Advances in Practice*, edited by Frances Lennard and Patricia Ewer, 204–10. Oxford, UK: Elsevier, 2010.

Slide, Anthony. *Nitrate Won't Wait: A History of Film Preservation in the United States*. Jefferson, NC: McFarland, 1992.

Smith, Abby. "Authenticity and Affect: When Is a Watch Not a Watch?" *Library Trends* 52 (2003): 172–82.

Smith, Abby. *The Future of the Past: Preservation in American Research Libraries*. Washington, DC: Council on Library and Information Resources, 1999. Accessed September 17, 2013. http://www.clir.org/pubs/reports/pub82/pub82text.html.

Smithsonian. "Early Sound Recording Collection and Sound Recovery Project," *Newsdesk*, December 14, 2011. Accessed September 28, 2013, http://newsdesk.si.edu/factsheets/early-sound-recording-collection-and-sound-recovery-project.

Smithsonian Museum Conservation Institute. "Care of Acrylic Paintings." Accessed September 29, 2013. http://www.si.edu/mci/english/learn_more/taking_care/acrylic_paintings.html.

Smithsonian Museum Conservation Institute. "Caring for Your Paintings." Accessed September 29, 2013. http://www.si.edu/mci/english/learn_more/taking_care/care_painting.html.

Smithsonian Museum Conservation Institute. "Painting Conservation Glossary of Terms." Accessed September 29, 2013. http://www.si.edu/mci/english/learn_more/taking_care/painting_glossary.html.

Smithsonian Museum Conservation Institute. "What Is a Painting?" Accessed September 29, 2013. http://www.si.edu/mci/english/learn_more/taking_care/what_painting.html.

Society of American Archivists. "Guidelines for a Graduate Program in Archival Studies." Accessed October 1, 2013. http://www2.archivists.org/gpas.

Society of American Archivists. "SAA Core Values Statement and Code of Ethics." Approved May 2011. Accessed September 17, 2013. http://www2.archivists.org/statements/saa-core-values-statement-and-code-of-ethics.

Stamp, Jimmy. "3D Printing during the Renaissance." March 20, 2013. Accessed September 18, 2013. http://lifewithoutbuildings.net/2013/03/3d-printing-from-the-renaissance-to-today.html.

St.-Laurent, Gilles. "The Care and Handling of Recorded Sound Materials." January 1996. Accessed September 28, 2013. http://cool.conservation-us.org/byauth/st-laurent/care.html.

Strang, T. "Choices and Decisions." In *Symposium 2003: Preservation of Electronic Records: New Knowledge and Decision-Making, Ottawa, 15–18 September 2003: preprints.*

Strassberg, Richard. "Library and Archives Security." In *Preservation: Issues and Planning*, edited by Paul N. Banks and Roberta Pilette, 166–77. Chicago: American Library Association, 2000.

Street, Seán. "Recording Technologies and Strategies for British Radio Transmission before the 2nd World War." *Sound Journal*. Accessed September 28, 2013. http://www.kent.ac.uk/arts/sound-journal/street002.html.

Stroeker, Natasha, and René Vogels. *Survey Report on Digitisation in European Cultural Heritage Institutions 2012.* London: ENUMERATE Thematic Network, 2012. Accessed September 18, 2013. http://www.enumerate.eu/fileadmin/ENUMERATE/documents/ENUMERATE-Digitisation-Survey-2012.pdf.

Stuart, Barbara H. *Analytical Techniques in Materials Conservation*. Chichester, UK; Hoboken, NJ: John Wiley & Sons, 2007.

Stutz, Roger A., and Bruce C. Lamartine. "Estimating Archiving Costs for Engineering Records." Paper presented at the annual meeting of the American Association of Cost Engineering, Dallas, TX, July 1997. Accessed September 24, 2013. http://www.osti.gov/scitech/biblio/484529.

Sun Records. "Elvis Presley." Accessed September 28, 2013. http://www.sunrecords.com/artists/elvis-presley.

Swanson, Marianne, et al. *Contingency Planning Guide for Federal Information Systems*. Washington, DC: National Institute of Standards and Technology, 2010. Accessed November 5, 2013. http://csrc.nist.gov/publications/nistpubs/800-34-rev1/sp800-34-rev1_errata-Nov11-2010.pdf.

Task Force on Archiving of Digital Information. *Preserving Digital Information*. Washington, D.C.: Commission on Preservation and Access, 1996.

Task Force on the Artifact in Library Collections. *The Evidence in Hand: Report of the Task Force on the Artifact in Library Collections*. Washington, DC: Council on Library and Information Resources, 2001. Accessed October 9, 2013. http://www.clir.org/pubs/abstract//reports/pub103.

Tedone, Melissa, ed. *From Gray Areas to Green Areas: Developing Sustainable Practices in Preservation Environments, 2007, Symposium Proceedings*. Austin, TX: Kilgarlin Center for Preservation of the Cultural Record, 2008.

Teynac, Françoise, Pierre Nolot, and Jean-Denis Vivien. *Wallpaper: A History*. New York: Rizzoli, 1982.

Thomson, Garry. *The Museum Environment*, 2nd ed. London: Butterworth-Heinemann, 1986.

Thompson, Jack C. *Manuscript Inks*. Portland, OR: Caber Press, 1996.

Tímár-Balázsy, Ágnes, and Dinah Eastop. *Chemical Principles of Textile Conservation*. Oxford, UK: Butterworth-Heinemann, 1998.

"Timeline: Digital Technology and Preservation." Accessed October 9, 2013. http://www.dpworkshop.org/dpm-eng/timeline/viewall.html.

*To Preserve and Protect: The Strategic Stewardship of Cultural Resources: Essays from the Symposium Held at the Library of Congress October 30–31, 2000*. Washington, DC: Library of Congress, 2002.

Trinkaus-Randall, Gregor. *Protecting Your Collections: A Manual of Archival Security*. Chicago: Society of American Archivists, 1995.

Turpening, Patricia K. "Essential Elements for Starting a Library Preservation Program." *Abbey Newsletter* 26 (6) (2003). Accessed October 1, 2013. http://cool.conservation-us.org/byorg/abbey/an/an26/an26-6/an26-608.html.

UNESCO. *Guidelines on Preservation and Conservation Policies in Libraries and Archives Heritage*. Paris, 1990. Accessed October 1, 2013. http://unesdoc.unesco.org/images/0008/000863/086345eo.pdf.

UNESCO. "Mechanical Carriers." *Safeguarding our Documentary Heritage*. Accessed September 28, 2013. http://webworld.unesco.org/safeguarding/en/all_meca.htm.

University of Massachusetts Amherst Digital Creation and Preservation Working Group. *Digital Preservation Policy*. Amherst, MA, 2011. Accessed October 1, 2013. http://www.library.umass.edu/assets/aboutus/attachments/University-of-Massachusetts-Amherst-Libraries-Digital-Preservation-Policy3-18-2011-templated.pdf.

Valente, A. J. *Rag Paper Manufacture in the United States, 1801–1900*. Jefferson, NC: McFarland, 2010.

Valverde, María Fernanda. *Photographic Negatives: Nature and Evolution of Processes*. 2nd ed. Rochester, NY: Advanced Residency Program in Photograph Conservation, 2005. Accessed October 4, 2013. https://www.imagepermanenceinstitute.org/webfm_send/302.

Van Bogart, John. *Magnetic Tape Storage and Handling: A Guide for Libraries and Archives*. Washington, DC: Commission on Preservation and Access, 1995.

Variable Media Network. "Definition." Accessed September 24, 2013. http://www.variablemedia.net/e/.

"The Vitaphone Project." Accessed September 28, 2013. http://www.vitaphoneproject.com/.

Von Waldthausen, Clara C. "Exhibition of Photographic Materials in Library and Archive Collections." *Topics in Photographic Preservation* 10 (2003): 178–90.

Walters, Tyler, and Katherine Skinner. "Economics, Sustainability, and the Cooperative Model in Digital Preservation." *Library High Tech* 28 (2010): 259–72.

Walters, Tyler, and Katherine Skinner. *New Roles for New Times: Digital Curation for Preservation*. Washington, DC: Association of Research Libraries, 2011.

Webb, C. "The Malleability of Fire: Preserving Digital Information." In *Managing Preservation for Libraries and Archives: Current Practice and Future Developments*, edited by J. Feather, 27–52. Aldershot, Hants, UK: Ashgate, 2004.

Wheeler, Jim. *Videotape Preservation Handbook*. 2002. Accessed October 5, 2013. http://www.media-matters.net/docs/resources/Traditional%20Audiovisual%20Preservation/WheelerVideo.pdf.

Williams, Hywel Gwynn, and Anna Henry. "Building a Digital Archive: Integrating Theory and Implementation." Paper presented at the International Council on Archives Congress, Brisbane, Australia, August 20–24, 2012. Accessed September 17, 2013. http://ica2012.ica.org/files/pdf/Full%20papers%20upload/ica12Final00280.pdf.

Wilson, Paul. "Historical Perspective on the Use of Microfilm in Libraries and Archives." In *Preservation Microfilming: Does It Have a Future?: Proceedings of the First National Conference of the National Preservation Office, National Library of Australia, 1994*, 46–56. Canberra, ACT: National Library of Australia, 1995.

Wilson, William K. *Environmental Guide for the Storage of Paper Records* (NISO TR01-1995). Bethesda, MD: NISO Press, 1995.

Wise, Andrea, Caitlin Granowski, and Belinda Gourley. "Out of the Box: Measuring Microclimates in Australian-Made Solander Boxes." In *Art on Paper: Mounting and Housing*, edited by Joanna Kosek, Judith Rayner, and Birthe Christensen, 55–58. London: Archetype Publications, 2005.

Wren, Diane J. *Books Gone Bad: Mold in Library Collections*. 2011. Accessed September 26, 2013. http://dianejwren.com/Mold%20Web%20Site/index.htm.

Yeide, N., A. Walsh, and K. Akinsha. *The AAM Guide to Provenance Research*. Washington, DC: American Association of Museums, 2001.

# Standards

........................................................................................................

AES-11id-2006 (r2012). *AES Information Document for Preservation of Audio Recordings—Extended Term Storage Environment for Multiple Media Archives.*

AES-22-1997 (r2003). *AES Recommended Practice for Audio Preservation and Restoration—Storage of Polyester-Base Magnetic Tape.*

AES-28-1997 (r2008). *AES Standard for Audio Preservation and Restoration: Method for Estimating Life Expectancy of Compact Discs (CD-ROM), Based on Effects of Temperature and Relative Humidity.*

AES-49-2005 (r2010). *AES Standard for Audio Preservation and Restoration—Magnetic Tape—Care and Handling Practices for Extended Usage.*

American Alliance of Museums. "Standards Regarding Collections Stewardship." Accessed September 29, 2013. http://www.aam-us.org/resources/ethics-standards-and-best-practices/collections-stewardship.

ANSI/AIIM MS23-2004. *Recommended Practice—Production, Inspection, and Quality Assurance of First-Generation, Silver Microforms of Documents.*

ANSI/AIIM MS45-1990. *Recommended Practice for the Inspection of Stored Silver-Gelatin Microforms for Evidence of Deterioration.*

ANSI/AIIM MS48-1999. *Recommended Practice—Microfilming Public Records on Silver Halide Film.*

ANSI IT9.21-1996. *Life Expectancy of Compact Discs (CD-ROM): Method for Estimating, Based on Effects of Temperature and Relative Humidity.*

ANSI/NISO Z39.48-1992 (R2009). *Permanence of Paper for Publications and Documents in Libraries and Archives.*

ANSI/NISO Z39.66-1992. *Durable Hardcover Binding for Books.*

ANSI/NISO Z39.73-1994 (R2012). *Single-Tier Steel Bracket Library Shelving.*

ANSI/NISO Z39.78-2000 (R2010). *Library Binding.*

ANSI/NISO Z39.79-2001. *Environmental Conditions for Exhibiting Library and Archival Materials.*

BS 1153:1992. *Recommendations for Processing and Storage of Silver-Gelatin-Type Microfilm.*

IEC 60908 (1999). *Audio Recording—Compact Disc Digital Audio System.* Ed. 2.0. (also known as "Red Book").

ISO 6200:1999. *Micrographics—First Generation Silver-Gelatin Microforms of Source Documents—Density Specifications and Method of Measurement.*

ISO 9706:1994. *Information and Documentation—Paper for Documents—Requirements for Permanence.*

........................................................................................................

ISO 11799:2003. *Information and Documentation—Document Storage Requirements for Archive and Library Materials.*

ISO 14721:2012. *Space Data and Information Transfer Systems—Open Archival Information System (OAIS)—Reference Model.*

ISO 16363:2012. *Space Data and Information Transfer Systems—Audit and Certification of Trustworthy Digital Repositories.*

ISO 18901:2010. *Imaging Materials—Processed Silver-Gelatin-Type Black-and-White Films—Specifications for Stability.*

ISO 18902:2013. *Imaging Materials—Processed Imaging Materials—Albums, Framing and Storage Materials.*

ISO 18911:2010. *Imaging Materials—Processed Safety Photographic Films—Storage Practices.*

ISO 18916:2007. *Imaging Materials—Processed Imaging Materials—Photographic Activity Test for Enclosure Materials.*

ISO 18918:2000. *Imaging Materials—Processed Photographic Plates—Storage Practices.*

ISO 18920:2011. *Imaging Materials—Reflection Prints—Storage Practices.*

ISO 18921:2008. *Imaging Materials—Compact Discs (CD-ROM)—Method for Estimating the Life Expectancy Based on the Effects of Temperature and Relative Humidity.*

ISO 18923:2000. *Imaging Materials—Polyester-Based Magnetic Tape—Storage Practices.*

ISO 18933:2012. *Imaging Materials—Magnetic Tape—Care and Handling Practices for Extended Usage.*

ISO 32000-1:2008. *Document Management—Portable Document Format.*

ISO/IEC 10149:1995. *Information Technology—Data Interchange on Read-Only 120mm Optical Data Disks (CD-ROM)* (also ECMA-130 and commonly referred to as "Yellow Book").

ISO/IEC 10918-1:1994. *Information and Documentation—Digital Compression and Coding of Continuous-Tone Still Images: Requirements and Guidelines.*

NFPA 40:2011. *Standard for the Storage and Handling of Cellulose Nitrate Film.* Accessed October 4, 2013. http://www.nfpa.org/codes-and-standards/document-information-pages?mode=code&code=40.

SMPTE RP-103:1995. *Care, Storage, Operation, Handling and Shipping of Magnetic Recording Tape for Television.*

SMPTE RP-190:1996. *Care and Preservation of Audio Magnetic Recordings.*

# Index

....................................................................

....................................................................

# About the Authors
# and Contributors

......................................................................

**Brenda Bernier** is the head of the Weissman Preservation Center and is the Paul M. and Harriet L. Weissman senior photograph conservator at Harvard Library. She is active in the field, teaching workshops and presenting new research. Working in such diverse institutions as the National Archives and Records Administration, the U.S. Holocaust Memorial Museum, and the Baltimore Museum of Art has shaped her conservation and preservation experience. She has a master's degree in photograph conservation from the Winterthur/University of Delaware Program in Art Conservation.

**Liz Coffey** has been working behind the scenes with film since 1995. She has immersed herself in theatrical and amateur film projection, TV newsfilm and regional film archiving, and she shoots the occasional Super 8 film. Liz is presently the film conservator for Media Preservation Services at Harvard University.

**Donia Conn** is an independent consultant for small and midsized cultural heritage institutions. She has worked in the fields of conservation and preservation for almost twenty years, specializing in book conservation and preservation training. She presents workshops and webinars on preservation and digitization topics, consults with institutions on disaster planning and preservation issues, and is adjunct faculty at the Graduate School of Library and Information Science, Simmons College, teaching courses on preservation management and collections maintenance. Donia is a professional associate of the American Institute for Conservation of Historic and Artistic Works (AIC). She earned her BA in mathematics from St. Olaf College and her MLIS with Advanced Certificate in Conservation from the University of Texas at Austin.

**Matthew Davies** worked at the Australian Broadcasting Corporation for ten years as a producer, broadcaster, and archivist before commencing work at the National Film and Sound Archive of Australia in 1993. He has worked in sound preservation, as operations manager of Preservation and Technical Services, and presently is senior curator for Sound Broadcast and Networked Media. Matthew is secretary of IASA's National Archives Section and president of the Australasian Sound Recordings Association.

**Richard Dine** has been the Training Specialist for the Holdings Protection Team at the National Archives and Records Administration (NARA) since February 2010, and prior to that he was a training manager at GE Capital. Since joining NARA, Richard has helped upgrade the required holdings protection training with new e-learning and instructor-led programs, and he has coordinated the production of several instructional videos. Richard holds an MBA from the Wharton School and a bachelor's degree from Georgetown University.

**Ross Harvey** is based in Australia. He was on the faculty of the Graduate School of Library and Information Science, Simmons College, Boston, until June 2013, and he has held academic positions at universities in Australia, Singapore, and New Zealand. Visiting professorships in 2007 to 2008 at the University of British Columbia and the University of Glasgow allowed him to observe digital preservation practice at firsthand. His research and teaching interests focus on the stewardship of digital materials in libraries and archives, particularly on its preservation. His most recent publications are *Digital Curation* (Neal-Schuman, 2010) and *Preserving Digital Materials*, 2nd ed. (De Gruyter Saur, 2011). Ross's website (elibank.net) provides more information, including full details of his publications.

**Heather Hole** is assistant professor of arts administration and art history in the Department of Art and Music at Simmons College, Boston. She is the author of *Marsden Hartley and the West: The Search for an American Modernism* (Yale University Press, 2007) and the curator of the traveling exhibition of the same name. In her previous position as curator at the Museum of Fine Arts, Boston, she played a key role in planning and installing the new Art of the Americas wing, which opened in November 2010. She holds a BA from Smith College and a PhD from Princeton University.

**Leslie Johnston** has over twenty years of experience in digitization and digital conversion, setting and applying metadata and content standards and overseeing the development of digital content management and delivery systems and services. Her research specializations include digital collection management system and infrastructure design, digital preservation systems and services, and standards for digital library collections. Leslie is the chief of repository development in the Office of Strategic Initiatives at the Library of Congress. Previously, she served as the head of digital access services at the University of Virginia Library; head of instructional technology and library information systems at the Harvard Design School; the academic technology specialist for art for the Stanford University Libraries; and as database specialist for the Getty Research Institute. She is an active participant in the Digital Library Federation since 2001 and has been active in the museum community, working for various museums, teaching courses on museum systems, editing the journal *Spectra*, and serving on the board of the Museum Computer Network.

**Michael F. Knight** is an archives specialist for the National Archives and Records Administration (NARA) Holdings Protection Team. Previous positions were at NARA as a reference and processing archivist, the National Park Service, Gettysburg National Military Park, the California State University Archives, Dominguez Hills, and the African American Museum and Library of Oakland, California. He chaired a panel session on holdings protection for the 2013 Society of American Archivists conference. Knight has published numerous articles highlighting the historical significance and preservation needs of collections he has worked with at local, state, and national cultural institutions. He has a BA in American History/Black Studies from San Francisco State University and an MLIS from the University of California, Los Angeles.

**Frances Lennard** worked as a textile conservator for fifteen years, at the United Kingdom's Textile Conservation Centre and in private practice, before returning to the Textile Conservation Centre, University of Southampton, in 2001 to lead the MA Textile Conservation program. She is now senior lecturer in textile conservation and leads the MPhil Textile Conservation program at the University of Glasgow. Her research interests focus on textile treatments.

**Martha R. Mahard** is a professor of practice at Simmons College Graduate School of Library and Information Science where she teaches courses in the management of photographic archives, moving image collections, art documentation, and digital preservation. She holds a Doctor of Arts degree in Library Administration from Simmons. Mahard retired from Harvard after a thirty-five-year career starting as a library assistant in the Harvard Theatre Collection in 1970. She became assistant curator and manuscript/special collections cataloger in 1981. In 1989 she became the visual resources librarian at the Harvard Graduate School of Design, in 1995 curator of visual collections in the Fine Arts Library, and in 2000 curator of historic photographs in the Fine Arts Library. At Harvard she served for four years as chair of the VIA (Visual Information Access) steering committee and chaired the working group that initially recommended the development and oversaw the implementation of a union catalog for visual materials at Harvard. She has lectured and published on a variety of topics including education for visual resources librarianship and the collaborative experiences involved in the successful implementation of VIA. Mahard has been active in the Art Libraries Society of North America, the Visual Resources Association, and the Visual Materials Section of the Society of American Archivists.

**Kevin A. McCoy** is director of the Security Management Division of the National Archives and Records Administration. He has thirty-eight years of federal law enforcement and security management experience and has completed numerous professional development law enforcement and leadership courses. Kevin is board certified in security management as a Certified Protection Professional and Certified Lodging Security Director. He has served at NARA for thirteen years and established the holdings protection team in the Security Management Division.

**Bob Pymm** is a senior lecturer and associate head of the School of Information Studies at Charles Sturt University in Australia. He coordinates a specialist online postgraduate course in audio-visual archiving. Prior to his academic appointment, Bob worked for more than twenty years in libraries, archives, and related cultural institutions. His teaching and research interests are in the areas of audiovisual materials, preservation, and popular culture and archives.

**Shelby Sanett** is the lead security management and program analyst, National Archives and Records Administration (NARA) Security Management Division, where she works in the Continuity of Operations program as the test, training, and exercise lead and chair of the Pandemic Working Group. She also works with the division's security programs to develop policy supporting security operations and procedures. She serves on the NARA Records Emergency Management Team, the FEMA Interagency Continuity Working Group, the Interagency Security Committee, and she represents NARA on the Society of American Archivists (SAA) Committee on Education, where she is the chair-elect. She is the past chair, SAA Preservation Section; and Member, International Council on Archives' Section on Academic Education and Training. Prior to joining NARA, she was the imaging and preservation services manager at Amigos Library Services, Dallas, Texas. She is past visiting assistant professor, Pratt Institute, School of Information and Library Science, New York, where she taught Preservation and Digital Preservation courses and is an adjunct faculty member at Simmons College, Boston, where she teaches a course in preservation management. Shelby holds a PhD from Charles Sturt University, Australia, an MLIS from the University of California, Los Angeles, and an MBA from the University of Phoenix.

**Elizabeth Walters** is the program officer for audiovisual materials for the Weissman Preservation Center, Harvard Library. Prior to becoming a preservation librarian she spent well over a decade working in the Japanese consumer electronics sector. She holds a bachelor's degree in East Asian Studies from Oberlin College and a master's degree in library and information science from Simmons College.

**Dawn Walus** is the conservator at the Boston Athenæum. She previously worked as a book conservator at the Weissman Preservation Center, Harvard Library, and she has held conservation internships and positions at the Preservation Society of Newport County in Rhode Island, the Brooklyn Museum of Art, the New York Academy of Medicine, the Rieger Art Conservation (Works on Paper) in New York City, and the Huntington Library, Art Collections, and Botanical Gardens in San Marino, California. She received an MA/CAS in art conservation from the Buffalo State College Art Conservation Graduate Program in 2009 and a BA in fine arts from Rutgers University in 1995. She is a member of the American Institute for the Conservation of Historic and Artistic Works (AIC) and the Guild of Book Workers.